Human Resource Management

in a

Business Context

Business in Context Series

Editors

David Needle
Head of Undergraduate Studies
East London Business School
University of East London

Professor Eugene McKenna
Chartered Psychologist and
Emeritus Professor
University of East London

Accounting in a Business Context (3rd edition)
Aidan Berry and Robin Jarvis
ISBN 1 86152 090 5, 448 pages

Behaviour in a Business Context
Richard Turton
ISBN 0 412 37530 3, 400 pages

Business in Context (2nd edition)
David Needle
ISBN 0 412 48410 2, 427 pages

Economics in a Business Context (2nd edition)
Alan Neale and Colin Haslam
ISBN 0 412 58760 2, 336 pages

Law in a Business Context
Bill Cole, Peter Shears and Jillinda Tiley
ISBN 0 412 37520 6, 256 pages

Quantitative Techniques in a Business Context
Roger Slater and Peter Ascroft
ISBN 0 412 37570 2, 416 pages

Books in the series are available on free inspection for lecturers considering the texts for course adoption. Details of these, and any other International Thomson Business Press titles, are available by writing to the publishers (Berkshire House, 168–173 High Holborn, London WC1V 7AA).

Human Resource Management

in a —

Business Context

Alan Price

INTERNATIONAL THOMSON BUSINESS PRESS
I ⓉP® An International Thomson Publishing Company

London • Bonn • Boston • Johannesburg • Madrid • Melbourne • Mexico City • New York • Paris
Singapore • Tokyo • Toronto • Albany, NY • Belmont, CA • Cincinnati, OH • Detroit, MI

Human Resource Management in a Business Context

Copyright ©1997 A. J. Price

First published by International Thomson Business Press

 A division of International Thomson Publishing Inc.
The ITP logo is a trademark under licence

British Library Cataloguing-in-Publication Data
A catalogue record for this book is available from the British Library

First edition 1997
Reprinted 1997

Typeset by J&L Composition Ltd, Filey, North Yorkshire
Printed in the UK by Alden Press, Oxford

ISBN 1–86152–182–0

International Thomson Business Press
Berkshire House
168–173 High Holborn
London WC1V 7AA
UK

International Thomson Business Press
20 Park Plaza
13th Floor
Boston MA 02116
USA

http://www.itbp.com

Contents

List of figures

List of tables

List of case studies

Series foreword

This book is part of the 'Business in Context' series. The books in this series are written by lecturers all with several years' experience of teaching on undergraduate business studies programmes. When the series first appeared in 1989, the original rationale was to place the various disciplines found in the business studies curriculum firmly in a business context. This is still our aim. Business studies attracted a growing band of students throughout the 1980s, a popularity that has been maintained in the 1990s. If anything, that appeal has broadened, and business studies, as well as a specialism in its own right, is now taken with a range of other subjects, particularly as universities move towards modular degree structures. We feel that the books in this series provide an important focus for the student seeking some meaning in the range of subjects currently offered under the umbrella of business studies.

With the exception of the text *Business in Context*, which takes the series title as its theme, all the original texts in our series took the approach of a particular discipline traditionally associated with business studies and taught widely on business studies and related programmes. These first books in our series examined business from the perspectives of economics, behavioural science, law, mathematics and accounting. The popularity of the series across a range of courses has meant that the second editions of many of the original texts are about to be published and there are plans to extend the series by examining information technology, operations management, human resource management and marketing.

Whereas in traditional texts it is the subject itself that is the focus, our texts make business the focus. All the texts are based upon the same specific model of business illustrated in Figure 0.1. We have called our model 'Business in Context' and the text of the same name is an expansion and explanation of that model.

The model comprises four distinct levels. At the core are found the activities which make up what we know as business and include innovation, operations and production, purchasing, marketing, personnel, and finance and accounting. We see these activities operating irrespective of the type of business involved and they are found in both the manufacturing and service industries as well as in the public and private sectors. The second level of our model is concerned with strategy and management decision-making. It is here that decisions are made which influence the direction of the business activities at our core. The third level of our model is concerned with organizational factors within which business activities and management decisions take place. The organizational issues we examine are structure, size, goals and organizational politics, patterns of ownership and organizational culture. Clear links can be forged between this and other levels of our model, especially between structure and strategy, goals and management decision-making, and how all aspects both contribute to and are influenced by the organizational culture. The fourth level concerns itself with the environment in which businesses operate. The issues here involve social and cultural factors, the role of the state and politics, the role of the economy, and issues relating to both technology and labour. An important feature of this fourth level of our model is that such elements not only operate as opportunities and constraints for business, but also that they are shaped by the three other levels of our model.

This brief description of the 'Business in Context' model illustrates the key features of our series. We see business as dynamic. It is constantly being shaped by and in turn shaping those managerial, organizational and environmental contexts within which it operates. Influences go backwards and forwards across the various levels. Moreover, the aspects identified within each level are in constant interaction with one another. Thus the role

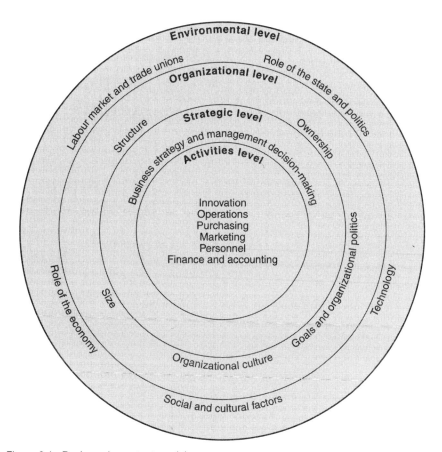

Figure 0.1 Business in context model.

of the economy cannot be understood without reference to the role of the state; size and structure are inextricably linked; innovation is inseparable from issues of operations, marketing and finance. The understanding of how this model works is what business studies is all about and forms the basis for our series.

In proposing this model we are proposing a framework for analysis and we hope that it will encourage readers to add to and refine the model and so broaden our understanding of business. Each writer in this series has been encouraged to present a personal interpretation of the model. In this way we hope to build up a more complete picture of business.

Our series therefore aims for a more integrated and realistic approach to business than has hitherto been the case. The issues are complex but the authors' treatments are not. Each book in this series is built around the 'Business in Context' model, and each displays a number of common features that mark out this series. First, we aim to present our ideas in a way that students will find easy to understand and we relate those ideas wherever possible to real business situations. Second, we hope to stimulate further study both by referencing our material and by pointing students towards further reading at the end of each chapter. Third, we use the notion of 'key concepts' to highlight the most significant aspects of the subject presented in each chapter. Fourth, we use case studies to illustrate our material and stimulate further discussion. Fifth, we present at the end of each chapter a series of questions, exercises and discussion topics. To sum up, we feel it most important that each book will stimulate thought and further study and assist the student in developing powers of analysis, a critical awareness and ultimately a point of view about business issues.

We have already indicated that the series has been devised with the undergraduate business studies student uppermost in our minds. We also maintain that these books are of value wherever there is a need to understand business issues and may therefore be used across a range of different courses, including some BTEC Higher programmes and some postgraduate and professional courses.

David Needle and Eugene McKenna

Acknowledgements

My thanks are due to TVU colleagues and students in many countries who have helped me develop and test the contents of this book. I am also indebted to the people who have contributed to its production, in particular to Mark Wellings at ITP for commissioning the work and Jenny Clapham for seeing it through to fruition; Eugene McKenna and David Needle for their rigorous and supportive editorial advice; and Lisa Williams for her professional scrutiny prior to publication.

Preface

Human Resource Management (HRM) is a distinctive approach to managing people. People make a business function efficiently and yet they cause the greatest difficulties. Indeed, for most of us interaction with people provides much of any job's challenge and satisfaction. It follows that success, or even survival, in business requires an understanding of people management. This book is intended to provide a comprehensive account of the critical issues in HRM, taking the reader from an introductory level to a relatively sophisticated understanding of an increasingly important business topic.

Like other texts in this series, the book follows the Business in Context model. It locates HRM and other perspectives of people management in a framework focused on the needs of business studies students. In fact, the model fits the subject well, providing a logical explanatory framework in which to explore the complexities involved in managing people at work.

At the outermost level of the model, we see that the activities of people managers are constrained by a series of environmental factors. For example:

- the economy, affecting business growth and subsequent demand for and availability of employees;
- the actions of government and supranational bodies such as the European Union in determining investment in education and vocational training;
- legislation on a wide range of employment issues, including hours, conditions, minimum pay, redundancy rights, consultation and so on.
- competing demands from stakeholders such as customers, trade unions, shareholders and senior managers.

At the organizational level, the dimensions of size, structure and culture constrain and sometimes determine the way in which HRM takes place. Organizations range from one-person 'start-ups' to multinationals employing hundreds of thousands of people. As a consequence, the problems which people managers face vary from simply managing themselves to the problems involved in controlling vast numbers. Not surprisingly, HRM in small businesses tends to be commonsensical, with an emphasis on solving day-to-day problems. People management is a natural part of the owner-manager's role, along with finance, production, marketing, customer service and everything else.

By contrast, large organizations require much greater sophistication and structuring of the human resource function. Even where HRM has been adopted as a philosophy and line managers have much of the operational responsibility, there is likely to be a major specialist function. Activities such as resourcing, counselling, employee relations, communications and training/development require expert handling but can be provided on an in-house or external consultancy basis.

The next level – strategic decision-making – is particularly relevant for this topic. HRM is viewed as a strategic alternative to traditional personnel management. Employees are a major cost to organizations of any size. Hence decisions about employee requirements are strategic issues with important consequences for the profitability and growth of organizations.

The final level encompasses the activities of people managers, including recruitment and selection procedures, performance assessment, training and development and employee relations. These are the areas traditionally associated with 'personnel'. In this volume we see that they are important but also form part of a much wider approach to managing people.

We commence the book by addressing the nature and scope of HRM as a philosophy of people management. We will see that there is no universal agreement on the meaning of HRM. In fact, there are varying and contradictory models. Yet they embody common elements which distinguish them from previous approaches to managing people – specifically personnel management. For this volume, these elements have been combined into ten major principles of HRM to provide a further integrative framework for the subject. This framework is used in combination with the Business in Context model throughout the book. Together, these perspectives are particularly appropriate to the discussion of a management philosophy which, it is claimed, is a coherent approach to the management of people.

Chapters 2–7 take us through the environmental, organizational and strategic levels, also covering the employment market, human resource planning, organizational change and the nature of resourcing decisions in some detail. The remainder of the book, Chapters 8–12, addresses the key activity areas: recruitment and selection, the management of diversity, performance management, human resource development, and employee relations.

Each chapter includes at least one and often several case studies designed to illustrate particular themes within a real-life context. In most cases questions have been added to provoke further discussion. The flavour of reality is emphasized throughout the book, with references to ongoing issues discussed in the quality press. HRM really happens out there, but it is rarely labelled as such. It comes as a surprise to many students (and journalists) that newspaper business and economics pages frequently carry accounts of human resource management in action. At the end of each chapter we also provide a number of review questions and one or more scenarios or 'mini-cases' which embody further real-life problems.

Alan Price
January 1997

Introduction to HRM

> This chapter introduces the concept of human resource management. It outlines HRM as a philosophy of people management and provides a framework for its role within the business context.

This first chapter will introduce you to the essential elements of human resource management (HRM), its origins and application. HRM is comparatively new to most countries but in the USA the term has been used for over fifty years as an alternative name for personnel management (Noon 1992: 23). For most of that time, the terms were used interchangeably. However, in the 1980s HRM took on a new connotation, one significantly different from traditional personnel management. It was identified with a strategic approach, linking the management of people to the achievement of business objectives (see key concept 1.1). This interpretation has been adopted in many parts of the world, particularly Australasia, the British Isles, Scandinavia and South Africa. In these regions and elsewhere, HRM has become increasingly influential but has taken a variety of forms to fit local business cultures.

A philosophy of people management based on the belief that human resources are uniquely important to sustained business success. An organization gains competitive advantage by using its people effectively, drawing on their expertise and ingenuity to meet clearly defined objectives. HRM is aimed at recruiting capable, flexible and committed people, managing and rewarding their performance and developing key competencies.	**KEY CONCEPT 1.1** *Human resource management*

Nevertheless, the concept of HRM is not straightforward. We will see that there is a considerable debate about its distinctiveness and definition, while evidence for the extent of its adoption remains contradictory. Some commentators regard HRM as a major advance; others dismiss it as a passing fad. This introductory chapter provides a framework which will allow you to understand and evaluate the different and sometimes ambiguous views of HRM.

HRM owes a great deal to older models of people management but its orientation is consistent with other modern management techniques. Often HRM is associated – or even confused – with initiatives such as total quality management (TQM), culture change and business process re-engineering. Each has its own rationale but there are underlying themes in common with HRM. They are all products of a late twentieth-century re-evaluation of management thinking. They reflect criticisms of western business practices, the impact of Japanese competition and the emergence of dynamic new industrial economies such as Singapore and Korea.

Within this chapter we will address a number of specific issues:

- Where do the fundamental concepts of HRM come from?
- What distinguishes HRM from other approaches to managing people – particularly personnel management?
- Is HRM a coherent and integrated approach to managing people?
- How prevalent is HRM?
- Does its use lead to greater organizational effectiveness?
- Is HRM here to stay or is it just another management fad?

We commence this chapter with a survey of approaches to people management which have contributed to the development of HRM.

People management

Arguably, HRM has become the dominant approach to people management in English-speaking countries. However, it is important to stress that human resource management has not 'come out of nowhere'. HRM has absorbed ideas and techniques from a number of areas. In effect, it is a synthesis of themes and concepts drawn from over a century of management theory and social science research.

There is a long history of attempts to achieve an understanding of human behaviour in the workplace. Throughout the twentieth century, practitioners and academics have searched for theories and tools to explain and influence human behaviour at work. Managers in different industries encounter similar experiences: businesses expand or fail; they innovate or stagnate; they may be exciting or unhappy organizations in which to work; finance has to be obtained and workers have to be recruited; new equipment is purchased, eliminating old procedures and introducing new methods; staff must be reorganized, retrained or dismissed. Over and over again, managers must deal with events which are clearly similar but also different enough to require fresh thinking. We can imagine that, one day, there will be a science of management in which these problems and their solutions are catalogued, classified, standardized and made predictable. Sociologists, psychologists and management theorists have attempted to build such a science, producing a constant stream of new and reworked ideas. They offer theoretical insights and practical assistance in areas of people management such as recruitment and selection, performance measurement, team composition and organizational design. Many of their concepts have been integrated into broader approaches which have contributed to management thinking in various periods and ultimately the development of HRM (see Figure 1.1). The most significant include:

- **Scientific management.** A hard-nosed and authoritarian approach to management developed by F.W. Taylor at the beginning of the twentieth century. Taylor believed in a combination of detailed task specifications and selection of the 'best man' for the job. It was the function of managers to think – workers were expected to do exactly as they were told. This, he felt, would result in the most efficient method of performing physical work. Additionally, he advocated premium payments as a means of rewarding the most effective (compliant) workers. Taylor's ideas led on to:

    - **Fordism** – a philosophy of production based on the continuous assembly line techniques devised by Henry Ford. This methodology dominated worldwide manufacturing until the 1980s.
    - **Time and motion** – stopwatch methods of measuring work, used to increase efficiency and minimize wasted time and effort.

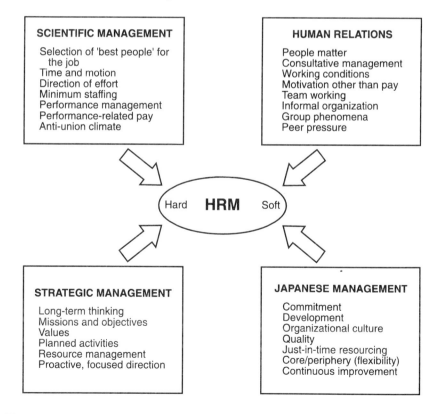

Figure 1.1 Influences on the development of HRM.

● **Continuous improvement** – an attitude fundamental to Japanese production methods, using employee knowledge and ingenuity continually to refine product manufacture and development.

These practices require management control over the precise detail of work in order to maximize efficiency and gain competitive advantage. Inevitably, this is achieved at the expense of employees who sacrifice the freedom to control their own work. 'Scientific management', under any name, creates an inevitable tension between the rights and expectations of workers and management's need to gain ever greater quality and cost-effectiveness. HRM is identified with attempts to deal constructively with this tension through assertive, but non-autocratic, people management. It is also linked to the use of performance-related pay and other ways of rewarding appropriate behaviour.

● **Human factors.** In Australia, New Zealand and – particularly – the UK, government-sponsored research by work psychologists during and after the First World War produced significant information on the relationship between boredom, fatigue and working conditions. They established that fatigue arose from psychological as well as physical causes. They demonstrated also that longer working hours did not necessarily increase productivity. Human factors psychologists established a tradition of performance measurement, job analysis and clarification of skill requirements. These underlie key HRM techniques such as competence assessment and selection methods.

● **Human relations.** In the 1920s and 1930s researchers in the USA demonstrated that work performance and motivation did not depend simply on pay and discipline. People worked for many other reasons. They wanted to be involved in determining their own work conditions. They responded to encouragement and the interest shown by management. Workers formed informal groups which established their own norms of behaviour, including acceptable levels of performance. Working groups exercised social pressure on their members to conform to these unconsciously determined rules. The human relations movement had considerable influence within US business schools such as Harvard, which later developed a 'soft', humanistic interpretation of HRM.

● **Behavioural science.** The human relations and human factors approaches were absorbed into a broad behavioural science movement in the 1950s and 1960s. This period produced some influential theories on the motivation of human performance. For example, Maslow's hierarchy of needs gave an individual focus to the reasons why people work, satisfying an ascending series of needs from survival, through security to eventual 'self-actualization'. In the same period, concepts of job design such as job enrichment and job enlargement were investigated. It was felt that people would give more to an organization if they gained satisfaction from their jobs. Jobs should be designed to be interesting and challenging to gain the commitment of workers – a central theme of HRM.

● **Management by objectives.** Based on work by Drucker in the 1950s, and further developed by McGregor, management by objectives (MBO) linked achievement to competence and job performance. MBO primarily focused on the individual, tying rewards and promotion opportunities to specific agreed objectives, measured by feedback from performance assessment. Individual managers were given the opportunity to clarify the purposes of their jobs and set their own targets. MBO developed into modern performance management schemes and performance-related pay.

- **Contingency.** Many researchers found it difficult to apply academic theories to real organizations. The socio-technical school developed models of behaviour and performance which took into account the contingent variables, or 'it depends' circumstances, attached to particular work situations (Burns and Stalker 1961; Woodward 1980). They argued that employees were part of a system which also included the equipment and other resources utilized by an organization. The system could not function optimally unless all its components – human and non-human – had been considered. The HRM concepts of coherence and integration derive, in part, from this line of thought.

- **Organizational development.** Also drawn from the long tradition of organizational theory, organizational development (OD) took a pragmatic approach to change. Theory and practice were mixed in a tentative process called 'action research'. OD familiarized managers with the idea that changes in processes, attitudes and behaviour were possible and that organizations should be thought of as whole entities.

- **Strategic management.** Directing people to achieve strategic objectives so that individual goals are tied to the business needs of the whole organization. Strategic management has become a dominant framework for organizational thinking since the Second World War. It is based on concepts first used for large-scale military and space programmes in the USA. Frequently, it employs project and team-based methods for planning and implementation. Lately, internal (including human) resources and key competences have been identified as crucial elements of long-term competitive success. Strategic management has become the major unifying theme of undergraduate and – especially – postgraduate business courses. The concern with strategy distinguishes human resource management from personnel management.

- **Leadership.** Many writers have concluded that a visionary leader is essential, particularly in developing and inspiring teams. McGregor's *The Human Side of Enterprise* (1960) linked leadership and management style to motivation. McGregor expressed the contrast between authoritarian people management ('Theory X') and a modern form based on human relations ideas ('Theory Y'). His ideas parallel those of 'hard' and 'soft' HRM. Effective managers do not need to give orders and discipline staff; they draw the best from their people through encouragement, support and personal charisma. Later authors (such as Peters and Waterman 1982) feature the leader's vision and mission as a quasi-religious means of galvanizing worker commitment and enthusiasm.

- **Corporate culture.** Deal and Kennedy (1982) popularized the belief that organizational effectiveness depends on a strong, positive corporate culture. They combined ideas from leadership theory and strategic management thinkers with prevailing beliefs about Japanese business success. Managers were exhorted to examine their existing organizational climates critically and work to change them into dynamic and creative cultures. The **excellence** movement inspired by Peters and Waterman (*In Search of Excellence*, 1982, and others) has been particularly influential with practising managers, despite criticisms of the research on which it was based.

Management thinking

These concepts have exercised strong influences on managers but, like fashions in hairstyle and clothing, management ideas come and go. Today's best-selling management concept will not survive long before being overtaken by the next 'big idea'. Significantly, however, a consistent theme has prevailed for twenty years: the most successful organizations make the most effective use of their people – their human resources. In fact, the emergence of HRM is part of a major shift in the nature and meaning of management towards the end of the twentieth century. This has happened for a number of reasons. Perhaps most significantly, as we will see in Chapters 2 and 3, changes in the structure and intensity of international competition have forced companies to make radical changes in their working practices (Goss 1994: 1).

From the 1970s onwards, managers in the west have felt themselves to be on a rollercoaster of change, expected to deliver improved business performance by whatever means they can muster. Their own careers and rewards have been tied to those improvements and many have been despatched to the ranks of the unemployed for not acting quickly and imaginatively enough. Caught between the need to manage decisively and fear of failure, managers have sought credible new ideas as a potential route for survival.

The shift of economic power to the Asia-Pacific region emphasized the weakness in traditional western – specifically, American – management methods. To meet competition from East Asia, industries and organizations in older developed countries have been forced to restructure. The Japanese provided both a threat and a role model which eastern and western companies tried to copy. Frequently, reorganized businesses have adopted Japanese techniques in an attempt to regain competitiveness. The term 'Japanization' came into vogue in the mid-1980s to describe attempts in other countries to make practical use of 'Japanese' ideas and practices, reinforced by the impact of Japanese subsidiaries overseas. Initially, the main interest lay in forms of technical innovation and manufacturing methods such as 'continuous improvement' and 'just-in-time'. More recently their ways of managing people have attracted attention.

Japanese practice indicates that human resources are an organization's key asset. A key feature of Japanese organizations is the emphasis on worker commitment, flexibility and development. Books such as Pascale and Athos's *The Art of Japanese Management* (1981) highlighted the competitive advantage which the Japanese gained through effective people management. The message came through that 'at bottom, it is the human resource among all the factors of production which really makes the difference' (Storey 1995: 5).

People management is a central strategic issue rather than a 'necessary inconvenience' (Goss 1994: 4). The component ideas of HRM parallel elements of Japanese people management. However, whereas HRM is a matter of rhetoric for most western managers, the Japanese view it as a way of life: an instrumental approach to ever-increasing efficiency focused on employee commitment and skill. Traditionally, Japanese companies have placed the interests of their employees first amongst their stakeholders (see key concept 1.2), followed by those of customers and lastly the shareholders. This is virtually the opposite situation to that found in free-market western countries such as Australia and Britain. However, as we shall see in Chapter 2, the recession in the early 1990s forced a number of Japanese companies to adopt western ways.

Employees have rights and interests other than pay. They are stakeholders in common with members of other recognizably separate groups or institutions with a special interest in an organization. These include shareholders, managers, customers, suppliers, lenders and government. Each group has its own priorities and demands and fits into the power structure controlling the organization. Employees have limited importance in free-market countries such as the USA and the UK in comparison with most European and many Asian-Pacific countries. Notionally, shareholders are paramount in English-speaking countries. In reality, top managers normally have effective control and pursue their own interests – often at the expense of their staff.

KEY CONCEPT 1.2 *Stakeholders*

Personnel management

The renewed emphasis on the importance of human resources drew attention to the practice of people management. Conventionally, this has been divided between line and personnel managers – now frequently called human resource managers. Personnel management has been a recognized function in the USA since NCR opened a personnel office in the 1890s. American personnel managers worked within a unitarist tradition, identifying closely with the objectives of their organization (see key concept 1.3). It was natural for HRM to emerge comparatively smoothly from this perspective. In other countries, notably the UK, the personnel management function arrived more slowly and came via a number of routes. Moreover, its orientation was not entirely managerial. In Britain its origins can be traced to the 'welfare officers' employed by Quaker-owned companies such as Cadbury. At an early stage it became evident that there was an inherent conflict between their activities and those of line managers. They were not seen as having a philosophy compatible with the worldview of senior managers. The welfare officer orientation placed personnel management as a buffer between the business and its employees. In terms of organizational politics this was not a politically viable position for individuals wishing to further their careers, increase their status and earn high salaries.

KEY CONCEPT 1.3 **Unitarism**	Unitarism has been defined as the spirit of a team defined by a common purpose. It embodies a central concern of HRM, that an organization's people, whether managers or lower-level employees, should share the same objectives and work together harmoniously. From this perspective, conflicting objectives are seen as negative and dysfunctional.

The second tradition – industrial relations – further compounded this distinction between personnel and other managers. In the acrimonious industrial relations climate which prevailed in the UK throughout much of the twentieth century, personnel/industrial relations managers played an intermediary role between unions and line management. Their function was legitimized by their role as 'honest brokers'. However, in the 1980s the Thatcher government reined in union freedom severely. There was a similar reduction in the importance of collective worker representation in other English-speaking countries. The perceived importance of collective bargaining reduced as managerial power increased. Trade union membership declined, along with centralized pay bargaining and other forms of collective negotiation – and with them, the importance of the personnel manager with negotiating experience. The focus switched from the collective to the relationship between the employer and the individual employee. To support this change, a variety of essentially individualistic human resource (HR) techniques have been applied to achieve business goals. These include performance measurement, objective-setting, and skills development related to personal reward.

By the 1980s, personnel had become a well-defined but low status area of management (see Table 1.1). Associations such as the British Institute of Personnel Management (now the Institute of Personnel and Development) recruited members in increasing numbers, developed a qualification structure and attempted to define 'best practice'. Although the knowledge and practices they encouraged drew on psychology and sociology, they were largely pragmatic and commonsensical and did not present a particularly coherent approach to people management. Moreover, in some instances training and industrial relations were considered to be specialist fields outside mainstream personnel management. Traditional personnel managers were accused of having a narrow, functional outlook. Storey considers that personnel management:

> has long been dogged by problems of credibility, marginality, ambiguity and a 'trash-can' labelling which has relegated it to a relatively disconnected set of duties – many of them tainted with a low-status 'welfare' connotation.
>
> (Storey 1989: 5)

In practice, the background and training of many personnel managers left them speaking a different language from other managers and unable to comprehend wider business issues such as business strategy, market competition, labour economics, the roles of other organizational functions – let alone balance sheets (Giles and Williams 1991).

For some, HRM was simply a matter of relabelling 'personnel' to redress

Table 1.1 Specialist personnel functions

Function	Description
Recruitment	Advertising for new employees and liaising with employment agencies
Selection	Determining the best candidates from those who apply, arranging interviews, tests, references and so on
Promotion	Running similar selection procedures to determine progression within the organization
Pay	A minor or major role in pay negotiation, determination and administration
Performance assessment	Coordinating staff appraisal and counselling systems to evaluate individual employee performance
Grading structures	Comparing the relative difficulty and importance of functions as a basis for pay or development
Training and development	Coordinating or delivering programmes to fit people for the roles required by the organization now and in the future
Welfare	Providing or liaising with specialists in a staff care or counselling role for people with personal or domestic problems affecting their work
Communication	Providing an internal information service, perhaps in the form of a staff newspaper or magazine, handouts, booklets and videos
Employee relations	Handling disputes, grievances and industrial action, often dealing with unions or staff representatives
Dismissal	On an individual basis as a result of failure to meet requirements, or as part of a redundancy or closure exercise, perhaps involving large numbers of people.
Personnel administration	Record-keeping and monitoring legislative requirements, for example related to equal opportunities

this situation. Sceptics argue that familiar personnel functions were repackaged and given a more up-market image – 'old wine in new bottles' (M. Armstrong 1987). Indeed, until the early 1990s 'Human Resource Management' textbooks tended to be slightly revised 'Personnel Management' texts covering familiar topics in a prescriptive manner. Torrington and Hall concur that the term has been adopted in order to get away from the ineffectual image of previous eras:

> personnel managers seem constantly to suffer from paranoia about their lack of influence and are ready to snatch at anything – like a change in title – that might enhance their status.
>
> (Torrington and Hall 1991: 15)

It has also been fuelled by longstanding criticisms by other managers. This includes a general prejudice which is often expressed within organizations and sometimes finds its way into print:

> Many of us have long held the view that personnel management, or human resource management as companies sometimes insist on calling it, is a

uniquely irrelevant executive function fulfilling no obvious purpose other than to stifle initiative, flair and creativity.

(*The Independent*, 12 May 1994)

Some commentators argued that personnel people should relinquish their ambiguous roles and adopt unashamedly managerialist positions. Others concluded that if human resources were fundamental to business success they were too important to be left to operational personnel managers. Major human resource decisions should be made by top managers and the consequences of those decisions should be carried through by line management. These considerations place HRM on a strategic rather than operational footing and therefore make HRM a concept of greater interest than personnel management to senior executives. In larger organizations there has been a reappraisal of the previously unfashionable and low-status personnel department. 'Personnel' cannot be regarded as peripheral if it controls an organization's people, since the rhetoric states that they are its greatest resources. Many businesses have adopted some form of HRM as a recognition of this importance. As Fowler famously stated, 'HRM represents the discovery of personnel management by chief executives' (1987: 3).

The new managerialism

In fact, line and general managers have been instrumental in the adoption of HRM – often pushing changes through despite the resistance of personnel specialists (Storey 1995: 7). Radical changes in business structures and supportive – largely right-wing – governments encouraged a renewed confidence in the power of managers to manage. The balance of power moved away from workers and their representatives with the collapse of traditional heavy industries. High levels of unemployment allowed managers to pick and choose new recruits. Existing employees felt under pressure to be more flexible under the threat of losing their jobs. As a result, managers were able to design more competitive organizations with new forms of employment relationships.

Encouraged by the writing of management gurus such as Peters and Waterman (1982) and Kanter (1989), managers eagerly adopted new forms of organization. Businesses moved away from multi-layered, rigid hierarchies and long-term career paths. Instead we have seen an increase in flatter, project-oriented forms of organizations resourced in a flexible way – including by short-term, part-time and contract workers. People managers found themselves needing a framework within which to comprehend and justify these innovative practices. The stage was set for HRM, which was presented as a coherent and integrated philosophy by its originators, covering every aspect of people management (Beer *et al.* 1984: 1).

The concept of HRM

What exactly is 'human resource management'? Many people find HRM to be a vague and elusive concept – not least because it seems to have a variety of meanings (see Table 1.2). Pinning down an acceptable definition

Table 1.2 Definitions of HRM

Human resource management involves all management decisions and actions that affect the relationship between the organization and employees – its human resources.

(Beer *et al.* 1984: 1)

A method of maximizing economic return from labour resource by integrating HRM into Business Strategy.

(Keenoy 1990)

A strategic, coherent and comprehensive approach to the management and development of the organization's human resources in which every aspect of that process is wholly integrated within the overall management of the organization. HRM is essentially an ideology.

(M. Armstrong 1992: 9)

Perhaps it is best to regard HRM as simply a notion of how people can best be managed *in the interests of the organization*.

(M. Armstrong 1994)

A diverse body of thought and practice, loosely unified by a concern to integrate the management of personnel more closely with the core management activity of organizations.

(Goss 1994: 1)

HRM is a discourse and technology of power that aims to resolve the gap inherent in the contract of employment between the capacity to work and its exercise and, thereby, organize individual workers into a collective, productive power or force.

(Townley 1994: 138)

Human resource management is a distinctive approach to employment management which seeks to achieve competitive advantage through the strategic development of a highly committed and capable workforce, using an integrated array of cultural, structural and personnel techniques.

(Storey 1995: 5).

---

can seem like trying to hit a moving target in a fog. This confusion reflects the different interpretations found in articles and books about human resource management. HRM is an elastic term (Storey 1989: 8). It covers a range of applications which vary from book to book and organization to organization.

Simple reflection on the three words 'human resource management' does not provide much enlightenment. 'Human' implies it has something to do with people; 'management' places it in the domain of business and organization; but 'resource' is a highly ambiguous concept which many people find difficult to relate to. Take the following letter to *The Scotsman* newspaper:

Sir,
While visiting a patient in Edinburgh's Western General hospital, I was shocked to see a six-foot long board with large letters proclaiming: HUMAN RESOURCES. This distinguishes people who work in the hospital – doctors, nurses, porters, office workers, painters, managers – from other resources such as computers, laser beams, toilet rolls, refuse bins, beds, etc.

If these human resources are ill, are they labelled 'out of order' or 'broken down' and when being treated, are they being repaired? Are babies listed as 'in process of being manufactured' with an expected date when they will be operational? Are old and dead people 'non-usable human resources' or can they be listed as 'replacement parts'?

When we define humans as resources, we are in danger of forgetting that we are dealing with people!'

(quoted in Bennis 1990)

In fact, much of the academic literature suffers from forgetting the human element in HRM. Most of us would not take kindly to being classified as a 'resource', along with our desks and computers. It seems that there is a fundamental difficulty in considering a person's worth or value to an organization. This arises from that person's humanity. People are **different** from other resources and cannot be discussed in exactly the same way as equipment or finances. This difference lies at the heart of the antagonism and ambiguity that surrounds HRM in practice.

Origins

HRM-type themes, including 'human capital theory' (discussed in Chapter 2) and 'human asset accounting', can be found in the literature from the 1970s. However, the modern view of human resource management first gained prominence in 1981 with its introduction on the prestigious MBA course at Harvard Business School. The Harvard MBA has provided a blueprint for many other courses throughout the world, making its interpretation of HRM particularly influential (Beer *et al* 1984; Guest 1987; Poole 1990). Simultaneously, other interpretations were being developed in Michigan and New York. These ideas spread to the UK in the 1980s, and also to Australia, New Zealand and parts of northern Europe. Today, the HRM approach is influential in many parts of the world. Typically, HRM has been portrayed as being:

- A **radically new** approach to managing people, demarcated sharply from traditional personnel management (Storey 1989: 4). Personnel management is commonly viewed as having an **operational** focus, emphasizing technical skills and day-to-day functions such as recruitment and selection, training, salary administration and employee relations. 'Personnel' is a detached and neutral approach to staff. HRM is more proactive, looking at people in economic terms as assets and liabilities to be actively managed. HRM is **strategic**, tying people management to business objectives. It attempts to manage people – not necessarily employees – in the long-term interests of the business.
- An **integrated** approach which provides a coherent programme, linking all aspects of people management. Whereas personnel managers employ a piecemeal range of sophisticated techniques for assessment or selection, HRM integrates these within a meaningful and organized framework. Each element fits into a pattern which ultimately meets business needs. Additionally, HRM is seen to be holistic: its concern is with the overall people requirements of an organization. There is a significant shift towards more conceptual, higher-level concerns such as the structure and culture of the organization and the provision of necessary competences.
- A **consistent** view of people management in which employees are treated as valuable assets. An organization's reward systems, performance measures, promotion and learning opportunities are used to maximize the utilization of its human resources. In particular, they

are focused on the the attitudes, beliefs and commitment of employees to achieve behavioural consistency and a culture of commitment.

- A **general** management function. Personnel management is viewed as the work of specialists; HRM is the responsibility of all managers. In some organizations human resource experts provide an internal consultancy service to line managers. There is a particular stress on the role of top management and an overall increase in the status of people management. Traditional personnel managers have little power or prestige.

From an organizational perspective human resources encompass:

- The people in an organization – its **employees**. They offer different skills, abilities and knowledge which may or may not be appropriate to the needs of the business. Additionally, their commitment and motivation vary. Some people identify with an organization and are motivated to help achieve its objectives. Others regard their employing firm as a vehicle for personal goals. Some may be overworked while others are underutilized. Invariably, there is a gap or mismatch between the **actual** performance of employees and the **ideal** requirements of a business. HRM focuses on closing this gap to achieve greater **organizational effectiveness**. This has been referred to as the 'matching model'.
- The **human potential** available to a business. This includes the recognition and development of unrealized skills and knowledge. Ingenuity and creativity can be tapped to develop innovative services and products. This also extends to people outside an organization – contractors, consultants, freelancers, temporary and part-time workers – who can add expertise, deal with unusual problems and provide the flexibility to give a **competitive advantage**.

Why should HRM have attracted such attention – particularly from senior managers? From a strategic viewpoint, Lengnick-Hall and Lengnick-Hall (1988) identify a clear rationale for adopting the HRM approach:

- HRM offers a broader range of solutions for complex organizational problems.
- It ensures that an organization's people are considered as well as its financial and technological resources when objectives are set or capabilities assessed.
- It forces the explicit consideration of the individuals who implement and comprise the strategy.
- Two-way links are encouraged between the formulation of strategy and its human resource implications, avoiding problems which might arise from:
  - subordinating strategic considerations to HR preferences;
  - neglecting an organization's people as a potential source of organizational competence and competitive advantage.

Different interpretations of HRM

We noted that the Harvard Business School generated one of the most influential models of HRM. The Harvard interpretation sees employees as resources. However, they are viewed as being fundamentally different from other resources – they cannot be managed in the same way. The stress is on people as *human* resources. The Harvard approach recognizes an element of mutuality in all businesses, a concept which has parallels in Japanese people management, as we observed earlier. Employees are significant stakeholders in an organization. They have their own needs and concerns, along with other groups such as shareholders and customers.

The Harvard view acknowledges that management has the greatest degree of power. Nevertheless there must be scope for accommodation of the interests of the various stakeholders in the form of trade-offs, particularly between owners, employees and different employee groups. The model also acknowledges the need for mechanisms to reconcile the inevitable tension between employee expectations and management objectives.

The Harvard view provides a **strategic map** of HRM territory which guides all managers in their relations with employees. Figure 1.2 demonstrates the relationship between this map and the Business in Context model. The Harvard interpretation identifies situational and stakeholder factors which largely coincide with environmental and organizational factors in our model. However, as we shall see in Chapters 2 and 3, the

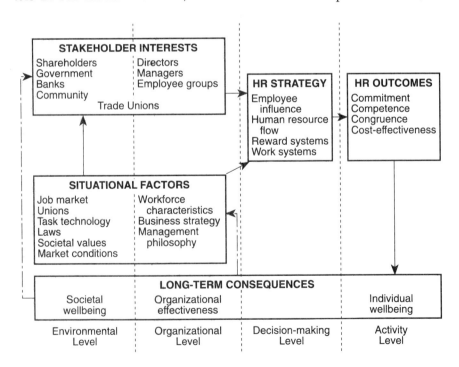

Figure 1.2 The Harvard perspective on HRM related to the Business in Context model.
Source: adapted from Beer *et al.* (1984).

influence of these variables on management is undervalued (Hollinshead and Leat 1995: 16). The emphasis is on psychological objectives – the 'human' side of human resource management – including:

- **motivating people** by involving them in decision-making;
- developing an organizational **culture** based on trust and teamwork.

Within the Harvard 'map' four strategic policy areas are addressed:

1 **Human resource flows**, managing the movement (flow) and performance of people:

- **into** the organization by means of effective recruitment programmes and selection techniques which result in the most suitable people;
- **through** the organization, by placing them in the most appropriate jobs, appraising their performance and promoting the better employees;
- **out** of the organization, by terminating the employment of those no longer required, deemed unsuitable or achieving retirement age.

Human resource policies must ensure the right mix and number of staff in the organization. This is achieved by means of the processes of resourcing and development of employee competences.

2 **Reward systems**, including pay and benefits designed to attract, motivate and keep employees.
3 **Employee influence**, controlling levels of authority, power and decision-making.
4 **Work systems**, defining and designing jobs, so that the arrangement of people, information and technology provide the most productive and efficient results.

These policies result in the 'four Cs':

- commitment of employees to the organization's mission and values in a way thought to be typical of Japanese workers;
- congruence, linking human resource objectives with the organization's goals;
- competence, developing an appropriate mixture of skills, abilities and knowledge;
- cost-effectiveness, delivering performance in a competitive manner.

The Harvard model is strongly influenced by behavioural research and theory and stands in the tradition of 'human relations'. This is a humanistic and anti-authoritarian viewpoint which holds that employees will only adopt an organization's objectives if they wish to. They will not demonstrate enthusiasm and commitment if they are forced to comply. Accordingly, although strategic decision-making is channelled through top managers there is an emphasis on participation throughout the organization.

A further key point is that HRM is the responsibility of all managers – not just human resource specialists. Responsibility for the delivery of HRM initiatives is pushed down to line managers wherever possible. The Harvard model applies HRM to **any** manager with staff responsibilities. It should consider issues such as delegation, leadership, participation, team-building and organization from a non-specialist perspective. This will be further explored in Chapter 4, in our discussion of organizational HRM. Taken to its extreme, it can be argued that if managers are sufficiently competent at handling people, then personnel or human resource specialists are unnecessary.

A harder approach – people as human *resources*

A different view of HRM is associated with the Michigan Business School (Tichy *et al.* 1982). There are many similarities with the Harvard 'map' but the Michigan model has a harder, less humanistic edge, holding that employees are resources in the same way as any other business resource (see key concept 1.4). People have to be managed in a similar manner to equipment and raw materials. They must be:

- obtained as cheaply as possibly;
- used sparingly;
- developed and exploited as much as possible.

Moreover, the same approach should be applied to all people who resource an organization – not just its employees. Human beings are 'matched' to business needs. They are recruited selectively and trained to perform required tasks. Whereas the Harvard approach was inspired by the behavioural sciences, the Michigan view was strongly influenced by strategic management literature. HRM is seen as a **strategic** process, making the most effective use of an organization's human resources. Hence there must be coherent human resource policies which 'fit' closely with overall business strategies.

KEY CONCEPT 1.4 **Hard and soft HRM**	Storey (1989) has distinguished between **hard** and **soft** forms of HRM, typified by the Michigan and Harvard models, respectively. 'Hard' HRM focuses on the resource side of human resources. It emphasizes costs in the form of 'headcounts' and places control firmly in the hands of management. Their role is to manage numbers effectively, keeping the workforce closely matched with requirements in terms of both bodies and behaviour. 'Soft' HRM, on the other hand, stresses the 'human' aspects of HRM. Its concerns are with communication and motivation. People are led rather than managed. They are involved in determining and realizing strategic objectives.

In fact, HRM is seen as a secondary product of strategy and planning rather than a primary influence. Within this model, the purpose of human resource strategy is to assist in the achievement of an organization's goals. This requires an alignment of all HR systems with the formal organization. Since the nature of HRM is determined largely by the situation and the environmental context there is little freedom of operation for human resource managers. At best, human resource managers can only choose from a menu of possible initiatives which fit business strategy. The Michigan School identified the following key areas for the development of appropriate HR policies and systems:

- **selection** of the most suitable people to meet business needs;
- **performance** in the pursuit of business objectives;
- **appraisal**, monitoring performance and providing feedback to the organization and its employees;
- **rewards** for appropriate performance;
- **development** of the skills and knowledge required to meet business objectives.

The Michigan model takes a top-down approach. In contrast with the Harvard viewpoint, control of human resources lies firmly in the hands of senior management. People are selected and trained to meet the performance needs of the organization. However, this is not sufficient. Their attitudes and behaviour must also fit the strategic requirements of the business. The Michigan model advocates that HRM requires that employees show **behavioural consistency** with the ways of thinking and operating necessary to achieve business goals. For example, if strategy focuses on sales, employees will be expected to be extravert, responsive and attentive to customer needs. On the other hand, an innovative strategy based on research and development will emphasize creativity, technical skill and long-term diligence. Behavioural consistency is an objective of change management, and both are discussed in Chapter 6.

Adopting HRM

So far, we have tried to establish a reasonably clear concept of HRM – despite the different emphases between the two major early models. At this point, however, we must inject a necessary element of caution. Human resource management has been presented as a radical alternative to personnel management. So much so that it has been regarded as a new paradigm (Kuhn 1962) – a framework of thinking – consisting of exciting, modern ideas which would replace the stale and ineffective prescriptions of personnel management. Enthusiasts saw the transition from 'personnel' to 'human resources' as an inevitable and unstoppable process – a paradigm shift. In fact, the process has proven to be somewhat slow.

HRM in the United States

As we have seen, HRM is primarily North American in origin, but in the USA, far from causing a revolution in people management techniques, acceptance of the new interpretation has not been universal. Kochan and Dyer comment that, despite an explosion of interest in human resource management:

> even today we find that the human resource function within many American corporations remains weak and relatively low in influence, relative to other functions such as finance, marketing and manufacturing . . . little progress has been made in developing systematic theory or empirical evidence on the

conditions under which human resources are elevated to a position where the firm sees and treats these issues as a source of competitive advantage. Nor is there much research that actually tests the effects of different strategies on the competitive position of the firm.

(Kochan and Dyer 1995: 333)

Why is this so? A number of explanations can be considered. First, there is the issue of perception: many US businesses fail to see the difference between HRM and earlier forms of people management. We observed at the beginning of the chapter that the term 'human resource management' had been used interchangeably with 'personnel management' in the USA. This continues to be the case. For example, many American 'HRM' texts are concerned with the functional activities of personnel specialists – their philosophy is little different from that of 1970s texts. In part, this is due to the managerialist and anti-union tradition of personnel management in the USA. For US practitioners, HRM was not such a radical departure from previous practice as it seemed to be for welfare-oriented personnel managers and industrial relations specialists in other countries.

Kochan and Dyer also point to the 'market failures' problem (1995: 333, 344). HRM is generally portrayed as having a long-term perspective. Within this context an organization's people are investments for the future. They are not to be hired and fired for short-term purposes. Yet we will see in Chapter 2 that this concept sits uneasily with the prevailing short-termist ideology of business in the English-speaking world. Long-term investment is expensive and requires the use of money which might otherwise be diverted to dividend payments. This draws unfavourable comment from shareholders. If all businesses in an industry were to take the same human resource initiatives there would be no problem. This is unlikely. Moreover, expensively developed staff can be creamed off by competitors unwilling to invest in training but prepared to pay a premium for competent recruits.

In Case 1.1 we see how the difficulties associated with long-term, soft HRM are reflected in the history of IBM. As one of the world's major businesses, IBM was used as an example of excellence by Peters and Waterman (1982). It hit its high point in 1984 with profits of over $6 billion – a sensational 25 per cent return on equity for shareholders. At that time it was the dominant force in world computing with 37 per cent of the total market. IBM was also featured by Beer and his colleagues as an example of a corporation which utilized the Harvard form of HRM. However, recent years have seen a significant shift towards a harder model as IBM encountered serious problems in the 1990s. Despite increases in overall revenues, the company was forced into major restructuring and job losses.

CASE 1.1 *Soft and hard HRM at IBM*	IBM symbolized the USA's technological and economic dominance in the postwar world. Ironically, the company resembled civil service organizations more than other industrial corporations. Its style was paternalist and hierarchical, offering employment for life and excellent career paths for its brightest workers. Company songs and slogans (such as THINK) were encouraged and benefits included IBM country clubs, designed to develop

a collective feeling. Despite IBM's reputation for aggressive sales activity, staff were required to behave in an 'honest, fair and square way'. This sober behaviour included wearing the familiar dark suits and white shirts which led to the nickname 'Big Blue'. This approach was eventually transmitted to Japan. In fact, during the 1950s Japanese management style was deliberately modelled on IBM.

The corporation was accused of being anti-union – but most of its staff seemed to like it that way. For example, an ACAS survey in 1977 showed that only 4.9 per cent of the company's British employees wanted a union. For half a century its culture was strongly based on lifetime employment and excellent working conditions, which were implicit in human resource policies which included:

- sophisticated human resource planning, recruitment and training procedures;
- a system of lifetime employment in which staff changed their jobs as and when required by the organization;
- equal status for all IBM employees in terms of fringe benefits, staff restaurants and other facilities, although company cars were restricted to senior management and some sales staff;
- centrally determined salaries – better than the rates of competitors – reviewed annually with increases based on a performance-objective system;
- considerable emphasis on training, particularly related to people management and averaging forty days a year for managers;
- an audit of staff opinion held every two years, focused on attitudes towards work methods, HR practices, pay and conditions;
- a model HRM approach with decision-making and people management delegated to line managers at the lowest possible level;
- formal communication procedures designed to encourage debate of business problems and to allow aggrieved staff to appeal against local management decisions.

(Needle 1994: 332)

IBM became one of the largest corporations in the world, with a global workforce reaching a peak of 405,000 in 1985. Its strength was based on an integrated product range of highly expensive mainframe computers, peripherals and software which locked users into IBM products once they had made their initial purchase. By the early 1990s, however, IBM was in serious trouble. According to one senior manager, the organization's bureaucratic paralysis meant that 'the management seemed to have totally lost contact with the product'. The personal computer had liberated customers from the mainframe. Despite the fact that the PC was an IBM invention, PC 'clones' were supplied more cheaply by competitors with much lower overheads. Profitability moved from the mainframe sector to the PC, and particularly to software producers such as Microsoft.

The company had been cutting costs for six years under the chairmanship of John Akers, a lifelong IBM man in his late fifties. Silver-haired and youthful, he was the image of the IBM corporate employee. The severity of the problem and Akers's bleak assessment of sales performance and poor productivity came to light in 1991. A middle manager who attended a confidential briefing inadvertently distributed his summary of the meeting through IBM's internal electronic mail network. This soon brought the media spotlight on to the corporation.

One publicized failure was the recruitment of 5,000 additional sales representatives – to boost the existing 20,000 – which resulted in increased revenues of less than 4 per cent. This was followed by a sharp about-turn – 17,000 job cuts. In IBM-speak these were referred to as 'management-initiated separations' (MIS). 47,000 IBM employees had already had an

MIS experience over the previous five years but this still left the company with a worldwide workforce of over 350,000.

Media and industry analysts increasingly criticized the momentum of change. Forecasts of reduced profits and static turnover led to calls for more radical action. IBM's strong points – its culture and structure – had apparently become its major weaknesses. The company was described as insular and complacent, slow to react to the move away from large expensive mainframe computers to powerful PCs and workstations. IBM's bureaucratic decision-making structure dragged down its ability to react at a time when the industry was becoming increasingly fast-moving. Procedures which functioned adequately when product development had a four-year cycle were hopelessly ineffective when the lead time had shrunk to a year. IBM had a tradition of producing virtually everything in-house, further increasing its insularity and inability to react quickly to market changes.

A loss of over $4 billion in 1992 led to Akers's replacement by the first outsider, who was destined to take the serious decisions which Wall Street analysts had demanded. The conclusion had been that Akers was too imbued in the IBM culture to be able to take sufficiently drastic measures. Louis Vincent Gerstner Jr, aged 51, was appointed Chairman in April 1993, with no experience of running a computer business. 'There will be no pussy-footing, no more salami-slicing,' he told shareholders a month later. Gerstner listed four immediate priorities:

- major staff reductions, reducing IBM's global workforce worldwide to about 250,000 and including the first compulsory redundancies in the company's history;
- defining IBM's core areas;
- improving customer relations;
- decentralization.

In 1993 Gerstner announced a record quarterly loss of $8 billion that included an $8.9 billion charge for laying off 50,000 employees that year – double the previous estimates. Gerstner said: 'Getting IBM's costs and expense structure in line with the revenue realities of our industry – right-sizing the company – is my highest near-term priority.' Gerstner appointed Gerald Czarnecki, an accountant and ex-banker, to take charge of 'human resources'. According to Czarnecki: 'IBM *did* deliberately foster paternalism, with a social contract between employer and employee. But economic realities forced us to rethink the relationship. Now we're no longer asking people for total commitment to us. They're eager to stay, but prepared to leave' (Sampson, 1995: 228).

The company still refrained from using terms such as 'layoff', but employees soon got the message. At the original IBM site, Endicott in New York State, the process was called ETOP – the Endicott Transition Opportunity Program. Cynical staff translated this as 'Eliminate the Older People'. Local mental health services reported a massive increase in requests for stress counselling. 'Surplused' staff felt stigmatized and rejected by the firm. For the company itself, however, the picture was looking better. By 1995 the company returned to profitability.

(*Sources*: *Guardian*, 28 July 1993, 'Layoff costs take IBM loss to $8bn peak'; Needle 1994; Sampson 1995)

Discussion questions

1 To what extent was IBM an example of 'soft' HRM in action prior to the 1990s?
2 Compare and contrast the people management styles of Akers and Gerstner.
3 What does this case show about the relative importance of employees in comparison with other stakeholders?

4 How has people management contributed to IBM's success and survival?

5 What are the short- and long-term implications of Gestner's strategy on employee effectiveness and morale?

The IBM case study emphasizes a number of difficulties associated with the adoption of 'soft' HRM. When business is good and continued growth seems probable, a company can afford to manage its people in a humane and considerate way. However, when the going gets tough and significant change is demanded, profitability becomes the prime consideration. The pressure for action from other stakeholders becomes overwhelming. It appears that in such circumstances managers have no alternative but to adopt a 'hard' approach. The choice between hard and soft models is governed as much (if not more) by the prevailing market situation as it is by any question of managerial humanitarianism.

HRM in the UK

When HRM was imported into other countries, it arrived with many of the contradictions inherent in American practice. Further confusion was created as its principles were considered in the light of local people man-agement traditions. As many commentators in Britain and elsewhere have been quick to point out, there is a 'central uncertainty' as to exactly what HRM is (Blyton and Turnbull 1992: 2). The nature of HRM has been the focus of a particularly vigorous debate in the UK. Its meaning and its distinctiveness from personnel management have been the topic of numer-ous articles, texts and conference papers.

Karen Legge (1989, 1995a, 1995b), for example, has been a steadfast critic of simplistic or evangelistic interpretations of HRM. The rhetoric of HRM claims that personnel and human resource management are distinctively different forms of people management. She demonstrates some flaws in this argument (Legge, 1989: 20; 1995a: 36). First, we have seen that 'hard' and 'soft' models of HRM themselves describe very different approaches. The 'soft' model can readily be identified with the welfarist tradition in British personnel management. Second, most texts do not actually compare like with like:

- Accounts of HRM are **normative** – they are theoretical models of how human resource management could or should take place. That is to say, they express an 'ideal' or set of intentions for HRM. They do not tell us how human resource management actually happens in the real world. Moreover, the intentions of soft HRM are often pious and contradictory. We saw earlier that they are derivative of much older concepts and techniques. What makes them 'HRM' is that their components are welded together into expressions of a particular – if divergent – philo-sophy of people management.

- In contrast, accounts of personnel management are generally **descriptive** of personnel practice. Models of personnel are grounded in decades of activity whereas HRM is still comparatively new and empirical evidence of its conduct is only beginning to emerge.

In short, we are comparing the **theory** of a young form of people management (HRM) with the **practice** of an older variety (Personnel Management). Comparing like with like, on the other hand, Legge concludes that there is not much difference between the normative, or 'ideal', models of personnel management and HRM. If we seek normative accounts of personnel management in the textbooks of the 1980s, we find the same terminology of 'integrating with organizational goals' and 'vesting control in the line' as in the more recent HRM literature of the 'soft' variety. However, she finds differences in emphasis:

- Personnel management focuses on the non-managerial workforce. HRM concentrates on managers and the 'core workforce'.
- HRM is vested in line managers in their role as business managers not people managers. The stress is on managing all resources to maximize profit.
- HRM models feature the role of senior managers in managing the culture of organizations.

Schools of thought

Paradoxically, attempts to define HRM too precisely seemed to have resulted in confusion and contradiction rather than clarity. However, and perhaps only for the moment, HRM has the advantage of appearing to be contemporary and innovative. This is particularly the case in comparison with personnel management. Nevertheless, personnel departments have refused to go away. A casual examination of job advertisements in the press will reveal that applications are still to be sent to 'Personnel Managers', 'Personnel Departments', and even 'Staffing Officers'. At the same time, advertisements for 'human resource' jobs are common – particularly at a senior level – even if applications are to be sent to the Personnel Office!

It is evident, therefore, that defining and accepting HRM comes down to a matter of opinion – or vested interest. Indeed, some interpretations have a strong constituency. It can be seen from Table 1.3 that each of these views has a natural audience able to identify its own interests with a particular interpretation. Hence it is possible to find accounts stressing one of the following:

- **HRM is really personnel management.** Human resource management is a modernized form of 'personnel', repackaged to enhance the status of personnel managers. It has a hard edge, entitling HR managers to the same respect as finance professionals. HRM is based on integrated and coherent recruitment, assessment and development programmes. It is sophisticated, requiring rigorous training under the auspices of a professional body or university.

- **HRM is a strategic model.** It employs the techniques of strategic management for the utilization of human resources. It focuses on senior managers' concern with achieving objectives and containing costs. HRM aims for a seamless link between business policy and recruitment, performance assessment, reward management, development and dismissal. HRM is a mechanism for control and the exercise of power by top management. It encourages employee attitudes and behaviour which are consistent with business goals. HRM is just one aspect of a senior manager's strategic repertoire. It requires a wide appreciation of the industry and the organization and fits with resource-based theories which are familiar from the business strategy literature. This interpretation owes its inspiration largely to the Michigan model.

- **HRM is people management.** It covers all aspects of managing employees in its widest sense and emphasizes the role of line managers in overseeing their own staff. From this perspective, HRM is a new generic label for all the techniques and tactics available to manage people. It concentrates on translating organizational objectives into operational achievement by winning employee commitment and gaining high-quality performance. HRM is practical and pragmatic. This interpretation derives from the Harvard model. However, as can be seen from much published material, and even university courses, there is a considerable risk that this approach can result in a loss of focus. The subject can easily be reduced to an incoherent and inconsistent collection of techniques and practices.

In fact, the value and popularity of HRM may derive from its openness to varied interpretations. It is possible to argue that the term is a useful 'catch-all phrase, reflecting general intentions but devoid of specific meaning' (Guest 1989). This allows it to be applied in a variety of circumstances. Individual authors and practitioners interpret HRM according to their own background, interests and intended audiences. Indeed, Keenoy and Anthony consider that we should not look too closely:

Table 1.3 Perceptions of HRM

Perspective	Audience	Focus	Interest
HRM as people management	General/line managers	Managing people as a direct, inter-personal activity	Commitment Performance Leadership Team-building
HRM as personnel management	Personnel specialists	Technical skills for assessment, selection, training, etc.	Appraisals Recruitment Selection methods Development
HRM as strategic management	Senior managers	People as assets (and liabilities)	Strategic planning Performance management Development Managing change

once we seek to explain HRM, to subject it to any analysis or criticism, it ceases to function as intended. Its purpose is to transform, to inspire, to motivate and, above all, to create a new 'reality' which is freely available to those who choose or are persuaded to believe. To explain it is to destroy it.

(Keenoy and Anthony 1992: 238)

Essential principles of HRM

At this point, and conscious of the risk of 'destroying it' (HRM), we will conclude the chapter with a discussion of the principles which appear to be essential to understanding HRM. First, why do we need a concept such as HRM? Surely, people management is a matter of common sense. Certainly, some good people managers have – from many years of experience – developed an internal model which guides them well in the way they deal with their employees. However, there are many indifferent managers who appear to have learned little from their careers. In any case, students need to acquire a comprehensible and communicable model without the benefit of years of experience. Second, if HRM has been in existence for two decades or so, has it not fulfilled its role? Unfortunately not. Comparing the early 1980s – the birth period of the subject – with the situation in the late 1990s, the need for a coherent approach to people management continues to be justified by some obvious deficiencies:

- In the 1980s personnel management had its own agenda: its priorities were not necessarily matched to those of the organization, and its professional training and structure focused on a narrow range of techniques at the practitioner level rather than emphasizing a global view of business needs. It is arguable that the 'personnel profession' has become aware of these criticisms and has gone some way towards addressing them. However, there is still room for improvement.
- Other managers practised people management through a ragbag of often dubious and counter-productive methods, usually developed from intuition and experience. This continues to be largely the case.
- In the 1980s theories of strategic management concentrated on areas such as finance and marketing, tending to ignore human resources. Since then, theoretical accounts have become much more people-conscious, but it will be some time before most managers become truly aware of the importance of HRM.

As a consequence, the people in an organization were, and are, dealt with in a largely inconsistent and parochial manner. The 'You are our most valuable asset and, by the way, you're fired' approach describes people management in so many organizations. As we shall see in later chapters, the evidence shows that a meaningful form of HRM still does not prevail in most organizations. Little has changed.

So how should we practice meaningful HRM? At this point we introduce a systematic framework devised for this book (see Table 1.4). It incorporates ten principles, each conveniently beginning with 'C' – in the best management-guru style. In fact, terms beginning with 'C' have a considerable track record in HRM and, therefore, the principles are not novel or surprising. The Harvard model has its central four Cs – commitment, congruence,

Table 1.4 Ten principles of HRM

Principle	Purpose	Action
1 Comprehensiveness	Includes all aspects of people management	People management must be organized, rather than left to ad-hoc decisions at local level
2 Coherence	HR management activities and initiatives form a meaningful whole	Clear link between individual performance/reward and business needs
3 Control	Ensures performance is consistent with business objectives	Participative management, with delegation of *how* an objective is achieved
4 Communication	Objectives understood and accepted by all employees; open culture with no barriers	Clear, simple and justified strategies; cascading process of communication with feedback to the top
5 Credibility	Staff trust top management and believe in their strategies	Top managers are sincere, honest and consistent
6 Commitment	Employees motivated to achieve organizational goals	Top managers are commited to the staff
7 Change	Continuous improvement and development essential for survival	Flexible people and working systems; culture of innovation; skills training
8 Competence	Organization competent to achieve its objectives – dependent on individual competencies	Resourcing strategies, selection techniques and human resource development systems in place
9 Creativity	Competitive advantage comes from unique strategies	System for encouraging and tapping employee ideas
10 Cost-effectiveness	Competitive, fair reward and promotion systems	Top managers pay themselves on equivalent basis to staff

competence, cost-effectiveness – three of which are incorporated in our ten principles. Torrington has similarly proposed a seven Cs model of international HRM, including 'consultancy' and 'culture'(1994: 7). However, our ten principles have been chosen because they are all measurable in some way. They can be used for 'benchmarking' or comparisons between different organizations, as we shall see in Chapter 4. In fact, the essence of HRM lies in the tension and balance between them.

Comprehensiveness

All people management activities should be part of a single, comprehensive system. This implies that the attitudes, behaviour and culture of every individual in an organization – especially those with people management responsibilities – should be integrated within a deliberate framework. This approach ensures that HRM is holistic and systematic, with every aspect – together with their interrelationships – brought into consideration. It reflects the perspective that business problems, especially those involving people management, are highly complex. The relevant variables are **den-**

sely interconnected (Checkland, 1981). In other words, simple solutions are rarely possible.

Coherence

The second principle addresses the internal balance and integration of the people management system. Strategies and actions must be consistent with each other. For example, if a business has a strategy of increasing sales of high-profit-margin products, rewards in the sales department should be focused on those products rather than less profitable items. Similarly, if the organization has chosen to take a team-based approach, recruitment and training should emphasize team skills rather than strong individualism.

Control

As with any other form of management, HRM is aimed at directing and coordinating employees to meet an organization's objectives. As such, it cannot be anarchic nor totally democratic in its approach. However, the nature of control must be consistent with the remaining principles. Human resource literature mostly advocates a participative approach with a high degree of empowerment and delegation. An autocratic approach is unlikely to encourage good communication and employee commitment.

Communication

Effective communication facilitates coherence. Serious attention must be given to communicating the organization's strategic objectives, together with the parameters – acceptable behaviour, cost and time – within which they can be achieved. Good communication is essential to the smooth running of the people management system. It must be a two-way process. This can involve a cascaded flow of information from the top and also feedback from lower levels through surveys, performance measures and open meetings. An open culture should be encouraged: employees need to feel confident that they can express their opinions and concerns without fear of retribution.

Credibility

Many organizations spend a great deal of money and effort in their attempts to communicate with employees. Often, however, employees dismiss glossy magazines and time-consuming team briefings as so much management propaganda. A degree of healthy cynicism is unavoidable, but in today's 'down-sized' workplaces this frequently extends into mistrust of and contempt for senior management. This feeling reflects the way many staff feel they are themselves regarded by management. Regaining trust depends on personal credibility which, in turn, can only come from honesty and sincerity.

Commitment

Earlier, we noted that the Harvard model of HRM places a strong emphasis on the notion of commitment. It embodies a 'can-do' approach, going further than is normally asked. Committed employees can give that competitive edge – the extra something which distinguishes a successful company from its lesser rivals. However, commitment is difficult to achieve. As we will find in our discussion in Chapter 5, it is dependent on confidence in the organization, the people who lead it, the reward mechanism and the opportunity for staff to develop themselves. More than anything, it depends on the degree of commitment which managers show to their own people. As we saw in the IBM case study, economic realities can jeopardize this commitment.

Change

Businesses must change to survive. However, change is a difficult management task. Effective change requires sure-footed, considerate people managers who can take employees through the process with minimum anxiety and maximum enthusiasm. It requires the recognition that an organization's people should not be the pawns of strategy but active participants in change. In Chapter 6, we will see that their detailed job knowledge, customer contact and ingenuity can be harnessed to provide ideas for improvement.

Competence

Organizations must have the capability to meet changing needs. In current parlance this is often expressed in terms of competences – skills, knowledge and abilities. These are qualities possessed by the people who work for those organizations. Competences can be brought into businesses through the recruitment of skilled individuals. They can also be developed within existing people by investing in training, education and experiential programmes. The establishment and cultivation of a high level of relevant competences leads to a distinct competitive advantage.

Creativity

Advantages can also come from the ingenuity of staff. Creativity is under-emphasized in management training but it can lead to new products and services, novel applications and cost-savings. Competences such as detailed knowledge of products and procedures are required before innovation can occur. A creative environment develops from a trusting, open culture with good communication and a blame-free atmosphere. Conversely, creativity is inhibited by lack of trust or commitment and fear of the consequences of change.

Cost-effectiveness

One of the original Harvard 'four Cs', it provides the hard kernel of an otherwise 'soft' model of HRM. Expressed in terms of profitability, it has been extensively used as the justification for large-scale job cuts. This aspect has attracted considerable criticism, primarily because of the obsessive way in which many senior managers have pursued 'down-sizing' at the expense of commitment to their staff. However, as a reflection of the value of its human assets, an organization has a duty to use its people wisely and cost-effectively. In itself, there is nothing wrong with an attention to cost – provided that it does not become the one and only management criterion.

These principles are developed further in later chapters. It can be seen that the ten principles are interlocked. Failure to observe any one of these principles can lead to the breakdown of the people management system. Throughout the remainder of the book we will find illustrations of such failure, usually attributable to management belief that HRM can be adopted on a 'pick-and-mix' basis.

Summary

In this chapter we introduced you to the concept of human resource management. It has evolved from a number of different strands of thought and is best described as a loose philosophy of people management rather than a focused methodology. It is a topic which continues to attract debate and disagreement. As a consequence, practitioners and textbooks use a diverse and sometimes contradictory range of interpretations. We found that HRM has a variety of definitions but there is general agreement that it has a closer fit with business strategy than previous models, specifically personnel management. The early models of HRM take either a 'soft' or a 'hard' approach, but economic circumstances are more likely to drive the choice than any question of humanitarianism. We concluded the chapter with a discussion of ten key principles which determine the coherence and effectiveness of the HRM approach to people management.

Further reading

The seminal Harvard model is described in Beer *et al.* (1984), *Managing Human Assets*. John Storey's (ed.) (1989) *New Perspectives on Human Resource Management*, a collection of reviews written by leading commentators in the field, has been influential in the HRM debate. It remains useful, although *Human Resource Management: A Critical Text*, also edited by Storey (1995), draws a more recent picture. Both texts give a good account of the disagreement and confusion over the meaning and prevalence of HRM. For example, Sisson's contribution in the 1995 volume evaluates the highly problematic role of traditional personnel management and the influence of HRM. *Reassessing Human Resource Management*, edited by Paul Blyton and Peter Turnbull (1992) also provides useful critiques of the subject. Karen Legge's (1995b) *Human Resource Management: Rhetorics and Realities* is a further useful summary, aimed at MBA students.

Review questions

1 Is managing people just a matter of common sense? If so, what value can we attach to theories and models?

2 What is HRM? Is it really different from personnel management?

3 Is HRM a fashion or is it here to stay? What is the probability that HRM will be the dominant framework for people management in the twenty-first century?

4 Evaluate the following statement:

> (HRM) is in reality a symbolic label behind which lurk multifarious practices, many of which are not mutually dependent on one another.
> (Storey 1992)

5 List the major tasks of traditional personnel management. How do these functions compare with those suggested in models of HRM?

6 The Harvard model of HRM is an idealistic representation of people management. In the real world it is bound to be displaced by harder models of HRM. Discuss.

7 HRM theorists argue that employees are assets and not just costs. What does this mean in practice?

8 Compare and contrast the 'hard' and 'soft' forms of HRM. Of the two, which is the best approach to people management?

9 Consider an organization of your choice and discuss the questions which follow:

- Are its people management practices closer to traditional personnel management or to HRM?
- Who is in overall charge of the organization's employees?
- Does it have a human resource strategy? Who is responsible for its implementation?
- Do line managers or specialists recruit and/or dismiss employees?
- How committed are employees to the organization?
- What changes would improve the situation?

10 How much does the concept of HRM owe to Japanese management practices?

Problems for discussion and analysis

1 The Craft Partnership is a cooperative of twenty independent producers. They are based at an old factory site on the outskirts of town which is divided into small workshops. Personnel, marketing and finance services are provided by an office manager and two staff. The cooperative has grown successfully over the last five years. Now they have the opportunity of taking on a much larger site adjacent to the tourist centre.

Opinion is divided among the partners on the way forward. Some are content to stay as they are. A few have said that they will leave and set up on their own if the cooperative gets much larger. Others are excited at the prospect of better facilities, room for growth, and space for new members in the cooperative. They also see big advantages in being accessible to tourists.

The office manager sees this as the opportunity to make more radical changes. She is concerned that the partnership is unwieldy and makes external finance difficult. She spends much of her time sorting out squabbles between partners and trying to get them to share resources sensibly. Some partners are overworked and others do not have enough to do. She can see many ways of increasing efficiency if the partnership becomes a conventional business. This could be done by creating a holding company, making the existing partners both shareholders and employees. A local venture company is prepared to make a substantial investment for a 50 per cent share in the new organization. However, this would require a formal structure with defined management roles. The company feels that the office manager would make a suitable managing director.

She has arranged a meeting with the partners and the venture company. How should she proceed? What is the reaction likely to be? What is the way forward?

2 The Royal Ocean is a well-established resort hotel. Its clients are in the middle- to upper-income bracket and many return year after year. It has developed a reputation for attentive service and is regarded as expensive but good value. In recent years, however, a new marina development further down the coast has provided extra competition. The new hotels are larger and more modern, boasting a choice of restaurants, bars and leisure facilities. They have affected the Royal Ocean's profitability seriously.

The hotel is on a restricted site and the owners, a small regional chain, cannot afford substantial capital investment. Like most hotels it has a highly seasonal pattern of business. Despite the competition, the Royal Ocean has no difficulty in filling rooms during peak periods. Occupancy rates have been affected mainly during quieter periods. The company has decided to encourage more business out of season through selective promotions to group travel organizers. During the low season, the country has a national holiday when, traditionally, the hotel has allowed most of its staff to take two days off. The small number of remaining employees have been sufficient to cater for the few guests. In the past, visitors at this time of year have tended to be middle-aged people seeking quiet relaxation. They have been happy to tolerate restricted service in the restaurant, bar and pool area.

This year, the hotel has achieved 80 per cent occupancy over the holiday period. The regular clients have been vastly outnumbered by families with young children. Rooms have been sold cheaply to low-income groups who are not expected to spend heavily on the more profitable services. Accordingly, the hotel general manager decided not to increase staffing to normal weekly levels. He felt that the low return would not justify upsetting employee morale.

However, the consequences have proven to be unfortunate. The regular clients have been angered by the inability of the hotel to provide even the basic service experienced in previous years. Most shops, restaurants and visitor facilities in the area are closed because of the holiday. The clients are forced to remain within the hotel. The restaurant has been besieged by noisy family groups. The pool area has become a playground. Clients have to wait for up to twenty minutes for an elevator because children are continuously going up and down in them. The previously quiet middle-aged regulars are complaining vociferously to any member of staff they can find. It seems that they are largely affluent professionals who are accustomed to having their way. They are becoming increasingly demanding and are threatening never to come back.

What can be done: now; in the future?

2

HRM and the business environment

This chapter examines the relationship between HRM and the business environment. It encompasses the influence of the state, the economy and national cultures on the management of people.

At first sight it may seem strange to devote a whole chapter to the relationship between HRM and the business environment. However, a moment's thought makes it clear that people management within individual organizations cannot take place in isolation from the rest of the world: 'HRM does not exist within a vacuum' (Hollinsead and Leat 1995: 7). As we saw in Chapter 1, this is reflected by the somewhat understressed inclusion of outside stakeholders in the Harvard model of HRM.

Many practitioners and academics have neglected HRM's environmental context, preferring to concentrate on technical detail. This is consistent with criticisms of traditional personnel management for its narrow focus on functional or 'micro' matters such as recruitment. In fairness, however, it must be recognized that personnel managers have always required a detailed knowledge of employment legislation, together with an understanding of industrial tribunals and trade union organization. Nevertheless, this represents a restricted selection from the wide range of environmental factors impacting on people management.

Often exponents of HRM have been no better than traditional personnel managers in this respect. Kochan and Dyer argue that despite the obsession with strategy, HRM theories have a fundamental weakness, 'a myopic viewpoint which fails to look beyond the boundary of the firm' (1995: 343). Without the ability or the interest to locate their activities in a wider environmental setting, human resource practitioners can lose contact with the 'bleeding edge' of organizational survival. To counter short-sightedness and parochialism, HR managers must widen their perspectives beyond their own organizations (Beardwell and Holden 1994: 613). In contrast to colleagues in marketing, production and finance, people managers seem less prepared to function in a competitive world.

This chapter addresses this wider perspective and introduces a number of fundamental issues which are developed further in later chapters, for example:

- What is the connection between education and skill levels and national success?
- To what extent is the nature of people management determined by prevailing political ideology and national culture?
- Is HRM simply a managerial reaction to the spread of market economies throughout the world?
- Is there a contradiction between HRM's long-term emphasis and the short-term priorities of the stock market?

We observed in the previous chapter that the essence of HRM lies in the competitive advantage to be gained from making the most of an organization's human resources. However, it is obvious that we are constrained by the availability of suitable people – a factor which is heavily dependent on environmental variables. As we shall see, they include:

- the implications of world and national economic conditions for business growth;
- the effect of inflation on the perceived value of wages;
- the traditions of local business culture;
- the particular nature of national employment markets.

In effect, therefore, these variables have a 'macro' effect on the utilization of human resources. Additionally, in this chapter we consider other effects caused by the activities of external stakeholders, such as:

- competitors' utilization of and demand for human resources;
- multinational organizations and strategic alliances leading to restructuring or integration on a global basis;
- economic and legislative actions by governments;
- resistance or cooperation from trade unions;
- pressure on senior managers to cut costs and maximize shareholder value.

We begin the chapter with an examination of situational factors at the international and national levels.

HRM and global competitiveness

We concluded the previous chapter by considering HRM as a people management system, acknowledging its intricate and interdependent principles. However, HRM is a system within other systems. The most complex of these is the international **business environment** (see key concept 2.1). The forces which act on people management are not purely internal to an organization. They include innumerable active players in the world economy, including international agencies, governments, competitors, unions, speculators and consumers – each pursuing their own goals.

KEY CONCEPT 2.1 *The business environment*	'All factors which exist outside the business enterprise, but which interact with it' (Needle 1994: 26). Traditionally, human resource managers have been closely involved with employment legislation, industrial tribunals and trade unions at a functional level. HRM's strategic emphasis requires a focus on other environmental variables. Government economic, social security, education and training policies affect the availability, cost and quality of available employees. International competition, strategic alliances and supranational organizations such as the European Union are exercising increasing influence on people management.

Changes in the business environment have major consequences for people managers. As we saw in the case of IBM, these forces may be so powerful that an individual organization loses the discretion to pursue its own strategies (Kochan and Dyer 1995: 337). In essence this means that factors outside a company's control will affect its requirements for human resources and the way they are managed. For example, unexpected changes in competitor technology or currency exchange rates may compel a business to abandon long-term human resource plans and shed staff in order to survive.

Growth and employment

The growth of the economy is the most significant overriding variable for people management since it determines overall demand for products and services, and hence employment. Table 2.1 shows a ranking of OECD countries in terms of gross domestic product (GDP), together with average growth rates between low points in two recent business cycles. The British economy has the longest industrial history but UK growth has been consistently slow – rarely exceeding 3 per cent per annum. There is a tendency for countries which are lower in the GDP league to have higher rates of growth in a 'catching-up' process. Consequently, high rates of growth in East Asia have accompanied medium growth in the developed countries. However, this is not universal – there has been consistently low growth in Africa, for example.

The reasons for differing rates of growth have been endlessly debated but the effective exploitation of human resources appears to be a crucial factor. The nature of the link between human resources and economic success is not simple. This is illustrated by attempts to provide an index of international competitiveness.

For some years the World Economic Forum (WEF), an international business organization, and the Institute for International Management Development (IMD), a Swiss business school, cooperated in the production of such an index. In 1996, however, they produced independent league

Table 2.1 International comparison of GDP and growth

Country	GDP per capita 1994 purchasing power (based on UK = 100)	Average growth rate % (GDP per capita) 1981–93
Luxembourg	166.9	3.0
USA	144.5	1.6
Switzerland	135.6	0.9
Norway	124.5	2.2
Japan	117.6	3.1
Denmark	116.4	2.0
Canada	115.6	1.0
Austria	114.5	1.7
Belgium	114.3	1.7
Germany	111.5	2.1
Iceland	109.2	0.8
France	108.8	1.3
Italy	105.8	1.8
Netherlands	105.3	1.5
Australia	104.1	1.4
UK	100.0	2.0
Sweden	98.7	0.9
New Zealand	92.1	1.0
Ireland	86.2	3.5
Finland	86.2	0.9
Spain	76.9	2.4
Portugal	69.9	2.5
Greece	64.1	1.1
Mexico	41.0	−0.8
Turkey	29.9	2.9

Source: adapted from *The Financial Times*, 25 April 1995; figures derived from OECD.

tables (*The Independent*, 30 May 1996). We can see in Table 2.2 that their conclusions differ markedly. For example, according to the IMD, the UK's competitiveness is slipping, whereas in the WEF version the country's rankings in 1995 and 1996 are the same.

Both organizations calculate their competitiveness indices by combining hundreds of different measures. These range from GDP per head to estimates of the competence of a country's managers. The main difference lies in the relative weightings given to the measures. The WEF regards government regulation and welfare provision as negative factors for national growth, whereas openness to international trade and investment are viewed favourably. Hence the UK's comparatively low pension burdens and flexible employment market are seen as strengths. The IMD, on the other hand, emphasizes investment in higher education and vocational skills – areas of weakness in the UK. Significantly, both organizations rate the quality of British management as low. These ratings reflect two important perspectives on the role of human resources in the competitiveness debate. We can regard them as the 'hard' and 'soft' versions of macro HRM.

Paradoxically, a competitive environment can drive organizations

Table 2.2 Relative competitiveness

Position	1995	IMD 1996	WEF 1996
1	USA	USA	Singapore
2	Singapore	Singapore	Hong Kong
3	Hong Kong	Hong Kong	New Zealand
4	Japan	Japan	USA
5	Switzerland	Denmark	Luxembourg
6	Germany	Norway	Switzerland
7	Denmark	Netherlands	Norway
8	Netherlands	Luxembourg	Canada
9	New Zealand	Switzerland	Taiwan
10	Norway	Germany	Malaysia
11	Austria	New Zealand	Denmark
12	Sweden	Canada	Australia
13	Canada	Chile	Japan
14	Taiwan	Sweden	Thailand
15	UK	Finland	UK
16	Australia	Austria	Finland
17	Luxembourg	Belgium	Netherlands
18	Finland	Taiwan	Chile
19	France	UK	Austria
20	Chile	France	Korea

Sources: International Institute for Management Development; World Economic Forum

towards greater similarity rather than innovative differentiation. Businesses in the same sector adopt surprisingly similar ways of managing their people – or any other resource. In part this is due to fashion. They watch each other, copying what seems to work. Staff also move between companies in the same field, taking people management practices with them. In fact, novel methods are not common. The principal idea-generators – management gurus and consultants – cannot make their fortune by selling a new practice to just one organization. On the contrary, they have a vested interest in peddling their wares as widely as possible. The increasing globalization of products and management practices encourages this process (see key concept 2.2). Organizations throughout the western world are swept by waves of fashion, taking to 'down-sizing', 'total quality', 'team briefings', or 'business process

KEY CONCEPT 2.2 *Globalization*	A systematic trend towards the integration of production and marketing with brand-named goods and virtually identical 'badge-engineered' products being made available throughout the world. This process has been fostered by 'transnational' and 'multinational' companies operating in more than one country. Such companies are relatively free to switch resources and production from one country to another. Typically this is done in order to maximize the benefit (to the corporation) of greater skills availability and lower employee costs. This has been described as the **new international division of labour**.

re-engineering'. The principle seems to be to do the same as everyone else, as quickly as possible, in order to avoid a competitive *dis*advantage.

Large organizations with overmanaged and rigid structures have become especially vulnerable to a host of smaller competitors able to introduce new products quickly, unencumbered by existing production lines and management systems. This is exemplified by the case study on IBM in Chapter 1 (Case 1.1). Career structures collapsed in such firms as they cut employee costs, flattened their management hierarchies and subdivided into nimbler small business units. In the interest of short-term profitability, experienced staff were 'let go' and training budgets cut. The remaining staff were in fear of losing their own jobs. As we shall see in Chapter 6, on strategic HRM, such companies are lean and mean and well able to survive but lack many of the human resource strengths necessary for sustained organic growth. Some of the most successful become predators, initiating few new ideas themselves but able to buy and absorb other – more innovative – companies.

This has produced a conflict between the rhetoric of HRM – emphasizing the importance of employees as a long-term investment – and the expendability of staff in practice. Most organizations have not taken happily to such hypocrisy. Economic instability has made employers wary of taking on full-time staff when times are good, only to have to shed them when order levels fall. This is a wasteful and costly process with damaging consequences on the morale of remaining employees. Instead, businesses have been attracted to forms of human resource which do not require a long-term commitment. Contractors, consultants, freelancers and temporary staff do not pose a redundancy problem if economic conditions turn sour and production has to be cut. As we will find in Chapter 3, depending on one's political perspective, employment has become increasingly **flexible** or **casualized**.

Economic turbulence

Businesses are not entirely passive or helpless. They are also active players in their environment. They can influence and, sometimes, control their markets. Effectively, major industrial sectors such as petroleum, information technology, aerospace and automobile manufacture are dominated by a small number of multinational corporations. At a local level, strategic alliances between small companies can have the same effect: establishing a degree of control and predictability on the market.

It has been estimated that some large corporations operating internationally, described as multinationals, are responsible for a greater proportion of international trade than most independent states. At one time, companies such as IBM in the USA, ICI in the UK, Volkswagen in former West Germany and Toyota in Japan were viewed as national champions. They were key players in those countries' economic activities. Their senior managers influenced governments. As long as profits flowed, shareholders, banks and employees were relatively content. In recent decades, however, industrial competition has become global. National champions have become multinational corporations moving functions around the world without loyalty to any nation. Research and development takes place in one country, manufacturing in a second, with sales in different continents.

This importance has given them the power to play one country against another and to take actions which would be unacceptable for companies operating within single states. Their ability to switch investment from one country to another has been a significant cause for concern. Multinationals are major determiners of action on the world scene, able to move their operations from country to country in defiance of government attempts to maintain minimum wages or workers' consultation.

Initially, corporations such as Ford adopted a policy of dual-sourcing in which two or more plants in a regional trading block such as Europe or North America had the same function, for example building engines. If there were engineering or industrial relations problems in one plant, the other could supply the required components. This insurance policy became less necessary as quality control improved, but it afforded the opportunity of shifting production, and hence employment, from the country with the greater labour costs to that with the cheaper. Potentially, this had the effect of driving down employee costs. Deliberate government policy has made dismissal cheaper and easier in the UK than in other European countries, thereby encouraging manufacturers in volatile industries to consider the UK for inward investment. However, this policy has backfired. Short-term expediency induced corporations to close UK plants because this was effectively easier than tackling less competitive European plants protected by social legislation.

Another feature of multinational activity has been the sourcing of components of manufactured products in different countries. Low skill items were the first affected, but more sophisticated items have followed. Wage levels and required skills are not constant factors and it can be argued that this form of sourcing is a natural and progressive feature of industrial growth. Alternatively, it could be described in terms of unscrupulous corporations chasing low wages around the world with the connivance of desperate and sometimes corrupt politicians. Described as *maquiladora* or *maquila* plants (duty-free factories) in Mexico, comparatively unrestricted manufacturing plants have mushroomed with their exports geared to the US market (Ransom 1994). The Mexican government copied similar plants in the 'Tiger' economies of South-east Asia, almost all owned by US multinationals. These firms now produce a quarter of Mexico's output, employing half a million workers in 2,000 plants. It is estimated that this will rise to 3 million people by the end of the century. Initially, they were predominantly small-scale sweatshops with largely female labour producing low-skill goods. The emphasis has switched to a more balanced workforce making technologically advanced parts for major US companies in the automobile, electronics and textile industries. Some of this employment has been exported from the United States, estimated at 100,000 jobs in the last decade.

The marriage of global telecommunications and advanced information technology has resulted in a phenomenon known as 'teletrading'. Airlines such as British Airways, Lufthansa, Swissair and Austrian Airlines have transferred data-processing work to Bombay and New Delhi (*The*

Independent, 3 July 1995). Similarly, Data Management Services, an associate of American Airlines, employs 1,600 staff in Barbados and the Dominican Republic handling much of the airline's data-processing work, along with claim forms for a number of US insurance companies. In fact, the company has become Barbados's largest private employer. Initially, teletrading focused on low-skill work handled by low-wage workers, but the trend is towards transferring more skilled programming and query handling.

Despite the criticisms of multinationals, many governments – including those of developed countries such as the UK and those of underdeveloped economies – have devoted much energy and money to attracting overseas investment. The British have focused on American and Japanese manufacturers such as computer and car makers. The Pacific rim countries have wooed the same companies. Developing countries in Africa, the Caribbean and South America have been more restricted, often dependent on mining and plantation conglomerates supplying the supermarkets of the North. Multinationals have ruthlessly played one country or region against another, accepting the highest subsidies and lowest controls over pollution and workers' welfare. Environmental and employee legislation in their 'home' countries has been cynically avoided by transferring production overseas. Trade unions have been slow and largely ineffective in providing employee protection to match the activities of global managers.

Admittedly, however, despite the bad press multinationals also produce clearly positive benefits. Multinationals have introduced innovative human resource practices, including mobility packages, cross-cultural and language training, greater sensitivity to national management practices, recruitment and development of local employees and some exciting international careers.

Even in quasi-monopolistic sectors, however, management is constrained by a range of environmental factors. Western economies have experienced alternating periods of global recession and recovery. Spurts of growth have been followed by cuts in both production and employment. In a dynamic economy businesses expect growth in sales, production and ultimately in employee numbers. Conversely, companies experiencing recession or intense competition may have to retrench – 'downsize' in modern management-speak. For instance, in the mid-1990s air travel recovered slowly from recession. Airlines struggled to meet competition and cut costs to remain in existence. Orders for new aeroplanes were deferred or cancelled. The consequences for aeroplane manufacturers were severe. The world's largest aircraft manufacturer, Boeing, was forced to cut production, leading to thousands of job losses. Similarly, losses at the Dutch company Fokker, leading producer of medium-sized aircraft, impacted heavily on its major German shareholder, Daimler-Benz.

The law of the market jungle rules – survival of the leanest, fittest and fastest. At the time of writing Fokker's prospects look uncertain, whereas Boeing has recruited more workers to meet an upturn in demand for its aircraft. 'Market Darwinism' forces businesses to change direction at short notice, seeking any possible competitive advantage. Businesses have to keep a worldwide watch for the next revolutionary improvement in productivity or service.

The globalization of human resources

Growth in international business has led to massive interest in the way people are managed in different countries – particularly in the management techniques underlying the 'economic miracle' of Japan. At one time the twentieth century seemed to be destined to be the American century. US corporations dominated world trade, and American business methods, focused on tight financial controls and marketing, were widely copied. As international competition and recession damaged the US economy, however, it became clear that management practices in countries such as Japan and Germany were more successful than American business school models.

The short-term attitudes of senior American executives have been much criticized. Managers with financial or legal backgrounds have gravitated to the top at the expense of those with technical or scientific expertise. This has led to a prevailing management style emphasizing cash management with fast measurable returns. Mergers and takeovers, disposals and closures fit neatly into this mindset, whereas longer-term research, product development and people management have been neglected. Senior managers elsewhere in the English-speaking world have followed the US lead. American practice was enthusiastically copied in the UK, where it fitted a longstanding class prejudice against 'dirty hands' and 'trade'. 'New Right' policies ensured government support for such attitudes, defended within the mythology of 'market forces'.

In Chapter 1 we saw that Japan served as a role model for western businesses in the 1980s. HRM owes much of its inspiration to the long-term and people, rather than cash, orientation of Japanese business. For some time it was believed that the Japanese had the 'magic answers' for people management and that these could be identified and translated into western businesses. Team working, quality circles and continuous improvement produced discernible benefits in car manufacturing in the UK, for example. However, in the 1990s the Japanese model lost some of its mystique. Despite a record trade surplus of $145.8 billion (£93.5 billion) in 1994, there was talk of Japanese industrial dominance having peaked (see Case 2.1). Ironically, major Japanese companies began to introduce western methods of people management.

In fact, no single approach to people management can be guaranteed to be more effective than any other. Different business environments generate different forms of managerial structures, which can be equally successful in world markets. Hegewisch and Brewster found that the country involved was much more significant in the way people management is handled than business size or commercial sector (1993: 22). Different approaches develop because organizations are dependent on the social, political and financial institutions of the countries in which they operate. Contrary to Margaret Thatcher's confident ideological statement that 'there is no society', it is evident that societies determine what organizational structures and managerial practices are acceptable and 'normal' (Tyson 1995: 46). The perception of normality varies widely from country to country and is attributable to the business cultures of those countries. We will see in later chapters that the concept of culture features prominently in the human resource literature, both at a corporate and a national level.

Trading blocks

Partly due to the activities of multinational firms, international trade has grown to colossal proportions in recent decades. The bulk of this trade is concentrated in three major trading blocks: the European Union, the North American Free Trade Area (NAFTA – Canada, Mexico and the USA) and the 'Tiger' economies – the newly industrialized countries (NIDs) of East Asia. These blocks comprise the 'triad' which now dominates the world economy (Chung 1991). The boundaries of the trading blocks are shifting and generally expanding. The European Union has accommodated Austria, Finland, and Sweden and is looking eastwards. East Germany has been absorbed by the Federal Republic. Former members of the Soviet empire, Estonia, Latvia, Lithuania and satellites such as Poland, the Czech and Slovak republics, Hungary and others are in the queue to join.

The integration of former communist countries into the free world brings different philosophies and practices of management into focus and possible conflict. Currently the eastern European countries have a much lower standard of living than most of the EU's longstanding members. The Czech Republic is closest to the western European norm, with earnings just 10 per cent lower than the Greeks. Tourism has boomed and exports to the EU have replaced business lost in the former communist countries. It seems reasonable to assume that inequalities between eastern and western Europe will gradually even out as businesses move to the regions with lower costs. However, the evidence of recent economic history indicates that this may not happen quickly – if it happens at all. The reality has been that whereas poorer areas have cut employee costs to maintain their competitiveness, more affluent regions have been unwilling to consider this tactic and have turned to more up-market quality products instead.

Countries such as South Korea, Taiwan and Singapore have shown much faster rates of economic growth than those of the west and have benefited considerably from the export of Japanese jobs. Comparatively low labour costs and strong adherence to the work ethic have appeared highly attractive to foreign investors. Adjacent countries are making efforts to join in this success. For example, Australia has made political moves away from its Anglo-Celtic ways in an effort to make the country more acceptable to its Asian neighbours. According to Chung:

> Business people from and in the Asian-Pacific area have become more self-confident, and they are demanding respect for Asian culture if European or American business people want to cooperate with them. The one-way street is a thing of the past, and what is needed now is the ability to engage in culture-specific dialogue. The ability to communicate interculturally has become a crucial factor for success in the global business of the future.
>
> (Chung 1991: 419)

Within the trading blocks, there is increasing scope for integration and rationalization. This is exemplified by the defence and aerospace industries in the EU. Cuts in defence expenditure following the end of the Cold War, together with ever-escalating costs for the development of new planes and other equipment, have encouraged a consolidation between the former national defence specialists. Joint development and marketing agreements will be replaced by closer working arrangements such as those employed by Airbus Industrie. The consequences for employment will probably include overall staff reductions within the sector, increased specialization and a demand for higher language and technology skills.

There are signs that the period of Japanese economic dominance may have reached its peak. Seasonally adjusted unemployment at the end of 1995 stood at 3.4 per cent, the highest level since the Second World War. A survey by the World Economic Forum placed Japan thirteenth in 1996 (see Table 2.2) in its table of competitive economies, and in 1995 the United States again overtook Japan to become the world's largest producer of manufactured goods. As we can see in Case 2.1, these problems have caused significant changes in traditional Japanese practices, possibly signalling the end of the 'jobs for life' policy of larger organizations.

Japanese growth has not been without problems in the past – but these have been overcome by renewed effort. The oil-price increases of the 1970s virtually eliminated the Japanese trade surplus – briefly – until productivity improvements allowed competitiveness to be regained. Again, in 1987 Japanese firms overcame a massive surge in the value of the yen by using workers' efficiency suggestions to improve production processes further.

However, Japan has found it difficult to establish the social flexibility to cope with a changed world (Kobayashi 1992: 19). The ease with which Japanese businesses upgrade their technology and production contrasts sharply with the country's rigid social structures, including their employment practices (Kilburn 1993).

CASE 2.1 *Change in* *Japan*	The recession of the 1990s seemed to be of a different order from those of the past. Japanese companies struggled against a further increase in the value of the yen during a period of low worldwide demand. To keep prices competitive, manufacturers in the early 1990s almost gave away their profit margin, and many famous names showed losses for the first time in their history. Matsushita, the world's biggest consumer electronics group, reported a 60 per cent fall in profits. Its president resigned and it was stated that the company would have to adopt western methods of 'hiring and firing'.
	Smaller Japanese companies without financial muscle suffered badly, with over 1000 businesses failing each month – despite the labour ministry's attempts to keep people in employment by paying subsidies. For some time, the larger companies tried to avoid compulsory redundancies through redistributing human resources, freezing recruitment and early retirement. For example, in 1993 Japan's biggest company, Nippon Telegraph and Telephone (NTT), announced it would be reducing its workforce from 230,000 to 200,000 within three years. This reduction would be achieved through early retirement and a cut in recruitment.
	Major companies also laid off 'temporary' workers, typically comprising 10 per cent of the staff. This was followed by reduction in overtime – possibly 20 per cent of an average worker's pay packet. Then came the first announcements of redundancies in core workforces. Nissan, the country's second-largest car maker, announced heavy losses and began a restructuring involving shedding 5,000 staff – 9 per cent of its employees. The most dramatic part of the announcement was the closure of the Zama plant which employed

2,500 workers. This was a showcase factory capable of making 260,000 cars a year, using the most advanced technology, including extensive employment of robots. However, Nissan did not anticipate any job losses at all from this move, offering transfers to other Nissan plants. The 1,500 workers left at Zama would be employed on administration, design, distribution and manufacturing specialist parts. The bulk of cuts would affect its privileged white-collar workers. An effectiveness measure has been introduced for each of its 3,000 managerial staff. A five-point scale links salary to achievement rather than seniority, and managers receive performance scores each month. Performance management is expected to reduce employee costs from 10 to 8 per cent of sales.

The rising value of the yen has made overseas production cheaper than domestic manufacturing for Japanese multinationals. This has had the effect of exporting jobs (see Chapter 6, Case 6.1). After a period of huge investment in Japan and overseas, much of the domestic production capacity is standing idle. Ironically the overcapacity has not been tackled by sacking workers. Initially, redundant executives were left within organizations as *Madogiwazoku*, the 'window-gazing tribe', with nothing to do but stare out of their windows. Western managers would not have hesitated to close surplus factories and make large numbers of workers redundant. Japanese businesses have to overturn their basic philosophy in order to come to terms with firing their people.

Instead, many Japanese companies have exerted pressure on higher-paid salarymen to leave of their own accord. Managers over 45 years old earning 10 million yen (£61,000) or more have been the main target. Ironically, people of this generation have been accustomed to doing what their employers asked them to do. Now they are being asked to leave, they find it difficult to say no. Companies exert psychological pressures on them, for example appealing to their sense of duty to get them to leave and thus help the company's financial situation.

In general, Japanese manufacturing companies employed large numbers of people they did not need. More critically, overstaffing in the Japanese retail and distribution system is remarkably high in comparison with manufacturing and with retailers in the west. One estimate puts the surplus at 1.5 million people in manufacturing alone, with around 4 million overall. If these workers were dismissed, the true level of unemployment would be 11–12 per cent.

Half the companies surveyed by Asahi Bank knew that they employed too many people. Almost 70 per cent believed they had too many people in their fifties and 60 per cent felt they had too many managers. The survey found that 56 per cent of companies thought the lifetime employment system would have to be reviewed, with 37 per cent believing it was already disappearing.

Japanese attitudes towards workers in overseas operations has been less sympathetic (see Chapter 12). American employees of Japanese subsidiaries falsely assumed that, if they perhaps did not have a job for life, their employment was at least virtually secure. Instead, American employees were shed quickly when orders fell. Americans were not the only people to lose their jobs: hundreds of Japanese executives were sent home to lower-status positions.

Underlying the reaction to the recession is a change in Japanese beliefs. The attitudes of the workaholic senior executives of the postwar era are not often shared by their middle-aged successors and even less so by young graduates. They have different values and are prepared to take on some of the risks of the western way of business. Whether or not the recession is quickly overcome, a falling birthrate and increasing independence of young people require long-term changes. Excellence in manufacturing has disguised organizational inefficiency. The commitment expected from employees (see Chapter 5) can no longer be guaranteed. Younger men and women with career aspirations are not prepared to work 'long hours for little money while waiting to fill dead men's shoes'. For the first time, there is a debate about fast-track career paths, appointment on merit and performance pay.

(*Sources*: *The Economist*, 18 December 1993; *The Independent*, 12 August 1993; Nakamoto, *The Financial Times*, 16 January 1996)

Discussion questions

1 To what extent can Japanese people management practices withstand global economic changes?
2 Why should Japanese multinationals treat Japanese and foreign employees in different ways?

The developing world

Developing countries are gradually being brought into the global industrial economy. China and India are reawakening as industrial powers. The return of Hong Kong to Chinese control should act as a catalyst to the development of neighbouring areas on the Chinese mainland. The 1993 United Nations Industrial Development Organization report (UNIDO 1993) indicated that international trade has replaced aid as the principal vehicle for industrialization. UNIDO's report showed that the developing world's share of manufacturing trade increased from 11.7 per cent to 14.5 per cent between 1975 and 1990. As we noted in our earlier discussion of multinationals, private capital is being moved around the world in search of profit from flexible and open economies. Complex factors attract this capital: it is not simply a case of the cheapest employees. Case 2.2 examines the situation in South Africa where foreign investment has been affected by a perception of the country as being strike-ridden. UNIDO indicates that the cheapest global human resources are available in Tanzania, averaging $6.32 per $100 worth of output against $24.98 in Germany. Yet German jobs are not being transferred to Tanzania. This is because employee productivity in Germany is 48 times as great and material costs in Tanzania are significantly higher. Tanzania's disadvantages outweigh the benefits to investors despite the poor levels of pay. In fact, direct employee costs rarely contribute more than 10 per cent of the total costs of manufacturing. They can be dwarfed by transport charges.

Japanese manufacturers have opened factories in the UK and other parts of Europe where employee costs are high in comparison with developing countries. They have done so in order to avoid EU import restrictions and cut transport costs. But they have also created jobs in developed rather than developing countries in order to make use of better skills and education.

Uncontrolled globalization has not gone unquestioned. The possibility of **social dumping** puts societies and national economies under intense pressure and is generally destabilizing (see key concept 2.3). The International Labour Organization (ILO) has attempted to introduce a social clause into the constitution of the new World Trade Organization (WTO) requesting that all signatories permit trade unions and collective bargaining. Industrialized western countries would retain open markets – but with the condition that competitor states did not allow the unfair exploitation of their workers. However, resistance was expected from a number of countries in East Asia and Latin America who might perceive this as cultural imperialism. Within their tightly controlled societies, worker representation is perceived as a source of dissent and social unrest.

The concept of social dumping describes the practice of switching production from countries with relatively high employee costs to those with cheap labour. It is an accusation made against large multinational corporations. Social dumping has led to long-term structural changes, including the closure of older heavy manufacturing industries such as steel and shipbuilding in established industrial countries.

KEY CONCEPT 2.3
Social dumping

With the demise of apartheid, President Nelson Mandela's government of national unity faced a formidable challenge: 4.7 million South Africans were unemployed – 32 per cent of the available workforce. Half of them were under the age of 30, with a further 400,000 school-leavers joining the queue for jobs each year. A mere 3–4 per cent of these were expected to find employment in the 'formal' sector in 1995. It was estimated that the economy needed to grow by 8–10 per cent a year to make a significant impression on these figures. In 1994 growth was only 2.3 per cent, with 3.5 per cent estimated for 1995.

CASE 2.2
South Africa

Reforming the economy
The strategy for reforming the moribund economy included:

- the privatization of South African Airways;
- partial sale of the telecommunications utility Telekom;
- encouragement of tourism;
- and an unbundling of private conglomerates.

Government policy did not include large-scale privatization along New Zealand or British lines. Politicians were unlikely to accept the image of closures, heavy redundancies and large capital gains for a few shareholders. The intention of privatization – where it happened – was to empower the disadvantaged and spread wealth more widely.

Foreign businesses began to renew investment. Ford and IBM bought back in to former subsidiaries which had been sold off in the 1980s. Microsoft, Apple, Pepsi and Proctor & Gamble were new investors. Pepsi made a point of putting black managers in charge of its operation. Rover said it would make South Africa its major production hub for Land Rovers in Africa. Other investors were holding back because of a perception of relatively high wage levels and low productivity, inflexible working practices and poor management.

Productivity levels
A Monitor Company report commissioned by the then National Economic Forum found that – in almost every industrial sector examined – identical products were being made at much lower cost or to a higher quality in other countries. Many industries could only survive through protectionism and subsidy. The Monitor report demonstrated how South Africa lost its international competitiveness because of low levels of productivity. They compared South African vehicle assembly with Mexico and the USA:

Country	Employee cost per hour (US$)	Employee hours per car	Employee cost per car (US$)
South Africa	5.6	63.5	355
Mexico	6.0	24.3	145
USA	38.0	18.56	705

The same pattern was found in the textile industry. Paradoxically, a long-term cure for unemployment requires short-term job losses in order to increase productivity. Both the public and private sectors are regarded as inefficient and overstaffed. Rising expectations amongst workers, however, means a clash with trade unions is likely.

Affirmative action

Seventy-five per cent of South Africa's population is black, but fewer than 2 per cent of its managers are black. Under apartheid, blacks had been prevented from having business accommodation in many city sites. They had been denied skills training and access to capital. Black empowerment required a nurturing of small businesses, backed by extra training and finance. Franchising and joint ventures with overseas companies offered considerable possibilities. Kentucky Fried Chicken and McDonald's actively sought black franchisees.

Many firms are using affirmative action programmes to recruit black professionals, partly in an attempt to appease the government and public opinion. Job-hopping – the 'pinball syndrome' – has become normal, with educated black employees moving from one job to another every six to eight months. People attempt to climb up the status and responsibility ladder much faster than their experience and training will allow. The number of skilled, experienced black professionals is so low that they are being offered salaries 20–50 per cent higher than their white counterparts. Jobs have imposing titles and may be accompanied by cars and cellular phones. In practice, these positions often turn out to be disappointing: the responsibilities bear no comparison to the titles. Black professionals become frustrated as high salaries are not matched with the opportunity to develop self-esteem.

Many employers are seen as cynical, hiring black faces for 'soft' jobs such as human resources but not for financial and line-management positions. Support in the form of training, development or mentoring is frequently absent. The process is usually initiated by the board of directors without consulting existing managers, who subsequently do little to help the new appointees.

Employee relations

The foreign investment community has an image of South Africa as a relatively high-wage and strike-ridden country. In fact, in the first nine months of 1995 some 870,000 days were lost due to strikes – compared with 2.5 million days in the same period of 1994 and 3.1 million in 1992.

Hopes of a long-term improvement in employee relations were based on new legislation and the creation of a National Economic Development and Labour Council (Nedlac). This is divided into four chambers, responsible for public finance and monetary policy, trade and industry, the job market, and development. Its task was to forge a consensus on broad economic and social policies. Representatives were included from government, employees, unions and civic associations.

A new Labour Relations Act was expected to reduce strikes by offering alternative methods for resolving disputes. Legislation included workplace forums (at employee request in any company with more than 100 workers. A Commission for Conciliation, Mediation and Arbitration was proposed to further the use of discussion rather than strike action.

(*Sources: The Financial Times*, 2 May 1995; *New York Times*, article syndicated in the *Guardian*, 5 August 1995)

Discussion question

From your reading of this case and recent media accounts, determine the effectiveness of the South African government's policies for increasing employment.

HRM and the state

Governments and supranational authorities such as the European Union influence human resource strategies and practices through a variety of mechanisms. In our case study on South Africa (Case 2.2), for example, there is a description of the government's attempt to focus and direct economic activity. In some countries, the size of the employment market (employable population) can be restricted or encouraged through controls on migration. However, South Africa's extensive borders cannot be policed sufficiently closely to prevent massive immigration from relatively poorer neighbouring countries. Governments can affect local human resource availability by encouraging or discouraging population movement, for example through housing policy. In South Africa the movement of people has a momentum of its own.

The availability of skilled and educated employees is governed by the provision of vocational and academic education. In principle, governments can change minimum school-leaving ages, the proportion of people in higher education and the age at which state retirement pensions become available. But these controls apply only where there is adequate schooling and access to higher education. Again, in the South African case the majority black population is disadvantaged by conditions laid down under the previous apartheid regime. State retirement pensions for all remains an impossible dream.

Also, as we observed in the case of South Africa, governments influence the number of people in employment by stimulating investment and consumer demand. Fiscal and economic measures affect market conditions, encouraging or suppressing overall economic activity and hence the requirement for human resources. This is reflected in the ease with which suitable recruits can be obtained and the level of reward they expect.

The state has a direct influence on the perceived value of pay. Many developed countries have minimum wages which ensure fair remuneration for workers. The UK Conservative government has argued against minimum wages on the grounds that such restrictions prevent the creation of new jobs. The 'New Right' belief in market forces holds that if people are prepared – or forced – to accept low-pay jobs it is beneficial to the national economy. This issue is discussed further in Chapter 3.

In most countries there are further measures within the power of government:

- interest rates, reflected in payments on mortgage loans, overdrafts, hire purchase and credit card debts;
- control of inflation, reducing the pressure for wage increases;
- tax and social security deductions.

For example, in 1995 the Mexican government announced a review of its state-run healthcare and pensions cover (*The Financial Times*, 28 April 1995). With 9 million affiliates and their dependants, it still does not cover over half the population – peasants, domestic workers and the self-employed. The social security institute (IMSS) employed 340,000 people with a budget of 46 billion pesos (US$7.6 billion). As the population ages, the size of the problem will get worse: the number of pensioners is increasing at twice the rate at which young people are entering the workplace.

Despite relatively low employee costs by North American standards, the government is worried about the effect of social security on Mexico's competitiveness. Contributions add 38.5 per cent to the employer's wage bill, with a further 32 per cent deducted from the employee's salary. The employment minister considered these non-wage costs to be a significant deterrent to job creation and foreign investment in Mexico.

The state further controls the nature of employment relationships between organizations and their staff by means of legislation. Typically this encompasses minimum employment conditions, trade union rights, equal opportunities, health and safety, and disciplinary and redundancy processes. State agencies may also be involved in the provision of training, job placement services and arbitration. In many countries there are separate employment courts or tribunals engaged in resolving disputes and legal actions between workers and their employers.

Market forces

One of the most significant functions of government is to set the political stance of a country. Governments may choose an economic position anywhere between the command economy favoured by the former communist states of eastern Europe and the **free market** of the USA. Since the late 1970s the free market has been dominant in the predominantly English-speaking countries. The concept was raised to the status of a near-religion by governments and economists of the Thatcherite persuasion – the New Right. Such 'economic rationalists' believe that market forces favour efficient business organizations and destroy inefficient ones. Social and political traditions exist which affect business practice, but they are of minimal importance in the face of uncontrollable market forces. The impression offered is that there is an optimum competitive form of organization within any particular industry or market sector. Successful firms will converge on this form.

In fact, this free-market model is only one of many alternative forms of capitalism (see Table 2.3). It derives from the 'liberal-individualistic' principles which guide economic, political and social conditions in those countries. These principles focus on the rights of the individual in preference to those of the collective. Its ideology is fundamental to the original Harvard

Table 2.3 People management in three types of market economy

Emphasis	Free market	Social market	Japanese
1 Environment	Laissez-faire 'hands-off' approach by government Individualist culture	Close cooperation between government and industry sectors Socially responsible culture	Strategic link between government and industry sectors Group culture
2 Organization	Top-down, power-driven Contractual	Cooperation between stakeholders Legislative framework	All stakeholders valued Trust and obligation
3 Decision-making	Concentrated at top	Consultative	Consensus
4 Functional	Finance foremost Rhetorical HRM	Engineering foremost Mutual consideration	Quality and service foremost Mutual loyalty

map of HRM territory and it is not surprising to find that the prevalence of HRM is greatest in free-market countries (Hollinshead and Leat 1995: 16).

Free market governments encourage private industry with minimal state controls. The ideology is short-termist, emphasizing the following:

- fast return on risk capital;
- business growth from deals, mergers and aggressive takeovers;
- hard-headed attitudes towards employees, including relatively easy recourse to redundancies and acceptance of low pay;
- limited employee protection from dismissal or radical changes in their working conditions;
- little emphasis on development or staff training;
- minimal social responsibilities.

The paradox here is obvious. Why should HRM – a fundamentally long-term concept – have taken off in such a dramatic fashion in countries whose business activities are primarily short term? The HRM approach advocates an investment in skills training, showing a commitment to employees and to developing their human capital. Yet free-market countries show the least respect for workers' rights and the long-term development of human resources as organizational assets. It is easier to explain the popularity of 'hard' HRM, with its concentration on staff numbers and their alignment to requirements. In countries such as Australia and the UK, 'soft' HRM has all the characteristics of rhetoric. It is talked about but only rarely implemented.

In some senses, HRM is compensatory. HRM theories advocate that individual organizations should decide, as a matter of strategy, to set up internal development mechanisms to compensate for the human-capital deficiencies of free-market states. This is entirely consistent with the New Right position on education and medical insurance. They are regarded as a matter of choice, to be paid for individually and with no state provision beyond the bare minimum.

Eccles (1989) concludes that the free market is at an inherent disadvantage when compared with social market or East Asian models. The consensus social market, sometimes called the 'Rhineland' model and found in Germany, Scandinavia, and the Netherlands, is a form of social capitalism featuring:

- government encouragement of investment in production and product development;
- regulation of workers' rights and employers' obligations, ensuring consultation on major changes and restrictions on staff dismissal;
- the provision of extensive social benefits, adding considerable social costs to the payroll of commercial organizations.

The social-market has produced higher economic growth, more harmonious societies (by and large) and better infrastructures than free-market capitalism. It is the dominant approach in the European Union. It can be argued that there is no need to introduce soft HRM in social-market countries such as Germany. Effectively, it is in place already. However, the integration of East Germany into the Federal German economy is an illustration of 'hard', not to say brutal, HRM in which millions of people have lost jobs and had their lives disrupted.

Although the social-market is at the heart of the EU, European countries display considerable variations in people management. Filella (1991) describes three regional clusters in western Europe:

- **Latin** (Spain, Italy and France) – with an oral tradition and a tendency towards docile dependency on authority reinforced by subtle institutional structures. People management is in a state of transition towards recognizable HRM.
- **Central European** – a legalistic tradition, with a relatively low status for HR departments and an emphasis on the role of line managers. Collective bargaining is enshrined in legislation.
- **Nordic** – where HR departments have considerable authority, strategies are detailed in writing and employee consultation is widespread.

Filella attributes these stages to the level of socio-economic development. The Latin model represents the most recent, the central model the intermediate stage, and the Nordic the summit of development. Brewster distinguishes the UK and the Irish Republic from the central cluster, with the UK, in particular, being somewhere between North American and central European practices (1995: 311). Clearly, these models are generalizations and individual countries will show their own particular characteristics. Culture and history strongly influence the manner in which people are managed at work in different countries. In fact, all models of this type fall into the trap of stereotyping national cultures on grounds which are uncomfortably close to racism.

For example, people management in France does not easily fit Finella's model. French management has a number of unique features as well as elements in common with free-market, social-market and 'Latin' versions. The characteristics of French industrial development have been bold, imaginative, long-term thinking together with heavy investment in specific areas of the economy (Barsoux and Lawrence 1990: 4). However, investment and protection have not always been targeted in suitable areas. The OECD highlighted the electronics industry as one which had received considerable assistance but failed to improve its worldwide standing. State-owned companies such as Air France were feather-bedded to the extent that considerable reductions were required in the workforce in the 1990s as airlines suffered from recession and overcapacity. The emphasis on technology and educational standards leads to employers valuing technical skills and the intellectual capacity to grasp the 'big idea'. Conversely, people management is not highly valued and tends to be primarily authoritarian, with considerable status differences between managers and staff.

East Asian economies have a number of similar features to social-market countries. The emphasis again is on long-term, organic growth and mutual respect between employers and employees. However, the system relies on social harmony and group cooperation rather than legislation and social protection for its maintenance. In Japan, and other East Asian states, government has played an important strategic role. Specific industrial sectors have been targeted for growth and suitable companies encouraged to participate.

As does Europe, East Asia encompasses a variety of different cultures and distinctive forms of people management. For example, South Korea and Malaysia employ significantly dissimilar ways of managing people to those of Japanese practice. South Korean industry has developed under the guidance of a government which has had close links with the military since the Korean War. The major businesses are themselves controlled by family groups but, unlike Japanese corporations, they have recruited senior managers freely from outside sources such as the civil service and the military. The consequence is a more authoritarian form of people management than that seen in Japan.

The state and intervention

Should governments take a strong hand in the use of a country's human resources? We noted that East Asian economic success has been guided by interventionist governments. In other countries the trend has been in the opposite direction. With the collapse of the communist command economies in eastern Europe and the predominance of New Right ideology in English-speaking countries, state-ownership has gone out of fashion. Government organizations have been shed in favour of privatized and contracted-out services. In the UK, and even more so in New Zealand, the government further withdrew from many areas of economic regulation. The faith in the virtue of market forces was such that when significant areas of the economy collapsed or were taken over by foreign interests, government reaction was minimal. Confusingly, deregulation has been adopted by political parties of varied hues. A comparison of New Zealand, Scotland and Wales, three small countries with related cultural and business traditions, illustrates the inconsistent pattern. The latter is discussed in Case 2.3. With similar population levels and a strong agricultural tradition, the three countries have endured considerable structural adjustments to their economies. These have arisen from three main factors:

- UK entry into the European Community in the 1970s, which restricted access to New Zealand's main overseas market and made Scotland and Wales peripheral parts of the EU;
- relatively high wage-levels and social welfare provisions in comparison with significant competitor countries;
- a reduction in the importance of low-margin, low-technology commodities, including steel and coal in the Scottish and Welsh cases.

As a fully independent country, New Zealand had the opportunity to exercise control over its own destiny. Despite being a relatively young state, it has a long tradition of bold initiatives in social and economic policy. The emancipation of women, a national health service and extensive social welfare were seen in New Zealand long before their adoption in larger countries. By the early 1980s the country's economy was in a dire state with raging inflation and unsustainable budget and trading deficits. From being a provider of basic agricultural products to the UK, New Zealand had to diversify its markets and maximize the profitability of its products.

In 1984 New Zealand's Labour – supposedly a left-of-centre, socialist party – government began a Thatcherite programme of privatization and withdrawal of subsidies. Organizations such as the Bank of New Zealand and Air New Zealand were transferred to the private sector and farmers were forced to compete on the world market at unsubsidized prices. Subjected to this shock treatment, many firms went out of business and considerable numbers of employees were discharged by large organizations. Between 1985 and 1989, New Zealand saw the greatest increase in inequality between rich and poor of any developed country (followed, perhaps not surprisingly, by the UK).

The 'conservative' National Party took Labour's policies further and by the mid-1990s the country showed high levels of growth and every indication of an economic transformation. Fully exposed to world competition, even the agricultural sector seemed to be successful. Most aspects of government were privatized or handled in a commercial fashion. The state had withdrawn so that intervention was at a minimum. The line was drawn when the government failed in its bid to abolish automatic state pension provision. Debate has raged over the true effect of minimalist government. It is too early, and there is insufficient evidence, to conclude the argument on one side or the other.

Scotland and Wales were also controlled by free-market governments throughout the 1980s and 1990s. However, in a centralized state such as the UK, specific 'regional' units may be treated in different ways. Unlike New Zealand, Scotland and Wales have had semi-colonial status, each with a Secretary of State supported by a large number of unelected quangos (quasi-autonomous non-governmental organizations). For most of the latter part of the twentieth century they have been under the rule of the Conservative Party – despite voting consistently and strongly against that party. This has produced some uncomfortable tensions between the wishes of the electorate and government activities. For example, the Conservatives' sell-off of state industries has led to the closure of Scottish offices, mostly in favour of control from England. A prime example is the major UK utility British Gas, which obtained a large proportion of its supplies from Scottish waters. The absence of a Scottish parliament meant that British Gas could close down its Scottish administrative structure with impunity. The London government simply denied having any responsibility for the actions of a privatized utility.

Despite the 'hands-off' approach which dominated Conservative governments in the UK, Wales benefited from a degree of interventionism. Direct inward investment was boosted by ensuring assisted-area status for substantial areas of the principality. The Welsh Development Agency (WDA) encouraged corporations such as Sony, Bosch and Ford to invest heavily in manufacturing. This was concentrated particularly along the 'M4 corridor' in southeast Wales. A third of Welsh manufacturing workers are employed by overseas companies. Thanks to the diplomatic initiatives of the Welsh Office and the WDA, Wales has one of the highest concentrations of Japanese-owned companies in Europe.

CASE 2.3
Development in Wales

In the 1980s the Secretary of State, Peter Walker, particularly trumpeted the virtues of interventionism. He launched the 'Valleys Initiative' in an attempt to revitalize the depressed former mining valleys in South Wales. The full initiative covered education and training, the environment, tourism, the arts, roads, voluntary effort, health, social services, housing, and the Welsh economy. The programme included (Walker 1991):

- new schemes to assist small businesses;
- research projects to promote new opportunities for Welsh firms, such as developing joint purchases and marketing by small firms;
- expert advice;
- a new centre for Quality Enterprise and Design;
- a Welsh Technology Development fund to help translate new ideas into sales;
- plans for the 3*i*s, Investors in Industry, to invest at least £2.5 million in the valleys in a single year, two-thirds more than in previous years;
- a trebling of spending on an advanced factory and workshop programme;
- a new campaign to improve the standard of retailing;
- new links between business and schools in each valley;
- a training commission to carry out a 'skills audit' and identify the skills likely to be needed by existing and potential employers;
- a marketing scheme to attract more visitors to the valleys;
- an enhanced road-improvement programme;
- UK 2000 to provide more practical projects to improve the environment, provide training and create jobs;
- increased funding for the Prince of Wales Committee;
- funding of two valley health centres and twelve other projects, including a day hospital and community hospitals;
- further capital allocations with £8 million to improve the housing stock.

Superficially, the benefit has been considerable. Road networks have been substantially improved; coal waste tips have been flattened and planted with grass and trees; many villages have been given a facelift. Much of this has been supported by European Union funding.

Despite criticisms that much of the effort was cosmetic, the growth rate in Wales exceeded that of most of the United Kingdom in the 1980s. With 4 per cent of the British manufacturing workforce, the Welsh share of UK manufacturing output rose from 3.8 per cent in 1980 to 5.1 per cent in 1990. This was based on comparatively high net capital spending, which increased from 6.8 per cent of the UK total to 7.7 per cent over the same decade. This allowed a considerable improvement in productivity and a sharp reduction in unit employee costs, offering further scope for advance in the Welsh economy in the 1990s and beyond. For example, between September 1994 and January 1995, a regional trends survey showed a balance of 49 per cent of companies in Wales reporting increased as opposed to reduced output. This compared with 8 per cent in Scotland. While many parts of the UK were reporting capacity problems due to poor levels of investment, businesses in Wales were continuing to invest in plant and machinery.

This optimistic scene has to be qualified by the fact that the former South Wales coalfield is one of the poorest regions in Britain. Average income per head remains low compared with most of the UK. Highly paid male jobs in the coal and steel industries have been replaced with lower-paid and comparatively low-skill jobs. These have been filled by female workers, so that the employment balance is virtually equal between men and women. Greater female participation disguises a major reduction in the number of males in the local employment market. Many former coal and steel workers have taken early retirement. Others have been registered as permanently sick by sympathetic doctors in order to qualify for higher levels of benefit. As a consequence, official statistics do not reflect the true unemployment rate.

Inward investment has limited value for skilled and educated people. Few of the manufacturing firms have head-office functions in Wales, offering minimal opportunities for administrative and upper-level employees. Educated young people continue to migrate to areas of the UK, such as the South-east of England, where such jobs are more common. Services, parts and raw materials are supplied from elsewhere, so that small local companies gain little benefit. Senior managers, at a distance in London or overseas, do not identify with the workforce in their manufacturing plants. Decisions to reduce numbers or introduce short-time working are made with little thought for the human consequences.

(*Sources*: Herbert and Jones 1995; Walker 1991)

Discussion questions

1 Is external investment in Wales simply due to the availability of cheap labour?
2 Does interventionism work?

Minimum wages

Should governments set minimum wage levels? This is a key point of dispute between left- and right-wing thinkers. Minimum wage legislation has been used by governments in many developed countries: Australia, Belgium, Canada, France, Greece, Japan, Luxembourg, the Netherlands, New Zealand, Portugal, Spain and the USA. For a considerable time, wages councils set minimum rates for defined economic sectors in the UK. Most of these councils were dissolved by the Conservative administration, although employers and unions argued for the retention of the system for agricultural workers. In the USA a federal minimum wage was set at about 50 per cent of average hourly earnings until the right-wing administrations of Presidents Reagan and Bush reduced its levels. In 1991 the minimum wage was set at $4.25. In the mid-1990s approximately 2.5 million workers were paid at this rate, although they represented a small proportion (2.4 per cent) of the US workforce. Most were over 21 and worked in service industries such as retailing, fast food and personal care.

Exponents of the free market – supported by much orthodox economic opinion – argue that the mere existence of a minimum wage destroys jobs. Any increase in existing minimum-pay rates further reduces employment levels, particularly for young people. However, there is recent but contradictory evidence to suggest that this may not be the case. For instance, fast-food restaurants are not in competition with cheaper overseas competitors – they simply compete with each other. Imposing a minimum hourly wage or increasing an existing one places all competing restaurants in a particular location on the same level. Provided the pay rate is not set too high, the effect on prices and service quality will be minimal and employment levels should not be affected.

In fact, comparison of job markets in different US states, some of which increased their own minimum rates above federal levels, shows that employment levels can grow when a minimum wage exists. Wage rates in service industries are so poor that they encourage a high turnover of employees and leave vacancies unfilled for long periods. When minimum wages bring potential earnings above welfare levels, more people enter the job market and fill vacancies.

European initiatives

The European Union has created a new dimension for people management. The European Commission has undertaken a number of initiatives which are aimed at improving economic conditions in less privileged regions. The differences in income between the EU's richest and poorest regions are dramatic, ranging from 30 per cent to 209 per cent of the average (*The Independent*, 5 April 1994). It was once believed that the division between rich and poor could be described simply in terms of location. The rich were concentrated in a belt from South-east England, through northern France, Belgium, and the Netherlands into northern Germany. The peripheral areas along the Mediterranean and Atlantic seaboard were thought to be poorer. In the 1990s the situation has become far more complex. For a variety of reasons, rich and poor regions are found next to each other in a patchwork throughout the community.

The EU has attempted to equalize wealth through the use of 'structural funds', of which 20 billion ecus (over £15 billion) were allocated in 1992. In particular, there was pressure from the then president of the European Commission, Jacques Delors, for the EU to adopt a unified and strongly interventionist approach to the problem of 17 million people without work. This was an area of conflict between the majority social-market position in Europe and the UK's free-market stance. The British government advocated a 'hands-off' approach to the issue, arguing that the 'market' would take care of the problem if employment laws were loosened and 'flexibility' encouraged. However, it is clear that having a pool of unskilled people in run-down industrial or mining areas is not sufficient to attract industry.

Companies need to be able to draw on an infrastructure of transport facilities, service companies and highly trained potential employees.

Human capital

Personal and national success are increasingly correlated with the possession of skills. Skilled individuals can command a premium salary in periods of high economic activity. Worldwide, unemployment levels remain high, while organizations have difficulty filling vacancies which require specific expertise. A shortage of skilled people can act as a limiting factor on individual organizations and on the economy as a whole. For example, in the UK small businesses report an inability to expand because of the difficulty of finding people with the right skills. Small firms are also vulnerable because their owners do not possess basic marketing and finance skills. It is in the interest of any country to maximize its human resources by investing in the skills of its workforce, its **human capital** (see key concept 2.4). Human capital is one component of a country's overall competitiveness.

KEY CONCEPT 2.4 *Human capital*	It can be argued that economic growth, employment levels and the availability of a skilled workforce are inter-related. Economic growth creates employment, but economic growth partly depends on skilled human resources – a country's human capital. The concept encompasses investment in the skills of the labour force, including education and vocational training to develop specific skills.

The most successful developing countries, for example Singapore and Malaysia, are investing heavily in the education and technical skills of their population. Similarly, South Korea aims for 90 per cent of its young people to have an 18-plus qualification, with 60 per cent undertaking higher education. Britain, conversely, was able to provide only 28 per cent of its youth with higher education at the beginning of the 1990s. Yet industry recognized the value of human capital – unskilled people were paid at just 40 per cent of the graduate rate. Belatedly, the UK government has set targets for higher levels of achievement (see Table 2.4).

Skill requirements are particularly critical at the managerial level. For example, the arrival of multinational corporations in China has produced an increased demand for professional managers. Chinese colleges produce large numbers of technicians but few accountants, lawyers or marketing specialists. Without a modern commercial tradition, western companies such as Motorola and Price Waterhouse are using in-house training programmes (Reuter source in *Scotland on Sunday*, 12 February 1995). Motorola's own 'university' in Beijing announced its intention of sending sixty students each year for on-the-job training in its plants elsewhere in Asia and the USA. Price Waterhouse opened its own $600,000 training centre in Shanghai.

Competition is not restricted to marketing and product development. It

Table 2.4 UK education targets for the year 2000

For the workforce	• 30 per cent qualified to NVQ level 4 (degree standard) or above
	• 60 per cent qualified to NVQ level 3, Advanced GNVQ or 2 A level standard
For young people	• 75 per cent achieving GNVQ level 2 competence in communication, numeracy, information technology by age 19; 35 per cent achieving GNVQ level 3 in these skills by age 21
	• 85 per cent achieving 5 GSCEs at grade C or above, an intermediate GNVQ or an NVQ level 2 by age 19
	• 60 per cent qualified to NVQ level 3, Advanced GNVQ or 2 A level standard
For employers	• 70 per cent of all firms employing 200 or more and 35 per cent with 50 or more employees to achieve the Investors in People training standard

Source: adapted from *The Times Higher*, 26 May 1995, based on UK Government *White Paper on Competitiveness*.

also entails competition for staff. The availability of skilled employees in the external job market may constrain growth. Additional expensive advertising may be required, together with the offer of enhanced salaries to attract suitable applicants. We saw in the first chapter that investment in training is limited by the non-activity of other businesses in a particular sector. Companies like Motorola and IBM, which invest heavily in training and development, are at risk of losing their investments (Kochan and Dyer 1995: 344). Their staff can be poached for higher wages by businesses which spend little on training. In turn, this may lead good trainers to conclude that training is not worthwhile.

Human capital theory also deals with personal investment in self-development, such as enrolling on a degree course. It presupposes that individuals balance the cost of education and training (time, loss of income, fees) against the benefits of a higher income in the future. As such it predicts that the young are more likely to invest in training because their losses are relatively less – and the potential gains greater – than for older people. In general, the income of employees with degrees and other higher education qualifications is significantly higher than that of people who ceased education at an earlier point. It has been suggested that the value of education may lie not in any real investment in skills but in its 'screening' power (Sapsford and Tzannatos 1993: 89). Recruiters assume that individuals with 'pieces of paper' are better candidates than those without. Qualifications are used as a cheap and easy selection filter. However, a survey designed by the US National Center on the Educational Quality of the Workforce at the University of Pennsylvania produced evidence to show that improved workers' education directly increased productivity (*The Times Higher*, 26 May 1995). The survey of owners and managers in 3,000 businesses showed that whereas a 10 per cent increase in capital investment (machinery, tools, buildings, etc.) produced a 3.4 per cent increase in productivity, a 10 per cent improvement in educational attainment increased productivity by 8.4 per cent. The survey found that organizations which used educational grades as selection criteria and were linked to schools through work placement arrangements or training

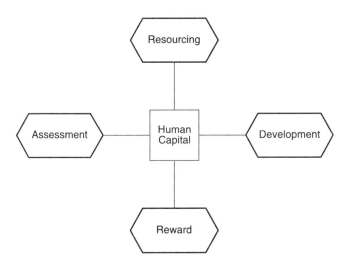

Figure 2.1   Human capital and major HR activities.

schemes also showed higher levels of productivity and innovation. However, most employers disregarded school grades and reports in favour of 'attitude', communication skills and previous work experience.

We can see from Figure 2.1 that human capital is a significant unifying concept in HRM. It links four major people management activities – resourcing, assessment, development and reward – with an environmental variable which is a key to both organizational and national success. Each of these areas is further explored in later chapters in this book.

Table 2.5 locates macro HRM in the context of a changing world and a background of economic uncertainty. In the next chapter we address key human resource issues at this level – such as the job market – in greater depth.

The legal framework

One of the most important environmental constraints on the job market and the activities of people managers comes from the law. We will conclude this chapter with a brief overview of some of the major legal aspects affecting HRM. An in-depth treatment can be found in the companion volume to this one *Law in a Business Context* (Cole *et al.* 1990), which discusses the impact of law on a number of business issues, including the management of human resources. They view one of the strategic purposes of law as being 'the creation of a balance between competing interests' and see 'the traditional depiction of justice by a pair of scales, or balances' as a clear illustration.

Law changes continuously and varies extensively in different parts of the world. Much of the legislation relating to business comes from custom or precedent. Precedents are also decided by judges working to the system that says 'like cases should be decided alike'. Within the Anglo-Celtic countries these have been systematized into a **common law** framework.

Table 2.5 Macro HRM in context

| | LEVELS OF ANALYSIS | | | |
	Environment	Organization	Strategy	Activities
HRM type	Macro HRM	Organizational HRM	Strategic HRM	Operational HRM
Features	Economy	Structure	Mission	Recruitment
	Labour market	Culture	Objectives	Development
	Culture	Power	Policy	Reward
	Political climate	Functions	Planning	Dismissal
Traditional responsibility	State	Senior management	Senior management	Personnel
Modern responsibility	Supranational	Managers	Senior and middle	Line managers
	National	Employees	management	HR specialists
	Multinationals			

Many of these countries, such as the USA, also have a written Constitution which provides a further code. Most European countries employ an entirely code-based system called **civil law** and descended from the law code of the Roman Empire. A further element is that of **equity**, which is discretionary and has relevance to cases involving non-monetary actions or injunctions, for example against an illegal strike. According to Cole, Shears and Tiley:

> Equity in a literal sense means fairness; in a technical sense those rules of law derived from petitions to the King or his Chancellor for relief from the inadequacy or harshness of the Common Law on the grounds of conscience.
>
> (Cole *et al.* 1990: 7)

The main source of new laws is government **legislation**. During the twentieth century, national governments have become law-making machines, creating a complex legal environment for businesses. Governments implement statutes for strategic reasons, ensuring, for example, that employees who are disciplined or dismissed are dealt with in a particular manner. Organizations which fail to meet their legal obligations must compensate aggrieved individuals appropriately. This applies not only to current employees but also to ex-employees and potential recruits such as job applicants.

Legislation in the European Union

Within Europe, national traditions have led to wide variations in legislation relevant to human resource management. The European Court of Justice has contributed to harmonization with an increasing body of case law (Gold 1993: 16). The different legal systems in the EU can be divided into three traditions (Due *et al.* 1991; Gold 1993):

- The **Roman-German** system prevailing in Austria, Belgium, France, Germany, Italy and the Netherlands. Government has a pivotal role in employee relations, guaranteeing a fundamental core of constitutional rights. These provide the foundation for national industrial relations. Legislation covers significant aspects of employment market conditions such as working hours and trade union representation.

- The **Anglo-Celtic** system in the United Kingdom and the Irish Republic. A minimalist approach to the role of the state with limited legislative protection.
- The **Nordic** system, covering Denmark, Finland, Norway and Sweden. The 'basic agreement' between employers and unions forms the foundation of employee relations. The state plays a limited role, intervening only at the request of these two parties.

Countries in the central and dominant group of the EU follow the Roman-German model. Not surprisingly, their way of thinking shapes most proposals to the Commission. However, debate on employee relations reflects changing business practices and a shifting balance of attitudes within an enlarging Union.

In our earlier discussion of globalization we observed that the EU is not sealed off from other trading areas such as East Asia and North America – its industries are often in direct competition. We also noted that the process of **social dumping** (see key concept 2.3) has led to the fitness of traditional methods of industrial relations within the EU being questioned. Institutionalized worker participation can function smoothly in a growing company, but what happens when employees are asked to participate in determining their own redundancies?

Many governments and employee groups have been concerned that social dumping can also take place from one country to another within the EU. They have proposed improvements in employment rights for all workers across the Union. Gold has described this approach as **social protectionist** in contrast to the **deregulatory** views of the UK Conservative government (1993: 17). The UK further refused to sign the 'Social Chapter' of the Maastricht Treaty in 1991, arguing that it would lead to higher employee costs and a reduction in the country's competitive position. It was agreed that the other eleven members at the time would implement a common social and employee policy whether or not the UK acquiesced.

Whereas HRM in the USA has been predominantly within non-unionized firms, this has not been the case in Europe. In Britain and Ireland, where HRM has had its earliest and greatest impact, there is a longstanding pluralist tradition of collective bargaining. In the pre-Thatcher era, the industrial relations scene in Britain could be described as confrontational and competitive, with unions and management in a state of frequent disagreement and strikes or other forms of industrial action commonplace.

During the Thatcher period the UK witnessed a massive reduction in union power: a phenomenon associated with large-scale redundancies and restructuring within the British economy. The old labour-intensive industries, where the major union power lay, were particularly affected by these processes. By the mid-1990s fewer than half of Britain's commercial-sector employees were covered by collective bargaining arrangements. UK-wide agreements were being eroded in the public sector, with government pursuing a policy of breaking up structures such as the National Health Service into local trusts with bargaining powers. There has been a marked move towards authoritarian styles of management in this period, with unions' rights to take industrial action considerably reduced – partly through government legislation but also due to an awareness of economic reality amongst the workforce and a reluctance to run the risk of further job losses. This has been described as a 'New Industrial Relations' within which 'management has seized the initiative to change working practices and unions have become less confrontational, more flexible, more accommodating to "local" conditions, and generally more "realistic"' (Goss 1994: 140). This new realism was reinforced by a succession of changes in legislation (see Table 2.6), with the following consequences:

- It became easier for people not to join a union. For example, rights for non-union workers within a 'closed shop' were strengthened and protection introduced for workers who lost their jobs or were victimized for not being members of a trade union when a closed shop agreement prevailed between a union and employing organization. There was also protection for employees who chose not to join a union because of personal conviction. In effect, closed shops became unworkable.
- Unions were made financially liable for their members' actions. A union could be held responsible for any damage caused by an individual member to property during a strike.
- The power of solidarity was curtailed. For instance, picketing was restricted so that only six people could picket at any one entrance and workers could only picket their own place of work. Secondary industrial action was limited to situations where the employers involved had a contractual relationship and the action was directly related to the dispute. This prevented any sympathetic action by other union members and was further reinforced by redefining a trade dispute to refer only to a dispute between workers and *their* employer (the previous definition had been 'employers *and* workers'); the dispute had to be *wholly* or *mainly* related to (formerly *connected* with) one or more specific issues – such as terms and conditions, recruitment or dismissal, duty allocation, discipline, and negotiation.
- The accountability of union leaders was increased. A secret postal ballot was required before any industrial action, including strikes, overtime bans and working to rule. Similarly, senior union officials were required to offer themselves for re-election every five years by secret ballot.

The topic of employee relations is discussed in depth in Chapter 12.

Summary

In this chapter we discussed environmental factors which have a 'macro' effect on the management of people. In our discussion we outlined some of the most significant ways in which governments and international bodies can determine the nature of employment, and outlined the major characteristics of three different market models. We introduced the concept of human capital – investment in skills. The chapter concluded with an overview of the legal constraints affecting people management.

Table 2.6 Summary of UK employee legislation under the Conservatives

1980 Employment Act	• Picketing: change in definition of lawful picketing – restricted to employees' own place of work; no more than six people; secondary action restricted.
	• Closed shops: 80 per cent support required in ballot to legalize closed shop agreements.
	• Statutory recognition procedure repealed.
	• Unfair dismissal and maternity rights restricted.
1982 Employment Act	• Change of definition of trade dispute – further restriction.
	• Employers awarded right to obtain injunctions and sue for damages.
	• Right of compensation if dismissed due to closed shop agreement.
	• Clauses requiring only union labour removed from commercial contracts.
1984 Trade Union Act	• Requirement for executive elections every five years by means of secret ballot.
	• Ballots required for political fund every ten years.
	• Secret ballots must take place before any industrial action.
1986 Public Order Act	• Trade union members able to obtain injunction if no secret ballot before strikes.
	• Compensation for members disciplined for not following majority decisions.
	• Inspection of union finances.
	• Unions no longer allowed to pay fines on behalf of officials or members.
	• Action taken to preserve post-entry closed shop made illegal.
	• Additional restrictions on election ballots and industrial action.
	• Control on election addresses.
	• Commissioner appointed to provide independent scrutiny of unions.
1989 Employment Act	• Restrictions on the work of young people and women lifted.
	• Small employers exempted from providing detailed information on disciplinary procedures.
	• Paid time off work for union duties restricted.
	• Abolition of redundancy rebates.
	• Written reasons for dismissal required only after two years' employment.
1990 Employment Act	• All secondary action made unlawful.
	• Liability of unions for any wildcat action taken by an official unless written repudiation sent to all members using prescribed set of words.
	• Workers taking unofficial action may be selectively dismissed.
	• No longer lawful to refuse employment to non-union members.
1992 Trade Union and Labour Relations (Consolidation) Act	• Consolidation of all collective employment rights, including trade union finances, elections, time off and dismissal.
1993 Trade Union Reform and Employment Rights Act	• Individuals able to seek injunctions against unlawful action.
	• Requirement for seven days' notice of ballots and industrial action.
	• Abolition of wages councils.
	• Union financial records to be available for scrutiny.
	• Increased penalties against unions failing to keep adequate accounts.
	• All strike ballots must be postal; independent scrutiny imposed.

Further reading

Two other books in this series are relevant to our discussion: David Needle's *Business in Context* (2nd edition, 1994), which places human resource management in its wider business framework; *Law in a Business Context* (1990), by Bill Cole, Peter Shears and Jillinda Tiley, outlines the legal framework. There is a burgeoning selection of texts on international comparisons in human resource management, including Sarah Vickerstaff (ed.) (1992) *Human Resource Management in Europe: Text and Cases,* and Paul Sparrow and Jean-Marie Hiltrop (1994) *European Human Resource Management in Transition.* One of the best discussions of Japanese business methods can be found in Arthur M. Whitehill (1991) *Japanese Management: Tradition and Transition.* The *International Journal of Human Resource Management* provides in-depth discussion of current developments in worldwide HRM. For more general reading, *New Internationalist* covers a wide range of topics with background – and sometimes direct – relevance to international human resource management.

Review questions

1 If businesses have little control over economic growth or recession, is there any point in attempting to follow long-term human resource strategies for employee development?
2 Define the concept of human capital in your own words. Is it possible to quantify a nation's/company's human capital?
3 It has been said that a successful multinational must have a strong presence in each of the three main trading blocks. What are the human resource implications for an organization undertaking this strategy?
4 In what ways do approaches to people management differ between 'social-market' and 'free market' countries. Relate these differences to hard and soft models of HRM.
5 What can be gained from comparing people management practices in different countries?
6 To what extent did changes in the law by the Conservative government in the UK enhance the development of a free-market approach to HRM?

Problems for discussion and analysis

1 You have been appointed General Manager at a new local subsidiary of a Japanese television manufacturer. The subsidiary is controlled by three senior Japanese managers who have been seconded from the parent company for a five-year period. Your first task is to identify and shortlist suitable locations for production and then participate in choosing suppliers and staff. Describe the likely decision processes and contrast them with the way a typical local company would have dealt with the same problem.

2 Leyanne has recently graduated with a degree in business studies, specializing in finance. She has been recruited as a trainee by a large conglomerate involved in airport management and cargo distribution. The company operates in Australia, Singapore, Europe and the Caribbean. Corporate headquarters are in Sydney, Australia, but the largest operational units are in Singapore and Germany. The organization prefers to develop its own management and expects a broad range of experience and a grasp of different cultural traditions. Leyanne is ambitious and wants to become a senior manager in the company. Outline a possible career plan for Leyanne, including aspects for which the company should take responsibility and issues for her own self-development.

The employment market

3

> This chapter examines the dynamics of the employment market. We consider how and why people choose to work and investigate the range of modern job patterns.

The employment or job market (see key concept 3.1) is the ultimate source of all new recruits. Human resource managers need to understand the dynamics of this market in order to deal properly with resourcing, set competitive salaries and obtain people with essential skills. They need to understand the expectations of prospective employees and have an insight into issues such as:

- Why do people work?
- What conditions and salaries are they prepared to work for?
- What expectations do they have of employers?
- How does the availability of human capital affect employment levels?
- What effects do the activities of competitors have on employee availability?
- What patterns of work are replacing traditional nine-to-five jobs?

These questions are addressed in this chapter. We begin by exploring the reasons why people seek employment and examine their expectations of working life. This is evaluated first from an economic perspective, introducing competitive market and institutional theories, and then from social and

The employment market comprises all those people who are available for work. Neo-classical economics views this potential workforce as forming a labour market. The market is affected by national or regional supply of and demand for appropriately skilled employees. It is constrained by demographic factors such as the number of young people leaving schools and universities and by cultural variables such as expectations for mothers to stay at home looking after children.	**KEY CONCEPT 3.1** *The employment market*

individual viewpoints. The chapter moves on to consider the issue of unemployment. Finally, the characteristics of the flexible job market are debated, including new forms of part-time working and the effects of greater female participation in the working economy.

Why do people work?

The simple answer in most cases is that they have to. Few of us have the private resources needed to maintain a satisfactory lifestyle without an income from employment. This seems obvious, but the issue becomes much more complex on examination. For example, many wealthy people (or lottery winners) continue to work even though they do not 'need' to. Moreover, unless they are in a desperate financial state, people pick and choose what work they are prepared to do. Professions such as nursing and social work attract large numbers of people despite relatively low rates of pay in many countries. Clearly, there are many other factors which have to be taken into account in understanding people's motives in the employment market. Economists, occupational psychologists and industrial sociologists have contributed to our knowledge.

As yet there have been few attempts to link economic theories of the employment market with HRM (Claydon 1994: 74). The task is all the more complicated because economists have provided several different and contradictory theories in this area. They can be divided broadly into two main approaches: competitive and institutional.

Competitive market theories

These are derived from the neo-classical economic concepts of **rational choice** and **maximization of utility**. The assumption here is that **individuals** choose jobs which offer them maximum benefits. The utility or value of these benefits – money, vacation time, pension entitlement and so on – vary for different individuals according to their personal preferences. People move from one organization to another if improved benefits are available. At the same time, employer organizations attempt to get the most from their employees for the lowest possible cost.

The outcome of this process is a dynamic and shifting equilibrium in which both employees and organizations compete to maximize benefits for themselves. Within a specific region or industry there is a balance between **supply** and **demand** for human resources. Pay and conditions for employees are determined by the relative scarcity or abundance of skills and abilities in the employment market. Competitive forces push wages up when demand for products – and hence employees – increases, and downwards when the economy is in recession. In the latter case a **market clearing wage** is eventually arrived at which is sufficiently low to encourage employers to increase recruitment and eliminate unemployment. This discourse reinforces the view that employees are objects to be traded like any other commodities in the market – human resources in the hardest possible sense. Supposedly, they offer themselves – their skills and human qualities

– for sale to the highest bidders. Within this mindset they could just as well be vegetables on a market stall.

In reality, it is obvious that the job market does not work in such a simple fashion: people do not move readily between organizations in search of higher wages; most firms do not cut benefits when unemployment levels are high and cheaper workers are available. Indeed, in the 1980s wages soared for those in work at the same time as unemployment levels increased. Such contradictions are partly explained by the omission of HR development issues such as training and career structures in competition theories. More generally, they assume that employment markets are purely external when, in fact, large organizations have internal job markets operating through the promotion and transfer of existing employees.

Competition theories assume that job-seekers have perfect knowledge of available jobs and benefits. Job-searching is an expensive and time-consuming business. The unemployed do not have money and those in work do not have time. The result is that few people conduct the extensive searches required to find jobs which meet their preferences perfectly. In practice, most individuals settle for employment which is quickly obtained and which exceeds the **reserve minimum wage** they have in mind. There is a considerable element of luck involved. Moreover, the job-seeker does not make the choice: in most cases the decision is in the hands of the employer.

Entry barriers to skilled jobs provide a further constraint on the competitive job market. Many jobs are restricted to people possessing key skills – often specific to a particular firm or industrial sector. In fact, the external job market is made up of many submarkets with widely different circumstances and constraints. For example, between 1989 and 1995 the job market for construction workers – particularly house-building – in the UK experienced a contraction of half a million posts. Conversely, other sectors were unable to find enough suitable workers. Although the reduction in housing construction is a feature of recession, the failure of many workers to find jobs elsewhere reflects the consistent trend away from unskilled manual work. As we shall see in later chapters, full employment is no longer likely to come from low-paid and low-skilled jobs.

The United States is an exception among developed countries, having generated more new jobs than any other through flexible job markets, minimal welfare benefits and comparatively low wages for unskilled work. However, the cost has been considerable social inequality and a high crime rate. The employment market is subject to a greater level of state control in most other countries. In the previous chapter we saw that the state has a major influence on the quantity and quality of workers in their employment markets by means of two types of intervention:

- economic, social and employment legislation;
- investment in human capital through education and training programmes.

However, underlying beliefs regarding the degree of employment protection, benefits for the unemployed and acceptable wages have become tougher. Against an agenda primarily set by right-of-centre politics, even left-wing parties have adjusted their views. Hence, 'New Labour' in the

UK has adopted policies which advocate the following (*Financial Times*, 9 January 1996):

- restrained and affordable public sector spending;
- control of inflation;
- encouragement of inward investment;
- tax rates which compare favourably with those of international competitors;
- employment protection which does not cause rigidity or inflexibility in the job market;
- maintenance of 1980s legislation restricting the scope of trade union activities;
- partnership between public and private sectors to revitalize investment-starved infrastructure, for example railways and roads;
- the reform of education to boost the nation's skill base;
- active participation in the European Union, including the Social Chapter.

On a European level, the pursuit of a single market has led increasingly to measures allowing the free circulation of employees and freedom of residence in any EU country. Other barriers are being removed with recognition of educational qualifications and further social and economic cohesion. Sweden has proposed the standardization of employment regulation and protection measures to further promote a single European job market with the goal of full employment.

As a result of unification, Germany has by far the largest job market in the EU. However, amalgamation of the highly productive and expensively rewarded west with the inefficient but poorly paid east has disrupted the German employment market. The equal valuation of the two currencies and a commitment to raise eastern wages to western levels delivered a fatal blow to hopes for a rapid spread of prosperity throughout the country. In fact, German industry has shed jobs in both parts. Overall, the unemployment rate passed 10 per cent by the beginning of 1996, with almost 17 per cent in the east. Even in the former West Germany, the unemployment rate of 9.4 per cent exceeded that of the UK.

Institutional theories

An alternative approach places its main focus within the firm rather than the external job market. Institutionalists do not accept the principle of individual maximization of utility, arguing that both individuals and organizations cooperate to some extent and take account of the preferences of others in similar situations. Individual workers are less concerned with maximum benefits than achieving a fair rate compared to their peers. But this comparison may be restricted to employees within the same organization: most people appear indifferent to benefits offered by other employers and large variations occur between firms in the same sector. Employers set wages for a variety of reasons ranging from profitability to tradition – competition with other firms is a relatively minor consideration (see Table 3.1). As a result, benefit levels within many firms are relatively rigid. Wage rates are

Table 3.1 Secretarial salaries in London

Grade	Description	Range
Level I	College leaver/less than twelve months' experience	£6,000–15,500
Level II	Junior secretary/minimum one year's experience	£8,000–19,000
Level III	Manager/team-level secretary/PA	£10,000–20,000
Level IV	Director/partner-level secretary/PA	£12,500–25,000
Level V	Chairman/CEO/senior partner-level secretary/PA	£13,000–31,000

Source: adapted from *Secretarial Salaries in Central London 1993–1994*, Gordon Yates Secretarial Recruitment Group in conjunction with *The Times*.

more likely to go up than down and are largely immune to influence from the external job market.

Competition theories assume that hiring and firing in reaction to changing market conditions is good practice. There are close parallels between this way of thinking and 'hard' HRM. In fact, most firms take active steps to avoid employee turnover. This is because turnover is disruptive and costs money. Recruitment advertising and redundancy payments are expensive, and training new employees represents a considerable investment in time and effort. Organizations may encourage workers to remain with them by means of HR policies which increase benefits such as annual leave and pensions in line with length of service.

Reflecting on our discussion in Chapter 1, we can conclude that institutional approaches to the job market have a greater affinity with 'soft' HRM. They recognize that group effects underlie notions of fairness and loyalty which are fundamental to the principle of commitment (see Chapter 5). They are consistent with the stakeholder concept, recognizing the important roles played by government and trade unions. For example, the **insider–outsider** model offers an explanation for simultaneously high wages and high levels of unemployment, as we will see in Case 3.1 (Lindbeck and Snower 1988). Insiders have stakeholder status whereas outsiders do not (see key concept 3.2).

Union negotiators are more aware of the interests of their employed members (insiders) and their pursuit of increased benefits than of the interests of the unemployed and non-members (outsiders). Equally, as we discussed earlier, employers know that replacing existing workers with others from the ranks of the unemployed has inherent costs. These costs and the associated disruption outweigh the advantages of employing cheaper workers from outside. Consequently, insiders can demand an **economic rent** or premium above competitive wages. Established workers can use their insider-power in other ways, including a refusal to cooperate with new recruits, if there is a perceived threat to this premium.

KEY CONCEPT 3.2
Insiders and outsiders

At the organizational level, human resource managers also affect the nature of the market as a result of their recruitment and redundancy strategies. When business is optimistic, recruitment numbers increase; if conditions are bad, employees may be shed. Technological change is a further complicating factor, leading to fewer but more highly skilled employees.

Figure 3.1 demonstrates some of the forces which shape the employment market, including elements discussed in Chapter 2, such as the major role played by government, particularly in the shape of legislation. The interactions between organizations and the job market are further debated in Chapter 6, when we consider human resource strategy. At this stage it is appropriate to note some omissions from most discussions of this subject. These include the influence of social class, age, status, gender and ethnic origin in the job expectations of employees and the attitudes of employers towards these characteristics. As we shall see in Chapter 9, suitable people can appear invisible to managers who associate competence for high-level jobs with a particular age, accent, sex or colour.

Social preferences

It is important to understand that participating in employment is not an 'all-or-nothing' decision. Individuals also determine the amount of time they are prepared to devote to paid work. This time allocation is affected by **expected market earnings**, taking travel, clothing and taxation into account. Traditionally, time given to **market work** is distinguished from that devoted to any other activity – described as **leisure**. However, it is

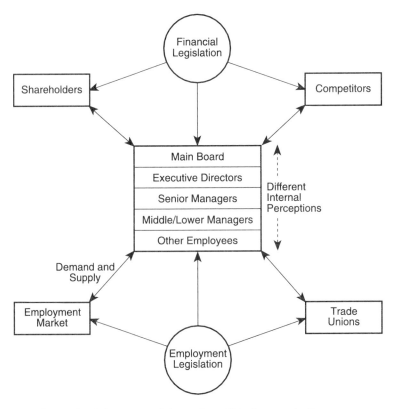

Figure 3.1 Competing influences on job creation within the organization.

recognized that time outside paid work is not necessarily devoted to pleasure. Far from lying on a beach sipping a cool drink, people spend much of their 'leisure' time on some form of work without pay. This could be housework, maintenance, looking after children, cooking or providing a voluntary service.

Deciding to take a job, or not, involves a trade-off between family members. If an additional member works, there must be a reduction or reallocation of that person's unpaid activities. Employment may change lifestyle significantly. In developed countries this can result in the purchase of labour-saving devices such as a microwave oven, changing from fresh to ready-prepared food and hiring a cleaner or childminder.

Becker (1965) recognized that the decision to seek employment can be complex and is likely to be taken in conjunction with other members of the household. The household is viewed as the 'decision-making unit'. The household chooses how to allocate its members' time, evaluating the comparative advantages of working as against not working. For example, the emphasis can be on working for money in order to buy the largest possible house, a brand new car, expensive holidays and consumer goods such as convenience foods. Alternatively, the household can minimize working time and maximize leisure, making do with a more modest home and car, spending effort on home-grown and home-prepared food. Doing without paid work in order to maximize free time is an **opportunity cost**. In other words, if paid work is available, not working has a cost for the household. There may be preferences for particular family members to stay at home – typically mothers – whereas others (fathers) are expected to earn a wage. As we will see later in this chapter, this pattern has changed radically in most industrialized countries in recent years.

Recognition of household preferences is important to people managers because there are strong cultural differences between one region and another. There are considerable pressures on potential and actual workers to behave in the way perceived as normal in their particular society. However, most organizations pay little attention to the domestic influences on an employee's motivation and performance. Employees are recruited and their performance assessed as if they were entirely free agents with no domestic responsibilities or interests outside work.

When is it worthwhile going to work? The total available resources of the household unit may be weighed up in the equation, including the time available for all its members, other income and total wealth. The financial benefit of work can only be gauged when tax, social security deductions, travelling, childminding costs and so on have been calculated. This benefit may prove insignificant.

Mathematical models have been developed to predict the number of hours which people are prepared to work. They take into account factors such as the availablity of overtime work, the effects of taxation, opportunities for self-employment and payment by results (Sapsford and Tzannatos 1993: 27). Empirical studies do not necessarily support this approach. In Case 3.1 we see that unemployment is an experience which can arrive like a tidal wave. There may be no opportunity to make a free decision on whether or not to work. During the 1980s recession, for example, it was common for both husband and wife to lose their jobs in quick succession (Morris 1987). Wives were often in highly vulnerable part-time jobs. Morris argues that his research contradicts the notion of the household decision-making model. He concludes that such models take no account of the local social network which influences beliefs and expectations of employment. Neither do they accommodate local differences in employment opportunities and cultural ideas of gender behaviour. Job choices also reflect individual career plans and preferences.

Individual preferences

We have seen that people do not behave as mere commodities. Human behaviour involves deep complexities which bring unpredictability and apparent contrariness into the employment market. Most people's motives and ambitions involve much more than seeking the highest salary. Money is important, but to a degree which varies between individuals. People will remain in comparatively low-paid jobs such as nursing because the satisfaction which comes from helping other people can be valued above a high salary. An economic model based purely on income will go some way to explaining employment behaviour on the large scale but it will not explain individual human behaviour. Other motivations come into play in determining people's approach to work. Psychologists have attempted to provide explanations at the individual level (see, for example, McKenna 1994: 63; Mullins 1996: 479).

It is common to ask the question 'what do you do?' For many of us, personal identity is provided by a job. Table 3.2 lists a number of other psychological benefits obtained from work. These include social needs such as companionship, group cohesion and a sense of belonging. In contrast, as we shall see in Case 3.1, unemployment carries connotations of worthlessness. For example, a Coopers and Lybrand study of unemployed executives found that 43 per cent did not reveal their lack of a job in applications (*Personnel Management*, March 1992: 3). In the next section we go on to explore some of the consequences of participating, or not, in the job market and the relevance of unemployment to the formation of modern work patterns.

Participating in the employment market

Who is involved in the job market? In Figure 3.1 we see that the resourcing of organizations is affected by national or regional availability (supply) and demand for appropriately skilled employees. On the supply side of this balance, people can be divided into three groups, the first two of which are described as **economically active**:

- The **employed**, those in paid work;
- The **unemployed**, those who are looking for paid work but are unable to find it;
- The **economically inactive**, those neither in paid work nor seeking jobs,

including people in education, with medical conditions, looking after dependants and the retired.

The proportion of people in each of these categories varies from country to country, depending on economic conditions and custom. Accurate figures for each group are not easily calculated. In particular, it is difficult to estimate true unemployment because the unemployed are identified on the basis of registration with state agencies. As an illustration, Table 3.3 shows official figures for a number of European countries in 1994. Usually the registration of individuals as unemployed is linked to the payment of unemployment relief or other social security benefit. If the benefit system is generous, people are more likely to register. Conversely, if benefits are

Table 3.2 Psychological benefits of work

Factor	Characteristics
Opportunities for control	Limited control over work, or no job at all, leads to higher levels of anxiety, depression, tiredness and psychosomatic symptoms, as well as lower general life-satisfaction and self-esteem.
Opportunities for skill use	People benefit from challenging jobs. Morale, self-esteem, sociability and life satisfaction are reduced when a worker's job is deskilled or lost. Some people can compensate through hobbies or voluntary work, but many are unable to fill the gap.
Goal and task demands	Jobs set demands on our lives in general. Many unemployed people find it hard to fill their time, often spending a high proportion of it sleeping, sitting around or watching TV, further contributing to lowered morale.
Variety	Work can increase variety, providing a contrast with home life. It also provides the income to pay for experiences such as cinema, music, sporting activities and holidays.
Environmental clarity	Work helps us understand and predict the world around us. Mental health is better if we are clear about our roles and purpose in life. Conversely, uncertainty is detrimental, especially over a lengthy period.
Availability of money	The unemployed have a lower income level (40–60 per cent on average) than those in work. This can make it difficult to repay credit and keep up mortgage payments, adding further stress. Expensive activities are curtailed, contributing to feelings of isolation and boredom.
Physical security	In western cultures people are brought up to value personal and private space. To provide feelings of personal security, self worth and wellbeing they need a home to call their own. Most people require a regular income to achieve this.
Opportunity for interpersonal contact	Interaction with other people reduces feelings of loneliness and provides emotional support.
Valued social position	Work provides a sense of identity and a feeling of worth.

Source: adapted from Warr (1987).

Table 3.3 Comparative levels of unemployment (1996)

Country	%
Spain	22.2
Belgium	13.8
France	12.6
Italy	11.7
Germany	10.6
Canada	10.0
Australia	8.8
Sweden	8.8
UK	7.2
Netherlands	6.7
USA	5.2
Japan	3.3

restricted the registered unemployment figure decreases. As a result, Mexico has the lowest official rate of unemployment in the OECD! The British Conservative government was also accused by the Opposition of massaging figures in this way.

As we can see from Case 3.1, developed countries have experienced considerable variations in unemployment levels. This is reflected in changes in public expectations and concern over the level of unemployment. In the UK, for example, whereas the unemployment level is about average for the EU, it is historically high but public concern appears to be minimal.

Others would work if jobs were easy to find but do not search when work is scarce. This has been called the **discouraged worker hypothesis**. Workers calculate the probability of finding a job in relation to the wage they are likely to get and conclude that the effort is not worthwhile. This hypothesis suggests that the number of active job-seekers decreases in times of high unemployment, leaving an unmeasurable hidden unemployment rate behind the official statistics.

Organizations in free-market countries focus on the **external** employment market, seeking new staff from outside the business. This is compatible with a competitive market approach in which employees are recruited when needed and dispensed with when no longer required. This view also provides a clear rationale for the hard HRM form of employee planning which we will discuss in Chapter 6. In the first chapter of this book we observed that the softer Harvard model of HRM emphasizes commitment between organizations and their employees. The latter approach is more consistent with social-market and East Asian capitalist models. In Germany and Japan – together with the ideal organizations of soft HRM rhetoric – the focus is on the **internal** employment market, in which:

- recruitment takes place almost entirely at the lower levels from the pool of available school-leavers and graduates;
- organizations offer a structured career on a lifetime basis;

● there is little movement, or labour turnover, between organizations.

You will remember from the earlier discussions on Japan that, until recently, major Japanese companies offered lifelong employment and career development. German organizations emphasize the recruitment of apprentices who will eventually fill middle and senior posts, whereas in free-market countries companies advertise vacancies externally at all levels. An OECD study quoted by Thomson and Mabey showed that people stayed with one employer for an average of around twenty-two years in Japan, Germany and France (1994: 1). This compared with around thirteen years in the USA, and similar average periods of time in Australia, Canada, the Netherlands and the UK. Drawing on data from the Price Waterhouse Cranfield survey of European HRM, Brewster and Bournois comment that:

> Sixty-three per cent of German organizations used apprenticeships to fill vacant clerical positions, whereas hardly any UK employers did so. For manual worker vacancies, UK employers were significantly more likely to advertise externally, the Germans much more likely to rely on apprentice-ships. Sixty-seven per cent of British employers advertised manual vacancies externally, and 41 per cent of German organizations.
> (Brewster and Bournois 1991: 6)

Intriguingly, the archetypal East Asian economy, Singapore, has seen high rates of employee turnover to match its remarkable growth rate due to competition for scarce skills. Similarly, Japanese companies have changed their traditional practices to attract electronics experts with premium tech-nological skills.

Projections of the future size of the employment market are critical to planned economic development. On a local basis, individual companies need to anticipate the availability of suitable recruits to meet business planning needs. These are normally calculated from the following:

● demographic trends, including the birthrate at least sixteen years previously;
● retirement rates;
● numbers of people in higher education.

Reductions in demand for manual work have seen many unskilled workers leaving the employment market. In the UK, the Institute of Public Policy Research found that the proportion of men of working age in employment fell from 91 per cent in 1977 to 80 per cent in 1992. However, the change was much greater for men over 55 (from 82 per cent to 59 per cent) and those without qualifications (from 88 per cent to 67 per cent). Reduction in the numbers of older men at work is a worldwide phenomenon (see Table 3.4). This reflects a variety of factors from choice to enforced redundancy on ageist grounds. We discuss ageism further in Chapter 9, on the management of diversity.

Table 3.4 Percentage of older males in the workforce (age 60–64)

Country	1960–1	1994	% decrease
Australia	79.6	48.7	39
Austria	66.0	12.7	81
Finland	79.1	23.9	69
France	71.1	18.2	74
Germany	72.5	34.9	51
Italy	70.1	37.2	46
Japan	81.9	75.6	8
Netherlands	80.8	18.0	88
Sweden	82.5	57.8	29
UK	est 87.4	52.2	40
USA	77.1	54.9	29

Source: World Labour Report 1995, International Labour Organization.

CASE 3.1
Unemployment in the UK

For much of this century the ideal of full employment was fundamental. In the 1950s and 1960s – Harold Macmillan's 'you've never had it so good' period – the average rate of unemployment was less than 3 per cent. Often it was as low as 1.5–2 per cent. Technically, this represented a state of full employment throughout most of the country since there is always a small proportion of people 'between jobs'.

The first indication of the new era of unemployment came from the 1973 oil crisis, when the price of petroleum increased by some 300 per cent. The shock to the economy led to UK unemployment passing the 1 million mark for the first time since the Second World War. This rate continued to rise until the 3 million point was passed a decade later. At its worst, in 1986, the official rate peaked at 12.3 per cent, or 3.4 million people. The recession of the late 1970s and early 1980s turfed out large numbers of people from Britain's manufacturing base. These were mostly located away from the prosperous south-east of England.

Effectively, the UK split into two zones, with the old industrial areas of the Midlands, the North and the West taking the brunt of job losses. The total number of jobs in Wales and the North-West of England fell by 10 per cent between 1979 and 1989. In the same period, the boom in the financial sector led to an equivalent level of job growth in the south of England. The job market actually increased by 26 per cent in East Anglia.

During the 1980s southern Britain maintained its negative views of the unemployed, that unemployment was an indication of unwillingness to look for work. At that time, high levels of unemployment were largely restricted to lower-class, inner-city areas which already had a stigmatized population:

> it was fashionable on the Right to argue that anyone could get a job if they tried, and that too many people were workshy. This was – and continues to be – rubbish, except in the case of a tiny minority. At present there are 101,000 vacancies advertised at Jobcentres to be distributed among the 2,909,000 unemployed.
> (William Keegan, *The Observer*, 20 December 1992, 'We wish you a Merry Crisis . . .')

However, by the late 1980s events had taken a new turn: in a further 'boom and bust' cycle, a second recession had arrived. This time its effects were experienced in those parts of the country which had escaped earlier job losses. At first, media coverage was scarcely sympathetic as the first victims were high-living city yuppies, but redundancies soon hit the middle-class suburbs. The high levels of borrowing for house purchase in the South-east and the link with consumer spending made this recession much more of a middle-class crisis than any in the past. Suddenly, people who thought that unemployment was something which happened to other people realized that it could also happen to them. Moreover, there was increasing awareness that there was very little that individuals could do to influence events – they had no power to prevent this happening.

Table 3.3 shows that the official unemployment level in the UK fell in the mid-1990s due to economic recovery and innumerable changes in the way that the unemployment rate is calculated (invariably producing a lower figure). Government schemes to assist the unemployed to obtain new jobs have been largely unsuccessful. A principal cause of continuing high levels of unemployment lies in a 'structural' change away from the old manufacturing industries, which were major users of unskilled workers, to technologically based activities requiring expertise. A further change has been a substantial growth in part-time work, predominantly taken up by women.

Discussion questions

1 Is unemployment a social stigma in your community?

2 Is full employment a realistic goal?

Employee supply

Individuals determine how much time they will devote to paid work for a variety of reasons. The proportion of people of working age in work or seeking jobs is described as the labour force participation rate. In 1993, for example, the highest proportion of people at work in the EU was found in Denmark – 67 per cent of the population over the age of 15. The UK took second place with 61.9 per cent, compared with the EU average of 55 per cent. The relatively high proportion in the UK is explained by three factors: the highest level of female employment in the EU; comparatively large numbers of young people (aged 15–24) in work rather than education; and more people between 50 and 64 still working.

The flow of young people into the workforce is fundamental to the employment market. The underlying **demographic** pattern is changing throughout the world (see Table 3.5). Whereas most developing countries have seen an explosion of growth in the youngest age groups, the developed world is experiencing a reduction in birthrate. This follows a baby boom after the Second World War which produced a wave of people in

Table 3.5 Demographic trends

- Populations in developed countries are stabilizing or declining. Birth rates are tending to fall below replenishment rates.

- Ageing populations in 'first world' countries may be counterbalanced by immigration, for example North Africans in France.

- Developing countries experience a period of rapid population growth as infant mortality rates are reduced – well in advance of birth-control measures being adopted.

- Most developing countries experience population pressure for decades until stablility is achieved.

- The population balance will change markedly between the developed and developing world. Eventually the developed world will decline in importance, in line with its reduced working population.

their forties and fifties in the mid 1990s. In Western Europe and North America, the numbers of people entering the employment market have been falling. This will reduce the overall size of their workforces, shifting the age balance towards older employees. This has been compensated for by a massive increase in the number of working women, especially in part-time jobs. In the United Kingdom the working-age population had reached a record 34.4 million by 1989, a growth of almost 2 million in the preceding decade. This remained stable during the early 1990s but will increase to 34.7 million by the beginning of the new millenium.

Migration has an important effect. Some countries are net importers (Australia) or exporters (Ireland) of people, whereas a few (UK) are in a state of near equilibrium. Within overall demographic trends, particular social and ethnic groups show different patterns. In the latter case it is possible to project the future ethnic balance. A Manchester University report on ethnic dimensions within the 1991 census showed that the population of ethnic minorities in the UK will eventually stabilize at around 10 per cent of the British population (*Guardian*, 20 January 1994). This represents a doubling of the 1991 total of 2.7 million, based on a projection of birth and death rates. The current ethnic population is heavily weighted to under-21s in comparison with the majority Anglo-Celtic population. In the London boroughs this means that 40 per cent of school leavers in the 1990s will come from ethnic minority groups. In terms of performance, some ethnic groups are showing greater career advancement than white groups. The greatest success is shown by Chinese, with 13 per cent in professional jobs, compared with 5 per cent for the general population. Equal opportunities and ethnic discrimination are discussed further in Chapter 9.

Germany has experienced significant changes because of its proximity to eastern Europe. In western Germany, the indigenous population both declined in numbers and aged in the 1980s: 23 per cent of the population was under 15 years old in 1970, dropping to 14.6 per cent in 1987; by contrast those over 65 increased from 13.2 to 15.3 per cent (Randlesome 1994: 93). However, the employment market was boosted by refugees from eastern Germany, people of German descent from other eastern European states and asylum seekers from elsewhere. Consequently, the working population increased from 26.3 million in 1970 to 28.2 million in 1987, contributing to a substantial increase in the unemployment rate. Following unification of the two German states, the long-term trend continues to show declining population. The forecast for the year 2030 indicates that:

- only 17 per cent will be aged below 20;
- 48 per cent will be between 20 and 60;
- 35 per cent will be over 60.

By the year 2030 Japan and Germany will have a significantly higher proportion of people over 60 than many of their major competitors, including the UK and the USA. In the UK, a slow decline in jobless figures in the mid-1990s was partly explained by demographic changes which led to the number of young people of school-leaving age dropping by one-third. The Office of Population Census and Surveys estimated that whereas 900,000 16-year-olds were available in each year between 1979 and 1983, this gradually declined to just over 600,000 in the 1990s. In addition, the proportion of young people remaining in education after the age of 16 grew from 52 to 71 per cent between 1988 and 1993.

The complex interaction between demographic trends, economic activity and the employment market is well illustrated in Australia. Despite its location, its business history in the 1980s and early 1990s had close parallels with that of North America and Britain, geared more to economic recession than boom. During a period of fifteen years, long-term unemployment increased from 50,000 to 350,000, creating a 'jobless generation', with up to 50 per cent of teenagers unemployed in some parts of the country. Their stresses were made worse by the poverty of unemployed parents, leading to fears of an underclass turning to crime and drugs. The problem is considerably worse among the indigenous aboriginal population, with unemployment running at three times the national average.

Australia's role as a migrant country, with a continually increasing potential labour force, has exacerbated these problems. A Monash University report (quoted in *The Times Higher*, 4 March 1994) concluded that if immigration continued at the prevailing rate there would be an increase of 2.9 million (25 per cent) in the working-age population by 2011; 826,000 would have been added between 1991 and 1996 alone, a time when public and private organizations were shedding employees. In contrast to that of its Asian neighbours, the Australian track record of job creation has been poor. A key factor appears to be the history of a low level of investment in research and development, achieving only 50 per cent of the OECD average. However, recent years have seen a substantial increase in business-funded research pointing towards a more optimistic trend for the future.

Employee demand

Demand for workers is linked to the economic cycle, increasing in boom times and decreasing in recession. Other factors include the adoption of new technology, productivity improvements and changing skill requirements. Superficially, calculating employment supply and demand seems easy. In practice, the combination of variable consumer demand, development of new products and technology, and economic turbulence make it extremely problematic. In the last decade, for example, commentators have confidently predicted both permanently high levels of unemployment *and* shortages of labour.

As we observed in the last chapter, the role of the state is important in this respect: through fiscal or monetary policy, governments can directly increase or diminish consumption and economic activity. Such actions lead quickly to changes in demand for human resources as firms relate their requirements to production or the provision of services. Activity in service and manufacturing services may follow different patterns. The decline in manufacturing in the UK, for example, has been dismissed as unimportant by some commentators who believed that production jobs would be replaced by new work in financial and other services. The reality is that these sectors have proven incapable of generating enough employment to compensate for the loss of full-time jobs in manufacturing. As we shall see shortly, there has been a widespread trend for well-paid jobs to be replaced with low-paid part-time work.

CASE 3.2 ***Working hours***	How much time do people want to spend at work? How long can they work effectively? For example, is it reasonable to expect employees to work ten, twelve, fourteen hours or longer at a stretch? How much annual leave is advisable? Should it be two weeks or eight weeks a year? These issues are basic to the employment relationship. They are matters on which managers and employees have firm opinions. But are their views based on cultural differences rather than on sound economics, psychology or physiology?

Simplistically, we can argue that productivity is directly related to hours worked, so that doubling the time spent at work leads to twice the output. This approach seems to be dominant in many American businesses. It has become common also in high-pressure working environments such as the dealing rooms of the City of London. However, it has been known for at least 150 years that this view is based on a false premise. An 1845 report from the British Inspector of Factories found that reducing the hours of work in a Lancashire cotton mill from twelve hours to eleven led to no diminution in production. This came as a surprise to the mill owners but did not lead to any widespread reform.

People can work long hours for a few intense periods, perhaps to pass an examination or meet a critical deadline. On a permanent basis, however, there is a point at which working extra hours actually reduces overall output. The lesson was learned again during the First World War (Smith 1948: 19). Over 50,000 female 'munitionettes' were employed at National Shell Filling Factories around the UK. The country needed a massive increase in armaments and the average daily shift was increased from ten to twelve hours. This often stretched to fifteen when travelling was included. However, the extra work time did not lead to additional production. In fact the workers produced less because the strain led to a slowing in the speed of work, greater sick leave and increased incidence of alcoholism.

Throughout the twentieth century the trend in Europe has been towards shorter working hours and longer holidays. John Maynard Keynes even predicted that the advance of automation would lead to a fifteen-hour working week. He forecast that the biggest problem we would have to cope with would be making use of all the spare time available. More recently there has been talk of a 'leisure revolution' based on the microchip. However, that seems further away than ever for most working people.

The nearest approximation to the leisure culture is to be found in Germany. Work attitudes in the former West Germany have shown a marked change in the latter part of the twentieth century. The postwar recovery has often been attributed to long and hard work. By the 1980s, however, German unions had negotiated some of the shortest working hours in the developed world. Surveys showed that many Germans worked only as long as they had to.

The UK has the longest working hours of any country in the European Community. In 1993, for example, full-time British workers usually worked 43.4 hours a week, compared to the EU average of 40.2. The difference between actual hours worked, however, was lower – just one and a half hours longer than the EU average of 39.6. This is due to higher levels of absence due to sickness and stress. Yet the UK government fought against EU plans to introduce a maximum of 48 hours a week for a wide range of employment categories. UK attitudes towards the issue are exemplified in the working hours of junior hospital doctors – typically up to 100 hours a week. Since April 1993 no junior doctor is supposed to be working more than the incredible 83 hours specified in their contracts. In many cases this is no more than 'paper compliance', with a large number being paid for 83 hours when, in fact, they are working even more for nothing.

A 1994 survey conducted for a catering group showed that many British workers also cut their lunch breaks. The average break was 32 minutes; 51 per cent of the staff surveyed took less than half an hour; 14 per cent took no break and worked through. The hardest workers – hospital doctors – took less time and ate less than other workers; 30 per cent had only one meal a day. A similar trend is occurring in mainland Europe, where traditional lengthy lunches are becoming a rarity.

In the USA, working hours have actually increased. It has been said that most people work to live but Americans live to work. In 1992 the average American worked 164 more hours a year than in 1970. Typically, new employees receive a mere two weeks' annual vacation. A competition for 'America's Most Overworked Person' awarded the title to Jack Dudley, Personnel Director of an American subsidiary of Siemens. He worked five or six days a week, getting up at 5 a.m. and arriving home after 8 p.m. – including four hours' commuting each day. Despite the title, Mr Dudley's working week was probably quite modest by American standards – the US Overachievers Anonymous organization has 10,000 workaholic members. American work attitudes can be related to relatively low tax rates and minimal welfare benefits. The rewards for extra work are substantial.

Workaholism has become institutionalized in Japan, where employees take only 60 per cent of their paid vacations. Half of middle-aged 'salarymen' return home after 8 p.m., rarely eating dinner with their families during the week. The working year in Japan averages 2,044 hours a year, in comparison with 1,900 in the USA and the UK and just 1,600 in Germany. With an average of 28.8 hours overtime a month, many employees are happy to put in 50 hours. A trade union survey showed that only a quarter of Japanese workers would like shorter hours. The attitude is most typical of the 'guilt generation' of older managers who grew up with the postwar boom. Totally wedded to their jobs, they do not know what to do with their spare time. After the death of a vice-chairman from *karoshi* – sudden death from overwork – Toyota are attempting to compel managers to take ten consecutive days off in a year.

Discussion questions

1 To what extent are working hours and annual leave culturally determined? What is the ideal length of the working week? On what basis?
2 What are the strategic and cost implications of a reduction in working hours?

Technology and skills

Developments in telecommunications and computing are dramatically changing the nature of work and the way it is performed and managed. At the time of writing, half of all workers in the USA use computers in their jobs. As this trend increases and extends throughout the world, the importance of skill and knowledge will increase commensurately. In general, low-skill jobs are steadily disappearing in the face of the professionalization of work. One of the major pressures on the old industrialized countries is the collapse in demand for unskilled workers in industries such as shipbuilding and textiles. Handy argues that in the early twenty-first century between 70 and 80 per cent of all jobs will require 'knowledge workers' (1989: 82). He estimates that more than one-third of jobs will require graduate-level training or professional qualifications.

In advanced economies a further reorientation comes from the move away from manufacturing towards service industries. Computer software, financial products, insurance and so on are heavily dependent on knowledge workers. Even manufacturing is changing its requirements. 'Fordist' industry based on mass production of a small range of products is being replaced by a 'post-Fordist' choice between numerous niche products produced by flexible people with flexible equipment. Niche production requires much higher knowledge standards than mass assembly. It also requires different, more adaptable, employees than the human robots of the assembly line.

Technology is also changing the organization of work. Most of the management techniques of the twentieth century have been based on paperwork and face-to-face communications. Meetings, memos and reports are transformed by information technology. People management must change to meet new realities. For example, banking was a sector in which long-term careers were the norm. Information technology is transforming the situation. Electronic transfer of funds, debit cards, 'hole-in-the wall' cash dispensers and cashback facilities at major supermarkets have dramatically reduced the need for counter facilities and administrators. The number and nature of banking jobs are changing in line with these developments. High street bank branches are destined to disappear in large numbers, together with the careers they once represented.

'Homeworking' or 'telecommuting' is a further much-quoted example. Managing people is complex enough when staff are located within defined business premises. The task becomes much more involved when people work from home and vary their working hours to fit around domestic pursuits. If a teleworker wants to do a few hours work before breakfast and have the afternoon off – why not?

Changes in the nature of work and continuing economic certainty have led to a diversification in working hours and job types. This fits with the current preoccupation with 'flexibility' – a subject we will consider in depth in later chapters. For example, in the UK most newly created jobs are part time.

Part-time working

Part-time employees contract to work for anything less than normal full-time basic hours. Part-time working has grown consistently in developed countries for thirty years. For example, in the UK part-timers made up just 4 per cent of the employment market in 1951. This had risen to 16.4 per cent in 1979 and 23.5 per cent in 1992. European figures varied considerably, with around one-third of all employees in the Netherlands working part time, 26.9 per cent in Norway, 10.2 per cent in France and just 9.5 per cent in Germany (*The Financial Times*, 12 December 1995). Advantages to employers include:

- more intensive work with less time used for breaks;
- lower absenteeism among part-time workers;

- potentially higher enthusiasm and commitment (less opportunity for boredom);
- little unionization among part-time staff.

The main forms of part-time work include the following:

- **Classical** – work that does not require full-time cover – typically taking a few hours a day, for example office cleaning, staffing a canteen.
- **Supplementary** – where a part-timer replaces overtime, perhaps performing an evening shift, or working short days to cover peak periods.
- **Substitution** – in which part-timers replace full-timers through job-splitting. It is common for older workers to be retained as part-timers before full retirement.

More recent types of part-time work include:

- **Key working** – typically found in service industries such as retailing. Service work differs from 'traditional' work. Peak activity occurs on days and at times when other workers are at leisure. Peak times may be so short that it is impossible for an employer to use full-time workers effectively. In these circumstances few 'core' full-timers are required. Correspondingly, a large number of 'peripheral' part-timers work at busy periods. Peripheral numbers can be shrunk or expanded as required. This allows greater flexibility than would be possible for a completely full-time workforce.
- **Job sharing** – where two people are responsible for one full-time job, dividing pay and benefits in proportion to the hours worked. Days or weeks may be split or alternate weeks worked. An advantage for some employees, job sharing can also benefit employers; for example:
  - sharers can overlap hours so that busy periods receive double cover;
  - jobs are at least partly covered when one person is away through illness or annual leave;
  - two individuals can bring greater experience and a broader range of views to a job than a single employee.

Job sharing allows skilled people to be retained if they give up full-time employment. However, there are some difficulties and disadvantages, such as:

- training, induction and administration overheads for two people;
- finding a suitable partner with matching skills and availability if one sharer leaves;
- communication on tasks which cannot be dealt with quickly ('hand- over' problems);
- responsibility for staff can be problematic – people may find difficulty in working for two supervisors;
- fair allocation of work.

Part-time workers come especially from specific groups, which include:

- **female parents with children**, the largest group, typically working when children are at school;
- **retired or semi-retired**, supplementing pensions, filling time and using their skills. Again, they tend to work during the day period;
- **moonlighters**, with full-time jobs elsewhere, supplementing income in the evening or at weekends – for instance driving mini-cabs, delivering free newspapers, bar work;
- **students**, supplementing pocket money or grants by delivering papers, pizzas, serving in fast-food outlets – they may also work in vacation periods or undertake seasonal work in the summer tourist industry etc.

Paradoxically, many managers question part-timers' commitment, seeing them as being primarily home-oriented. They are excluded from interesting and senior positions. Part-time workers get few training and promotion opportunities. Managers have contradictory beliefs about women part-timers. On the one hand they believe them to be reliable, loyal and flexible. At the same time, they also consider that they take time off to be with children and give precedence to partners' careers.

Working women

Attitudes towards 'working wives' have changed dramatically in the western world. A number of trends have coincided so that we have seen the virtual disappearance of that Victorian middle-class ideal, the nuclear family, with mother staying at home to look after the children and father going to work. It has become normal for married women to work, to the point where, in many countries, it is expected that married women **should** be in paid employment. Why has this happened? A number of explanations can be offered:

- **The Victorian ideal was a myth.** There was a steady fading away of the **male breadwinner** concept – belief that a working wife reflected a 'failed' husband. The man-at-work, woman-at-home pattern was never universal. Women have always provided a high proportion of labour, and this has continued to be the case in developing countries. Often, however, this work went unrecognized because it was not permanent employment but an extension of home activities, for example agriculture, casual work, and paid work done for others within the home. It has been said that women perform two-thirds of the world's work, for which they receive one-tenth of the world's income, and own a mere one-hundredth of its resources.
- **A revision of the model of work.** By extension it can be argued that the notion of 'work' is based on a male model which makes an artificial distinction between work in the home and employment elsewhere (Wilson 1995: 10). In many ways, this distinction is becoming blurred and increasingly meaningless. Homeworking, or telecommuting, has been well publicized. This involves executives and other professionals working from home using computers, modems, telecommunications and so on. This has been hailed as a radical transformation of working life, neglecting the fact the home has always been the place for a great

deal of work – for example most craft industries until the nineteenth century.

- **The added-worker hypothesis.** People are forced to maximize paid work to supplement family income, for example to pay housing costs. The hypothesis predicts an increase in employment participation rates during periods of high unemployment. This is because partners work to compensate for the lost income of main wage-earners who are made redundant. It can be argued that this was the case during the periods of high unemployment in the late 1980s and early 1990s. However, the reverse prediction that 'secondary' wage-earners would cease paid employment as unemployment levels fall is unlikely to become a reality. This can be attributed to two further social changes: higher consumption and the introduction of labour-saving devices.

- **Higher consumption** of market goods is fuelled by advertising and social comparison. The growth of a consumerist society requires higher levels of disposable income. Household income needs to increase in line with growth in the choice of consumer goods. If the people next door have one, why can't we?

- **Labour-saving devices.** Automatic washing machines, microwave cookers, and so on reduce the time required to maintain domestic life.

- **Changes in relationships.** The dominant-male, secondary-female pattern of marriage (perhaps another myth) is being replaced by a greater diversity in relationships. The result is greater independence and freedom for women to establish themselves in paid work.

- **Tax structures.** Part-time hours worked by one partner are more tax-efficient than overtime worked by the other partner.

- **Employment protection legislation.** Full-timers are a less attractive prospect for employers than part-timers.

Temporary workers

Temporary contracts have become significantly more common in recent years. Over 10 per cent of workers in the EU have temporary jobs, with the highest level (30 per cent) in Spain (European Commission data, quoted in the *Guardian*, 23 September 1995). A UK Labour Force Survey found that 1.6 million British workers were employed on a temporary basis. The largest temporary staff agency, Manpower Inc., had 560,000 'staff' registered on its books in the USA – more than any other private-sector employer. Its worldwide turnover exceeded $5.6 billion in 1994. US tax structures, unemployment insurance and contract law make overtime and contingency working more attractive to employers than hiring new employees. Moreover, it is estimated that temporary workers are 20–40 per cent cheaper for employers than permanent staff.

Apart from the familiar 'temps' obtained from specialist agencies, two main groups of temporary workers can be highlighted:

- **Contingent employees.** In the UK there are 500,000 professional and highly skilled people working on temporary contracts, for example 'interim managers'. These are generally freelance executives over the age of 40. Most assignments last for forty to eighty days, allowing for short-term problems to be handled without long-term commitment to expensive staff. Specialist expertise can be bought in for specific tasks or projects. Contingent managers have been rated highly in functions such as human resources, finance, information technology, marketing, operations and property.

- **Seasonal employment.** Seasonal workers are hired to cope with fluctuations in demand – to keep down stock volumes, and hence cost. For example, the chocolate industry has especially high periods of demand at times when gifts are commonly given, such as Christmas.

Implicitly, two classes of workers are created. One class has employment rights. The other is disposable. In the public sector, government action – particularly in New Zealand and the UK – has seen the distancing of many activities (and workers) who were formerly civil servants or local government employees.

From the employee's point of view, it is undeniable that part-time and temporary work are both convenient for and attractive to many people. However, they are no substitute for the loss of full-time jobs. The twentieth-century concept of the nine-to-five job and a lifetime career is disintegrating in favour of much more flexible arrangements. Levels of insecurity and stress are rising as people have increasingly uncertain working lives. It has become a truism that most people will experience at least two or three careers in their lifetime. Handy sees work becoming part of a portfolio of activities (1989: 146). At any one time, individuals may have a number of part-time jobs, together with leisure or study periods. Flexibility and career development will be further explored in Chapters 4 and 8.

Summary

In this chapter we discussed some important features of the employment market. We considered factors which lead to people seeking work and joining that market. We examined key economic and psychological concepts and identified a number of links with fundamental elements of HRM. Participation in the job market was investigated, comparing rates in different countries. Different working patterns were described, as a prelude to later discussion of flexibility.

Further reading

The companion volume *Economics in a Business Context* (Neale and Haslam 1994) provides a more detailed outline of labour economics. Sapsford and Tzannatos's (1993) *The Economics of the Labour Market* is a concentrated discussion of the subject aimed at advanced students. HR specialists may find Claydon's (1994) discussion useful as an alternative perspective (see Beardwell and Holden (1994) *Human Resource Management: A Contemporary Perspective*). Psychological theories of work participation are to be found in

Warr's (1987) *Psychology at Work* (2nd edition). Charles Handy explores future working patterns based on the idea of flexibility in a number of his works, including *The Age of Unreason* (1989). Stephen Wood (ed.) (1989) *The Transformation of Work?* also provides an in-depth discussion of flexibility and related issues.

Review questions

1 How is it possible to regard jobs as being in a 'market'?
2 Describe in your own words what is meant by the labour force partici-pation rate.
3 Is full employment a practical goal for every country?
4 How will demographic trends affect employment in your country in the twenty-first century?
5 How do competition and institutional models of the job market relate to hard and soft versions of HRM?
6 Outline the advantages and disadvantages of part-time jobs for employ-ers and employees.
7 Why has the introduction of technology not led to a 'leisure revolution'?

Problems for discussion and analysis

1 Rob is a student on placement with a thriving media marketing com-pany. He enjoys the challenges of dealing with customers and other staff. He prefers placement work to university, where, academically, he is an average performer. Rob enjoys some parts of his course but dreads other aspects – particularly the end-of-semester assessments. He was pushed into higher education by an ambitious father whose own career was limited by his lack of qualifications. Personally, Rob cannot wait to complete the course and get on with his career.

Rob's placement company has lost a number of key staff to a competitor. Senior managers have looked at the younger staff and highlighted Rob as a potential high-flyer. He has the energy and the enthusiasm to cope with the long hours and the considerable travel-ling required. They have offered Rob a higher-level position which is now vacant. The rewards are high and the prospects for the next few years are excellent. However, Rob has been told that he cannot accept this position and return to full-time education to complete his final year.

Rob has to make a choice quickly. What factors should he take into account in making his decision?

2 Jefford Trading is a medium-sized business selling high-quality designer furnishings. It was originally started twenty years ago from one small shop, and Jan and Keith Jefford have built the company into a multi-shop retailer with ventures around the country. In the last three years business has become a struggle: other firms have entered the same

market and rental and other costs have risen sharply. The company continues to make a profit but further expansion will be hard work.

There are fifty-seven employees. Apart from the founders there is one other director, Paul Stevens, the Company Secretary (aged 49), who looks after major contracts and personnel. He is competent but not ambitious. There are five middle managers, all graduates under the age of 35 picked by Paul, with responsibilities for Buying, Distribution, Finance, Marketing and Retailing, respectively. The Distribution and Retail managers are responsible for most of the staff. Junior managers run the shops, all without higher education qualifications but keen. The other head-office staff are of mixed ages with little potential for advancement.

The Jeffords have worked long hours developing the company, taking few holidays and little money out of the company. Keith is 48, looks much older and has some health problems. Jan is 43, more determined but worried about her husband. The managers have suggested that they take over the running of the company, allowing the owners to sit back and enjoy life.

The Jeffords' accountants have little faith in the managers: they believe them to be too young and inexperienced. The accountants have advised the sale of the company and investment of the proceeds. The Jeffords accept this is sensible advice but would prefer to keep the company going.

You have been brought in as a consultant to advise them. What would you do?

Organizational HRM

4

> This chapter relates the people function to three key
> organizational dimensions: goals, size and structure.

This is a world of organizations: more and more elements of life which
were once a matter of personal action are now integrated into organizational frameworks. Modern society depends on people working together
effectively to solve problems and achieve objectives which are beyond the
scope of individuals. It is a truism to say, therefore, that all people management takes place within organizations. But what are these organizations?
We talk about familiar corporations such as the BBC and IBM as if they
were objects. Yet we cannot see them in their totality. We recognize them as
entities but they are also intangible:

> Although organizations are real in their consequences, both for their partici-
> pants and for their environments, they are essentially abstractions. They
> cannot be picked up and dropped, felt or fulfil any of the other tests that
> we apply to physical things.
>
> (Butler 1991: 1)

The very idea of something which everyone is aware of but no one can fully
grasp is fascinating in itself. It has spawned an entire field of academic
enquiry – organization theory. Key concept 4.1 outlines some of the main
characteristics identified by organization theorists. In this chapter we focus
on how they can be understood in terms which have meaning for people
managers.

Firstly, we must recognize that the term 'organization' is wide-ranging: it
can be used to describe bodies as disparate as Microsoft and scout troops.
For our purposes, the concept has to be defined more narrowly. The key lies
in the nature of control within organizations functioning on business lines,
exercised through the employment relationship between staff and management. Business organizations such as Volvo or News International are
set apart from 'social arrangements' – for example lunch clubs or photo-
graphic societies – by a preoccupation with controlled performance

---

KEY CONCEPT 4.1 Organizations

Organizations are the means by which human and other resources are deployed so that work gets done. They can be defined by a number of characteristics (Daft 1989; Arnold et al. 1991):

- they are **social entities** created by humans;
- they have **purpose** expressed in the form of **common goals**;
- they are unrestricted in range – from corner shops to multinational corporations;
- each organization has a **boundary** which leads to the inclusion of some people and excludes others;
- within this boundary, people are patterned into a **structure** composed of formal and informal **relationships**.

(Huczynski and Buchanan 1991: 580). They set financial, service or production targets which determine the activities of their employees. People managers have a critical role in monitoring and controlling performance in order to achieve these targets. In the first chapter of this book we stressed that HRM is a 'holistic' approach to people management. To make the best use of an organization's human resources it is necessary to manage not only its people but also its corporate structure and culture (discussed in Chapter 5). This should be done in a considered and integrated manner, in line with business objectives.

The formal allocation of people management responsibilities is fundamental to the process. Businesses vary considerably in this respect: small firms tend to incorporate people management within line or general management; larger organizations are likely to have specialist functional roles. We noted that these roles might have titles such as 'personnel officer', 'personnel manager', 'staff administrator' or 'human resource manager'. These titles do not give much indication of the activities undertaken or the power vested in the jobs. In fact, they differ significantly from one firm to another. This chapter explains some of the major reasons for these variations. We set out to investigate the following issues:

- Why do organizations structure their people management systems in different ways?
- How do organizational goals influence the management of human resources?
- Does the size of an organization impose limitations on the choice of alternative structures?
- What are the advantages and disadvantages of these structures?
- How does the work of a human resource specialist vary from one form of organization to another?

We begin this chapter by placing organizations in their environmental context: the competitive business world. This is followed by a discussion of how and why organizations are formed and the implications for the nature of the people function.

Organizations and the business environment

Competitive pressures on businesses and national economies have increased markedly in recent decades. As a consequence, the organizations which impact on our lives are constantly changing. Powerful entities have arisen at the international level – the European Union being a prime example – and multinational corporations increasingly dominate particular sectors such as cars and aerospace. New competitors are emerging and forcing older organizations to adapt and reform themselves in order to survive.

Like Russian dolls, most organizations are parts of larger entities. They are the complex products of a world subject to the international division of labour, geographic rationalization and product differentiation. There is nothing unusual in a business section in Cork reporting to a Dublin-based department within the Irish operating division of the European subsidiary of a US multinational. For marketing purposes some firms deliberately obscure these relationships. Walking down a typical high street or shopping mall in a developed country, we find an apparent diversity of retail traders. In fact, many are brand names controlled by just a few conglomerates.

In Chapter 2 we saw that organizations also interact with their environment through the regulatory, economic and cultural framework in which they operate. Different levels and types of organization supervise, support and impede each other's operations with contradictory demands (Brunsson 1989: 1). External stakeholders such as governments, financiers, customers and shareholders exercise their influence through legislation, tax benefits, interest rates, consumer demand and the purchase and sale of shares. Organizations reflect the values and norms of society, supplying products and services which meet the needs of the culture in which they function. They structure and manage themselves in ways which are acceptable to those societies. Inevitably, therefore, there are differences in the nature of organizations between one country and another. For example, French companies have a tradition of bureacratic, hierarchical organization, whereas German firms have tended towards flatter, less rigidly differentiated structures (Sparrow and Hiltrop 1994: 270).

Different structures affect the way in which people are managed. HRM is intimately bound up with the way firms are organized. Businesses throughout the world require the same basic human resource activities: they recruit new employees; they develop and train their staff; they have reward systems; they have control and feedback mechanisms; and people must interrelate and make decisions (Brewster and Tyson 1991: 9). But these issues are handled in different ways, reflecting the expectations and acceptable behaviour patterns within national business cultures. Similarly, employee values and attitudes are shaped to a considerable extent by people's native culture. Since national cultures are so pervasive, we will see in Chapter 5 that they strongly influence the cultures within organizations (Hofstede 1980).

This chapter focuses on organizational structure but we must be aware that structures are influenced by culture. People have strong feelings towards the organization in which they work. Siemens, Saab and QANTAS, for example, are psychological entities to which employees react positively or negatively (Schein 1988: 8). Internal stakeholders – employees, managers and owners – expect organizations to operate in an acceptable manner, but the notion of acceptability is culturally determined and varies from one country to another. For example, Korean employees expect and accept more authoritarian management than their Japanese neighbours. Expectation and acceptability are important factors in determining the range of possible organizational structures which can operate successfully in a particular country. This is particularly significant in relation to the principles of HRM we considered in Chapter 1 – since, for example, individual commitment depends on whether or not expectations are realized.

To a considerable extent, therefore, environmental factors constrain the operations of commercial enterprises; but, conversely, businesses must control elements of the environment to ensure their own survival. Organizations are not passive – they can take a number of actions which increase their freedom in meeting environmental demands. Managers do so by devising strategies for survival and growth which can prove to be beneficial or counter-productive. They can influence public perception through advertising, or achieve competitive advantage by developing new products.

Equally, an organization's prospects can be improved by deploying its human resources in a novel and effective way, drawing on their competences and creativity. Throughout the world, the use of human resources is moving away from the employment of inflexible, full-time workers with expectations of lifelong careers in a single organization. Businesses can make strategic choices between a range of alternatives: part-timers, contingent workers, contractors, franchises and so on, as we shall see in our discussion of flexibility later in this chapter.

Some organizational strategies have been misguided. In the 1980s and 1990s most large corporations indulged in tumultuous restructurings, variously described as 'downsizing', 'rightsizing', delayering', and 'focusing on core areas'. These dramatic disruptions have been justified largely on financial grounds. Often the consequences for employees – including those remaining – have been negative. Older redundant workers have had to accept early retirement. Others have faced long periods of unemployment. Morale has slumped and stress has increased amongst surviving employees, who are expected to work harder in a climate of uncertainty. In many organizations blind pursuit of cost-effectiveness has destroyed the credibility of senior managers in the eyes of their staff, leading to a marked reduction in employee commitment. In this chapter we seek to pinpoint more positive approaches in the organization of people management.

Dimensions of organization

How can we differentiate one organization from another? Large companies spend considerable amounts of money on developing strong images for themselves. Corporate logos, decoration schemes, uniforms, marketing literature and advertisements are all designed to create a favourable impression on customers and share analysts. But public image tells us little about an organization as an employer. In fact, it obscures the nature of people management.

From our perspective, the first question to ask in any organization is: who manages the people? In Chapter 1 we noted that early HRM models placed the responsibility for people management with line managers. This is a debate in itself: should the management of people be part of the role of every manager in an organization; or does it demand an expertise which can be expected only from trained specialists? Opinions have changed markedly, due sometimes to fickle fashion and sometimes to the idiosyncratic opinions of senior managers. One view is that managing people is what business is all about and therefore that every manager and supervisor should deal with the individuals within their area of responsibility. Conversely, it can be argued that the detailed aspects of people management such as resourcing and reward management are too complex for the average sales manager, accountant or engineer – untrained in the behavioural sciences – to handle them satisfactorily.

In reality, examples are found along the entire range from specialist to non-specialist. The decision to manage people in a particular way depends on a number of factors, including the basic organizational aspects which we shall consider next: goals, size and structure.

Organizational goals

> Organizations are formed with the intention and design of accomplishing goals; and the people who work in organizations believe, at least part of the time, that they are striving towards these same goals. We must not lose sight of the fact that, however far organizations may depart from the traditional description . . . most behaviour in organizations is *intendedly rational behaviour*.
>
> (Simon 1955: 30)

As we have seen, the rhetoric of HRM attaches great importance to strategy and the linking of employee performance to organizational goals (see key concept 4.2). What are these goals? They are expressions of a company's purpose and long-term objectives. Often written in the form of a mission or values statement, they give purpose or direction to an organization. They are intended to influence the behaviour of employees, but few small companies have a written statement and many larger companies provide woolly verbiage without clear meaning. We will discuss mission statements in more detail in Chapter 6 when we consider HR strategy.

The logical starting-point for human resource management lies in an organization's goals – the reasons for its existence. Most modern businesses express these goals in the form of a mission statement. The allocation and control of human resources serves to assist or constrain the achievement of these objectives.	**KEY CONCEPT 4.2** *Organizational goals*

Taken at face value, mission statements appear to show that businesses have clear objectives. Traditionally, competitive market models portray the firm as a single decision-unit engaged in maximizing profits. This approach ignores the possibility of conflict between owners, managers and employees. Organizations are political structures – usually surface unity is purely cosmetic. Needle observes that, as abstract entities, organizations do not have goals – their public objectives are those of some dominant person or group (1994: 99). Hidden behind the published goals of a business we find a series of conflicting agendas held by various individuals or work units. So, for example, the human resources or personnel department may have its own priorities – inconsistent with those of senior management. The HR department may be concerned with being 'professional', using the best selection techniques and careful job evaluation, whereas senior executives may be more concerned with short-term employee costs.

Size

Organizations can range from single-person businesses to multinational corporations employing hundreds of thousands of people. Generally, the sophistication and importance of people management is greater in larger organizations. However, sophistication does not necessarily lead to effective people management. In small companies all management functions – including human resources – are dealt with by the owners. By 'professional' standards these activities – especially selection and training – are often inadequately handled, yet the quality of the employment relationship can be high. Owners and employees work on a down-to-earth, personal level. Some are genuine friends with mutual trust and confidence. Conversely, larger organizations employ highly trained human resource practitioners using advanced selection, assessment and reward techniques. But size also brings problems in meeting the principles of comprehensiveness, coherence, control and communication, resulting in the possibility of remote and conflict-ridden relationships between people at the top and bottom of the firm.

To make sense of size differentials, it is useful to divide business enterprises into three categories (Curran and Stanworth 1988):

- **Small to medium-sized enterprises (SMEs)**, further subdivided by the European Commission into:

    - micro-enterprises, with less than ten employees;
    - small enterprises, with between ten and ninety-nine employees;
    - medium-sized enterprises, employing 100–499 people.

- **Large commercial** enterprises with over 500 people.
- Organizations within the **public** or state sector. These continue to have distinctive characteristics despite government attempts to place them on a business-like footing.

The distribution of these categories varies considerably between different countries. The UK has more medium-sized to large firms than the European average – including forty-eight of the European Union's 100 largest industrial companies. EU legislation requires that all companies headquartered in the EU with 1,000 or more employees and at least 100 in two or more member countries should set up Europe-wide Works Councils. Warwick University's Industrial Relations Unit examined large European firms to see how many would meet the criteria (Sisson *et al*. 1992). They found that 332 of the 880 companies which did so had headquarters in the UK, 257 in Germany and 117 in France. France has a considerable divergence in company sizes, including a large proportion of family-based SMEs with fewer than 200 staff, but also several major conglomerates with over 50,000 employees (Poirson 1993). There is an emphasis on small firms in smaller countries. For instance, in Denmark 80 per cent of companies have less than 50 employees (Amoroso 1990).

HRM in small organizations

Serious appreciation of HRM in SMEs is a comparatively recent phenomenon. HRM researchers have largely ignored the SME sector, preferring to concentrate on large organizations with recognizable 'personnel' structures (Hendry 1994a: 106). Yet the SME sector is an important aspect of any country's economy, already employing large numbers of people and embodying future growth potential. But the information available on people management in these organizations is sparse. Researchers attempting to investigate the topic have found access difficult, largely because small-business owners are busy and perhaps regard academics with some suspicion. Yet smaller companies should be fruitful subjects for study because many conduct people management in the direct fashion advocated by HRM models.

Until the late 1970s and early 1980s it was assumed that small businesses were a thing of the past: 'big is beautiful' was the prevailing view. Since then it has become clear in countries such as Hong Kong, Singapore and latterly the UK and the USA, that small firms are the basic seeds of a successful economy. They are a dynamic force for growth in comparison with the relatively slow movement of large and bureaucratic organizations. For example, in a number of East Asian countries the Chinese family-owned business is a key economic unit. Few of these businesses are large, as younger members tend to spin off their own enterprises.

There is evidence of a widespread increase in small businesses throughout the capitalist world in recent years. But in most countries the total economic value of the sector is not known with certainty. This is because a proportion of indeterminate size lies outside the tax system. In the UK it is estimated that in 1993 there were 3.6 million businesses, the vast majority of which were small (*Labour Market Trends*, December 1995); 2.6 million employed only the owner. According to Barclays Bank, a mere 4 per cent of UK businesses have an annual turnover exceeding £1 million.

It is estimated that smaller companies are responsible for 40 per cent of private-sector turnover. Just 17,000 businesses employed more than 100 people at the end of 1993. The 3,000 largest, each with more than 500 people, provided employment for 37 per cent of the working population. Companies with fewer than 100 staff employed 10 million people in the

UK. This represented over half the employees in the private sector – up from 40 per cent in 1979. In recent years there have been an average of approximately 200,000 business start-ups a year – peaking in 1989 – a much higher rate than that of many competitor countries. Of these firms, few grow large and 40 per cent fail in the first three years.

Only a small proportion are responsible for new jobs. This depends often on the intentions of the owner (see Table 4.1). For example, 18 per cent of firms in the south-east of England create 92 per cent of new jobs in that region. Throughout the UK a mere 4 per cent of small firms account for 50 per cent of new jobs. Overall, during the 1980s small businesses created 2.5 million new jobs in the UK – at a time when large businesses lost 250,000 – and are generating 100,000 new vacancies a year. The best survival prospects are those businesses which are based on new technology. However, whereas 80 per cent of the companies supported by US venture capitalists are technology-based, a mere 20 per cent fall into this category in the UK.

In western Germany, start-ups increased from approximately 160,000 in 1980 to 290,000 in 1985 and 320,000 in 1990 (Randlesome 1994: 189). Small firms employing 20–200 people were responsible for 46 per cent of the country's wealth in 1993 – compared to 32 per cent in the UK.

Defining the role of HRM in small organizations is problematic because of the limited research findings available. Table 4.2 summarizes the position of SMEs in relation to the ten principles of HRM outlined in Chapter 1. It is obvious that the nature of people management varies widely in small businesses, but they tend to be characterized by a number of factors, illustrated in Figure 4.1:

Table 4.1 Types of business owner

Craftsmen	They are self-employed in order to spend as much time as possible expressing their creativity.
	This freedom would not be possible in a large organization.
	They would prefer to make the product or provide the service personally and are reluctant employers.
	They probably experience difficulties in marketing or sales, and resent spending time on paperwork and administration.
	Many are 'hobbyists' and fail to create a viable business.
Promoters (opportunists)	Their ambition is to create personal wealth through 'deals'.
	Many have a succession of different businesses with varying degrees of success.
	They are not committed to a specific product or service.
	Proactive individuals, they are focused on marketing and finance, and capable of rapid rates of growth in the right circumstances.
Professional managers	They aim to develop businesses with the hierarchical characteristics of larger organizations.
	They aim for controlled and sustained growth and take a long-term view of their businesses.

Source: based on Hornaday (1990).

Table 4.2 HRM in small and medium-sized enterprises

Principle	Range	Comment
1 Comprehensiveness	All people management handled by owner/small executive team	Tends to the extreme: comprehensively good – or totally ineffective
2 Coherence	Dependent on owner's personality	May be haphazard and idiosyncratic
3 Control	Often completely centralized	Can be either autocratic or 'clubby'
4 Communication	Highly variable; objectives may be a mystery to staff	Dependent on owner; often an open culture with direct communication
5 Credibility	Highly variable; employees tend to develop a fixed opinion of the owner	Owner's personality is visible to all
6 Commitment	Can be exciting and challenging for people of the right type	People who relate to the owner will stay – others will quickly leave
7 Change	Varies between static and growth businesses	Change usually reactive rather than strategic
8 Competence	Dangerously dependent on the abilities and knowledge of the owner and core staff	Often erratic and personalized resourcing; 'development' unsystematic and restricted to the chosen few
9 Creativity	Most SMEs do the same as their competitors; the few exceptions are destined for success	Creative owners generally make use of their own ideas
10 Cost-effectiveness	Often run on a shoe-string: minimal staffing and low pay	Most owners do not reward themselves and their staff on the same criteria

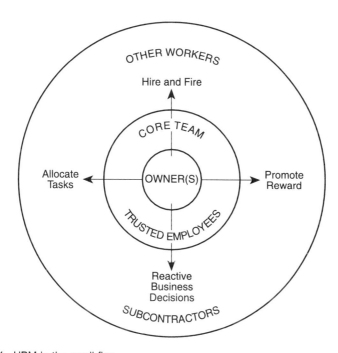

Figure 4.1 HRM in the small firm.

- **Centralized control.** A spider's web – with the owner at the centre. Limited financial and organizational resources ensure that people management is a non-specialist activity. The small business tends to be direct and informal. The character of the principal determines the climate, the morale of the workforce, and whether it is a friendly or unfriendly place to work. Employees have poorly defined responsibilities and little authority. The principal normally controls all major functions. Job tasks, pay rates and benefits are negotiated with the owner. The boss hires and fires, determines pay and conditions, and requires considerable flexibility from the workers.
- **Strategy.** There is little forward planning. Decisions are taken when problems are encountered. Staff development and training are often neglected. Succession and career planning are rare. Performance assessment is rudimentary and arbitrary.
- **Fire-fighting or crisis management.** Employees are expected to be totally flexible, prepared to work long or irregular hours. They must perform a variety of tasks without necessarily having appropriate skills or training.
- **People function.** Companies with fewer than fifty employees are unlikely to have an identified human resource function.

Entrepreneurs start small businesses in order to obtain freedom, challenge and personal income. Starting one's own business offers a way around the lack of equal opportunities outlined later in Chapter 9. Women are strongly represented in the SME sector. Immigrants often overcome prejudice, language difficulties and barriers in the employment market by starting their own businesses, as we can see in Case 4.1. People of Asian origin now control some of the most successful SMEs in the United Kingdom.

CASE 4.1
The Asian
small business
in the UK

Asian-owned businesses have become a prominent feature of UK retailing. Having spread from the textile and grocery trades, they now include some of the largest privately owned businesses in the country. It is estimated that 70 per cent of the independent neighbourhood retail outlets in the UK are owned by Asians. In London Asians own 90 per cent. This amounts to a substantial turnover: in 1990 the neighbourhood sector of retailing – 80 per cent of which is independent – achieved sales of £31 billion, compared to £21 billion in out-of-town centres. Asians own 30,000 of the 36,600 independent grocery outlets, a further 30,000 of the 46,000 confectionery, tobacconist and news (CTN) shops, and a significant percentage of chemists and off-licences. There are also 7,000 Tandoori and Balti restaurants.

Their growth has not been without difficulty. Many business founders arrived from the Indian subcontinent and East Africa in the 1950s and 1960s, many arriving with nothing more than a suitcase. Faced with barriers into higher-paid jobs and often having a tradition of retailing, many chose to develop their own businesses. According to Dadu Patel, owner of a £20 million property business including pharmacies, hotels and shopping centres:

If each household has six members earning £200 a week, that brings in £1200. Allow £400 for mortgage and general expenses and that leaves £800 to save. In five years the family has £200,000 without scrimping, and then you can really start to build a firm business base. The bank knows that if they lend to one Patel, the whole family is involved, and so have been exceedingly good to us.

The recession hit Asian businesses like any other but one event hurt them more than most – the collapse in July 1991 of the Bank of Credit and Commerce International (BCCI). The main UK banks were slow to lend to ethnic minority groups, having little appreciation of different cultures and having little expert knowledge of the activities – such as import/export – in which their businesses specialized. In contrast, BCCI became a major lender. With a branch network employing mostly Asian staff, they were able to deal with customers in their own languages and were sensitive to their particular needs. After nineteen years in Britain, the bank had more than 7,700 loan accounts valued in excess of £1 billion at the time of its closure.

A further setback came when several large supermarket groups decided to open on Sundays and petrol stations began to exploit their long opening hours to offer convenience goods. Small Asian shops had taken advantage of early and late hours and Sunday opening for years, selling essential items at a profitable premium. Further threats are on the horizon as major supermarket groups – blocked by planning restrictions from opening further out-of-town megastores – return to the high street with their own convenience outlets. Never-theless, despite these difficulties there is evidence that many Asian businesses are suffi-ciently well established to survive and grow: they are moving into new sectors, breaking out of the isolation imposed by their own culture and white racism.

There are indications, however, that the phenomenon of the small Asian-owned business may be coming to an end. The Policy Studies Institute has concluded that those of the next generation are not inclined towards the long hours worked by their parents. With declining racism and increased participation in higher education, young British Asians are more likely to become employees in large organizations, with many gravitating towards professional jobs.

Sources: Independent on Sunday, 12 January 1992, 'Cornerstone of success', N. Fielding; Metcalf *et al.* (1996) *Asian Self-Employment*, Policy Studies Institute)

Discussion questions

1 Have corner-shop owners really broken through employment market barriers?
2 What is the future likely to hold for people in this sector?

The picture is different for employees, however. Staff in small businesses can feel insecure because of the lack of structure and planning. Career aspirations are frustrated as most owners either do not wish their busi-nesses to expand beyond their personal span of control or do not have the management skills necessary for effective delegation. As we saw in Case 4.1, few corner-shop owners have the skills or inclination to develop large businesses and many of their children are disinclined to carry on with the family firm. In contrast, the best entrepreneurs have a range of general business skills – including people management – or have the good sense to obtain specialist assistance from various sources:

- **consultants**, providing advice on recruitment, pay and benefits, man-agement structures and organizational change associated with growth;
- **training agencies**, providing local or regional skills training;

- **networks**, in which small businesses can link together to pay for resourcing and development assistance, possibly through chambers of commerce and business clubs.

Entrepreneurial structures can only function up to a certain size. When they become too large for personal relationships they must evolve into a more clearly defined organization. The nature of people management must change fundamentally when this occurs. However, it is possible to preserve some of the informal and non-hierarchical characteristics of the small business by forming a cooperative.

Cooperatives

This form of organization has a considerable history. In the UK, for example, such enterprises date from the establishment of a corn cooperative by workers in the Chatham and Woolwich areas of south London in the eighteenth century. In the nineteenth century, retail and wholesale cooperative societies brought fair-priced groceries to the working classes. By the 1970s, however, the number of cooperatives in the UK had dwindled to around twenty. Since then the trend has been firmly upwards. The work team has been a fashionable obsession amongst human resource theorists and consultants in the 1990s. In the small cooperative the work team *is* the organization. This offers us an opportunity to examine the supposed benefits of team working in a relatively pure form. According to Foley and Green (1989: 8), cooperative relationships are based on six principles:

- an open and voluntary membership;
- a democratic method of control, usually based on 'one-member, one-vote';
- limited interest on the capital invested;
- fair and equal distribution of any profit;
- education in the principles of cooperation;
- cooperation among cooperatives.

Cooperatives arise in three ways:

- as new business start-ups, deliberately created in this fashion;
- as buy-outs of existing factories or companies by the workforce;
- through the conversion of existing enterprises into cooperatives.

Of these, the first has been the most common. They tend to be providers of services, usually benefiting from the different skills of the participants, rather than manufacturers. Most start-ups of this nature have been established with groups of fewer than five people who feel that the cooperative relationship fits their social values and their need to structure their own work. But some are larger. For example, the inhabitants of an entire island – Papa Westray (Papay) in Orkney – have established a community shop, youth hostel and hotel as a joint enterprise to revitalize their island economy. Survival in such a location requires hardy, resilient and self-sufficient people (Hewitson 1996). They do not fit readily into a formal organization arranged according to some neat management theory. So how are fundamental questions of who does what, when and how dealt with in a situation composed of strong personalities? Superficially we seem to have HRM without the M! And yet it works.

However, there are many instances of cooperatives failing. An examination of such organizations can tell us a great deal about the advantages and disadvantages of the 'softer' aspects of HRM such as participative management, commitment and the functioning of self-organized teams. Using our familiar principles of HRM, Table 4.3 summarizes the nature of people management in smaller cooperatives.

Larger cooperatives may employ managers but ultimate power lies in the democratic voting system. Similar structures are found in legal and medical practices, where specialists are independent but obtain administrative support and accommodation from the practice in which they operate. Success in such a system requires much tolerance and goodwill. Many cooperatives have failed because of a lack of clear strategy and leadership; often the maintenance of a harmonious relationship has obscured the need for financial viability. However, some have expanded to a considerable size; for instance, the John Lewis Partnership is a major retailing force in the UK.

Table 4.3 HRM in cooperative businesses

Principle	Range	Comment
1 Comprehensiveness	Cooperatives are uniquely focused on their working members	Actual people systems such as resourcing and training are not necessarily sophisticated
2 Coherence	Medium to good, depending on mutual understanding between members	Where specific aspects have not been discussed and agreed, members may 'do their own thing'
3 Control	Generally decentralized	Assertive members can have undue influence
4 Communication	Tends to be fairly good with shared and well-understood objectives	Generally open, with intermittent conflict and possible political factions
5 Credibility	Strategies have to be discussed and agreed (or accepted) by all	Management and staff are the same in smaller cooperatives
6 Commitment	Belonging implies commitment	People vary – there are committed activists and less committed 'passengers'
7 Change	May be slow because of the need for agreement	A sensitive and highly political subject; may be the major cause of conflict
8 Competence	Competent intially but needing to bring new partners in as requirements change	What happens to the partners whose skills are no longer appropriate?
9 Creativity	Can be high	Where members are free to deal with own areas of work
10 Cost-effectiveness	Depends on the realism of the partners	Transparent and equitable as pay is agreed among members

Even large cooperatives face structural problems which impact on people management because of their size.

HRM in large organizations

As organizations grow larger and technology becomes more complex, it becomes increasingly difficult to coordinate the people involved in an enterprise (see key concept 4.3). Beyond a certain size it is impossible for one person to know what people are doing or even what their names are. It is necessary to introduce some form of managerial structure as a framework for control and coordination. Large businesses – including sizeable cooperatives – have to be organized in a deliberate, formal way, probably with groups of workers reporting to individual managers or supervisors.

KEY CONCEPT 4.3 **Coordination**	Tasks divided amongst a group of individuals must be synchronized and integrated in some way so as to achieve the overall objectives of the group. Jobs must fit into a coherent flow of work. Coordination may be routine, because of structure and control mechanisms, including a performance management system or direct action by management. Coordination involves the distribution of decision-making. This can be formal, with rigid rules and regulations, or informal, giving the freedom to make local decisions.

With a formal structure there is likely to be a clearer division between specialist functions, including that designated to look after aspects of people management – usually labelled 'Personnel' or 'Human Resources'. Someone, at least, has to keep basic records. Typically HR managers are closely involved in the effective distribution of people and the development of management structures. The focus is on matching human resources to strategic objectives. Larger organizations display some degree of specialization, centralization and hierarchy (see key concepts 4.4, 4.5, and 4.6). This applies to people management as much as any other activity.

KEY CONCEPT 4.4 **Specialization**	There is a division of work between individuals or departments, allocating responsibilities for specific activities or functions. HR managers are concerned with the organization of the HR function and resourcing of all other functions.

KEY CONCEPT 4.5 **Centralization/ decentralization**	This depends on where decisions are taken. The human resource function may be held within a separate headquarters department or devolved to local sections. Alternatively, it may be allocated to line managers, with an in-house 'consultancy' provided by specialists for procedures such as selection, development and performance measurement.

For a long time, large organizations were **bureaucratic**, typified by precise job titles, grading structures and segregated departmental activities.

This refers to patterns of responsibility and authority, usually represented by a tree and branch organization chart. The hierarchy reflects senior managers' perception of the organization. **Vertical complexity** of an organization is indicated by a tall or flat hierarchy. Taller organizations tend to be bureaucratic but have clear lines of command. Each individual has one boss. Flatter organizations are fashionable. They demand more responsibility and self-control from staff, but decision-making responsibility and authority are less clear.	**KEY CONCEPT 4.6** *Hierarchy*

Status and responsibility were matched accordingly. We noted earlier that French organizations have continued to follow this pattern. The 'people function' was identified with the personnel department, which primarily had a supportive, maintenance role in a comparatively rigid framework. This department held an intermediate position – part of the 'glue' which held the balance between two organizational aspects:

- **differentiation**, allowing specialist tasks to be fulfilled by relatively expert people;
- **integration**, combining all those tasks into a coordinated whole.

Nowadays organizations are structured more diversely and the people function has taken on a variety of forms. The diffusion of HRM ideas, on the one hand, and simple cost-cutting, on the other, has led to a move away from 'all-embracing' personnel departments in many companies, particularly in Scandinavia and the UK. Line managers have become more involved in activities such as selection, recruitment and performance appraisal. Typically, there is a division of work between various aspects of people management. Senior management may take responsibility for human resource strategy; line managers assume operational responsibiltity for their people; human resource specialists provide specific services ranging from administration to selection programmes and counselling.

In line with the fundamental HRM principles of comprehensiveness and coherence, the basic elements of people management must be interdependent. Supervision, recruitment and selection, training and development, reward systems and performance management cannot be considered in isolation. Each activity has implications for a number of other functions and subtly influences many more. Interactions throughout an organization's systems have to be assessed before changes can be made in any one function. The move away from permanent, nine-to-five jobs towards short-term contracts, part-timers and subcontracting offers a particular opportunity for human resource specialists with expertise in training, contracting and controlling workers in these categories.

Large organizations cannot be discussed as a homogeneous group. Their human resource and other management functions are dependent on their structure.

Structure

Organizations can be regarded as people management systems. They range from simple hierarchies along traditional lines to complex networks dependent on computer systems and telecommunications. Structures may be relatively formal, following strict reporting lines. Alternatively, they may be based on informal working relationships. Structures are power and control systems which constrain or facilitate the freedom of employees to act and make decisions.

Chandler (1962) argued that structure follows on from strategy. Human resource managers can encourage strategies which foster both cost-effectiveness and employee commitment. Whether as line managers or specialist practitioners, they are able to use employee information and assessments to gauge the effectiveness of a particular structure. As managers they can influence or determine changes leading to improved employee performance and productivity. Organizational structures can be classified into a number of types, including functional, divisional, matrix, federations and networks:

Functional structures

Early organizational design divided enterprises into relatively simple parts, splitting them into defined activities such as production, marketing or personnel. This is still a common structure in medium-sized companies but it has become unusual in large – particularly multinational – organizations, except, paradoxically, Japanese corporations (Sparrow and Hiltrop 1994: 284). Such a design normally divides human resource management between specialized activities dealt with by a designated department (see Figure 4.2) and day-to-day aspects handled by the operational functions.

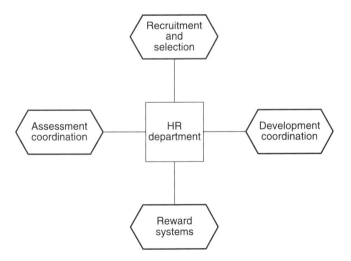

Figure 4.2 The main activities of the HR department in a functional organization.

As we can see from Table 4.4, there are both advantages and disadvantages to such an arrangement. On the one hand, functional organizations are simple to understand with clear lines of command, specified tasks and responsibilities. Staff can specialize in a particular business area such as production or marketing and follow well-defined career paths. This is equally true of human resource specialists, who can develop expertise in specific areas such as employee relations or reward management. Table 4.5 details a number of specialist roles performed by human resource specialists in functional and other large organizations.

However, there are also major disadvantages to functional structures. People managers have to tread carefully because this form of organization is prone to interdepartmental conflict, often degenerating into 'them and us' tribal warfare. Coherence and good communication are particularly hard to achieve between virtually independent functions. Moreover, HR development is complicated as it is difficult for individuals to gain a broad range of experience and an overview of the organization as a whole. Additionally, functional organizations have a tendency towards rigidity and ever-increasing layers of management. Since the 1980s, however, larger

Table 4.4 HRM in functionally structured organizations

Principle	Range	Comment
1 Comprehensiveness	Different functions are likely to be treated differently	Specific people systems such as resourcing and training may be sophisticated
2 Coherence	Low to medium, as functional managers block or value different aspects, e.g. performance-related pay	Organization is divided into separate camps
3 Control	Split between functions	Some functions are more powerful than others
4 Communication	Good vertically within a function – dreadful horizontally between functions	Prone to 'us and them' misunderstanding and warfare between departments
5 Credibility	Promotion and reward policies not understood if they do not fit functional needs	Parochial view restricts comprehension of overall business objectives
6 Commitment	Focused on functional department, not whole organization	People march in different directions
7 Change	Structural change regarded as threatening	Managers fight to preserve departmental power
8 Competence	High at functional and individual levels	Limitations on developing generalists with all-round abilities
9 Creativity	Limited	Little cross-fertilization between functions
10 Cost-effectiveness	Can be good if management kept to minimal levels	Specialist managers expect professional rates; jealously between functions

Table 4.5   Specialist HR roles in large organizations

Role	Activity
Human Resource Director/ Manager	Head of specialist people management function.
Personnel Administrator	Formerly a clerical function concerned with maintaining paper records. Latterly requires expertise in creating and developing computer databases of human resource information.
Employee Relations Manager	A longstanding specialist role with responsibility for collective bargaining and liaison with trade union officials. Now extends to employee involvement and communication.
Recruitment Specialist	Less common than they used to be. Trained in interviewing techniques and psychometric testing. May be occupational psychologists in larger organizations. This activity is often outsourced to specialist firms.
Training and Development Specialist	Previously concerned with direct training. Now becoming an internal consultancy role (see Chapter 11). Often possessing a psychology qualification.
Human Resource Planner	Statistical and planning expert providing projections of human resource requirements for strategists.
Employee Counsellor	Comparatively new but increasingly common role. May be part time or outsourced. Requires counselling qualification and knowledge of stress reduction techniques. Typically replaces the welfare role of personnel management.
Health and Safety Officer	Ensures that legislation on workplace health and safety is complied with. Liaises with local authority and other enforcement officials.

Source: considerably adapted from Torrington and Hall (1995).

organizations of this type with tall and bureaucratic hierarchies have suffered the brunt of reorganization and delayering. Case 4.2 provides a simple illustration of delayering. Restructuring is further considered in Chapter 6, on human resource strategy.

CASE STUDY 4.2
Home Products

Home Products came into existence in 1975 and grew to be a medium-sized importer and distributor of plastic and wood domestic goods. Spread over the entire country, a network of distribution points and sales offices was gradually built up, employing eighty staff. By the early 1990s the company began to make heavy losses. Eventually, the Managing Director was replaced and management consultants were brought in to recommend changes in the structure of the organization.

The consultants examined the operation of the company in detail. They found a traditional, functionally split company with a low level of computerization and a high level of middle management for its size. They recommended the streamlining of the company, development of a team-based structure and investment in networked personal computers. Over a period of two years the company was transformed by eliminating expensive layers of management. Apart from financial savings, the improved communication and devolved decision-making produced a higher quality of service to customers. Before and after organization charts are shown in Figures 4.4 and 4.5.

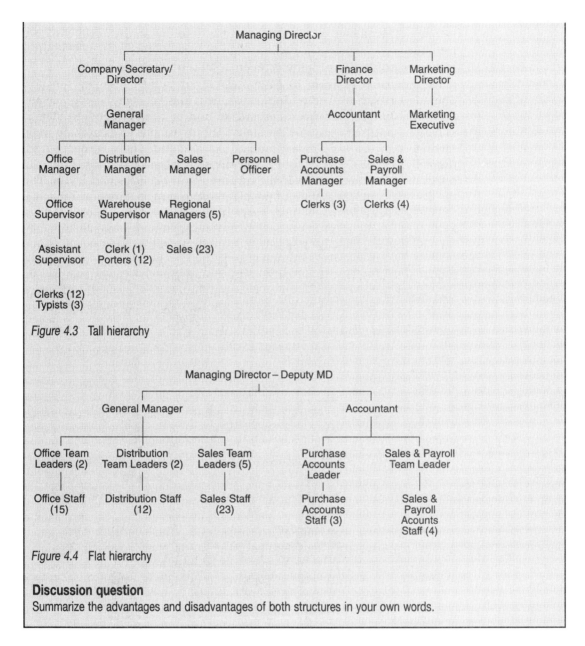

Figure 4.3 Tall hierarchy

Figure 4.4 Flat hierarchy

Discussion question
Summarize the advantages and disadvantages of both structures in your own words.

Divisional organizations

Split into self-contained units, able to react to environmental changes as quickly as small companies, they are also described as multidivisional or 'M-form' organizations. Divisional structures may be based on specific products or product ranges, as in the pharmaceutical industry, or alternatively on a territorial basis.

Divisions encourage team spirit and identification with a product or region. Managers can develop broad skills as they have control of all basic functions. The performance of business units and their employees can readily be monitored since costs and productivity are tied to product or territory. This allows organizations to increase investment with certainty, introduce new divisions for additional products and dispose of ineffective or unwanted divisions without repercussions on the remainder.

Each division is likely to have a devolved human resource function. There is a risk, however, of duplicating activities between head office and divisional human resource departments and of conflict between staff in successful and unsuccessful divisions. The divisional level may be intermediate between corporate headquarters and individual business units (Purcell 1995: 66). As a result, the division plays a coordinating role, reconciling decisions taken at the corporate and business unit levels. This results in a complex picture of people management, outlined in Table 4.6.

The key issue for people managers is the relationship between division and corporate head office. According to Purcell, 'there are no obvious roles for a corporate personnel department' (1995: 73). A few large organizations do without HR specialists at this level but most assign a role, usually of a policy nature, to the centre. Hence the central HR departments in companies such as Ford, Barclays and Sainsbury are comparatively large. This makes sense where the activities in different locations or divisions are closely related. In practice, the more diversified and unrelated the divi-

Table 4.6 HRM in divisional organizations

Principle	Range	Comment
1 Comprehensiveness	Successful and unsuccessful divisions are likely to be treated differently	Centrally provided people systems such as performance management may be sophisticated
2 Coherence	Corporate HR strategies may be neutralized at divisional level	Divisional people managers behave independently
3 Control	Divided between divisions and head office	Scope for conflict and confusion
4 Communication	Can be good within divisions; more problematic between divisions and head office; poor between divisions	Prone to resentments and misunderstandings between head office and divisions
5 Credibility	Corporate HR strategies not understood if they do not fit divisional needs	Parochial view restricts comprehension of overall business objectives
6 Commitment	Focused on division – not whole organization	Divisions quasi-independent
7 Change	Emphasis on acquisition and demerger	Managers fight to preserve integrity of division
8 Competence	High at functional and individual levels	Limitations on developing generalists with all-round abilities
9 Creativity	Scope for considerable creativity in suitable divisions	Small firm climate encourages cooperation between functions
10 Cost-effectiveness	Tendency for managerial/administrative jobs to be duplicated	Little consistency between divisions

sions, the more likely it is that HRM is fully devolved to divisional level. In very diverse conglomerates, even senior managers are recruited and developed locally.

Apart from the degree of differentiation, people management functions are affected by organizational strategies. Recent moves to delayer large organizations and reduce the number of managers have affected HR specialists as much as anyone else. Their activities have been 'balkanized' or parcelled up into discrete areas (Sisson 1995: 96). Based on information from a survey of nearly 100 large firms, K. Adams (1991) found that HRM was organized in a number of ways:

- Traditional 'personnel'-type departments providing a full range of HR services.
- In-house agencies, or cost centres, performing one or more activities such as recruitment. Their costs are automatically charged to client divisions or departments.
- Internal consultancies which 'sell' their activities to other parts of the organization, perhaps in competition with external services.
- Business within a business arrangements which provide an internal and an external service to clients inside and outside the organization.
- External consultancy arrangements, subcontracting HR activities to outside agencies.

Marginson *et al.* (1993a) also differentiated between UK-owned and foreign-owned organizations in the UK. Foreign-owned companies tended to move their managers between divisions in different companies and to grade them on the same rating scales. They were more likely than British companies to have a central department responsible for training and development. Twice as many foreign-owned companies had HR directors on their main board in comparison with British-owned firms. Foreign-owned companies were also much more likely to spend money on training and communication and to have a corporate committee of senior managers to establish HR policies (Marginson *et al.* 1993b).

Federations

One variant of the divisional form which has a particular relevance because of its human resource implications is the 'federation', a loosely connected arrangement of businesses with a single holding company or separate firms in alliance. For example, at the time of writing (1996) the Cable & Wireless group functions as a worldwide federation of equals with a small corporate centre. HRM operates on a partly formal, partly informal basis. The central human resource function offers an extensive support facility for international managers. This form of organization has attracted criticism from stock market analysts who find difficulty in comprehending its subtle informality. Recent top management changes are likely to lead to this structure being abandoned in favour of a more conventional form.

Matrix structures

As we have seen, both functional and divisional forms suffer from the 'them and us' problem between different parts of the organization. A number of large businesses have experimented with matrix structures to try and overcome these difficulties. Matrix structures focus on project teams, bringing skilled individuals together from different parts of the organization. Individuals are responsible to their line manager and to the project manager for different aspects of their jobs.

Their effectiveness is dependent not only on the provision of skilled people but also on clear information on location and activities. This is difficult to achieve and many matrix experiments have resulted in failure, largely due to the 'matrix muddle': a general confusion of roles and responsibilities. Some activities may be duplicated because no one understands the structure and others may be neglected because it is assumed that somone else is responsible. Some of these difficulties have been overcome in more recent 'network' structures.

New structures

Older accounts of people management within organizations propose a highly structured, directive role for managers. This kind of management style and the rigid organizational context which it requires are inconsistent with the 'tight–loose' frameworks advocated by gurus such as Peters and Kanter. They propose new relationships which offer the flexibility to respond quickly to changing market demands but also allow retention of effective managerial control. Such organizations require a fine balance between centralization and decentralization. The key lies in organization design (see key concept 4.7).

KEY CONCEPT 4.7 *Organization design*	The **design** of an organization patterns its formal structure and culture. It allocates purpose and power to departments and individuals. It lays down guidelines for authoritarian or participative management by its rigidity or flexibility, its hierarchical or non-hierarchical structure. Appropriate design is crucial to the effective use of resources and long-term success and survival.

In recent years the emphasis has been towards differentiated but **integrated** organizations. This paradoxical view stresses that individuals work for the business rather than for specific departments which might compete rather than cooperate with each other. Communication and information distribution systems in earlier parts of the century were based on paper memos and reports. Paper-based systems could only work if functional activities were broken down into defined, quasi-independent sections.

Today, developments in telecommunications and computing allow raw or analysed data to be collected electronically and distributed to any point in the organization. This makes it easier for an organization to be managed as a whole. As we have seen, such an organization is likely to be slimmed down, 'delayered' and focused on core activities. Non-core functions, including HR activities such as recruitment and training, can be subcontracted. Integrated information technology allows previously unimagined control mechanisms and organizational forms. The boundaries between organizations become increasingly blurred and the nature of people management takes on a new and complex level of intricacy. For example, we can ask how one manages 'employees' who have no employment contract with one's own organization?

Managers, including human resource specialists and others, must play a new role. They cease to be checkers and order-givers. Instead they become:

- **enablers**, structuring organizations to allow employees to achieve objectives;
- **empowerers**, devolving decision-making to the lowest level;
- **facilitators**, encouraging and assisting employees.

In such a context, people managers are no longer supervisors. Their organizations move from being rigid hierarchies and power distinctions towards an environment where people take responsibility for their own work. Various forms of integrated structure are technically and ideologically feasible within relatively loose arrangements which encompass different organizations, agencies and specialist contractors.

Networks

In the context of organizational design, networks extend firms beyond their own boundaries. Focused organizations concentrate on core activities – those areas in which they believe they have particular strengths. Other functions are provided by subcontractors, which may be different business units within the firm or entirely independent providers. For example, one organization manufactures and sells its products but purchases its research, design and computing functions from other firms within the network. Snow *et al.* (1992) distinguish a number of network types:

- **Internal networks**, comprised of business units, mostly owned by the parent organization, each specializing in one function. These units network with other internal units and also interact with external suppliers and customers. This is a development of the divisional system.
- **Stable networks**, basically working to the core–periphery model of flexibility which we will consider later in this chapter. A small core of professional and managerial staff subcontracts most of its activities to external providers. Television stations frequently work on this basis.
- **Dynamic networks**, a further extension where the core acts as a broker for independent suppliers, producers and distributors.

Case 4.3 describes a particular approach to networking: workflow. This has been shown to be an effective means of improving quality and customer-responsiveness matched to greater cost-effectiveness. In general, networking takes some familiar producer–wholesaler–distributor concepts, extends them into new industrial sectors and binds them into a seamless structure with no visible boundaries between individual parts of the network.

Human resource management takes on issues in networked structures which are outside the familiar bounds of the employee–employer relationship. Traditional personnel management is replaced by operational managers with strengths in people management – true 'human resource managers' (Thomson and Mabey 1994: 5). People managers in networked structures are diplomats, encouragers and resource-allocators. Table 4.7 outlines the main characteristics of HRM in network structures.

CASE 4.3
Workflow

Networking software allows employees to manage themselves. They are both 'customers' and 'performers' within a business. The workflow concept breaks each transaction into four stages within a closed loop:

- **Preparation.** A customer – someone within the organization wanting something done – makes a request. Alternatively, a performer – an employee wishing to provide a service – makes an offer.
- **Negotiation.** The two parties define the work to be done and agree on requirements.
- **Performance.** The assignment is conducted and the customer advised of its completion.
- **Acceptance.** The loop is closed when the customer is satisfied that the requirements have been met.

Performance is controlled by the workflow process rather than a manager because the transaction is not complete until the customer has made a formal acceptance. The work itself can be further subdivided into sub-loops and delegated into further customer–provider relationships. Although the concept is simple, it is possible to see how it can become extremely complex to keep track of a relatively easy task such as launching a new product. The workflow idea has only become feasible with the introduction of powerful computer packages. Software can monitor each sub-transaction to ensure that the whole activity is progressing as required. IBM used the process at its Austin, Texas, personal computer plant. They attributed significant productivity improvements to its use, including:

- reduction of the workforce from 1,100 to 423;
- reduction of average manufacturing time from 7.5 to 1.5 days;
- cuts in development time from two years to eight months.

The progress software pinpoints problems as soon as they arise and before they can turn into complaints. The workflow approach can also encourage commitment as employees coordinate their own activities.

(*Source*: *The Economist*, 11 December 1993)

Discussion questions

1   What role can a human resource manager play in establishing and maintaining the workflow process?
2   Why do you think the workflow process enabled IBM to increase productivity to such an extent?

Table 4.7 HRM in networked organizations

Principle	Range	Comment
1 Comprehensiveness	Dependent on design of organizational structure. Is it formalized or ad hoc?	Flexibility of the organization allows expertise to be bought in for any need
2 Coherence	Amorphous nature of organization can lead to incoherence	Reward, performance and development systems apply to some – but not to others
3 Control	Project or customer-driven	Dependent on software systems
4 Communication	Tends to consist of informal connections forged to solve problems and achieve task goals	Self-managed and problem-solving approach leads to direct communication
5 Credibility	Evident that organization is there to meet project or customer needs	Emphasis on performance gives high credibility to the network
6 Commitment	Focused on project – not whole organization	No long-term commitment to the organization required
7 Change	Organization changes continuously	Structure and processes driven by customer needs
8 Competence	Focus on skilled knowledge of workers	Dependent on the identification and availability of the most suitable people
9 Creativity	Emphasis on people devising their own approach to work	Freedom for creativity comes from self-management
10 Cost-effectiveness	Theoretically, human resources are perfectly matched to work	Minimal supervision requirement

Virtual organizations

Advances in technology allow firms to extend the network concept to form enterprises with no permanent structures. They bring people together for specific projects. Teams dissolve on completion, to reappear in new combinations for other tasks. The network is composed of expert nodes. These are people who add value through their knowledge. Traditional hierarchical structures have no role in this model. Departments, divisions and offices disappear, leaving an amorphous mass of people connected electronically and meeting only when required.

The characteristics of the various types of organizational structure are summarized in Table 4.8.

Flexibility

In Japan . . . it began after the 1973 oil shock . . . [and] has recently concentrated on how to handle reductions in labour demand, whereas in the USA attention has especially centred on changing work rules which are thought to inhibit intra-organizational job mobility. In Britain . . . much of the concern has been with the balance between non-standard and regular contracts.

(S. Wood 1989: 1)

Sociologists have long perceived industrialization as a process leading through a sequence from agriculture, to heavy industry, to service economies. In Chapter 2 we noted that the process is particularly visible in the older industrial countries such as the UK and the USA. These countries are described sometimes as 'post-industrial' in that the service element of their economies is a bigger proportion than manufacturing. This is reflected in the nature of employment, which has changed from predominantly manual and blue-collar jobs to white-collar work. Work has been revolutionized by the introduction of information technology which puts a premium on skilled, competent 'knowledge workers'.

We have already observed that one of the most pronounced trends in recent years has been the replacement of full-time, long-term jobs with other types of positions. These include part-timers, 'temps', consultants, franchisees and so on. Business strategies have focused increasingly on flexible working in order to reduce employee costs of products and services (see key concept 4.8). As we have seen, this is exemplified in the concept of the virtual organization.

Flexibility has become a much-used term. New Right politicians argue that, at the environmental level, competitiveness comes from the reduction

Table 4.8 Summary of organizational structures

Type	Focus	Benefits	Disadvantages
1 Functional	Department e.g. sales, accounts, personnel	Simple to understand Clear lines of command Specialist expertise Career structures	Slow to react 'Us and them' Hierarchies tend to grow into vast pyramids Managers have difficulty in gaining organization-wide perspective
2 Divisional	Product or market, e.g. pharmaceuticals Geographical territory, e.g. brewing region	Self-contained units Can be evaluated separately Can be added to, closed or sold as wholes Team-based, loyalty to division and product Managers obtain overall experience	Conflict between divisional and organizational objectives Morale difficulties in unsuccessful divisions Duplication of functional activities, e.g marketing, human resources
3 Matrix	Project or team	Strong focus on project, client objectives	Complex Conflict between reporting lines Conflict over allocation of resources
4 Federations	Loose relationship	Informal, flexible	Disliked by City commentators
5 Network	Nodes Individuals as resources	Talents focused on tasks Seamless organization – no departmental boundaries Open to external contributors	No job security Potentially anarchic

> A prominent buzzword in New Right ideology, the concept covers a combination of practices which enable organizations to react quickly and cheaply to environmental changes. In essence, flexibility is demanded from the workforce in terms of pay, contractual rights, hours and conditions, and working practices. This extends to the employment market, requiring a willingness to move location, change occupation and accept radically different terms of employment from job-seekers.
>
> **KEY CONCEPT 4.8**
> *Flexibility*

of perceived 'rigidities' in the employment market. Rigidities in the job market have been pinpointed as causes of industrial decline and flexibility has become an unquestioned 'good'. Rigidity includes lack of mobility, refusal to accept new conditions, unorthodox working hours and so on. By scrapping minimum pay rates, removing legislation which limits employers' rights to hire and fire, and generally deregulating the job market, they believe that they will allow businesses to achieve the maximum degree of competitiveness.

Simplistically, it can be argued that the terms have an implicit political agenda: rigidity equates with worker protection and therefore left-wing, socialist attitudes; flexibility matches with hard HRM, exploitation of workers and hence a right-wing, capitalist approach. So, for example, left-leaning governments in Spain have been accused of encouraging rigidity. Hence Spanish unions have been allowed to resist movement of people from one part of the country to another; temporary part-time contracts have been opposed. Even worse:

> Rigid hiring regulations and the difficulty involved in dismissing personnel do nothing to facilitate the entry of foreign companies into Spain. Companies who are thinking about investing in Spain will discover that if they want to get rid of an employee they will have to pay him/her the equivalent of 42 months' salary – one of the highest indemnity rates in all of Europe.
>
> (Vicente 1993: 217)

Flexibility takes a number of forms:

- **Numerical flexibility**, matching employee numbers to fluctuating production levels. This is difficult to achieve with 'regular' workers on full-time, long-term contracts.
- **Functional flexibility**, abolishing demarcation rules and skill barriers so that workers can take on a variety of jobs.
- **Pay flexibility**, offering different rates of pay for the same work, depending on geographical location and skills availability.

A further requirement is **flexible specialization**. Consumer demand increasingly reflects individual tastes. Purchasers want an ever-wider choice of goods, making it difficult, if not impossible, for mass production techniques to satisfy the market. The Fordist assembly line is outmoded – even if it does offer cars in colours other than black. Producers must switch equipment and employees from one product to another in a flexible but economic way. Staff must have versatile skills. Proponents of flexible specialization hold that mass production – the dominant industrial force of the twentieth century – and Taylorism and Fordism are obsolete. Organizations will become like major Japanese businesses. They will employ a multi-skilled, highly flexible core workforce able to turn their hands to a wide variety of tasks.

Atkinson's (1984) **flexible firm** model combines flexibility with Japanese concepts of 'core' and 'peripheral' workforces (see Figure 4.5). Core workers are employed on standard contracts. Peripheral workers are employed by subcontractors, or on short-term contracts. However, Atkinson's model does without mutual obligations essential to the Japanese system:

- Core workers provide functional flexibility – but without lifelong employment.
- Peripheral workers and subcontractors are not rewarded with close, long-term relationships.

Against a background of high unemployment, workers have been forced to accept a reduction in employment rights, unsociable working hours, short-term contracts and reduced pay rates. This is a development which has occurred throughout the industrialized world. It has been driven by competition – particularly from the Japanese – whose production techniques embody a process of continuous improvement. It is also a development which has attracted a considerable degree of theoretical and ideological debate. Flexibility enables organizations to react quickly and cheaply to environmental changes. In free-market countries there is a trend towards replacing full-time, long-term jobs with other employment relationships. Nevertheless, this is still a minority situation. For example, in the UK 70 per cent of those who have worked for over twenty years have been employed by the same organization during that time.

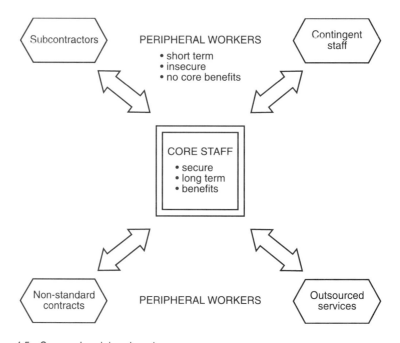

Figure 4.5 Core and peripheral workers.

The idea of flexibility has definitely taken root, but its theoretical basis has weaknesses. On the one hand, it is consistent with the concept of the 'virtual organization' discussed earlier, forming and re-forming to meet particular demands. Conversely, it is doubtful whether we are really moving to a 'world of quasi-bespoke production concerned with gratifying fleeting market whims' (Hyman 1988; quoted in S. Wood 1989: 15). Rather, niche marketing is concerned with defined 'varieties' of mass-produced products. Consumers are not purchasing unique cars made to their specific requirements, but red 2.0 litre GL model, or white 1.3 litre basic models from a controlled choice – built in factories which Henry Ford would find recognizable. The availability of such varieties has more to do with computer-controlled robots, switchable from one programme to another, than with a flexible, multi-skilled workforce.

Further problems arise in practice. Where are the necessary skilled people supposed to come from? A true transition to total flexibility requires a system for training non-permanent workers. Most employers are not equipped to provide this. Companies in countries such as Australia and the UK have been heavily criticized for underinvestment in the training of their permanent employees. Ironically, the same countries have a weak record in the provision of such training on a national basis as well. We will return to this issue in our discussion of training and development in Chapter 11.

Summary

Organizations are taking increasingly divergent forms. The key aspects of size and structure constrain the people function. HRM is conducted in a variety of ways due to these constraints and also because of strategic decisions taken to meet organizational goals. Businesses can choose to vary their structures and their people management systems for a number of reasons. Increasingly, flexibility is required from employees and managers to meet new circumstances. Centralized personnel departments have largely been replaced with more specialized units, some of which may be subcontracted outside the organization. Nevertheless there are opportunities for human resource specialists dealing with complex issues arising from new organizational structures and flexible working patterns. These include contract arrangements, selection, control, assessment and training.

Further reading

The literature on large organizations is vast. Thompson and McHugh's (1990) *Work Organisations: A Critical Introduction* and Schein's (1988) *Organizational Psychology* provide comprehensive accounts of the major issues in organizational theory. Handy's (1993) *Understanding Organizations* (4th edition) packs a wide range of ideas and theories of organization into a very readable book. In contrast, material on the 'people' aspects of small businesses is comparatively scarce. Burns and Dewhurst's (eds) (1989) *Small Business and Entrepreneurship* has useful material. The organization of HRM is discussed in Purcell's and Sisson's chapters in *Human Resource Management: A Critical Text,* edited by Storey (1995). The first chapter of Torrington and Hall's (1995) *Personnel Management: HRM in Action* (3rd edition) also gives a useful summary of the functions of HR specialists in large organizations.

Review questions

1 What are the principal dimensions by which organizations vary? What are the implications for the management of their human resources?

2 How does the size of a small business limit the practice of human resource management?

3 Outline some of the ways in which people management skills can be made available to entrepreneurs.

4 What are the major differences between the following types of organization:

- functional structures;
- divisional structures;
- networked organizations.

How is people management likely to be organized in each of these? What priorities and constraints will human resource specialists experience within each type of structure?

5 Discuss the consequences of advances in information technology on business organization and the work of employees.

6 Few small companies become major corporations. In terms of people management, why do you think this is so?

7 How would you implement a major reorganization in a large company involving a change from a tall, hierarchical structure to a flatter organization based on self-managing teams?

8 What are the advantages and disadvantages of flexibility to employees and employing organizations? Is total flexibility possible?

9 Distinguishing between numerical and functional flexibility explain how demands for flexibility would differ between organizations in the following sectors:

- public service, e.g. local government;
- production;
- retailing;
- the hotel industry.

10 What opportunities are there for human resource specialists in diversified, flexible organizations?

Problems for discussion and analysis

1 New Age Finance is a venture recently started by two experienced graduates. They have launched a range of financial services geared towards middle-aged suburban house owners. The products have proven to be very successful and have attracted the interest of a large insurance company which have agreed to fund a major expansion. A sales forecast suggests that around forty sales and administration staff need to be in place by the end of the year. The business plan envisages regionally grouped sales staff with administrative functions located at head office.

   What are the possible organizational structures for this company? On what basis should the decision be made for the chosen structure?

2 The Rapid Supply Company is a large electronic and mechanical parts wholesaler, supplying independent outlets throughout the country. The company purchases and distributes items from manufacturers throughout the world, supplying many to special order. The Progress department chases orders from placement to delivery. Dealing with customers, warehouse and manufacturers, the department has to maintain a careful and diplomatic relationship with both suppliers and customers. As a wholesaling organization, Rapid Supply credits its success to the ability to obtain and deliver a wide range of parts. Five years ago the company was purchased by its managers from a large multinational conglomerate. The business has thrived due to the determination and hard work of managers and key staff. Its market share has increased by 30 per cent in the last two years. The catalogue range of parts has grown extensively, with an additional fifty-three listed manufacturers.

   The owners and the venture capital company supporting the organization have decided to float the business on the stock market next year. This will allow them to realize a proportion of their investment and will make millionaires of the senior executives. To maximize the potential share value of the company, their advisers have recommended a number of cost-cutting efficiency exercises. These include a reduction in warehouse stocks, increasing the proportion of items supplied to special order.

   The progress department is divided into two sections: the five record clerks enter changes and information from manufacturers onto individual order records; the six order-chasing clerks deal with telephone and postal enquiries from customers. The former lead a comparatively peaceful life, steadily working through the daily pile of paper acknowledgements and amendments. In contrast, the order-chasing clerks have a hectic existence; they are barraged with phone calls, frequently experiencing abuse from irate customers. The department's work has increased considerably over the last two years but staff levels have been held down. Progress is managed by Julie Dee, a tough, self-reliant and detached person. She is polite but adamant with customers and staff, and can rebuff the most irate client. She seems to have an impenetrable shell. Around her, young employees wilt and fall under the onslaught of enquiries. The average length of employment is three to four months but there are a few experienced people who have worked in the department for several years.

Most enquiries are from customers requesting updates on delivery of their goods. The order-chasers first check goods-inwards records to see if the items have arrived. If they have been received, customers are forwarded to the despatch section to arrange a delivery date. More often, the parts have not arrived, requiring onward phone calls to the manufacturers and return calls to customers. At its simplest, a progress enquiry can be dealt with during the customer's first telephone conversation; at its worst, a succession of calls might be required over several days. Matters are complicated by delays elsewhere in the system. There is no guarantee that the goods are not in the warehouse even if they are shown as 'not arrived' on the computer screen. They might not have left the manufacturer, may be in transit, or may actually have arrived at the warehouse but not been recorded yet.

Order-chasing irritates other staff and the suppliers. There have been complaints from manufacturers about progress calls from Rapid Supply regarding parts which were delivered to the warehouse days ago. An instruction has been sent round stating that Progress clerks must check with the warehouse first, before going on to the manufacturers. This has caused a great deal of friction between Progress and the warehouse. Progress staff complain about the apparent slowness of recording receipt of goods; the warehouse complains of being pestered about parts which sometimes are not due for several days. There is further conflict with the despatch clerk, whose telephone is frequently engagaged for lengthy periods. Similar problems are experienced with suppliers, as, often, several calls or fax messages are required in order to obtain an answer. Manufacturers require that their own acknowledgement numbers be quoted: sometimes these have been entered incorrectly, or not entered at all, by the records clerks.

Progress clerks have a difficult role to play and run the risk of upsetting everyone they deal with. Customers become irate if they encounter one of several circumstances:

- if the progress telephone system is engaged;
- if they are put on hold and lines take a long time to answer because they are dealing with other enquiries;
- if they cannot be provided with an immediate answer.

Progress staff become frustrated in the following circumstances:

- Often, as soon as one customer is cleared, another comes on the line, making it impossible to deal promptly with the first enquiry (this could be true for a whole succession of calls).
- On particularly busy days, especially when staff are missing for any reason, it proves impossible to follow up all the calls; as a consequence many customers phone back, increasing the overall volume of calls and making it even more difficult to deal with enquiries.

As the work level has grown, individual enquiries have increasingly trailed from one day to another. Enquiries by fax and post do not seem quite as urgent and tend to be left to last. This has made some valued customers extremely cross, demanding to speak to the manager. Julie now spends much of her time dealing with complaints about the service received from her staff.

The marketing department has completed a customer survey which shows high levels of dissatisfaction with Progress. The senior managers are furious and have seconded you to work alongside Julie and 'sort things out'.

What will you do?

5

Culture and commitment

This chapter reviews the implications of corporate and national cultures for HRM. Commitment is evaluated as a prerequisite for successful people management.

Management practices vary throughout the world. Culture, history and language obviously underlie much of this variation. More than any other business function, the practice of people management is closely linked to national culture (Gaugler 1988). This is readily seen in many recent texts (Sparrow and Hiltrop 1994; Torrington 1994; Hegewisch and Brewster 1993; Brewster and Tyson 1991; and others). They catalogue significant differences between major countries and indicate a wide diversity in philosophies of people management. Comparing one country with another we find that basic activities are regarded with different degrees of importance; they are carried out differently; and the activities undertaken by HR managers vary from one country to another. As a consequence it is possible to distinguish practices which are **universally** applicable from those based on a particular **national** culture.

Cultural differences are also seen at the organizational level. The human resource literature places considerable emphasis on corporate culture. We saw in Chapter 1 that the classic Harvard model of HRM emphasizes the link between a culture which fosters appropriate employee attitudes, behaviour and commitment in order to achieve competitive performance. This requires sophisticated people management systems which facilitate the following:

- careful selection and development of people with suitable characteristics;
- accurate performance assessment and reward packages to encourage desirable behaviour.

In particular, the Harvard approach views employee commitment as the key determiner of competitive performance. People working within a culture of commitment are prepared to work longer, apply greater ingenuity to resolve a problem, try that much harder to win an order. Commitment comes from a climate of trust. There must be a shared understanding between employees at all levels as mutual stakeholders in the future of an enterprise. Workers cannot be expected to make suggestions leading to a reduction in the time and effort required to perform a task if there is a risk of job loss as a result.

It is easy to see how commitment can arise in a high-trust culture such as Japan. It can also be understood within the context of the consensus social market where jobs have a considerable degree of protection, employees are consulted through works councils and there is generous social security provision for people without jobs. But how can commitment arise in free-market businesses where there is an imbalance of power between different stakeholders? Why should people be committed to organizations whose senior managers reward themselves disproportionately for the efforts of others?

We begin this chapter by outlining aspects of culture at both national and corporate levels.

Culture and international HRM

> Culture is the great social matrix within which we are born, we grow, and we die. It gives meaning to human action, and we transmit it to our biological and spiritual descendants (our children and our students). It has many philosophical, political, and practical implications: it tells what is good and bad; how to live and die; how to talk, dress, and love; things to eat and when to eat them; how to express happiness and sadness; what to consider desirable and what to detest.
>
> (Bunge and Ardila 1987: 225)

International comparisons of HRM focus on the similarities and differences between people management practices in different countries (Sparrow and Hiltrop 1994: 3). For example, Pieper (1990) finds that most comparative texts ask questions such as:

- How is HRM structured in individual countries?
- What strategies are discussed?
- What is put into practice?
- What are the main differences and similarities?
- To what extent are corporate policies and strategies influenced by national factors such as culture, government policy and educational systems?

The answers to these questions are not simply of theoretical interest. They provide lessons which we can learn from other cultures (Brewster and Tyson 1991: 2). For the international manager operating in more than one country they define the cultural elements and behaviours which must be learned in order to be effective. We noted in Chapter 2 that the market place is global and the key players are multinational organizations. Modern people managers cannot confine themselves to an understanding of people management in their own countries. Everyone must develop an awareness of international HRM.

Torrington (1994: 5) argues that international HRM has the same basic dimensions as HRM in a national context, but with added features:

- It operates on a greater scale.
- Strategic considerations are more complex.
- Operational units vary more widely and require coordination across more barriers.

Torrington considers that we all operate within the 'learned frameworks' of our own cultures. People managers need to transcend these frameworks. Human resource managers often have responsibility for developing and training staff for subsidiaries in several countries. They must provide training programmes to meet the needs of international managers, including:

- language training;
- cultural awareness;
- economic and political understanding;
- appreciation of different legal systems;
- awareness of management style and conventions.

Respecting cultural differences

> One of the major dangers of any discussion of HRM is that it is easy to fall into the trap of ignoring the difference between national cultures.
>
> (Sparrow and Hiltrop 1994: 60)

There is a misleading assumption that the social, class and cultural values underlying management ideas are – or should be – 'normal' for every country. Scientifically based management methods are regarded as culturally neutral and universal (Chung 1991). In fact, they are mostly North American and based on that particular culture, but western managers have regarded methods such as performance-related pay and particular methods of selection as best practice **everywhere**.

Rooted in nineteenth century imperialism, this misconception is based on the belief that important ideas are conveyed in one direction – from western 'civilization' to less developed countries. Political and industrial world power moved from Europe to the USA as long ago as 1945 but the transmission of ideas continues to have a colonial pattern. English is the major business language, allowing the spread of largely American business concepts via colonial/post-colonial routes and multinational corporations (Brewster and Tyson 1991). These methodologies were accepted as 'received wisdom' in large areas of the world, including Africa, the Middle East and India. They were also adopted by countries in Europe and Asia which were brought within the American orbit after the Second World War. North American business ideas continue to flourish in both these continents as a managerial lingua franca in highly diverse markets where no single local culture dominates.

Cultures and standards

Cultures are human creations but, unlike bridges, buildings, roads and other material objects of our making, cultures are subjective (Triandis 1990: 36). They are made up of elements such as attitudes, beliefs, norms, roles and values (see key concept 5.1). We take our own culture for granted. In fact, we are scarcely aware of it until we interact with another. Each culture has a **worldview**: a set of values and beliefs. This is meaningful to its members but alien to others. As a consequence, we look at people from other cultures, see that their ways are different and often dislike these ways. It is normal to 'use our own culture as the standard and judge other cultures by the extent they meet the standard' (Triandis 1990: 34). This ethnocentrism can be related to the concept of the **in-group**: those people we identify with (see Table 5.1). It can be argued that the export of western (American) management methods by multinationals and business schools – including HRM and its associated paraphernalia of assessment, performance-related pay and related ideas – is an example of ethnocentrism on a massive scale.

The anthropologist Edward Tylor (1871) defined culture as 'knowledge, belief, art, morals, law, custom and any other capabilities and habits' acquired through membership of society. In a narrower sense the term is used to describe the differences between one society and another. In this context, a culture is an all-pervasive system of beliefs and behaviours transmitted socially. Specifically it consists of the set of **values** – abstract ideals – and **norms** or rules held by a society, together with its material expressions (Giddens 1989: 30).	**KEY CONCEPT 5.1** *Culture*

Cultural variety

Cultures should not be confused with countries or so-called 'nation-states'. There is a danger in examining cultures as 'wholes': there are differences not only **between** cultures but also **within** cultures (Brewster and Tyson 1991). For example, Australian culture can be identified with that of the majority Anglo-Celtic population, but the nation's culture also encompasses a number of distinctive subcultures. These include those of the indigenous Aboriginal population and a number of significant immigrant

Table 5.1 Characteristics of the 'in-group'

Studies of ethnocentrism show that everyone tends to:

- define their own culture as 'natural' and 'correct' and other cultures as 'unnatural' and 'incorrect'
- perceive in-group customs as universally valid – what is good for us is good for everybody
- think that in-group norms, rules, and values are obviously correct
- consider it natural to help and cooperate with members of one's in-group
- act in ways which favour the in-group
- feel proud of the in-group
- feel hostility towards out-groups

Source: based on the work of Campbell and associates; cited in Triandis (1990: 35).

groups, such as the Italian, Greek and Vietnamese communities. More accurately, aboriginal culture is itself plural, composed of hundreds of different cultural and linguistic groups. Hofstede (1991: 10) argues that an individual's culture has several levels:

- **national** – according to country (countries for migrants);
- **regional** and/or **ethnic** and/or **religious** and/or **linguistic**;
- **gender** – different assumptions and expectations of females and males;
- **generation** – differences between age groups;
- **social class** – linked to educational opportunities and occupations;
- **organizational** – different organizations have their individual cultures.

We can see readily that this mixture provides an intriguing cocktail for a selector to attempt to disentangle; for a performance assessor to misunderstand; a management developer to 'correct'. All in all, there is massive scope for a clash of cultures – and prejudices. As we shall see in Chapter 9, on the management of diversity, the real meaning of 'equal opportunities' in this context is a major issue.

The perception of time

How we manage people depends to a great extent on our perceptions and expectations of others. We assess, we select, we reward on our own criteria. We have our in-built standards, the origins of which we rarely question and which, as we have seen, we interpret as 'normal'. Given that this is the case, can we identify firm dimensions of difference which people managers can be taught to recognize and respect? Triandis (1990) identifies a number of such dimensions, or cultural syndromes. One example is **cultural complexity**, which particularly affects the perception of time. Think about time for a moment and consider how many basic business activities depend on people 'doing something within three hours', 'arriving for an interview at 10 a.m.', 'achieving an objective in six months' and so on. In fact, our judgement of other people depends heavily on our conception of time. How do we feel about people who do not turn up to an interview on time or fail to complete a task within the agreed period? If we live in an industrial culture we will regard them unfavourably. But what if their concept of time is not the same as ours? Of course, an hour, a day, or a month is the same for everyone, but we vary in our beliefs about the significance of these periods. Albert Einstein showed that time is relative and this notion is as significant for human resource management as it is for space travel.

Triandis argues that different cultures have different attitudes towards time. Time-keeping is treated tolerantly in undeveloped societies – with few things to do, one can do them in any order. However, as societies become industrial and technological, people must pay increased attention to time. In industrialized countries there are many things to do and they must be coordinated with other people. Hence, time becomes more important. Time is regarded as something precise and highly significant. So, if a manager moves to a less developed country what standard is it fair for that person to expect?

Another significant time characteristic is that of short- or long-term orientation. East Asians tend to have a much longer time perspective than, for example, nationals of Australasia, Nigeria, North America, Pakistan and the UK. In Chapter 2 we will see that there is a link between the market characteristics of these countries and their cultural attitudes towards time. Recall also that in Chapter 1 we identified HRM as a philosophy of people management which is long term in its intent. The root of this orientation lies in comparisons of US and Japanese management and criticism of the former's short-term attitudes towards human resources. In effect, the adoption of HRM requires short-termist cultures to take on Japanese attitudes towards time. As we saw in earlier chapters, this does not come naturally and provides a partial explanation of the failure of many organizations to take on true HRM.

Hofstede and Bond (1988) attribute the long-term orientation of East Asians to 'Confucian Dynamism'. It embodies values from the teaching of Confucius such as perseverance, a need to order relationships by status, a sense of shame and a habit of thrifty saving. Kahn also saw the rise of the East Asian 'Tiger' economies as being due to the Confucian ethic, including factors such as sobriety; placing a high value on education; a need for accomplishment in various skills; seriousness about job, family and obligations; a sense of hierarchy (1979: 121). However, as we will see later in this chapter, it has been pointed out that since Kahn contributed to the argument, the Tiger economies have come to include countries with Buddhist or Islamic rather than Confucian traditions.

Roles

Triandis also relates cultural complexity to the way we define our working and other roles. In complex societies roles become increasingly **specific** – compartmentalized into separate mental boxes. We can be finance managers, parents and social club officials, and behave differently in each role. In less complex societies, on the other hand, roles are **diffuse**, affecting every aspect of people's lives. Religion, politics and matters of taste are important in diffuse cultures. They are less important in role-specific cultures. Developed countries tend to be role-specific, avoiding role confusion. Theory and best practice in key HRM areas such as selection, performance measurement and development assume an equal opportunities approach in which people are dealt with without favour or prejudice. However, this notion is alien to diffuse-role cultures, in which it is natural to favour members of one's own family or community. Diffuse-role cultures value politeness and courtesy – even towards people who are disliked – something which would be regarded as hypocrisy in role-specific cultures. Again, human resource texts assume that outright, if tactful, honesty is required in rejecting job applicants, counselling for performance weaknesses and dismissal. In short, if we feel that someone is not up to the job we more or less say so. This approach can appear arrogant and aggressive to people from diffuse-role societies.

Related cultures

Haire *et al.* (1966) surveyed 3,500 managers in fourteen different countries and estimated that 28 per cent of discernible differences in management attitudes were culturally based and identified four main cultural groups: Nordic-European, Latin-European, Anglo-American and developing nations. This started a trend to try and divide the world's complex pattern of cultures into neat, analytical groupings – with all the attendant risks of historical inaccuracy and gross insensitivity. Take, for example, a recent attempt by Leeds *et al.*:

> we can distinguish a number of reasonably clear country clusters . . . which parallel the work of other commentators. . . . These would include:
>
> 1 Scandinavia: Denmark, Finland, Norway, and Sweden.
> 2 Anglo: Ireland and the UK in Europe but also other English-speaking countries including Australia, New Zealand and Canada (excluding Quebec), and the United States.
> 3 Germanic: Austria, Germany, and Switzerland.
> 4 Latin and Mediterranean: Italy, Portugal, and Spain.
> 5 Near Eastern: Greece and Turkey. The Turks and Greeks are close culturally, and both are proud of their European and Oriental associations. However, the Greeks have also been considered very close to the Italians culturally.
> 6 Northern (quasi) Latin: France and Belgium have frequently been placed in a separate cluster of two. However, France is often also put in the Latin and Mediterranean group.
> 7 Miscellaneous: regions such as Alsace (France), the Flemish and German-speaking Belgium and countries such as Luxembourg are difficult to categorize. They possess their own special identity as well as cultural traits based on national identity, and are also influenced by values from neighbouring countries such as Holland and Germany. Holland . . . has been placed in the Nordic group . . . but shares many of the traits associated with the Anglo group.
>
> (Leeds *et al.* 1994: 23)

The authors speculate on the historical origins of these patterns and qualify this classification with the caveat that reality is much more complex. However, they do not accept Thurley and Wirdenius's criticism of 'the tendency to over simplify national culture and make comparisons based on exaggerated cultural stereotypes' (1990: 33).

Strangely, many authors seem to have picked up the curious French habit of using the terms 'Anglo' or 'Anglo-Saxon' when describing countries in Australasia, the British Isles and North America. Notwithstanding the considerable irritation this creates for those of us with Celtic origins, it also demonstrates an ignorance of ethnic relationships which leads one to question the overall value of the exercise. If the Irish can be wrongly classified as 'Anglo-Saxons' (Ronen and Shenkar 1985; Sparrow and Hiltrop 1994), how much faith can be placed in the supposed validity of any other grouping?

Psychology and culture

Classification difficulties aside, there is no denying that cultural differences can be deeply embedded. Chung (1991), for example, draws on the psychology of thinking styles to explain differences between business cultures, arguing that Europeans are taught to think in a linear way, whereas Asians see things as a whole (see Table 5.2). We can see from Table 5.2 that, according to Chung, Europeans value rational logic while Asians think intuitively in circles and leaps. Whereas Europeans are individualistic and depend on legalistic controls, Asians are community-minded and prepared to build and work on the basis of trust. European thinking is comparatively short term whereas Asians look further ahead. This model provides a cultural explanation of the different forms of people management: contract-based in the west; commitment-based in the east. Despite the additional insight this model provides, however, we have, once again, a case of two groups of very diverse cultures being lumped together to suit an argument.

Culture and business behaviour

As we can see in Case 5.1, western observers have recently come to appreciate the diversity of cultures in Asia. Religions go beyond Confucianism to include Buddhism, Islam, Christianity and others, with wide-ranging effects on people management. In Malaysia and Indonesia, for example, a predominantly Moslem culture has produced distinctive role differences between men and women at work. There can be restrictions on the employment of female workers in 'male' areas of a factory and in promoting women to be in charge of men. For western people managers this can cause a conflict between moral commitment to equal opportunities and respect for local traditions, an issue we will develop further in Chapter 9, on the management of diversity.

The constitutional context and the role of the state also vary considerably throughout the region, with political arrangements ranging from democracy to one-party rule. At the level of individual behaviour, we can also see

Table 5.2 Ways of thinking

	European	Asian
Thinking styles	Causal, clear-cut, single-track thinking – one thing follows another	Network, whole vision, complex, taking in different perspectives
Decision styles	To suit controls Individual, free To suit the majority	Based on trust Group solidarity Reaching consensus
Behaviour	True to principles Based on legal principles Dynamic, facing conflict Open, direct, self-confident, extravert	To suit a situation To suit a community Harmonious, conservative Restrained, indirect, with self-assurance, introvert

Source: adapted from Chung (1991).

below that variations in rules on politeness and directness produce contrasting ways of conducting business. In Case 5.1 we see that:

- national cultures vary widely within the region;
- courtesy and politeness are valued highly in all these cultures;
- business structure is family-based in some, but not all, of these countries;
- there is widespread contact and cooperation between Chinese communities throughout the region;
- business practices are changing because younger people are being trained in western-style business schools.

CASE 5.1
Diversity in Asia

Western observers have tended to regard Asian countries as having one business culture, primarily based on the Japanese model. In fact the region contains a wide diversity of cultures, including several large countries such as Bangladesh, China, India and Pakistan – some of which are not homogeneous in themselves – and a number of smaller countries with very different traditions and economic problems. Failure to appreciate the contrasts between cultures is not confined to westerners: the variations in business practices in these countries are just as surprising to the Japanese.

Perhaps the only issue they have in common is a keen attention to etiquette and politeness. Rudeness and overeagerness can be the downfall of visiting executives, who must expect some obligatory courtesies. Thereafter, however, diversity begins. In Singapore and Malaysia, long accustomed to western business, negotiations can be relatively direct, whereas in Indonesia and Thailand the participants must engage in further elaborate ritual. Sensitivity to these variations is essential for negotiations to succeed.

As a relatively recent creation, Singapore pays less attention to tradition than countries such as Thailand and business is less dependent on family or clan connections. In a region where corruption is still not uncommon, Singapore's stringent legislative system encourages transparent honesty in business activities. Familiarity with western ways and good command of English also lead to a greater readiness amongst Singaporeans and Filipinos to ask questions or challenge instructions than, for example, among Thais and Malays.

Chinese minorities are widespread throughout South-east Asia and have their own ways of conducting business, sharing a similar management philosophy. In many countries they dominate business, but in Malaysia and Indonesia they are constrained by nationalist sensitivities. Throughout the region, and especially among the Chinese communities, there is a gradual trend away from family-owned business towards free-market joint-stock arrangements. In conjunction with this development, and partly due to contrasting business traditions, it is becoming common for younger managers to be trained according to American principles.

(*Source: The Financial Times*, 4 December 1995, Edward Luce: 'SE Asia: singularly different'.)

Discussion questions

1 Outline the main similarities and differences in people management between the countries described in this case study.
2 To what extent do you consider that the western concept of HRM is likely to replace prevailing forms of people management in these countries?

Cultural training

Human resource managers have a considerable role to play in preparing staff for work overseas. Given the range and sensitivity of cultural differences, as illustrated in Case 5.2 it is clear that people working in an international context can benefit from tuition in the business customs and social manners of the countries they will work in. Human resource managers can play a major part in developing programmes for sales and other staff whose behaviour must be fully acceptable in target countries. For example, it is clear from Case 5.1 that export managers travelling to other countries in east Asia need to have considerable awareness of cultural differences. Consultants from the west have even greater hurdles of understanding to overcome.

What kind of training can HR managers arrange for travelling staff? This is elaborated on in Chapter 11 when we examine development programmes for international managers. At this stage it is sufficient to say that training can encompass language, social behaviour, local business structure and practice, and table etiquette. However, the most critical area is that of non-verbal behaviour. Stories abound of contracts being lost because of inappropriate expressions, overeagerness, unacceptable familiarity and general insensitivity. Argyle (1991) details a number of key behavioural features which differ from one culture to another. These are outlined below.

Non-verbal behaviour:

'Normal' gestures, expressions and physical stance vary from one culture to another. For example:

- **Proximity, touch and gaze.** Cultures can be classified as contact or non-contact. For example, Arabs and Latin Americans stand much closer to each other than East Asians and northern Europeans. In Greece, staring is regarded as an expression of interest and politeness, even at a complete stranger in the street. Conversely, a Caribbean employee may avoid eye-to-eye contact with a manager during a conversation, having been taught to regard this as discourteous. Opportunities for misunderstanding here are boundless.
- **Expressiveness.** The Japanese are reluctant to be too expressive for fear of causing offence. Many northern Europeans are also reticent about showing emotion. By contrast, African-Caribbeans are more likely to be open about expressing opinions, including negative emotions and attitudes.
- **Gestures.** It is dangerous to make use of one's own familiar gestures in another country. In all innocence you may indicate a threat or pornographic meaning.
- **Accompaniments of speech.** People often expect listeners to show obvious attention while they are talking. Failure to do this can be interpreted as lack of interest or boredom. This feedback is not expected in all cultures. According to Argyle, 'black Americans often

annoy white interviewers by their apparent lack of response while listening' (1991: 235).

- **Symbolic self-presentation.** Dress, badges and uniforms have significance for individuals in a particular culture but may mean nothing to outsiders.
- **Rituals.** Seating positions at a dining or conference table may be highly significant to one culture – for example Japan – and virtually irrelevant to another.

Customs or rules

The way in which business is conducted is conditioned by historical practice and different concepts of morality. Important differences between cultures include:

- **Bribery.** A bribe in one culture is a gift in another. In many cultures it is normal to pay a commission to people involved in a transaction. People such as civil servants, managers and sales representatives expect a percentage of the contract value. Western European and North American tradition regards this as unethical, if not illegal.
- **Nepotism.** Cultures which feature personal obligations to large extended families expect powerful individuals to look after relatives, for instance by giving jobs or contracts. This 'social welfare' system is normally governed by codes of conduct which regulate its abuse.
- **Gifts.** Every culture expects its members to give presents in certain circumstances such as weddings or birthdays. Some cultures extend gift-giving to everyday business meetings. For example, the Japanese spend a great deal of money on standard presents from special gift shops.
- **Buying and selling.** The importance of bargaining varies from 'fixed-price' cultures where haggling is regarded with distaste, to others where negotiation is expected in any transaction.
- **Eating and drinking.** Each culture has taboos on various foods. For example, the eating of pork is unacceptable in religious Jewish and Moslem communities. Alcohol is particularly problematic. It is a feature of business transactions in parts of Europe, but drinking is increasingly frowned upon in North America and abhorred in many Arab countries. The ritual of eating, commonly described as 'table manners', also varies considerably. The international manager risks causing offence and prejudicing business if local eating customs are not observed.
- **Rules about time.** Being on time is regarded as polite and a demonstration of business efficiency in western countries. Conversely, lateness is taken as normal in other cultures – the more powerful the individual, the later that person will appear.

Language

The use of language has critical implications. For example, in appraisal feedback meetings or interviews people managers must be aware of cultural differences covering:

- **Directness.** Westerners often begin an informal meeting with a joke. At this stage in a Japanese relationship such familiarity would be regarded as extremely offensive. The Japanese expect formality until each other's status and authority are clearly understood. People of different status would not expect to conduct discussions at an informal level. Americans discuss business in a direct way.

  Northern Europeans, being sometimes reserved and formal, are closer to East Asians – but only slightly. According to Chung, 'Asians prefer indirect communication, they want the correct form, they esteem absolute politeness and reserve with self-control' (1991: 419). The Japanese, for example, may leave sentences unfinished to allow listeners to draw their own conclusions. Westerners live with confrontation and conflict, but this would cause considerable loss of face in Japan. The extent and importance of **face** is difficult for a westerner to understand.

- **Politeness.** All cultures employ polite forms of address which are expected in particular circumstances. For instance, senior staff expect to be addressed more formally than colleagues at the same level. In several languages the word for 'you' has to be used carefully. In French, for example, respect is shown to individuals by using the plural 'vous' rather than the singular 'tu'.

  Politeness is socially supportive behaviour which maintains harmony and respect between individuals. It varies considerably both in importance and practice in different cultures. Politeness is so important in Japan that it is even regarded as rude to say 'no'. Foreign business visitors are famously advised that 'yes' does not mean agreement but 'yes, I have heard you'.

Torrington describes the end-product as 'inter-cultural self-confidence' (1994: 19).

National and organizational cultures

We have identified some of the broader implications of culture on people management. In this section we examine some specific contributions to cross-cultural understanding, including the classic research conducted by Hofstede (1980). In our earlier discussion we touched on the danger of stereotyping. For example, France has a culture which is perceived in a highly stereotyped way in other countries. Images of beret-wearing peasants and long, leisurely lunches with impeccably cooked food obscure the complexity and variety of French culture. Our cultural stereotypes are composed of a few accurate notions mixed with generalizations and misconceptions, some dating from previous centuries. They take no account of change in a modern, technologically advanced country which also has distinctive regional cultures. Is it possible to define real differences between countries such as France and others, avoiding the trap of stereotyping?

Organizations are microcosms of national cultures, reflecting crucial differences. Hofstede (1980, 1994) compared several thousand IBM employees in over fifty countries using attitude questionnaires (see key concept 5.2). He found significant differences between employees in one country and another, despite their similar jobs and membership of an organization which, as we saw in Case 1.1, is renowned for its strong corporate culture. Using factor analysis, a sophisticated statistical method, Hofstede analysed their responses and attributed the variation to four main dimensions: power distance, collectivism versus individualism, masculinity versus feminity, and uncertainty avoidance.

KEY CONCEPT 5.2 *Attitudes*	Attitudes are dispositions held by people – towards or against – people, things and ideas. They have individual components based on factors such as personality and understanding, and social elements derived from shared experiences and cultural history. Attitudes are complex systems of belief, evaluation, emotion and behaviour (Eiser 1994; McKenna 1994: 251).

Power distance

How marked are the status differences between people with high and low degrees of power? Questions tested the following:

- Were people afraid of expressing disagreement with their managers?
- Was management style perceived as paternalistic, autocratic, participative and so on?
- Did employees prefer a particular management style?

Table 5.3 shows ratings on power distance and other aspects. Individuals in countries with autocratic management styles prefer their own bosses to have that style. Individuals in countries with low power-distance scores preferred consultation. Consistent with our discussion in Case 5.1, it is not surprising to find that the highest score was found in Malaysia, where workers have been known to ask western managers to be more 'bossy'. In a culture where respect for authority is a valued quality, participative management can make people feel uncomfortable (Beardwell and Holden 1994: 603).

Collectivism versus individualism

Is a culture focused on individuals or groups? Hofstede describes most societies as 'collectivist' in a non-political sense (1994: 50). In these cultures people obtain their identity from an extended family or a work organization. This is particularly relevant to people management, and HRM in particular, since most of its concepts come from the USA, a strongly individualistic country. Indeed, Hofstede found the highest scores for individualism in the USA, followed by Australia and the UK – both countries

Table 5.3 Cultural dimensions

Dimension	High	Medium	Low
Individualism (v. collectivism)	Argentina Australia Belgium Brazil Canada France Ireland New Zealand Spain UK USA	Austria Germany Israel Italy Japan Netherlands Scandinavia South Africa Switzerland	Chile Greece Hong Kong India Iran Mexico Pakistan Peru Portugal Singapore Taiwan Turkey Yugoslavia
Power distance (inequality between levels in organizations)	Belgium France Hong Kong Iran Nigeria, Philippines Singapore South America Spain Taiwan Thailand	Japan	Australia Germany Italy UK USA
Uncertainty avoidance (intolerance of ambiguity)	Argentina Austria Belgium France Germany Greece Iran Israel Italy Japan South Africa Spain Switzerland Turkey		Australia Canada Ireland Netherlands New Zealand Scandinavia UK USA
Masculinity (competitiveness)	Austria Italy Japan Switzerland Venezuela	Canada Greece Hong Kong India Jamaica Pakistan South Africa UK USA	Chile Costa Rica Netherlands Scandinavia Yugoslavia
Work centrality	Japan	Belgium Israel USA Yugoslavia	Germany Netherlands UK
Job satisfaction	Canada Germany Netherlands Scandinavia UK		Greece Italy Japan Portugal Spain

Source: after Hofstede (1980) and others.

which have followed US management developments keenly. Individualistic cultures are characterized by:

- an emphasis on care for self and immediate family – if necessary, at the expense of others;
- 'I' consciousness – heightened awareness of the distinction between oneself and other people;
- self-orientation – looking for advantage and career progression for the individual;
- keen defence of the right to a private life and personal opinions;
- emphasis on decisions being made individually;
- emotional independence from the work organization;
- autonomy and individual financial security.

The least individualistic scores came from Latin America and East Asia. High power distance and collectivism usually go together. France and Belgium are exceptional, combining medium power distance with high individualism. In collective cultures such as Taiwan, socially respected jobs are valued highly. In contrast, individualistic cultures value personal success, responsibility and self-respect. Triandis points to key differences leading to reward and promotion: 'People in individualistic countries have the tendency to emphasize *ability* more than is necessary, and to under-emphasize *effort*. In collectivist cultures, the reverse is true' (1995: 33). Hui argues that Hofstede's notion of the collective is too vague: people in collective cultures relate to particular in-groups – not to everybody (Hui 1990: 193). For example, the Japanese identify with the organization in which they work. The important distinction is a sharper distinction between 'in' and 'out' groups in collectivist cultures than in individualistic cultures, where boundaries tend to blur. Hence, recruitment may be restricted to members of a particular in-group, especially the extended family. Collectivist cultures emphasize harmony, and avoidance of shame or loss of face. These are social elements of culture emphasizing obligations to others within the in-group. This point is further developed later in this chapter in our discussion of commitment in Japanese organizations.

Masculinity versus feminity

Hofstede rates the aggressiveness of a culture as masculinity - its level of individual assertiveness and competition (1994: 80). Positive responses to questions relating to high earnings, recognition, advancement and challenging work rated highly on masculinity. Good working relationships, cooperation, living in a desirable area and employment security were scored at the 'feminine' end of the dimension. Japan scored highest on this dimension, with the lowest levels in Scandinavia and the Netherlands. This dimension has practical consequences for people management:

- **Recruitment.** Applications in 'masculine' cultures are expected to be couched in positive, achievement-oriented language. Interviews are searching and sometimes aggressive. In contrast, applicants from 'feminine' cultures are expected to be modest about their achievements, giving the opportunity for interviewers to 'discover' undeclared talents. Thus Americans applying for jobs in the Netherlands can appear brash and boastful, whereas Dutch people may appear soft and unassertive to American interviewers.

- **Meetings.** In Scandinavia and the Netherlands, meetings are held to achieve cooperation, exchange ideas and solve problems. The intention is positive and participative. In masculine cultures such as Australia and the UK meetings are more competitive and are used for displays of power, posturing and political point-making.

The masculine–feminine dimension helps to explain the different forms of market found in Chapter 2 and the styles of management and employee relations prevalent in those markets. The welfare-focused social markets in Scandinavia and the Netherlands emphasize mutual respect and care for all members of the community at the expense of individual wealth. Employee relations take place within a context of extensive worker participation and protection. The 'masculine' countries, on the other hand, feature highly competitive free markets, an imbalance of power and income between management and workers, and comparatively low levels of social security. There are exceptions, of course, since Japan and Germany are high on masculinity but do not show the same range of characteristics.

Uncertainty avoidance

How do people deal with conflict, particularly aggression and the expression of feelings? Hofstede's fourth dimension measures people's reactions to unusual situations. High uncertainty avoidance favours precise rules, teachers who are always right and superiors who should be obeyed without question. Low uncertainty avoidance leads to flexibility, and a situation in which arguing with superiors is acceptable and students are happy with teachers who do not claim to know everything.

> In weak uncertainty avoidance cultures, like the USA and even more in the UK and, for example, Sweden, managers and nonmanagers alike feel definitely uncomfortable with systems of rigid rules, especially if it is evident that many of these were never followed. In strong uncertainty avoidance cultures, like most of the Latin world, people feel equally uncomfortable without the structure of a system of rules, even if many of these are impractical and impracticable.
>
> (Hofstede 1994: 145)

The characteristics of national business cultures are further defined by the particular mix of these four dimensions. In Chapter 4 we outlined a range of organizational structures. Hofstede argues that the choice of structure is strongly influenced by the prevalent culture. For example, matrix structures have never been popular in France because the idea of having more than one boss to report to does not meet the French need for clearly defined authority. A culture with high power distance and strong uncertainty avoidance prefers a functional 'pyramid of people' hierarchy. Lower power distance but high uncertainty avoidance, as in Austria, Germany and Israel, encourages a 'well-oiled machine': an organization with a clear structure, rules and procedures. Anglo-Celtic and Scandinavian cultures, with low power distance and uncertainty avoidance, favour a flexible structure focused on human relations – a 'village market'. Finally, the large power distance and low uncertainty avoidance typical in East Asia feature a strong boss, equivalent to the father, and hence an organizational model based on the family.

Hofstede's statistics have been questioned but the thesis remains popular. It fits conventional wisdom and common stereotypes. Such research has relevance for HRM in cross-border mergers and acquisitions. Olie (1990) found that British–Dutch mergers were more successful than German–Dutch mergers. Netherlands and UK cultures had greater synergy than those of the Netherlands and Germany. Similarly, Olie observed the difficulties of American managers in the US subsidiary of a Japanese bank. Americans expected firm performance targets from head office. Japanese managers could not understand why the Americans could not identify their own objectives based on the parent's banking philosophy. Olie also found differences between Britons and Americans. Directors from the two countries disagreed about the information required for decisions. The Americans wanted far more data than the British.

Converging cultures?

The accelerating trend towards the internationalization of business is eroding these cultural differences. For example, the development of business within the European Union has led to talk of 'Euromanagers' (Tyson *et al.* 1993). But attempts to create pan-European businesses can still founder due to national differences, as can be seen in Case 5.2. Throughout the world, younger and more travelled managers are more alike in attitudes and practices than colleagues less open to foreign influences. They prefer to associate with people who have similar ideologies and personalities, even if they come from different cultures. Additionally, technological development is leading to an increasing convergence of business methods.

Corporate culture

> people are a company's greatest resource, and the way to manage them is not directly by computer reports, but by the subtle cues of a culture.
>
> (Deal and Kennedy 1982: 15)

In this section we turn to the cultures which distinguish one organization from another, whether or not they are in different countries. It has long been recognized that the organization cannot simply be described in terms of its formal structure. Often this is no more than window dressing – the illusion of order which senior management believe they have created. Behind and in parallel with the 'official' system there is the reality of action and power commonly described as the 'informal' organization: 'those patterns of coordination that arise among members of a formal organization which are not called for by the blueprint' (Schein 1988: 16).

Formal organization design is concerned with only certain activities which are felt important to the organization. All other aspects of working life, from gossip on the line to complaining about management, are the territory of the **informal organization** (see key concept 5.3). Real action depends on this informal structure of opinion leaders and power brokers (Brunsson 1989: 7). The formal organization is there for 'demonstration and display to the outside world . . . defined as rituals'. Management literature earlier in the twentieth century frequently regarded informal behaviour as undesirable: 'Basing their actions on the logic of formal organization, they try to neutralize or do away with the informal behaviour through directive leadership, management controls, and pseudo human relations programs' (Argyris 1957: 231). This was typical of the North American business schools, which tended to view organization structure as a prescriptive matter of 'one best way', with scant regard for functional purpose or cultural location. This form of management served to increase feelings of dependence, submissiveness and subordination amongst employees. Ironically, workers coped by increasing the scope of the informal organization, using it as a mechanism to counter management initiatives.

An organization is both a formal and an informal entity. The formal aspect of an organization is its official structure and public image, visible in organization charts and annual reports. The informal organization is a more elusive concept, describing the complex network of psychological and social relationships between its people. The informal organization is an unrecognized world of cliques and politics, friendships and enmities, gossip and affairs.	**KEY CONCEPT 5.3** *The informal organization*

By the 1980s, however, the informal organization was regarded in a new and more favourable light. Though it had previously been perceived as something to be ignored or bludgeoned out of existence, it was realized that some features of the informal organization could be harnessed for competitive advantage. This notion developed along with the concept of corporate culture – a central theme of the 'excellence' literature (Peters and Waterman 1982) as well as of the literature on HRM and total quality management (see key concept 5.4). Its major exponents presented a 'strong' corporate culture as a key factor in enhancing competitive performance through greater employee commitment and flexibility (Deal and Kennedy 1982). Employees in strong cultures know what is expected of them. Conversely, staff in weak cultures waste time trying to discover what is required. Employees identify with a strong culture and take pride in their organization.

The creation – or even the definition – of such a culture is not easy. In managing people to achieve organizational goals, organizations prefer clarity, certainty and perfection (Pascale and Athos 1981: 105). However, those same organizations have people as their basic building blocks. Their human relationships involve ambiguity, uncertainty and imperfection. The trick of good management is to honour, balance and integrate these. One

KEY CONCEPT 5.4 *Corporate culture*	The simplest – and probably most often quoted – definition is Bower's (1966) 'the way we do things around here'. Trice and Beyer elaborated on this, describing it as 'the system of ... publicly and collectively accepted meanings operating for a given group at a given time' (1984: 654). Hofstede describes corporate culture as 'the psychological assets of an organization, which can be used to predict what will happen to its financial assets in five years' time' (1994: 18).

way to do so is somehow to use the information channels of the informal organization to transmit and reinforce messages of commitment to management goals.

Unlike many other 'new' management ideas, corporate culture has endured and appears to have had a 'material effect upon the politics of work' (Willmott 1993: 515). We will see in Chapter 6 that a whole industry has arisen to supply management of change programmes, much of it devoted to changing and strengthening corporate cultures. However, it is worth noting that although a wealth of literature exists publicizing the importance of culture change, most of it is relatively uncritical.

The Deal and Kennedy model of corporate culture

We have noted that, together with Peters and Waterman's *In Search of Excellence* (1982), Deal and Kennedy's *Corporate Cultures* (1982) was inspirational in this area. As a prelude to discussion of the role of corporate culture in people management, it is appropriate to outline Deal and Kennedy's model. It incorporates five critical elements: the business environment, values, heroes, rites and rituals, and the cultural network.

1 **The business environment.** In line with our discussion in Chapter 2, Deal and Kennedy argued that the activities of governments and competitors, changes in technology, customer demand and general economic conditions are instrumental in shaping the cultures of organizations with survival potential. The orientation of organizations within this environment – for example a focus on sales or concentration on research and development – develops specific cultural styles.

2 **Values.** Values are at the heart of corporate culture. They are made up of the key beliefs and concepts shared by an organization's employees. Successful companies are clear about these values and their managers publicly reinforce them. Often values are unwritten and operate at a subconscious level.

3 **Heroes.** Heroes are personifications of the organization's values, achievers who provide **role models** for success within the company. Heroism is an element of leadership which has been virtually forgotten by modern managers: 'since the 1920s, the corporate world has been powered by managers who are rationalists, who do strategic planning, write memos, and devise flow charts' (Deal and Kennedy 1982: 37). Heroes, on the other hand, create rather than run organizations; are intuitive rather than decisive; have all the time in the world because they make time; are

experimenters rather than routinizers; are playful; get things 'just right'. Heroes have vision and go against the existing order if necessary in order to achieve that vision. Deal and Kennedy describe this process in terms of 'making success attainable and human' (1982: 39). A figure-head such as Richard Branson is presented as **being** the Virgin group, serving the purpose of 'symbolizing the company to the outside world' (Deal and Kennedy, 1982: 40).

4 **Rites and Rituals.** Ceremonies and routine behavioural rituals reinforce the culture. Examples include product launches, sales conferences or the Friday afternoon 'beer-bust'.

5 **The cultural network.** This is the carrier of stories and gossip which spread information about valued behaviour and 'heroic myths' around the organization.

Table 5.4 outlines an anthropological classification of the elements of corporate cultures.

Deal and Kennedy produced a framework with two key dimensions: the **risk** attached to the company's activities and the speed of **feedback** to

Table 5.4 Elements of corporate culture

Company practices	Rites: planned, dramatic events in the life of the organization.
	Ceremonial: a series of rites such as the launch of a product, a graduation ceremony, the annual shareholders' meeting.
	Ritual: standardized, unimportant activities such as the Friday afternoon pub session which used to be commonplace.
Company communication	Stories: based on true events.
	Myths: untrue stories, old-timers' stories.
	Sagas: heroic company histories.
	Legends: involving heroes and heroines in the organization's history.
	Folk tales: fiction with a message indicating successful behaviours which led to promotion or reward.
	Symbols and slogans: these are powerful components of a corporate identity, serving to create a recognizable image for people inside and outside the organization. They include colour schemes, letterheads, logos and uniforms.
Physical cultural forms	Artefacts: tools, furniture styles, appliances and other equipment used in a factory or office. Some companies collect these in a haphazard way over the years; others have central purchasing policies which ensure harmonization.
	Physical layout: as may equipment, offices, production areas and canteens may be laid out in an ad-hoc manner or they may be planned to follow an organizational theme.
Common language	Organizations develop their own terminology and means of expression. For example, in Disneyland theme parks, the staff are not employees but cast members who wear costumes (uniforms) onstage (at work). Guests (customers) use the attractions (rides). The use of such terminology helps employees to slip into their roles and reinforces their belief in the characters they play. At Land Rover, employees are called associates, and all wear company overalls, including the Managing Director.

Source: adapted from Trice and Beyer (1984).

employees. Taking the extreme combinations of these two dimensions, they described four types of culture:

1 **Tough-guy culture** – characterized by entrepreneurial, high-risk-taking individuals, receiving quick feedback, but with a low level of teamwork. Such companies tend to follow a cycle of boom and bust, with the possibility of high earnings during the successful period.
2 **Work hard, play hard** – where work is fun and there is plenty of action with low risk and quick feedback on success. A high-volume sales company is a typical example. The individual works alone but has a supportive team.
3 **Bet-your-company** – high-risk, long-term industries usually requiring significant technical expertise, such as the oil and aerospace businesses.
4 **Process culture** – low-risk, low-feedback organizations, typical of traditional models of public institutions, banks, civil service, etc., where the focus was on the actual carrying out of the work. In this kind of culture, status issues such as the right to sign off memos and use graded titles were of paramount importance.

Different kinds of people have varying degrees of success in these cultures. Someone who reacts well to a high-pressure, fast-moving 'work-hard, play-hard' culture will be unhappy and unsuccessful in a process culture. With the wrong cultural style an individual can lose self-esteem and confidence. Deal and Kennedy reasoned that 'culture shock may be one of the major reasons why people supposedly "fail" when they leave one organization for another' (1982: 17). Cultural fit is often ignored in selection procedures, leading to unhappy and non-productive experiences for some.

Corporate culture and people management

The concept of corporate culture continues the tradition of human relations and 'theory Y'. It fuses the two and moves further away from the logic of scientific management and Fordism towards a view of self-motivated employees who have internalized the values of the business (Wilmott 1993: 524). If the culture is strong, people do not need orders or directives. Social norms constrain individual discretion so that employee values are those of the organization. In HRM terms the focus on values and norms is important to achieving behavioural consistency and commitment to the objectives of the business. The key point is that corporate culturism requires the management of culture so that the 'correct' values are acquired. In effect, 'normal', rational techniques of management are applied to the affective (emotional) domain (Wilmott 1993: 532). In other words, culture management is a 'hard' approach in thoroughly 'soft' territory. However, there is an underlying tension between the 'humanizing' and the 'control' aspects of people management which is evident in this process. Whereas theory Y (McGregor 1960) was unashamedly humanistic, delegating discretion and freedom of choice to individual workers, corporate culturalism advocates 'a *systematic* approach to creating and strengthening core organizational values in a way that *excludes* (through attention to recruitment) *and eliminates* (through training) *all other values* (Willmott 1993: 524; emphasis in original).

People are promoted, appraised and rewarded according to management perception of their acceptance of core values. Hence, the view in the Deal and Kennedy approach and much of the corporate culture literature is that culture can be created and managed from the top. In this respect it is a departure from older ideas about informal organizations which are more closely aligned to the view that an organizational culture emerges from social interaction (Meek 1988: 293). In fact, the literature appears to transfer culture from the informal to the formal organization. As such it becomes the property of management and open to manipulation on their part. This has become the underlying logic for major change initiatives in many large organizations (this is discussed further in Chapter 13).

Furthermore, there is a common assumption that a unified culture – a **monoculture** – exists to which all members of the organization belong. Earlier, we saw that narrow, simplified stereotypes of national cultures are misleading: most countries are **pluralities** with different regional, ethnic and class cultures. In the same way, every organization has different cliques and minority groups with varying perspectives on culture. Far from being a management tool, culture can be regarded as a form of collective consciousness, reflecting the diversity of opinion, politics and ambition to be found in any organization. Indeed, as a product of the great mass of employees interacting with each other, it is often anti-managerial.

Legge asks 'If senior managers seek to manage "organizational culture", what exactly is it they are seeking to manage?' (1995b: 185). We can distinguish, therefore, between **corporate culture** as it is presented in most of the literature, and **organizational culture**. The former reflects the view that culture is something which an organization 'has'; the latter, that an organization 'is'. Corporate culture is portrayed as something created by management which employees must accept. If we choose the organization culture view, however, we must acknowledge its long-term interactionist basis. From this perspective, it is difficult to see how senior management can control the culture of a firm – it is too diffuse, embedded and ever-changing. Indeed:

> Corporate culture – that shared by senior management and presented as the 'official' culture of the organization – may be only one of several sub-cultures within any organization, and may be actively resisted by groups who do not share or empathise with its values. If the corporate culture makes no sense of the organizational realities experienced by the employees other than senior management, it will not become internalized outside that small sub-group.
>
> (Legge 1995b: 186)

This idea of a small 'official' corporate culture floating on top of a multi-cultural informal organization is mirrored earlier in Handy's classification of cultures (see Table 5.5). Senior managers typically form a dynamic club culture which they believe to be universal in the organization, whereas, in reality, it sits uncomfortably on top of a depressed and antipathetic role culture. From the managerial point of view, therefore, culture is a major variable to be influenced rather than a creation to be managed.

Table 5.5   Corporate culture and organization types

The club culture	Typical of a small company. A personal, informal culture focused on the owner. The **leader** is all. This form of culture is suitable for new ventures needing strong personalities and fast responses.
Role culture	Hierarchical, with an organizational chart portraying an orderly set of **job boxes** (roles). Individuals are less important than the roles they fill. A role culture is **managed** not led, with a formal communication system. Such a culture is best for stable, unchanging organizations with **routine** tasks. There is a strong tendency to adopt the role culture with increasing size, leading to the evolution of a mechanistic, bureaucratic organization.
Task culture	The main focus is on groups such as project teams. Organization is based on trust and respect and geared to plans not procedures. This is a **problem-solving** environment – exciting and challenging but expensive to run. Work is based on projects. There is little job security: staff leave when tasks are finished.
The person culture	This is radically different. It is suited to professionals who are self-managing and require minimal structure or supervision. The focus is on talent and professional expertise – management has low status. This is reflected in non-managerial titles such as Dean. Such a culture is best suited to professional practices and educational establishments.

Source: based on Handy (1993).

Commitment

Organizational commitment is a key concept in HRM (see key concept 5.5). It is one of the four Cs featured in the seminal Harvard model discussed in Chapter 1 and one of the measurable principles in our ten C framework (see Chapters 1 and 4). HRM rhetoric claims an integration and coherence for people management in organizations which adopt its philosophy. Integration is dependent on a strong and binding link between employee behaviour and the goals of the organization. According to this viewpoint, commitment to the mission and values of the organization is a fundamental principle. As a concept it is clearly related to that of 'strong' corporate culture. Commitment goes further than simple compliance: it is an emotional attachment to the organization.

> **KEY CONCEPT 5.5**
> **Commitment**
>
> Commitment is defined as the degree of identification and involvement which individuals have with their organization's mission, values and goals (Mowday *et al.* 1979). This translates into their desire to stay with the organization; belief in its objectives and values; the strength of employee effort in the pursuit of business objectives (Griffin and Bateman 1986).

Commitment has been the subject of research for some time because of its strong psychological connotations. Initially, attention was paid to commitment as **behaviour**. For example, Salancik (1977) identified four behavioural elements:

- **Explicitness.** Is it clear that an act of commitment took place? Can it be denied? Was it consciously determined?
- **Revocability.** Can we change our minds? Can the act be undone?
- **Volition.** Is an act performed under our own volition or under the control of someone else?
- **Publicity.** Has an expression or act of commitment been made in public?

Commitment arises as individuals perform acts such as joining a firm, working long hours and speaking well of the organization to customers or friends. Employees reflect on their own behaviour and conclude that because something has been done in front of others, of their own free will, there must be a commitment to the organization. In other words, free choice and public behaviour reinforce a feeling of commitment. This has been described as a 'neat theory' and there is some evidence in support of it (Arnold *et al.* 1991: 147).

Lately, the emphasis has shifted: the concept of commitment has been related to a significant framework in social psychology – the three components of **attitudes** (McKenna 1994: 251, 287). These are belief (cognitive), feeling (affective), and action (behavioural or conative). Each can be positive or negative. The emotional (affective) component seems to be of greatest significance, able to influence or override the other two. From this viewpoint, commitment is seen as having three key elements (Allen and Meyer, 1990):

- **affective** – the individual's emotional attachment to an organization;
- **continuance** – an individual's perception of the costs and risks associated with leaving the organization (equivalent to the behavioural component);
- **normative** – the obligation and responsibility a person feels towards the organization (equating to the cognitive component).

Research on attitudes indicates that these components usually show a considerable degree of consistency with each other but this is not always the case. For instance, employees can feel proud of a company and believe that they owe it an obligation for past good treatment, training or promotion. However, they may be aware that pay is relatively low and other organizations offer more attractive prospects. It is clear, therefore, that commitment is not as simple a concept as some HR theorists would have it. Many of us hold ambivalent attitudes towards our employing organizations.

In Case 5.2, we discuss an attempted merger between the Swedish car maker Volvo and the French Renault. Volvo has long been associated with progressive attitudes towards people management and mutual commitment between its various stakeholders. The alliance was motivated by financial and strategic considerations, but the deal foundered on the stresses placed on the commitment relationship. The key issues in this case are as follows:

- Volvo demonstrated a long history of innovative work practices and commitment to its workforce. This commitment appeared to be weakening because of increasingly difficult market conditions.

- Volvo commenced negotiations with another car manufacturer, Renault, which had an entirely different national and corporate culture.
- The potential deal made financial sense but threatened Volvo's commitment to its workers.
- As Renault would be the dominant partner, the workforce would be at the mercy of the French management with its alien business culture.
- Shareholders also questioned the wisdom of the deal and Volvo's commitment to them.
- The views of these internal and external stakeholders gave sufficient weight to allow a 'boardroom coup' and the termination of negotiations.

CASE 5.2
Volvo

In the 1970s Volvo was a model for the future of work – a partnership between management and employees. The company's policies recognized workers as human beings and moved manufacturing away from the production line towards team-based methods. Volvo's long-term commitment to its workforce placed it – together with many other Swedish companies – in the 'social-market' or 'soft HRM' model of capitalism (see Chapter 2). Workers were offered job security, high wages and comparatively short working hours. By the late 1980s competition was severe and the company struggled to maintain its generous policies in a worsening financial situation.

In the 1990s a relationship developed between Volvo and the French car manufacturer Renault. It began with a cooperation agreement. This involved Volvo taking a 20 per cent shareholding in Renault and Renault taking 10 per cent of Volvo shares. Then, in September 1993, Pehr Gyllenhammer, Volvo's Chairman, and Louis Schweitzer, his Renault equivalent, signed a deal in Paris which announced their intention to merge on 1 January 1994. Both groups had shed thousands of workers in previous years and there were immediate fears that the merger would lead to further job losses. According to Mr Schweitzer, designated Chief Executive of the new Renault–Volvo Automobile (RVA), they would expect savings of Fr30 billion (£3.3 billion) within the car and truck operations. RVA would maintain two distinct ranges of vehicles and separate dealerships. These savings would come from rationalizing research and development, lower investment costs and joint purchasing. They would also be able to launch new cars more quickly using common components. Pehr Gyllenhammer presented the deal as a large French investment in Sweden. The remainder of Volvo would be concentrating on other core activities such as Branded Consumer Products which had a leading share of the Scandinavian food, drinks and tobacco market.

The merger would have produced the world's sixth largest vehicle manufacturer, with over 200,000 employees and sales of 2.4 million cars and small commercial vehicles a year. Despite the high-quality market served by Volvo it was the junior partner, with a total production of 300,000 vehicles in 1992 leading to a loss of 1.8 billion Swedish Kroner. The Volvo directors felt that this was too small a company to support the ever-increasing development costs of launching new models. There was never any doubt that Renault would be in charge, with a holding of 65 per cent of the joint company. Renault still under French government ownership with an intention to privatize it by the end of 1994. The deal was supported initially by the major institutional shareholders such as insurance companies. However, it enraged private Swedish shareholders, who could not accept the effective takeover of Sweden's largest company and industrial flagship. The media took a keen interest and the Volvo share price dropped immediately.

The Volvo shareholders' meeting to vote on the merger was postponed from 9 November to the 2 December 1993. This was because top managers felt they were unlikely to be able to muster sufficient support. On 2 December – virtually at the last minute – the Volvo board decided not to proceed with the merger. Pehr Gyllenhammer, the Volvo Chairman for twenty-two years, resigned immediately along with three other directors, including Raymond Levy, the former Renault Chairman, who had been instrumental in setting up the link. The reason for not proceeding was a revolt among the top managers. The Managing Director, Soren Gyll, said that the necessary support had not been available to proceed with the plan, either from within the company or among the shareholders. Mr Gyll had consistently backed Pehr Gyllenhammer in public but had become disenchanted with the latter's handling of the issue and had held secret meetings to discuss his misgivings with other managers.

Discussion questions

1 Why do you think that the negotiations fell through?
2 If shareholders had not objected to the deal, would the views of the workforce have been sufficient to prevent it going through?

It is evident from the Volvo case study that there were major cultural differences between the two companies, at both national and organizational levels. In Hofstede's (1994) terms, whereas French managers contemplated an intellectual decision which could simply be imposed, the Swedish company's low power distance and high 'feminity' culture made this impossible. More generally, the nature of commitment has strong cultural underpinnings. This is most clearly shown in Japan.

Commitment and culture

Western companies have long strived to obtain the degree of commitment shown by Japanese workers. However, Japanese organizations have a significant and possibly insurmountable advantage: Japanese culture. The Japanese managerial scale of values is different from those of western cultures (Whitehill 1991). Most crucially, commitment is a two-way process – managers are committed to their people (Pascale and Athos 1981: 191). Physical status symbols, which are so important to western managers – such as named car parking spaces, large personal offices and executive dining areas – have little value for the Japanese. In contrast, traditionally minded Japanese managers and workers share fundamental values which lie at the heart of their commitment:

- **The work ethic.** Being seen to work hard and typically being in the office for long hours. Central to this culture is the belief that 'duty – in the form of work – must come first' (Briggs 1991: 41). Dissatisfaction, boredom and exhaustion are brushed aside in the commitment to duty. Indeed, surveys show poor job satisfaction in many Japanese companies. Commitment, therefore, is not to specific corporations so much as to 'duty' in general. Because of this cultural underpinning, it may be that western managers are pursuing a futile goal in copying Japanese 'commitment'. If the national culture does not feature a similar pressure

- for example the Protestant work ethic – organizations may never achieve the same levels of employee commitment.

- **Conformity.** As we observed in earlier chapters, individuals have little importance in comparison with the in-group. There is a psychological need to belong and not to be isolated from one's community. The high degree of interdependence leads to the 'high-trust' characteristics of Japanese business culture. Western companies are far more individualistic. Conformity comes from external control, as we shall see later in Chapter 10, on performance management, not from a deep compulsion. The result is that workers often conform only when the boss is watching. The unpredictability of individualists also leads to an inevitable reduction in mutual trust.

- **Avoidance of shame.** The Japanese manager has obligations and responsibilties derived from traditional culture rather than an employment contract or job description. Failure to discharge these according to the normal social rules can bring shame – loss of face – and isolation to managers and their families. This may be brought about, for example, by a breach of obligation (psychological contract) such as the guarantee of continued employment for one's staff. In the past this has reinforced a high-trust relationship and mutual commitment. However, as we observed in Chapter 2, the 1990s have brought economic reality to bear on traditional values and large organizations in Japan have been forced to shed people, albeit by oblique methods such as early retirement and coerced resignations. Many western managers have no concept of shame. Any obligation to staff is tempered by the need to maintain their own careers.

Commitment also depends on organizational culture. Indeed a 'culture of commitment' is frequently cited as a goal of organizational change. Paradoxically, however, change programmes designed to instil modern business methods and 'lean-mean' management structures can rebound, leading to a reduction in employee commitment. In the UK, attempts to reform the National Health Service have produced considerable argument and a clear reduction in morale. In Case 5.3 we consider how the new managerialism has clashed with the public-service values of nursing and medical staff, weakening staff commitment built over half a century.

CASE 5.3 **The UK** **National Health** **Service**	For several decades after the Second World War, the National Health Service (NHS) was the pride of the United Kingdom. The country became accustomed to a high standard of healthcare, provided virtually free of charge at the point of access and paid for by payroll National Insurance contributions. Successive governments have faced the escalating cost of increasingly sophisticated treatments, rising consumer expectations and the implications of demographic change. In an effort to contain the mushrooming budget and introduce commercial management and marketing techniques, the Conservative government published *Working for Patients* in April 1991, outlining plans for the reform of the NHS. For the first time, a distinction was made between providers and purchasers of healthcare

with the intention of creating a competitive market for services. With money following the patient, it was argued that the changes would lead to improved quality of service, enhanced choice, increased accountability and reduced costs. Doctors in community-based general practice (GPs), plus district health authorities have become fundholders with budgets based on the estimated health needs of their vicinity. Hospitals and other providers were encouraged to become autonomous business units, termed NHS trusts, with the freedom to improve efficiency and quality as they saw fit. Boards of management were appointed, accountable to the Secretary of State for Health. It was argued that a new culture would arise, dedicated to patient care, with greater commitment arising from market competition and local autonomy.

Arguments continue to rage over the consequences of these changes for patient care. In fact, the NHS has become largely a managed market as providers and purchasers have attempted to plan major developments, such as hospital closures, in order to minimize disruptions to previous patterns of use caused by fundholders shopping around for the quickest and cheapest healthcare. Government ministers have produced statistics apparently indicating an increase in the numbers of patients treated since the changes were introduced. Critics have argued that many patients have been double- or treble-counted, with each change of consultant or specialist regarded as a separate treatment. Improved methods of recording information and new treatment methods also affect statistics for reasons unrelated to NHS reform. The first independent evaluation, published in February 1994, argued that there had been little improvement in quality of care or patient choice, with only fundholding general practices showing any significant benefit. However, this was at the expense of equity of treatment.

The imposition of a management structure has led to a culture clash with health professionals and considerable political debate. Speaking in April 1994, Dr Sandy Macara, Chairman of the British Medical Association's ruling council, argued that winners under the market system had been some fundholding general practitioners, some trust hospitals, bureaucracy and 'the new breed of manager'. Losers had been non-fundholding GPs, most hospitals and community units, hospital doctors and patients – and, above all, truth – 'with dedicated deceit about waiting lists, misleading league tables, dubious productivity statistics . . . and denial of the undeniable fact of twin-tracking'. Dr Macara argued that patients had been left 'confused, bemused and frequently cheated . . . as they follow the money which was supposed to follow them, and fall by the wayside when the money runs out'.

In addition to the apparent lack of vision at the top as to where the service is actually going, it can be argued that one negative aspect of the reforms has been the increase in management required to organize the complexities of the new system. The number of managers in England rose from 16,091 in 1989/90, before the market-style changes, to 20,478 in 1992/93, and their pay bill more than tripled. Conversely, numbers of nurses fell by 27,235 over the same period. The government has defended the trend, asserting that the NHS was 'undermanaged' in the past. However, trusts in Scotland have been issued with non-binding guidance on how to set managers' pay, based on a job evaluation system, and the Welsh Secretary of State has cracked down on management costs and numbers.

Andrew Foster, whose Audit Commission research into NHS reforms was published in April 1994, was reported as commenting that while managers were attempting to make the changes within complex organizations, a significant number had failed to take advantage of them and in some instances almost all had failed in critical areas of staff management (reflected in, for example, low job satisfaction, extremely costly sickness levels and high staff turnover).

(*Sources*: *Guardian*, 19 January 1994, 1 August 1994; *The Independent*, 11 and 13 April 1994.)

Discussion questions

1 Why has the new market approach led to dissatisfaction and reduced commitment among NHS staff?

2 Are all employees equally dissatisfied?

3 Is it justifiable to argue that such problems are inevitable when essential changes are made in a relatively longstanding organization?

Commitment strategies

If there is a risk that commitment may be a casualty of change initiatives, as in the NHS case study, how is it best protected and developed? The answer seems to be that it must be regarded as a specific strategic objective in itself. This is best achieved by giving it a clear focus (M. Armstrong 1992: 102). In addition, it must be remembered that 'hearts and minds' commitment cannot be gained by top-down imposition of changes which run counter to the beliefs of employees. In the case of the NHS, the root of staff disaffection lies in the different perceptions of management and employees of the quality of service provided to patients. There is little consensus on the criteria for measuring quality.

Elsewhere, however, total quality management programmes have been shown to be particularly effective in obtaining commitment. This may be due to their systematic and apparent objectivity, employing project management and other documentation to verify quality standards. These standards are externally justified: they are required to satisfy customers and are not seen as a local management invention. Commitment is reinforced by in-built feedback mechanisms which inform staff and management of quality levels.

A more sinister implication is the extension of this mechanism within Japanese production techniques into insidious forms of control – 'management by shame' and 'management by blame' (Garrahan and Stewart 1992). Social pressure and individual feelings of guilt help to pressurize workers into meeting ever-rising performance standards.

More positively, a commitment programme should involve a thought-through package of measures which address the following areas and issues:

- **Communication**, outlining the direction which the organization's strategy is taking and the purpose of any changes. Staff need to understand why decisions have been taken before they will cooperate in their implementation. Additionally, they must be encouraged to contribute to the process from their experience and ideas.
- **Education** – where change involves new technology, systems or procedures there must be a suitable training package available to

provide confidence in their use. Training also builds commitment and respect through direct contact with managers involved in planning developments.

- **Ownership.** Commitment is encouraged by involving people in decisions, projects and making them responsible for implementing specific actions.
- **Emotional identification** is more likely in an atmosphere of enthusiasm. This can be created by acknowledging and encouraging responsibility and recognizing hard work and results.
- **Performance** assessment and reward structures should be focused on commitment.
- **Rewards** in the form of pay, bonuses and prizes can be linked to visible commitment behaviour. The introduction of performance-related pay has been extensive in recent years. Normally this has been justified as a means of increasing commitment. However, as we shall see in Chapter 10, evidence shows that performance-related pay can encourage a small proportion of good performers at the expense of demotivating the majority. In practice it reduces morale and leads to accusations of unfairness.
- **Employment contracts** can include clauses to prevent employees from publicizing information or opinions which might disadvantage the organization. Regrettably, such 'gagging' clauses have been used by management in public-sector organizations, such as the NHS, where staff feel committed to public service rather than a particular hospital trust, for example.

Justifying commitment

In practice, western managers have often imported the concept of commitment without a supporting framework which parallels that provided by Japanese culture. Some have appealed to the good sense of employees – a type of management rhetoric which presents commitment as voluntary. Supposedly, people are won over by the sound sense of strategic objectives and the 'obvious' view that commitment produces positive benefits for both staff and management. What are these benefits? Firstly, management is made easier. A committed workforce consists of self-motivated staff who can function without the need for orders or managerial control. Left to themselves, they will work in a manner consistent with business objectives. Secondly, employees gain from management trust. They are empowered to make decisions and are rewarded through achievement. But, as in Case 5.3, what if the rhetoric is not matched by reality?

There are a number of contradictions inherent in the notion of commitment. Earlier, we discussed commitment in terms of three elements: emotion, belief and behaviour. As a combination of these, commitment can range from **affective identification**, a real intellectual and emotional identification with the organization, to mere **behavioural compliance**, simply presenting an appearance of the attitudes and behaviours expected by senior managers (Legge 1995a: 44). For instance, it can be confused with the phenomenon of 'presentism' – the idea that putting in long, and perhaps ineffectual, hours is a demonstration of commitment to the organization.

Kunda (1991 cited in Willmott 1993: 538) found evidence of 'distancing' in a study of middle managers in a company where the rhetoric of commitment and corporate culturism was strong. Managers deftly played the game of appearing to be committed to the organization's culture, while in reality maintaining a sense of detachment from the process. In fact, many western organizations have a prevailing climate of cynicism, with employees and managers alike acting out their roles with little faith in the outcome of their actions. Watson, questioned managers in one organization and obtained the following response from one participant: 'We are a pretty committed bunch but I don't think ZTC knows what to with that commitment' (1994: 74).

Committed to what?

Individuals may identify with their work at a variety of levels: their job, profession, department, boss or organization. Realistically, commitment may be diverse and divided between any or all of these. For example, there may be a significant conflict between commitment to the organization and commitment to a trade union. Multi-union situations diffuse commitment even further: they encourage identification with themselves and their own sectional interests; they become combatants in a power game and compete with each other for management attention. Single-union agreements and healthy consultation arrangements help to unify and refocus commitment to the strategic objectives of the company. Japanese 'enterprise unions', linked to and funded by individual organizations, further enhance a unified focus. Abolition of union representation removes the alternative focus completely, at the expense of a useful mechanism for developing a cohesive workforce.

Commitment conflicts with the notion of **flexibility**. Numerical flexibility has been a predominant feature of recent years, with 'downsizing' and 'delayering' being an obsession of many large companies. A climate of fear has been created for those people remaining. Staff keep a wary eye on senior managers who have demonstrated a ruthless ability to cut employee costs. The workload has not been diminished in equal measure to the reduction in staff, imposing extra burdens on remaining staff.

Extra work, longer hours and fear of redundancy have increased stress and reduced commitment to employing organizations. Peak performance in the short term requires a significant level of commitment, but this can only occur if managers 'ensure that a perception of healthy longevity is achieved' (Watson 1994: 111). In other words, insecurity does not lead to motivated employees.

This is so obvious that one is hesitant to make the point. Nevertheless many people in charge of organizations behave in a way which suggests that it is beyond their awareness. Employees are far more likely to be committed to their employing organization if they can feel confidence in their employers' commitment to them. Recent evidence shows that such confidence is misplaced in many free-market companies, which are seemingly controlled by people concerned largely with furthering their own careers. There is no possibility of achieving real commitment without mutual trust.

Summary

We commenced this chapter by recognizing that international HRM can be considered analytically. However, descriptions of cultural differences tend to be stereotypical and do not pay sufficient attention to the diversity found in regions such as Asia. We discussed the work of Hofstede (1994) on dimensions such as cultural complexity, power distance, individualism, assertiveness and uncertainty avoidance. The concept was extended to corporate culture with an account of Deal and Kennedy's (1982) model and more recent debates on the subject. We concluded with a discussion on commitment, a key aspect of HRM theory.

Further reading

Leeds *et al.* (1994), in *Human Resource Management in Europe* (ed. Kirkbride), provide a good survey of cultural approaches to international HRM in its European context. Torrington (1994) takes a wider view in *International Human Resource Management: Think Globally, Act Locally.* Sparrow and Hiltrop's (1994) *European Human Resource Management in Transition* integrates detailed discussion of essential HRM theories and practices with international elements, including culture. Hofstede's (1994) updated version of *Cultures and Organizations: Software of the Mind* provides a stimulating account of his research and ideas. Deal and Kennedy's (1982) *Corporate Cultures* is one of the classic texts on culture within organizations. Thompson and McHugh's (1990) *Work Organisations* gives the concept a more critical treatment. Legge (1995b) brings the subject up to date and relates culture to commitment in *Human Resource Management: Rhetorics and Realities.*

Review questions

1 To what extent do national cultures determine corporate cultures?
2 How can the concept of 'in-groups' help to explain the inadequacies of equal opportunities policies?
3 Is it possible to describe national business cultures without resorting to stereotypes?
4 Explain the following terms in your own words:

● power distance;
● uncertainty avoidance;
● role specificity.

5 How does the notion of time vary around the world?

6 Explain the difference between organizational 'culture' and 'structure'. Is there a relationship between the two concepts?
7 Define commitment in your own words. Why is the term significant in the human resource literature?
8 If Japanese commitment is dependent on Japanese culture, how useful is the concept likely to be in other parts of the world?
9 To what extent is true commitment attainable? Is it just an example of management rhetoric?
10 What is the relationship between the concepts of 'strong culture' and 'commitment'?
11 Is it possible to obtain commitment in a situation where redundancies are inevitable?

Problem for discussion and analysis

Ark Nurseries is a specialist wholesaler of fresh and freeze-dried herbs and vegetables. These are grown within the country or brought in from other parts of the world and packaged in a small, chaotic factory. Most of the sales are to small retailers and restaurants in middle-class areas. The company was founded ten years ago and has prospered as its products have become familiar and customers have been increasingly interested in a more varied range of foods. The Managing Director (MD) founded the company with her late husband and has taken complete control of the company since his death three years ago. She was always accustomed to working hard and now spends virtually all her waking hours on the company. Her main interest is selecting and marketing new products and she is happy to spend a lot of her time travelling to meet growers and attending trade fairs and exhibitions. She is frequently away from the office for weeks at a time.

The number of staff has gradually increased over the years, most of the more senior managers having been with her for several years. She deals directly with her managers, usually on a one-to-one basis as problems come up, and dislikes committee-type meetings. An outgoing and energetic person, she takes decisions quickly, based on intuition and her experience of the market. She takes advice from her staff but does not feel obliged to follow it. Generally, she is a talker rather than a listener and is accustomed to having her way. She insists on vetting all staff recruitment, promotion and pay increases and takes all equipment-purchasing decisions herself. There is no one specifically in charge of human resources, each functional manager being responsible for their own staff. Pay is good for the area and employees are generally pleased to work for the company. The factory has a five-day week and is open for ten hours a day. There is no appraisal or performance management system, with senior staff being paid salaries and factory workers receiving wages based on a piece-rate system.

The sales manager has just clinched a deal with a major supermarket group which has agreed to take Ark produce for its sixty stores. The MD was surprised by his success but is delighted that it has finally been achieved. The contract was announced last week but reactions within the company have been mixed. The Managing Director has spent years trying to break into this market and is astonished by the attitude of most of her senior staff. They have been accustomed to steady but undramatic growth and are now faced with tripling sales over the next three years. They argue that their regular growers could not meet the demand at the right level of quality, especially as the supermarket group will expect stringent standards and exact financial penalties for late delivery.

Over the last few days, fierce arguments have broken out between the MD and her staff and there have been threats of resignation. However, the MD is convinced that the contract is feasible and that resignations will not happen because of the unemployment situation.

As a human resources consultant how would you analyse the situation and how could you help?

6

Strategic HRM

This chapter examines human resource strategy, its integration with corporate planning, and the development of human resource policies.

In Chapter 1 we saw that many theorists consider a strong link with strategy to be the key difference between HRM and earlier philosophies of people management. Exponents of HRM emphasize the importance of an organization's people in achieving its overall business objectives. Strategic HRM takes a long-term perspective and is concerned with issues such as corporate culture and individual career development, as well as the availability of people with the right skills. It incorporates redundancy and recruitment planning and is increasingly focused on the concept of the flexible workforce (discussed in Chapter 4).

In this chapter we address a number of fundamental questions:

- Is strategic HRM a reality?
- Are people managers involved in high-level decision-making?
- Are human resource concerns valued as much as financial, production or marketing issues?
- How can human resource strategies and practices be adapted to meet perceived threats and opportunities in a changing business environment?

If people are truly an organization's greatest assets, then their careful selection, deployment and development can lead to a competitive advantage. The first part of this chapter examines how this can be done. The second part concludes the chapter with a discussion of the implementation of change strategies from the human resource perspective.

People strategies

What *is* this thing called strategic HRM? It seems to be part of the brave new worlds of strategic management and human resource management. But have these terms any real meaning? How many people actually put either strategic management or human resource management into practice? And if they do, what do they look like and what impact, if any, do they make on organizational performance?

(M. Armstrong 1994)

Strategy is about choice. The underlying assumption is that firms can make deliberate decisions about their markets, the products or services they provide, prices, quality standards and the deployment of human and other resources. Strategic thinking is based on rational decision-making, taking into account the competitive and financial pressures on an organization and the resources available to it, including its people. It imposes orderly, logical thinking on a messy real world, modelling the present situation and predicting the consequences of specific actions (see key concept 6.1). In order to evaluate these outcomes there is an emphasis on quantitative statements – such as the number of people needed – based on an explicit set of objectives.

A strategy is the means by which an organization seeks to meet its objectives. It is a deliberate choice, a decision to take a course of action rather than reacting to circumstances. It focuses on significant, long-term goals rather than day-to-day operating matters.

KEY CONCEPT 6.1
Strategy

Under the influence of the Harvard MBA, business strategy has become an influential and integrative discipline at the organizational level. The emphasis on a planned approach to development and growth brings together the functional elements of operations management, marketing, finance and human resource management into a cohesive whole. Strategic management is a process by which organizations determine their objectives, decide on actions and suitable timescales, implement those actions and then assess progress and results (Thompson 1993: xiv). Fundamentally, it is the task of senior managers, although more junior employees contribute to the process and the implementation of strategy.

As we observed in Chapter 1, rhetorical accounts paint a picture of HRM as being focused and managerial, unified and holistic and driven by strategy:

A strategic orientation is a vital ingredient in human resource management. It provides the framework within which a coherent approach can be developed to the creation and installation of HRM policies, systems and practices. [. . .] The aim of strategic human resource management is to ensure that the culture, style and structure of the organization, and the quality, commitment and motivation of its employees, contribute fully to the achievement of business objectives.

(M. Armstrong 1992: 47)

Hence it is claimed that human resource strategies combine all people management activities into an organized and integrated programme to meet the strategic objectives of an enterprise. In Chapter 1 we also noted that HRM is different from personnel management primarily because of its supposed emphasis on the link between people policies and overall business strategy. For example, Guest distinguishes traditional personnel management from HRM 'by virtue of the way in which the former ignored, but the latter embraces strategy' (1993: 213). This contrasts with the 'technical-piecemeal' approach of personnel management.

Personnel management, we are told, is essentially reactive, whereas HRM, exemplified by HR strategy, is proactive. The personnel model focused on short-term, largely operational matters of little interest to strategists. HRM, by contrast, takes a longer perspective and is closer to the heart of the organization. HRM is portrayed as 'having an agenda which addresses "business-related" issues' (Beardwell and Holden 1994: 6). It takes a proactive stance towards the competitiveness and efficiency of the organization, unlike the mundane and reactive day-to-day orientation of personnel management. However, this distinction is by no means unanimously accepted: 'HRM's claim to take a strategic approach to employment touches a particularly raw nerve among personnel managers. "*Of course*" personnel management has "*always*" advocated a strategic approach' (Hendry 1995: 12). Moreover, human resource strategies are not easy to identify. For example, Marginson *et al.* (1988) found that 80 per cent of senior people managers claimed to have overall HR strategies – but few could describe what those strategies were! In fact, both academics and practitioners have found it difficult to understand what HR strategy means in practice. Hendry (1994b), for example, acknowledges that strategy is the dominant theme in HRM but is also a misunderstood concept. He concludes that 'the perspective writers on HRM offer on strategy is often glib and lacking in sophistication' (1994b: 2). Hendry attributes this to HR theorists being 'strategically illiterate' (1994b: 2). They use strategic concepts which are outmoded and defective. The problem is compounded by a lack of case studies to give us insight into the way strategies arise in practice.

Why do academics stress the importance of strategy? A number of reasons are apparent:

- Strategic literature emphasizes the internal resources of a business as the source of competitive advantage. Such resources must possess four qualities for advantage to be maintained:

  - they must add value to the organization's activities;
  - they must be rare and (preferably) unique;
  - competitors should have difficulty in copying them;
  - they must be unable to be replaced by technology.

  These criteria arise from human resources in the form of skills, expertise and experience (Storey 1995: 4).
- HRM models focus strongly on strategy. Certainly, this is the case. However, models of human resource management derive largely

from American business schools. The prevailing philosophy in these schools has been analytic and strategic. This line of reasoning offers an explanation but not a justification. In fact, it is circular because if one asks why they devised strategic models for HRM, the answer might simply be that 'they would, wouldn't they'.

- Strategy is intellectual and, therefore, interesting – to academics. It is analytical and can be conceptualized in terms of models, abstractions and even numbers. In other words, it deals with a business subject within an orthodox academic framework. This contrasts with forms of operational management which deal with 'boring admin'. Day-to-day management tends to be commonsensical, uses ragbags of techniques which – from experience – have been found to work, and deals with messy problems. It is unteachable and difficult to intellectualize. Students without business experience find discussion of real-life people management hard to relate to. It does not have the tidiness and coherence of a proper subject with 'right' answers. Far easier to regard it with contempt!

- Degree courses major on strategy. Since the advent of the Harvard MBA, there has been a steady trend towards a final-year focus on 'business policy' for undergraduate business studies degrees. The underlying rationale is the provision of an integrative subject which prepares students for high-level business jobs. It is taught by looking backwards – retrospective examination of case studies which are prepared within recognized frameworks. Essentially, it is a case of 'where did they go wrong' and, occasionally, right.

  Intriguingly, however, employers consistently ask for practical business skills such as presentation and teamwork – not strategic thinking. Essentially, strategy is for senior managers. In a time of mass higher education few students will ever become senior managers, and those who do will not achieve such jobs for at least a decade.

- Strategy is important. It deals with high-level decisions, concerning itself with the 'big agenda'.

If strategy is deemed to be so important by academics, how much impact has strategic thinking had on practitioners? Firstly, the emphasis given to strategy by HRM theorists has led to significant interest from senior managers. For example, there is a stress on the importance of maximizing the performance and potential of an organizations's people. This does not come from an altruistic and soft-hearted interest in their welfare. It derives from a hard-headed appreciation of the long-term contribution they can provide to the business. 'Soft' HRM focuses on an organization's people as assets so that time spent on training and development is an investment in **human capital** (see Chapter 2). This investment provides long-term benefit for an organization.

Hence strategic HRM can fit the interests of senior executives. But what of lower-level managers? There are two major difficulties for HR practitioners brought up in the personnel tradition. Firstly, as we have noted, knowledge of wider business functions has not been a strength of the personnel profession. There is a gulf in personality between those attracted to strategy and the people actually dealing with human resources at company level. Differing interests and outlooks on life can lead to a serious failure of communication.

On the one hand, business school strategists have tended to minimize human resource considerations because of the ambiguity and uncertainty attached to human behaviour. Humans are the most unpredictable of strategic resources. On the other hand, personnel departments generally employ practitioners who view themselves as pragmatists dealing with practical issues such as recruitment, pay and discipline 'on the ground', remote from the grand theories of strategists (Beardwell and Holden 1994: 7).

The second difficulty comes from their historic role of independent arbitrators between staff and management. As conciliators and apologists personnel managers depended on the ability to find compromises and reconcile the two sides rather than developing a clear agenda of their own. As a result, they make uncomfortable stakeholders, unable to fight their corner. Instead they are forced to react to the decisions of more powerful stakeholders. In practice then:

> personnel specialists find strategy difficult. Personnel specialists have not developed the strategic skills needed to contribute to their organization's effectiveness. Current education and training programmes give them little insight into how to link business, technical and human resource management skills in times of great uncertainty. Personnel specialists do not speak the language of top management in marketing and manufacturing and often seem to clam up when confronted with all the noughts on a company balance sheet.
>
> (Giles and Williams 1991)

Herein lies the source of difficulty between the planning mentality and human resource management. Good people managers, through intuition or experience, are profoundly aware of their lack of control over people. In a high proportion of situations, the most carefully constructed and devious tactics will fail to get people to behave in a desired way. Experienced managers will regard this as normal and inescapable. People are not puppets and it is not surprising that they do not behave as such. Coming to terms with this is very much a matter of personality. Managers with a high tolerance of ambiguity, able to operate in fluid, uncertain situations, gravitate towards jobs with a considerable people element.

In contrast, human quirkiness and unpredictability do not fit the planning mindset, which demands ordered, rational and entirely predictable behaviour. Communication between dedicated planners and people managers can be a painful business. To the HR manager a plan can seem to be a statement of intentions, an attempt to forecast an ideal world – but not one to be stuck to rigidly. If circumstances change, surely the plan can be bent to accommodate this? To the planner, human resource thinking seems woolly and vague. HR managers do not convey a feeling of confidence: they are far too tolerant of deviant behaviour and seem incapable of **making** employees toe the line. They are incorrigible 'firefighters' and hence unsuitable for senior, strategic roles.

Forming HR strategies

Identifying the relationship between HRM and strategy, it seems, is simpler in theory than it is in practice. Frequently, strategic HRM is a matter of rhetoric. Organizations can usefully be grouped into five alternative categories on the basis of their approach towards human resource strategy (Torrington and Hall 1995: 47):

- Businesses in which there is no consideration whatsoever of human resource issues in the preparation of organizational strategy. This is typical of firms twenty years ago and is still found in many small companies.
- Organizations in which there is a growing understanding of the role of human resources in implementing corporate strategy. Human resource strategy cascades down from organizational strategy, very much along the lines of the Michigan model (described in Chapter 1). The purpose of HR strategy is to match the requirements of organizational strategy, ensuring the closest possible fit in terms of employee numbers, skills and so on.
- Businesses in which the relationship becomes two-way, with some ideas initiated by HR managers. There is an element of debate about the people management consequences of particular strategies before they are implemented.
- Organizations in which the HRM concept has been accepted and people are seen as the key to competitive advantage. Corporate and human resource strategies are developed simultaneously. They are coherent and comprehensive.
- Companies where human resources become the driving force in the development of strategy. There is an overriding emphasis on developing their skills and capitalizing on their competences.

In practice, organizations may adopt any of these approaches, although, at present, the first and last type are rarely encountered among large businesses.

Strategies can encompass many issues. Whether or not a business gives prominence to its human resource strategies, when the organization takes decisions on its intended market and product or service range it also determines the types of job and skills required (Purcell 1995: 63). Where organizations are genuinely concerned with their people, HRM normally focuses on certain strategic sub-goals, or second-order strategies in Purcell's terminology, as shown in Table 6.1. For example:

- Resourcing an organization with the most suitable people at the right time, in the right place. In the next chapter we will consider this issue in depth, but for the moment we will note that, from a strategic viewpoint, there are two important elements:
  - knowledge of and participation in the formulation of 'official' strategy;
  - awareness of underlying developments which will produce

'surprises' which lead to about-turns in the official policy, typically with little or no notice.

- Planning the redeployment or dismissal of staff who are no longer required for specific tasks. The emphasis varies between free-market and social-market companies, with the former taking a hard-HRM line and the latter being committed to a softer approach.
- Determining the cultural characteristics appropriate to an organization's business objectives. Implementation requires us to plan the socialization, performance assessment, development and change programmes needed to realize that culture.
- Developing key skills for new products or equipment. This includes consideration of external and internal resourcing, training programmes, formal education, and job rotation.

Examining HR strategy within the framework of our ten principles of HRM we can see in Table 6.2 how each element, or combination of elements, can be made the focus of strategy. Guest (1987), for instance, identifies a circular relationship between a number of strategic goals:

- As we have seen, HRM aims for a **high level of commitment** from employees, so that they identify with the organization's goals and contribute actively to its improvement and success.
- In turn, this enables the organization to obtain a **high-quality output** from workers who want continually to improve standards.
- Within this environment, there is an expectation of **flexibility** from workers, a willingness to depart from fixed job definitions, working practices and conditions.
- **Strategic integration** – all these strands link the organization's strategy. They are directed towards agreed objectives and interact with each other in a cohesive way.

These goals require support from top managers and the integration of human resource strategy with business policy.

Table 6.1 Levels of strategy affecting HRM

Level	Organizational focus	Environmental constraints
First-order strategies	Long-term objectives Range of activities, markets, locations	Supranational authorities Government Culture and tradition
Second-order strategies	Internal operating procedures, organizational structure	Capital market Product market Consumers
Third-order strategies	Strategic choice in HRM	Job market Workforce Law
Outcomes	Style, structure, conduct of HRM	

Source: adapted from Purcell (1989).

Table 6.2 Principles of strategic HRM

Principle	Definition	Action
1 Comprehensiveness	Human resource management should be closely matched to business objectives	Clear, unambiguous mission statement supported by strategies and organization able to meet objectives
2 Coherence	Allocation and activities of human resources integrated into a meaningful whole	HR strategies developed at board level and integrated with all other strategies
3 Control	Effective organizations require a control system for cohesion and direction	People management must be organized, rather than left to ad-hoc decisions at local level
4 Communication	Strategies understood and accepted by all employees; open culture with no barriers	Clear, simple and justified strategies; cascading process of communication with feedback to the top
5 Credibility	Staff trust top management and believe in their strategies	Top managers are sincere, honest and consistent
6 Commitment	Employees motivated to achieve organizational goals	Top managers show commitment to staff
7 Change	Continuous improvement and development essential for survival	Flexible people and working systems; culture of innovation; skills training
8 Competence	Organization competent to achieve its objectives – dependent on individual competences	Resourcing strategies, selection techniques and human resource development systems in place
9 Creativity	Competitive advantage comes from unique strategies	System for encouraging and tapping employee ideas
10 Cost-effectiveness	Competitive, fair reward and promotion systems	Top managers pay themselves on equivalent basis to staff

Business goals

We saw in Chapter 4 that organizations are formed to achieve certain goals. Strategic thinking focuses on these long-term objectives. Human resource strategies are derived from overall business objectives in the same way as investment or marketing strategies. We noted also in the previous chapter that commitment is seen to be particularly crucial for competitive advantage. For true commitment to occur, conventional management wisdom sees the need for employees to accept and believe in an organization's goals.

A **mission statement** communicates these goals to everyone in a company (key concept 6.2). Mission statements have a particular significance in large companies, where communication can be difficult and, as we have seen, departments and 'political' groups frequently focus on their own sectional interests. A small business may not need such a statement since its employees and owners have a clear understanding of its reasons for existence. Mission statements can be wide-ranging. For example, BAA, the airport management company, states that:

Our mission is to make BAA the most successful airport company in the world. This means always focusing on our customers' needs and safety, seeking continuous improvements in the costs and quality of our services, enabling our employees to give of their best.

(BAA *Company Report*, 1995)

KEY CONCEPT 6.2 *Mission statements*	A mission statement should convey the essence of what an organization is about: why it exists, what kind of business it intends to be, and who its intended customers are. The mission is translated into objectives or goals within the strategic management process.

What prevents such a statement from being no more than a set of banal platitudes? It can be tied to some form of performance measure, perhaps in the form of detailed objectives. As part of its fundamental strategies, Christian Salvesen, the Scottish-based distribution and specialist hire company, makes the statement that:

Christian Salvesen's strategy is to concentrate on a limited number of activities in which the company has a demonstrable and maintainable competitive edge, based on market leadership or technological superiority, and in which the company has the resources both in terms of finance and people to grow the business.

(BAA *Company Report*, 1995)

This mission statement is locked into the company's **first-order** strategies (see Table 6.2). These are major decisions on its long-term aims and the scope of its activities (Purcell 1995: 67). Salvesen is an example of a diversified firm which has made both acquisitions and diversifications in recent years. The company has attempted to rebalance its activities to give long-term growth and profitability. The human resource implications are evident in terms of industrial relations, job security, career expectations and human resource development.

It has to be conceded that many businesses have a mission statement simply because it is the done thing to have one. Often they serve no clear purpose. This is not the case in large Japanese firms:

A statement of mission, or overall philosophy, is particularly significant within the Japanese management system. It is this broad policy declaration which establishes the corporate culture within which regular employees will spend their working lives. Becoming 'socialized' within the corporate culture, and internalizing the company spirit (*shafu*), are important foundations for building the Japanese employee's remarkable loyalty and dedication to the company.

(Whitehill 1991: 123)

Hence the mission statement plays a crucial role in developing the uniquely Japanese forms of organizational culture and commitment discussed in Chapter 5. This is illustrated in Case 6.1, which examines the relationship between fundamental business concerns and 'people principles' at Nissan UK.

Nissan UK has closely linked overall business policy to its human resource strategy. The key business principles have been defined as:

CASE 6.1
Nissan UK

- **quality** – build profitably the highest-quality car sold in Europe;
- **customers** – be No. 1 in customer satisfaction in Europe;
- **volume** – always achieve required volume;
- **new products** – deliver on time, at required quality, within cost;
- **suppliers** – establish long-term relationship with single-source suppliers, aim for zero defects and just-in-time delivery, apply Nissan principles to suppliers;
- **production** – use 'most appropriate' technology, develop predictable 'best method' of doing job, build in quality;
- **engineering** – design 'quality' and 'ease of working' into the product and facilities; Establish 'simultaneous engineering' to reduce development time.

In common with other Japanese corporations, Nissan has a human resource focus. Its business principles are followed by a number of 'people principles':

- **selection** – hire the highest calibre people, look for technical capabilities and emphasize 'attitude';
- **responsibility** – maximize the responsibility of all staff by devolving decision-making;
- **teamwork** – recognize and encourage individual contributions, with everyone working to the same objectives;
- **flexibility** – expand the role of the individual – requires multi-skills, no job descriptions, generic job titles;
- **kaizen** – continuously seek hundreds of 0.01 per cent improvements; give 'ownership of change' to employees;
- **communications** – 'every day face to face';
- **training** – establish individual 'continuous development' programmes;
- **supervisors** – regard them as 'professionals at managing the production process'; give the supervisor much of the responsibility normally assumed by indirect departments; make them the genuine leaders of their team;
- **single status** – treat everyone as 'first-class' citizens, eliminate all illogical status differences;
- **trade unionism** – single-union agreement with Amalgamated Engineering Union emphasizing the common objective for a successful enterprise; built-in dispute resolution.

(*Source*: Wickens, Peter D. (1991), 'Innovation in Training Creates a Competitive Edge', in Stevens, John and Mackay, Robert (1991), *Training and Competitiveness*, NEDO/Kogan Page.)

Discussion questions
1   What links can you see between Nissan's business and people principles?
2   To what extent are Nissan's people principles a function of Japanese business culture?

Strategy formation

The orthodox view of strategy is that it is a deliberate, conscious process coming from the top of the organization (Ansoff 1968). Figure 6.1 outlines a sequence of activities from this perspective. However, this model cannot

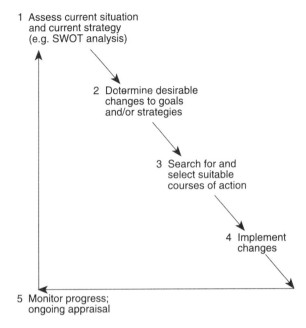

1 Assess current situation
   and current strategy
   (e.g. SWOT analysis)

2 Determine desirable
   changes to goals
   and/or strategies

3 Search for and
   select suitable
   courses of action

4 Implement
   changes

5 Monitor progress;
   ongoing appraisal

Figure 6.1 The strategy process.
Source: adapted from Thompson (1993).

explain the strategic organization and the means of evaluating their relative usefulness. A business can choose between recruiting and training its own direct sales people or subcontracting the function to outside agents. It has to be recognized that all options may not be apparent and that trial and error may be the only practical method of evaluation. Other factors such as competition, organizational politics or the absence of resources may limit the choice. For example, in order to reduce costs and increase quality Ford outlined plans in 1996 to reduce its workforce worldwide, partly by outsourcing component manufacture to subcontractors located alongside its car assembly plants.

Senior managers may believe that by determining strategy they have decided the future of the organization. In fact, as we have seen in previous chapters, the structure and culture of the organization and the commitment of lower-level managers can influence or hinder the implementation of strategy. This is particularly evident in decentralized and loosely controlled organizations which require higher levels of consultation and communication to ensure cooperation. Later in this chapter we will consider these issues in relation to organizational change.

Coherent strategies and integrated practices sound fine in theory but how are they to be translated into action? This 'surface neatness' hides an organizational reality which is far from simple (Blyton and Turnbull 1992: 2). Mintzberg argues that the strategies which are actually carried through into practice include an unintended element which he terms 'emergent strategies' (1994: 26). This might result from poor strategic thinking, poor implementation or a sound state of realism. It reflects the view that strategic management should not be confined to the top layers in an organization. Emergent strategy rarely comes from the centre, but rather from bright ideas and initiatives at a local level which were unpredicted but were found to work and then adopted more widely:

> big strategies can grow from little ideas (initiatives), and in strange places, not to mention at unexpected times, almost anyone in the organization can prove to be a strategist. All he or she needs is a good idea and the freedom and resources required to pursue it.
>
> (Mintzberg 1994: 26)

Other aspects of strategy involve people making decisions about capital equipment, finance or marketing; HR strategy requires people to make decisions about themselves. It is:

> important . . . to think of strategy as a game that people play, because when it is discussed more seriously there is a strong tendency to slip into talking about it as a response that 'the organization' makes to an 'environment'. [. . .] The inevitable result is a lack of insight into the real complexities of strategic management because in reality organizations and their environments are not things, one adapting to the other, but groupings of people interacting one with another.
>
> (Stacey 1993: 2)

However, it is a deadly serious game, with people's careers and livelihoods at stake (Stacey 1993: 9). The reality is that faced with a choice between profit and the wellbeing of employees most commercial organizations will select the former. 'Softer' human resource issues continue to be secondary and subordinate to financial matters. Regardless of well-meaning statements to the contrary, within the free-market capitalist model there is an emphasis on short-term improvement in financial performance. In western organizations, financially knowledgeable managers have taken the lead as the 'bottom line' of profit or loss drives business. As is evident from the experience of the Royal Bank of Scotland (see Case 6.2), strategic actions derived from technological or financial considerations can have direct and relatively immediate effect on an organization's people. Human resource initiatives are accommodated within a broad financial picture in which benefits to or changes in people management compete with other resources. In reality, long-term HRM goals such as training and developing skills for the future are rarely considered. If employee commitment, flexibility and product quality are valued, they are sought for profit and not pursued as beneficial for workers.

New technology has required major changes in human resource strategies within the banking industry. Introduction of ATMs (automatic telling machines), the hole-in-the-wall cash dispensers and debit cards which replace cheques, have slashed manual requirements. The Royal Bank of Scotland has pioneered many of the changes in the UK. Its delayering exercise was initiated in 1990 with the announcement of the loss of 600 head-office and support jobs, followed a few months later by the decision to restructure the branch network. In common with other banks, there was a shift away from processing paperwork at branch level. In the short term, back office work was transferred to administration centres but eventually most of the work will be electronic. Within a year staff levels had been reduced by 1,000, half through natural wastage; 506 people were asked to leave, of whom 431 took

CASE 6.2
The Royal Bank of Scotland

early retirement and 49 accepted voluntary redundancy. Of the 1,000 only 26 people were made compulsorily redundant.

The focus was on staff over the age of 50 as Inland Revenue regulations restricted benefits to younger leavers. This made it an expensive initiative, but the bank considered the redundancies to be cost-effective in the longer term. The result was a flatter operation, reducing the number of management layers from seven to four. Amongst the first to go were the Managing Director and his deputy; 16 (23 per cent) of the 68 senior executives were shed; 17 (11 per cent) of the 160 senior managers. Half of the total job losses came from managers and assistant managers, mostly in the branch network.

Discussion question

To what extent is the human resource strategy described in this case a matter of strategic choice rather than an inevitable reaction to technological change?

Translating strategy into action

At this point we turn to the issue of implementing human resource strategies. The classic approach follows the 'matching' process outlined in the Michigan model of HRM (outlined in Chapter 1). The goal is a realization of the organization's strategic human resource requirements in terms of numbers and, more importantly, attitudes, behaviour and commitment. According to Miller, the key lies with 'the concept of "fit": the fit of human resource management with the thrust of the organization' (1989: 36).

M. Armstrong (1992: 53) argues that the significant issue in HR strategy is that of integration with overall business strategy. In practice, this integration is difficult to achieve. Armstrong outlines some crucial difficulties:

- **Diversity of strategic processes, levels and styles.** As we have seen, many organizations do not use neat, traditional approaches to business strategy based on rational planning. In line with the criticisms of Mintzberg and others, it may be more sensible to be open-minded and intuitive. However, from the perspective of people management it becomes difficult to discern appropriate HR strategies and the corporate strategies they are supposed to match. Further, in a diversified organization composed of strategic business units (SBUs), each unit may have its own idiosyncratic strategies. Consequently it becomes difficult to provide corporate HR strategies – such as management development – which can be reconciled with the different needs of individual SBUs.
- **The evolutionary nature of business strategy.** It is not possible to provide a rational HR strategy if corporate strategy is evolving quickly and in a piecemeal way. In fact, the concept of 'rational' strategic planning is culture-bound: it is a product of free-market economies. Other cultures naturally employ a more diffuse, emergent or evolving method of business planning (Legge 1995b: 104).
- **The absence of written business strategies.** This occurs particularly in smaller companies and overwhelmingly in cultural contexts where evolutionary planning is the rule. This does not help to clarify those corporate strategic issues with which HR strategy is expected to fit.

- **The qualitative nature of HR issues.** Business plans have tended to be expressed in numerical terms: financial data, sales forecasts, competitive position. As we shall see later, traditional 'manpower planning' fitted this mould. Equally, human resource strategy has been identified with the 'hard' rationalist model of HRM. However, 'soft' or qualitative issues such as culture, motivation and employee relations have become increasingly important – even in free-market countries.

Armstrong's solution to these problems is to emphasize the need for human resource practitioners to achieve an understanding of how business strategies are formed. They should adopt a wider point of view and an understanding of key business issues such as:

- **Corporate intentions** for growth or retrenchment, including strategic alliances (mergers, acquisitions, joint ventures – discussed earlier), product and market development, disposals.
- **Methods of increasing competitiveness** such as improvements in productivity, quality and service, reducing costs.
- A perceived need for a more positive, **performance culture**.
- Other **cultural consequences** of the organization's mission such as 'commitment, mutuality, communications, involvement, devolution and teamworking' (M. Armstrong 1992: 55).

Case 6.3 explores the long-term development of a strategic process at ICL aimed at achieving a number of specified commitments from its people. Specifically, the strategy aimed to turn the company from one which was technology-led tactical and short term in approach, which tried to do everything, was internally focused and parochial, wrapped up in procedures and geared to UK requirements. Instead, stress was placed on becoming global and marketing-led, but only in specialized, long-term markets, and on being innovative and open-minded. This required an education process to produce a change in the attitudes and behaviour of ICL's employees.

International Computers Limited (ICL) was formed in 1968 from a forced marriage of two British computer firms, ICT and English Electric Computers. The product of an interventionist Labour government, it was funded to compete with world leaders like IBM as part of prime minister Harold Wilson's 'white heat of technological revolution'. Progress was disastrous until Robb Wilmot was appointed Managing Director in 1981.

Under Wilmot and his successor, Peter Bonfield (from Texas Instruments), ICL was steered away from proprietary mainframe manufacturing towards more specialist niche markets. Currently amongst the world top three in point-of-sale systems, ICL's products are a familiar sight at supermarket checkouts. More importantly, ICL has consistently turned in profits, year after year, whereas most other computer manufacturers have made losses (see Case 1.1: IBM).

Until Wilmot's arrival ICL was an inward-looking, bureaucratic company. He replaced the traditional hierarchical form of management with a matrix structure. In 1984 the company became part of STC, a relationship which provided few positive advantages apart from a new interest in psychological testing – STC had a long tradition of extensive psychometric

CASE 6.3
ICL

assessment. ICL introduced psychometric methods for recruitment, training and career development and also for team-building and counselling. STC–ICL placed a particular emphasis on integrating psychological assessment with business strategy and forward planning.

Personnel policies and statements of values and beliefs were translated into action through the Investing in People programme at the end of the 1980s. The programme was outlined in four management handbooks, which covered the following areas:

- New employees, outlining the recruitment and selection process, psychometrics, interviewing and assessment centres.
- People planning, in order to have the right numbers and skills in the right place at the right time.
- Performance management, outlining the setting of objectives, performance assessment and links with the annual pay review.
- Development, focusing on improved personal performance, career planning and the use of assessment, development centres, self-insight and psychometric tests.

In 1990 Fujitsu acquired 80 per cent of ICL. The two companies were already familiar with each other as Fujitsu was ICL's chip supplier. Fujitsu adopted a 'hands-off' approach, allowing ICL management to take a radical outlook. Fujitsu had many of the properties of a typical mainframe manufacturer, heavily directed towards the Japanese market, whereas ICL took on open systems on a worldwide basis. Having revised its business strategy, the company decided it needed seven commitments from its staff:

1 **Commitment to change** – welcoming change energetically and resourcefully.
2 **Commitment to customers** – their needs and expectations.
3 **Commitment to excellence** – requiring a 'can-do' attitude amongst its people.
4 **Commitment to teamwork** – effective teams achieve more than individuals.
5 **Commitment to achievement** – reward depends on results.
6 **Commitment to people development** – ICL's main strength lies in the quality and skills of its people.
7 **Commitment to creating a productivity showcase** – everything must be of showcase standard.

The process of change depended on a four-step performance management system which included individual objectives tied to business strategy; a performance rating process measuring achievement of these objectives; a separate pay review based on the achievement of objectives; and a review of the ability of parts of the company to meet future human resource needs.

Organizationally, ICL was split into twenty-six 'self-empowered units'. A number were joint ventures set up in combination with companies such as General Electric of the USA. These units were small enough to focus on specific markets so that staff knew precisely what was expected of them and thus could be highly responsive to customer needs. ICL based its organization on the technology which it employed, with the different units held together by a messaging and data distribution system which, according to Bonfield, acted as 'electronic glue'. This system extended to its trading partners.

(*Sources*: Beattie and Tampoe (1990); M. Armstrong (1992); *Guardian*, 8 July 1993, Richard Sarson: 'Firm grasp on the future'.)

Discussion question
To what extent could the ICL approach be applied to other organizations?

As a result of this programme, the process of career development in ICL became clearer (Beattie and Tampoe 1990), with each person knowing the point at which they were aiming at any given time – the next step on the career ladder. This case illustrates the all-encompassing nature of human resource strategy. As part of the development process, building blocks of experience were planned for each person. This required preparation of concise skill and experience profiles. Attention was also paid to the value of training courses, which were committed to practical use of course content on the job and making training of real value rather than something undertaken as a 'good thing'. People were offered growth opportunities in their jobs, being exposed to new areas and experiences. Specific development positions providing challenge without great experience were identified for people with high potential, but at an early stage in their careers. In line with ICL's global policy, particular emphasis was placed on gaining exposure to the international aspects of the business. Career management was seen as the joint responsibility of both the individual and the company.

The reality of HR strategy

Organizations vary considerably in the formality of their strategic planning, which range from detailed 200–page documents to unwritten 'orientations'. Neat theoretical approaches with successive stages of analysis, choice and implementation are rarely seen in practice. The organizational characteristics of a firm, and the environmental constraints upon it, affect and sometimes transform the process:

> Seldom is there an easily isolated logic to strategic change. Instead that process may derive its motive force from an amalgam of economic, personal and political imperatives. [. . .] The application of over-rational, linear programmes of HRM as a means of securing competitive success is shown to be at odds with experience both in the UK and elsewhere.
>
> (Whipp 1992: 33)

Whipp concludes that control of the environmental, organizational and strategic aspects of both competition and human resources is so problematic that the relationship between the two can only be indirect and fragile. Another critical factor is that the human resource is but one of the resources of the firm. Strengths and weaknesses in other areas, such as marketing and finance, may obscure the best people management.

Whipp also points to the environmental context within which HR strategy is implemented. We have discussed cultural influences already. Individual companies also have their own control and industrial relations traditions. Attempts to import HRM into British companies and link it to business strategy have foundered because many organizations have no tradition of strategy.

The greatest difficulties are experienced in large, diversified organizations with a wide range of interests. They are highlighted in recession when the business needs do not fit with 'soft' HR values. HR strategies may focus on redundancies, and sacking employees inevitably damages or destroys a caring corporate image. Legge (1989) outlines a strategy described as **tough**

love – being cruel to be kind – in which employees are expected to be both dedicated and disposable. In fact, human resource strategy may only be unproblematic in the ideal circumstances described by Guest (1987):

- It should take place within a purpose-built modern location, a **green-field** site employing carefully selected 'green' labour. Such staff would have no previous experience of the industry in which the company operates and therefore would be untarnished by an 'undesirable' industrial subculture. They would not be hide-bound by traditional but outmoded ways of doing things.
- The organization requires highly **professional management**, preferably Japanese or American.
- Employees should be given **intrinsically rewarding work** rather than uninteresting functions for which pay is the sole motivation.
- Workers should have **security of employment** and not be constantly in fear of losing their jobs.

Guest acknowledges that these conditions are difficult to achieve in practice since most organizations, Japanese transplant factories excepted, have pre-existing staff, buildings and equipment which cannot be discarded. They bring with them patterns of power and behaviour which may be contrary to the HR philosophy.

More positively, human resource strategies can be aimed at improving an organization's competitiveness by increasing its 'knowledge base' or competence (Whipp 1992). This includes shedding old values and techniques in favour of new ones. It requires a collective change of the organization's shared worldview – including perceptions of the company and the market. Organizational competences are the sum product of the competences of the workforce. This suggests that people management should drive rather than follow business strategy, by building employee competences through selection, assessment, reward and development. In the next chapter we elaborate further on the building of organizational competence with an examination of a fundamental aspect of people management: resourcing.

Change strategies

Enthusiasts have seen a transformational power in HRM, quoting major corporations such as IBM and Marks & Spencer which emphasize HRM-type values in their mission statements (Tyson 1995: 28). In fact transformation, or change, is an inevitable consequence of many human resource strategies. In the remainder of this chapter we will consider various kinds of change initiatives from both a strategic and an implementational perspective. Change initiatives fall into one of two types: turnaround change and organizational transformation (Bertsch and Williams 1994).

- **Turnaround change** – financially driven, often to ensure corporate survival by cutting unprofitable products and services. It involves the redesign of organizational structures, disposal of non-core activities and large-scale redundancies. This kind of change is painful but straightforward since existing hierarchical control systems can administer the process.

- **Behavioural transformations** – changing behaviour patterns throughout the company. Hierarchical control is inadequate because different power centres are likely to conflict and differences between business units make behavioural consistency a difficult objective to achieve.

Whatever the strategic purpose and product of change, its organization is likely to take the form of one of three models (Buchanan and Boddy 1992):

- **Project management.** This is a rational, linear problem-solving approach, very much in the tradition of classical business strategy, outlined earlier in this chapter. Decisions are generated at the top and orchestrated by a project manager who assigns objectives, allocates budgets and responsibilities, and sets deadlines. The project management model embodies a control mechanism which monitors progress in the determined direction.
- **Participative management.** This model takes more account of the skills and concerns of people affected by the change at lower levels of the organization. It involves a degree of emergent strategy. This approach is more time-consuming for managers and runs the risk of deviating into side issues. Participative management may lead to changes being blocked by inflexible interest groups. In general, however, it is more compatible with concepts of empowerment, commitment and team management.
- **Political perspective.** This framework goes further in accepting and dealing with interpersonal and cultural aspects of change. It reflects an awareness of power distribution within an organization and of the reasons for resistance. It is most useful when there is a lack of clarity or agreement over the objectives of the firm or the need for strategic change. This approach has particular relevance in comprehending the effects of mergers and takeovers. It requires front-stage political 'performances' from senior managers, together with Machiavellian intrigue in building behind-the-scenes power blocks and undermining resistance.

Each model has its merits and disadvantages. Individual organizations may also employ combinations of more than one approach.

Restructuring

Restructuring is the most common form of major organizational change (see key concept 6.3). According to its protagonists, restructuring should not be a defensive cost-cutting process but rather a proactive attempt to achieve innovative products and services: 'focus without fat' (Kanter 1989: 58). The goal should be **synergy** (see key concept 6.4).

Restructuring usually involves **reorganization**, a move from one form of organization to another. For example, a business may change from a divisional to a network structure (see Chapter 4). This requires the breaking up

KEY CONCEPT 6.3 *Restructuring*	Breaking up and recombining organizational structures. Advantages include reduced costs, elimination of duplication, greater efficiency. Disadvantages include disorder, interfering with normal activities; destruction of long-term commitment; loss of direction, especially in careers; overwork from excessive cost-cutting. Recent strategic thinking has also emphasized the importance of relating business objectives to core organizational competences. In other words, organizations should do what they are good at, leading to a new trend for companies to **demerge** – to split into focused activity areas on which separate management teams can concentrate.

KEY CONCEPT 6.4 *Synergy*	Making the new whole worth more than its old parts, sometimes described as '2+2=5'. Synergies involve economies from integrating activities – horizontally or vertically – but also unrealized potential for new ideas, products or processes by melding expertise from the different sources into centres of excellence.

of the previous hierarchy or departmental structure. Some organizations are notoriously prone to reorganizations at intervals of two to three years or less, with the consequences of the last restructuring not being fully absorbed and analysed before being swept up in the next. The difficulty for corporate management comes in the attempt to achieve both synergy and workable new diversified or decentralized structures at one and the same time (Marginson 1993: 7; cited in Purcell 1995: 70). Public statements through the media and shareholder information normally present such changes as deliberate and thought-through, the implication being that restructuring would be dealt with by means of a project management approach. However, the notion that restructuring is usually decided at the most senior level on the grounds of balance-sheet rationality is often illusory (Purcell 1995: 70). As we observed in earlier discussions on strategy and management, when faced with uncertainty, complex situations and conflict within the organization, managers typically resort to 'political' decision-making.

Unfortunately, as we concluded earlier, employees are a secondary consideration of change in free-market organizations (Wilmott 1995: 313). Participative management is squeezed out in favour of the project management or political approach. Developing on Wilmott's question 'will the turkeys vote for Christmas?' (1995: 306), it is evident that they are generally kept in the dark until it is too late. Hence, little account is taken of the people who will be disrupted by the process and those who have to maintain quality and value during a period of major upheaval. Often the principal role of people managers is to sort out the resulting mess and smooth ruffled feathers.

There are also financial costs associated with 'churn' – simply moving people around. This has been estimated as £1.5 billion a year in the UK alone (*The Financial Times*, 22 November 1995). The costs can be as great as

£2,000 per employee from the first year that people are shuffled until new structures settle down.

Shrinkage

As we observed earlier, focusing on core activities and disposing of others has become particularly fashionable. In some cases, businesses have decided that management control and shareholder value are best served by a demerger, for example the hiving off of Zeneca from ICI or the split of British Gas into distribution and retailing companies. More commonly, shrinkage involves downsizing – reducing the number of employees. In either case, HR managers are involved in communicating the change, conducting union negotiations and arranging redundancies or redeployment.

A particular concern is the cost-effectiveness of individual employees and departments. The more expensive they are, the greater is the degree of justification required to retain them. For example, the 'delayering' initiatives of recent years have focused on expensive middle managers. Kanter suggests that 'overhead' functions such as divisional headquarters have a duty to justify themselves to the business units they are meant to support (1989: 94). Approval and checking delay decision-making, hindering the ability to compete. Wherever possible, these should be eliminated completely or transferred to the business units whose activities are involved. Decentralization is a dominant force, leaving small, slimmed-down central functions.

Restructuring can be dangerous if companies treat people purely as costs rather than as assets. Kanter points to the inevitable 'discontinuity, disorder and distraction' which interfere with people's normal activities. She concludes that 'top management typically *overestimates* the degree of co-operation it will get and *underestimates* the integration costs' (1989: 62).

Cowboy management in these circumstances can destroy long-term commitment since restructuring removes many of life's certainties. Most of us try to create a state of order and predictability around our jobs. Restructuring can destroy this. No longer can we count on a job for life with any one company, but some sense of direction is essential to preserve motivation and obtain the best performance. Neither can people be expected to cope with overwork caused by excessive cost-cutting. According to American experience, much downsizing is really 'dumb-sizing', since two-thirds of the companies who have slashed workforces in recent years report no increase in efficiency. Often the principal role of human resource specialists is in rescuing the situation after the change has happened. Motivation and commitment must be rebuilt and skills training made available for staff involved in new tasks.

Incremental change

In the 1960s and 1970s, change often came under the label of organizational development (OD), relying on a methodology described as **action research**. This was an undramatic – but effective – long-term change process based on incremental improvements, effectively on a continuous flow of emergent strategies. With the advent of modern change pro-grammes such as business process re-engineering (BPR), this low-risk and long-term approach has gone out of fashion. However, as we can see from Table 6.3, its underlying principles are similar to Japanese methods of continuous improvement and the methodology has considerable parallels with the radical change initiatives described later in this chapter.

Competitive pressures often demand a faster, more dramatic process than action research. Many modern managers would question whether their organization had the time required. More pertinently, we can ask if ambitious executives on short-term contracts have enough time to make their mark with such a slow methodology. It is likely that a glossier and more public method will be better appreciated. This is provided by **pack-aged**, or 'off-the-shelf', approaches, which begin with top management and are cascaded down the organization. They are normally dramatized, with considerable emphasis on communication and a spotlight placed on the lead personality.

In the 1980s most large organizations engaged in **total quality manage-ment** (TQM) programmes, focusing on continuous improvement, quality assurance and zero faults. TQM programmes are geared to organizational processes such as production. HR involvement includes the selection of flexible people who are amenable to increasingly demanding levels of quality.

Business process re-engineering (BPR)

Re-engineering is a methodology of the 1990s (see key concept 6.5) which has inspired many change strategies. The technique was first publicized by Hammer (1990) in a Harvard Business Review article entitled

Table 6.3 Themes of organization development

1 Top management support	Initiatives will not succeed unless higher management levels are fully committed to the change process and its maintenance.
2 Problem-solving and renewal process	Allows adaptability and viability to be generated in an organization which may be living in the past. This should allow the organization continually to redefine its purpose.
3 Collaborative diagnosis and management of culture	The process of change must involve all levels within the organization in a search for ideas which will lead to improvement. This is a non-hierarchical, shared evaluation of the culture and long-term goals of the organization.
4 Formal work team	Focusing on work groups, group dynamics and team development.
5 Consultant-facilitator	Bringing in an external change agent or catalyst experienced in the mechanics of change, able to spot resistance and unbiased by any prevailing agenda.
6 Action research	A primary feature of classic organizational development which is absent in many modern packaged initiatives.

Source: adapted from French and Bell (1990).

> A 'fundamental rethinking and radical redesign of business processes to achieve dramatic improvements in critical contemporary measures of performance, such as cost, quality, service and speed' (Hammer and Champy 1993).
>
> **KEY CONCEPT 6.5**
> ***Business process re-engineering***

'Re-engineering work: don't automate, obliterate'. In typical guru fashion he outlined amazing benefits in a range of companies, proclaiming the existence of seven fundamental principles of re-engineering:

● Organize around outcomes, not tasks.
● Those who use the output should perform the process.
● Information processing work should be subsumed into the real work that produces the information.
● Geographically dispersed resources should be used as though they were centralized.
● Link parallel activities instead of integrating tasks.
● Decisions should be taken where work is performed and control built into the process.
● Information should only be captured once – at source.

BPR appears under the guise of a number of similar terms and a variety of definitions. Depending on the definition used, re-engineering can involve change in individual work tasks, in interpersonal work processes within a department, between sections of a business, or beyond the boundaries of a firm in a networked or virtual organization. Critics argue that perhaps it is no more than organization and methods (O&M), TQM and just-in-time 'dusted down and repackaged' (Burke and Peppard 1995: 28).

Nevertheless, BPR has swept across the western business world. Companies such as AT&T, BT, Ford, Mercury and Rank Xerox have used the methodology. A recent survey found no fewer than 3,500 articles on the subject in an online database search (Jones 1995: 44). Why is it apparently so popular? Instead of 5–10 per cent improvements from other methods, the proponents of re-engineering promise 30 per cent, 50 per cent or even more. BPR requires a total rethinking of the organization from the bottom up – rather than tinkering with an existing situation.

Hammer and Champy present a **process** perspective in contrast to the functional basis of most businesses. Hence, organizations and departments are not re-engineered, but processes are. For instance, the process of order fulfilment is everything from an order request to delivery to the customer, regardless of department or level. Hammer and Champy argue that traditional hierarchical structures 'stifle innovation and creativity'. Instead, new technology should be introduced to cut out stages and people in a process. Moreover, a multi-skilled team should be employed, able to deal with a process as a whole. In all, they describe ten interrelated changes which Grint (1995: 83) traces to much earlier origins (see Table 6.4). In fact, an examination of these change principles reveals some strong links between

Table 6.4   Origins of change principles in business process re-engineering

1 Switch from functional departments to processes	Principle of 1950s socio-technical systems and Volvo Kalmar experiment
2 Move from simple tasks to multi-dimensional work	1970s Quality of Working Life and job enrichment
3 Reversal of power relationship from superordinate to subordinate empowerment	Seen in both above
4 Shift from training to education	A criticism of British 'education' since the nineteenth century
5 From payment for attendance to payment for value added	Common in Ancient Greece
6 Bifurcation of link between reward for current performance and advancement through assessment of ability	The 'Peter Principle' – every employee tends to rise to his or her level of incompetence
7 From concern for boss to concern for customer	See modern Japan
8 Managers become coaches rather than supervisors	Hawthorne experiments – USA 1930s
9 Flattening of hierarchies	Kalmar experiments
10 Executives move from being scorekeepers to leaders	Human relations

Source: adapted from Grint (1995).

BPR and concepts, such as empowerment and facilitatory management, associated with HRM elsewhere in this book.

Business process re-engineering also has close parallels with the notion of a 'learning organization' which we will discuss in Chapter 11. BPR works on the principle that an organization cannot learn before it has first unlearned. BPR does this by starting with a 'blank piece of paper' approach, using techniques such as cognitive mapping and soft systems methodology. These are diagramatic methods aimed at tapping creativity and ensuring that a holistic approach is taken:

- Have a vision.
- Identify and understand the current processes.
- Redesign the processes.
- Implement the redesigned processes.

Matters become even more confusing when one asks 'who does it?' It is simultaneously presented as an **empowering** programme, with fine rhetoric about team working, multi-skilling and flattened hierachies, and as a top-down exercise demanding (as ever) commitment from senior executives! Of course, consultants have to remember who pays the bill. Perhaps the true emphasis is reflected in the key roles required for re-engineering, as presented by Hammer and Champy:

- **Leader** – a visionary and motivator.
- **Process owner** – sufficiently senior to oversee the entire process to be re-engineered.

- **Re-engineering team** – composed of insiders who understand present activities and outsiders to question assumptions.
- **Steering committee** (optional) – to oversee the organization's re-engineering as a whole.
- **Re-engineering czar** - the operational head of the organization's re-engineering activities.

Clearly, this is a directed process. Employees may be 'permitted and required to think, interact, use judgement, and make decisions' but this applies only to the workers who are allocated jobs after the process has been re-engineered, eliminating one or two departments along the way. The attractiveness to senior executives is evident in the promise of redundancy; the benefits to employees are somewhat less obvious. Clearly, therefore, Willmott's 'turkeys' may be less than keen to cooperate, but this appears not to be a problem to the proponents of BPR:

> any employee hostility to BPR is interpreted not as warrantable resistance but as irrationality or inertia which can be overcome by effective leadership and commitment from top management. Hammer notes that the disruption and confusion generated by re-engineering can make it unpopular. But he is equally confident that any opposition can be effectively surmounted by top-level managers.
>
> (Willmott 1995: 311–2)

Burke and Peppard (1995: 34) identify a number of further barriers to implementing BPR:

- There is a paradox in that people with knowledge of a particular process are unlikely to have the authority to redesign it, and vice versa.
- Redesign disturbs existing patterns of power in an organization. The power base may not coincide with senior management but with a 'dominant coalition' with a vested interest in frustrating BPR.
- The firm's culture may work against a process-based organization and consequent changes in work practices, job content and relationships.
- Within multinational companies, processes may cross national boundaries, bringing in further difficulties.

Given the importance of employees in implementing BPR, and the embodiment of strong ideas about people management in its basic texts, it is surprising to find that human resource issues have scarcely been addressed (Wilmott 1995: 306). Tinaikar *et al.*, in a survey of 248 articles on BPR, found that:

> Almost all of the articles (95.9 per cent) portray BPR as being concerned with only technical issues. The few articles discussing social issues such as empowerment of the lower levels, resistance to change, etc., focused primarily on the managerially relevant benefits of BPR. Cost-cutting through technology and downsizing, or the politically correct 'rightsizing', were some of the most common themes. However, the implications of this potential job loss through BPR were singularly neglected.
>
> (Tinaikar *et al.* 1995: 109)

They conclude that the human aspect has been trivialized in the BPR literature. However, it is not unreasonable to wonder if this lack of concern for people may be partly responsible for the high failure rate of re-engineering initiatives.

Strategic alliances

Redesign or restructuring may take place within one organization or go beyond its boundaries, perhaps as a result of the combination of one firm with another. There are several relevant variables to consider at the strategic stage:

- **Strategic intent.** Regardless of negotiated positions and public positions of the partner companies, what are their long-term intentions? Are they committed to a joint venture? Does one partner intend to achieve control? Managers will be wary of losing their power.
- **Consolidation.** How much autonomy and organizational independence is to be allowed? Mergers and acquisitions tend towards much greater consolidation than joint ventures and consortia. Employees feel threatened by the obvious opportunities for staff reduction.
- **Cultural integration.** Is cultural plurality to be respected? Does the alliance intend a common culture? If so, will it be based on the culture of the dominant partner or a negotiated hybrid? Being forced to change familiar ways is threatening.

Alliances and mergers draw on the capacity and potential of participants but they have a poor history of success. Surveys shown that over 50 per cent of mergers and acquisitions fail to achieve strategic objectives – often disastrously. A McKinsey & Company study of mergers between 1972 and 1982 (involving 200 of the largest US corporations) found increased value to shareholders in just 23 per cent of mergers. One-third of successful mergers were in relatively small takeovers of closely related businesses. The explanation seems to have attracted yet another analogy with poultry, although the meaning is quite different: 'You don't put two turkeys together and make an eagle!' (unnamed economist, quoted in Peters 1987: 8). Often the advantages are outweighed by the disadvantages (Porter 1990):

- **Restructuring costs**, including redundancy payments, consultancy and legal fees, accommodation transfer.
- **Strategic difficulties**, the harmonization of goals and objectives.
- **Organizational problems.** Difficulties in coordinating two different structures; overloading the parent organization's management systems; reorganization taking attention away from day to day activities.
- **Behavioural problems** and barriers. Managers fight to preserve their territories or take over others; motivation falls when staff feel they have been taken over by remote managers:

> Most of the evidence suggests that a failure to acknowledge the human dimension undermines many potentially successful ventures. [. . .] There is a feeling that if 'the figures are right' all else will follow smoothly. Wrong! It is precisely 'all else' that can frustrate the best laid plans of marketing men and accountants as cultures fail to gell and key executives engage in destructive battles for dominance.
>
> (Mackay 1992: 10)

The nature of the power relationship is particularly significant. Many studies show that acquisitions are notoriously unsuccessful because of the manner of the takeover. Specifically, the benefits of an acquisition or merger can be destroyed by the way in which the merger process is handled. Staff working for new owners tend to feel defensive and threatened. It is almost as if they have been colonized. Similar feelings are experienced when internal restructuring results in merged departments or the absorption of one section by another. Frequently, takeovers are handled insensitively. Acquisitions and mergers bring power differences into sharp and highly visible focus. There is a temptation to charge into the acquired firm or department or to take a condescending attitude. Many takeovers have parallels with the Sack of Rome. The new managers are inclined to feel superior and to regard methods which are different from their own as inefficient or second rate: 'Arrogance and organizational chauvinism on the "conqueror's" part lead to defensiveness and concern on the other side. People sense a loss of power to determine their own fate' (Kanter 1989: 65). Arrogance can destroy the essence of the company. Strangers in suits wander about the organization, misunderstanding what they see. Observation is accompanied by sniggers and sneering comments, serving to boost the acquiring management team's egos and sense of superiority. Mackay describes this as 'tribal warfare' (1992: 10) – one culture trying to assert preeminence over the other. The consequences are serious. This is not simply a matter of upsetting workers, important though that may be in terms of its consequences on morale and cooperation. There is a considerable risk of throwing the baby out with the bathwater by obliterating the victim's processes before their consequences and rationale are fully understood. Case 6.4 describes the merger of Sperry and Burroughs to form Unisys, which has been presented as a model of successful communication.

Unisys originated in a 'hostile' takeover of Sperry by Burroughs. Initially, the merger was heavily criticized by Wall Street analysts. However, the Chief Executive, Michael Blumenthal, had a clear vision of the combined firm and set out to confront anxieties and uncertainties directly. Good communication was required to prevent the 'merger syndrome': conflict, apathy, depression, departure and low productivity. This syndrome comes from unanswered questions going through the minds of the staff who have been acquired:

CASE 6.4
Unisys

- Will I lose my job?
- Will I be promoted or demoted?
- Will my salary and benefits change?
- Will I have to move?
- What will the organization be like: will its values, the kind of people employed and commercial objectives change?
- How long will the transition period take?

Blumenthal formed a merger-coordination council, including senior executives from both businesses, supported by taskforces which investigated ways of structuring and consolidating the merged organization. Efforts were also made to create a unified culture with:

- 'The Power of 2', a clear vision of the new business;

- supporting speeches by senior managers;
- the development of a sense of partnership between the two companies;
- sensitization groups and counselling sessions;
- newsletters reporting merger activities;
- a 'name the company' competition;
- continuing feedback to the employees throughout the process.

The merger was not devoid of problems. There were instances of 'in-fighting' between rival executives, of politics, distrust and fear of losing jobs to the 'other side'. Nevertheless, in terms of staff turnover and satisfaction, the merger seemed to be successful.

(*Source*: Mackay 1992: 14.)

Employee fears and anxieties can be minimized, but research shows that people who have been 'taken over' continue to be suspicious and uncomfortable in the new organization for some time.

Behavioural transformation

We noted earlier that the most difficult form of change involves modifying employees' attitudes, behaviour and commitment. Initiatives may come about as a result of deliberate strategic planning. Frequently, however, the process begins with a vague feeling amongst board members that there is 'something wrong' within the organization even though they are uncertain as to what it might be. The feeling may be fuelled by customer dissatisfaction, failure of innovation, conflict between departments or financial difficulties. The popularity of guru ideas and the spread of HRM have encouraged many senior executives to look to their people in order to improve overall organizational performance, quality of service and productivity:

> It is impossible to plan an effective change programme without first defining what cultural change aims to achieve and how this differs from the existing situation. The objective of many organizations in managing cultural change is to move from a static or rigid culture to one that is flexible and adaptable.
>
> (Fowler 1993: 25)

Fowler suggests that the process could begin with a theoretical comparison of static and adaptable cultures. Such a scale might include thirty items and would focus on the nature of the initiative, for example quality or customer care. The current organization is then scored on this scale. Frequently, detailed and accurate information does not exist in a form which allows this to be done. This can be gathered from a 'where are we now?' exercise, normally taking the form of **survey research and feedback**. Typically, this involves the use of questionnaires and structured interviews at all levels of the organization. Research can focus on employee attitudes towards:

- the organization;
- its methods;
- communication channels;
- company culture;
- customers;
- mechanisms for initiating and sustaining innovation and change.

Data is collated and a preliminary analysis fed back to the 'top team' and other interested parties, such as trade unions. After discussion – possibly involving a reappraisal of the company's mission and core values – action is agreed with the consultancy. To gain full cooperation it is best to discuss and agree the programme with employees and their representatives. Conventionally, the purpose and manner of any change is introduced to staff through presentations, discussions, videos, staff magazines and newspapers.

An example of this kind of process can be seen at Christian Salvesen Group, who issued a pilot questionnaire to head-office and other staff in 1993. The survey was designed to find out what employees thought about the company. Apart from some positive comments, three areas of concern were highlighted by the Chief Executive, Chris Masters:

> First, as an organization we are still not making the maximum use of the talents of our people. We need to work much harder to ensure that we fully recognise these talents, that where appropriate we improve on them, and that we increase the opportunities for our people to develop within the whole company rather than just one part of it.
>
> Second, we need to improve our internal communications. I believe passionately that the more our people know about the business and what we are trying to achieve the better and I believe that all of us have a part to play.
>
> Third, we still suffer from internal politics in some of our operations. Internal politics are a destructive force in any organisation. I am determined that Christian Salvesen should be an open company in which people are valued just as much for the contributions they make as for the position they hold.
>
> Openness and honesty is the way forward and that is what we all must promote.
>
> (Christian Salvesen Group company magazine: *Salvo*, winter 1993: 4)

Action to improve such a situation could involve a cascading process in which groups of interested employees are asked to consider the data in relation to the company's core values. Staff could then be encouraged to suggest improvements and innovations and to take responsibility for seeing them through. There are instances of successful behavioural transformations in existing businesses, using a culture-change approach. For example, at Land Rover staff – or rather associates – on the production line were asked to work to the maxim 'each associate has two jobs, their work and the improvement of their work'. Many employees were middle-aged and had been with Land Rover for most of their working lives. Yet they adopted the Japanese 'transplant' ways which supposedly require 'green labour'. Associates were grouped in teams and trained for a variety of jobs so that anyone missing due to illness or other cause could be covered by the team. Personal responsibility for their own performance, together with an emphasis on teamwork, produced a productivity gain of 28 per cent in two years.

Negative change

Implicitly, anyone opposing change is viewed as negative. Often, however, change is a destructive process and the end-product is inferior to the original. This may be disguised by redefining quality requirements so that the lowering of standards becomes invisible or obscured. Newcomers to the situation know no better. Many may be involved in the change process and have a commitment to perceiving it as being necessary.

A redefinition of quality coincides inevitably with a change in the nature and flow of information, making a true 'before and after' comparison impossible. The proponents of change are unlikely to present their initiatives as failures; antagonists will never be happy with modifications in methods they have cherished. In the absence of objective evidence, debate is reduced to political confrontation, with opponents of organizational change labelling new approaches as 'change for change's sake'. In fact, this is rarely the case. Change is difficult and disruptive and is not lightly entered into, but the true reasons for change may differ from its public justifications.

For example, we noted earlier that change is commonly associated with new management. This is not a coincidence. New managers have to work hard if the status quo is left alone. They are forever at the mercy of old networks and power balances. It is far easier to highlight deficiencies in the current situation, pronounce it to be lacking in quality, and sweep it away to be replaced with another of their own making. Power-holders in the old networks can be eliminated or sidelined; there are always ambitious replacements available who are willing to become loyal to the new regime. Young or formerly disaffected staff will show a naive enthusiasm for their newfound opportunities. Even better – from this somewhat cynical perspective – people can be imported from outside the organization who will be anxious to perform as required.

Summary

Strategic thinking has its basis in rational thinking. In practice, strategists have accepted that there must be a place for the unexpected. Strategy and planning provide a framework for human resource requirements over a defined period but traditional personnel managers have experienced difficulty in understanding and implementing strategy. Human resource strategies tend to focus on numbers and also attitudes, behaviour and commitment in line with harder 'matching' models of HRM, but their implementation is problematic.

People managers are involved in dealing with the consequences of reorganization, including closure and redundancies. In a more positive way, they are concerned with growth and strategic alliances. Some of the problems they face include relocation, changing roles and retraining for new skills. More difficult issues come from attempts at cultural change or behavioural transformations. These are notoriously expensive and unsuccessful but are sometimes inevitable and can hold the key to future success.

Further reading

Hendry's (1995) *Human Resource Management: A Strategic Approach to Employment* provides a comprehensive discussion of HR strategy in its widest meaning and includes a number of case study examples. Mintzberg's (1994) *The Rise and Fall of Strategic Planning* is a happily cynical discussion of strategic planning which does not cover HRM explicitly but outlines its business planning context. Legge (1995b) includes a useful chapter on the link between HRM and business strategy in *Human Resource Management: Rhetorics and Realities*. Carnall's (1991) *Managing Change* provides a prescriptive guide to change management, outlining a project management approach. Applications of specific change management techniques, including just-in-time, are further discussed in *New Wave Manufacturing Strategies: Organizational and Human Resource Management Dimensions*, edited by Storey (1994), and in *Organizational Change: A Processual Approach*, by Dawson (1994). The latter provides a number of illuminating case examples from Australia. Hammer and Champy's (1993) *Reengineering the Corporation: A Manifesto for Business Revolution* outlines their thinking. *Examining Business Process Re-engineering: Current Perspectives and Research Directions*, edited by Burke and Peppard (1995), provides a critical overview of the subject.

Review questions

1 What is a strategy? What is meant by first-, second- and third-order strategies?
2 Is HRM really 'strategic'? How does human resource strategy fit into the business planning process?
3 In your own words, describe the difference between strategic and operational HRM.
4 Is it possible to demonstrate that human resource strategies are vital for business success?
5 Within any organization, how are management styles and corporate culture likely to influence human resource strategy?
6 What are the ideal conditions for the implementation of a human resource strategy?
7 Describe the likely consequences of a merger on the human resource strategies of component companies.
8 Outline the role of human resource strategy in the management of change. What problems arise from:

● restructuring?
● behavioural transformation?

9 Discuss the human resource implications of:

- change from a divisional to a network structure;
- merger with a larger company.

10 Why do many change initiatives fail to produce sustained change?
11 When would you use an external consultant rather than an in-house human resource specialist to organize a change programme?

Problems for analysis and discussion

1 Supreme Sportscars makes high-powered luxury cars. Due to the limited manufacturing capacity, sales have been steady at 190 vehicles a month since 1992, with a two-year waiting list. The factory is poorly equipped, with a large proportion of the work being done by traditional hand methods. However, the company has always been profitable at this level. The staff are loyal but modestly paid. They take pride in their craftsmanship and the reputation of the cars. They have close relationships with the lower-level managers, most of whom were promoted from the ranks.

Five years ago, the company was acquired by a major US manufacturer. Initially, the American company had significant expansion plans based on a small and cheaper sports car. Under a new Chief Executive, the corporate strategy has changed and now the parent company is looking to dispose of Supreme, possibly by means of a management buy-out. Design of the small car is virtually complete but nothing has been done to increase production capacity. There are two key executives at Supreme. The current Managing Director is Arnold Davies, a 45-year-old marketing man. He was recruited by the parent company last year after a career spent mainly in promoting and advertising washing machines and refrigerators. He has few academic or technical qualifications but is an intelligent, decisive man with a reputation for getting things done. A flamboyant character, he drives a bright red Supreme from the top end of the range. The staff have accepted him but do not have great respect for his managerial qualities. He believes in leading from the front and has asked your management consultancy to advise him on the merits of a management buy-out.

You are aware that a large multinational car manufacturer is interested in acquiring Supreme and badging its own cars under this name. They would establish a new production facility to make these cars. They would not consider a joint venture but they might be prepared to take some of the management team and the design unit. The parent company of Supreme is wary of selling the company to the multinational in case this encourages further competition for their other products.

The Divisional Accountant, Jeff Mathias, is an important figure in any decision. He is a long-term staff member of the US company, well qualified and experienced. He is a quiet but firm person, known to be open to new ideas but also very loyal to his employers. He is respected by the other managers, although the nature of his work isolates him from the day-to-day running of the factory. He is well paid but is conscious that he will never become rich working for the US company. Mathias is also aware that the parent company is about to announce major job cuts worldwide because of heavy losses in the US and declining sales in Europe.

This is your first impression of the problem. How would you proceed with collecting relevant information, determining the crucial issues and devising the decision strategy?

2   The West Five Care Trust controls four hospitals in a suburban area. Two of the hospitals are modern and have extra accommodation space. The other two are old but prestigious specialist units located in expensive areas. The trust considers that it would make considerable financial sense to close the older hospitals and transfer their functions to the modern sites. Several specialist consultants are extremely unhappy about the consequences and have launched a public campaign to save the specialist units. This has angered the General Manager, who has only just presented the plan as a proposal to the management committee. He considers the consultants to be disloyal as they have taken a confidential business matter to the press. He is also baffled since the new hospitals would offer them far better facilities.

The General Manager was recently recruited from industry and has been keen to exercise his right to manage. In his first six months, he successfully contracted out cleaning and catering, brushing aside union opposition. He has also instituted stringent cost-control measures and now vets all budget requests personally, including expenses for attending conferences.

As Human Resources Manager how would you analyse the situation and how could you help?

7

Resourcing: plans and strategies

This chapter outlines the role of strategy and planning in the employee resourcing process. Forecasting, information collection and decision-making are considered in the context of flexibility.

Resourcing is a major issue for people managers. Not surprisingly, HRM and other management literature puts great emphasis on the process of selecting and socializing new recruits (Guest 1992; Storey 1989). Textbooks in the personnel management tradition devote considerable space to **how** recruitment and selection are best conducted (for example, Torrington and Hall 1995: 212). As we will see in Chapter 8, the topic range has a well-rehearsed familiarity because selection methods are regarded as basic tools for personnel managers. Indeed, the underlying 'best practice' model has achieved the status of a holy writ in the UK. Any deviation is regarded as heresy in certain quarters.

Many recent HRM texts have followed this line. Others, particularly those written by commentators with a firmly academic background, have gone to the opposite extreme, sniffily avoiding discussion of mere 'tools'. Instead the subject is skirted or else discussed at a high – and somewhat unreal – sociological level. We can take our choice, it seems, between superficial accounts of selection techniques and incomprehensible debates about postmodernist resourcing. Neither approach is adequate.

The basis of people management lies in how work gets done and who does it. Therefore, the rationale behind **why** we should decide on one solution rather than another is fundamental to HRM. There are important issues involved at all levels of analysis. At the environmental level, employee resourcing takes place against a background of:

● fluctuating economic conditions and global competition;
● choice and availability within the local job market;
● competition for scarce skills.

At the organizational level, the structure and functions of an enterprise are composed of the tasks which people perform. Allocating work to unsuitable or inadequately skilled people reduces the effectiveness of the whole organization. The consequences can be significant and – particularly with high-level or specialized work – may be critical to its future performance. Employee resourcing is no longer a matter of recruiting and selecting new people to fit existing posts. As we saw in earlier chapters, organizations have a range of 'flexible' alternatives.

At the strategic level, employee resourcing involves decisions on:

- subcontracting or creating vacancies;
- allocating tasks;
- choice of selection methods.

As an activity, it is a major element of the work of human resource specialists, involving considerable technical expertise.

Employee resourcing is also a subject of vital importance at a personal level because most of us have to apply for jobs: probably the first practical aspect of human resource management we encounter. In many cases it is a frustrating and sometimes baffling process of rejection. Readers in employment may well participate on both sides of the issue – as selectors or as applicants. Inevitably, therefore, resourcing deserves serious discussion. In this chapter we focus initially on **why** resourcing decisions are taken.

The first section of the chapter begins with a consideration of the environmental constraints on resourcing and discusses the implications of the move towards flexible organizations. Next we determine the nature of resourcing strategy and consider various types. In the second major section we discuss human resource planning, examining the hard or 'people as numbers' approach – involving forecasting methods – and soft planning which takes commitment and culture into account. In the next part of the chapter we consider the use made of information gained from job analyses. We discuss the role of the job description and person specification in resourcing decisions. The chapter moves on to a debate on the merits of the 'best practice' approach in flexible organizations. Finally, we discuss strategy and planning in relation to redundancies.

Resourcing

Employee resourcing is a fundamental aspect of people management (see key concept 7.1). We can define four key stages:

- **Strategy and planning.** Determining future human resources needs in terms of availability, expertise and location. We observed in Chapter 6 that HRM literature stresses the integration of resourcing activities with other people processes, such as performance management and human resource development, as well as the overall objectives of the enterprise.
- **Research** and data collection. Determining the nature of work to be done and the criteria or competences necessary to perform it.

Additionally, obtaining adequate information about the people who possess these competences, whether as employees, consultants or sub-contractors.

● **Marketing.** Making the work known – and attractive – to potential applicants in the internal and external job markets. Conventionally this function is contained within the term 'recruitment'.

● **Decision-making.** Selection or allocation. Choosing individuals to perform the work.

KEY CONCEPT 7.1 *Employee resourcing*	Resourcing is the process by which people are identified and allocated to perform necessary work. Resourcing has two strategic imperatives: first, minimizing employee costs and maximizing employee value to the organization; second, obtaining the correct behavioural mix of attitude and commitment in the workforce. Employees are expensive assets. They must be allocated carefully and sparingly. In terms of costs and efficiency, effective resourcing depends on the care taken in deciding which tasks are worthwhile and the levels of skill and ability required to perform them.

Marketing and decision-making are discussed in Chapter 8 on recruitment and selection. In this chapter we will concentrate on strategy and planning and the research necessary to establish the need for particular jobs.

Environmental constraints on resourcing

Unlike many other aspects of people management, employee resourcing involves direct interaction between organizations and their environment. In Chapter 3 we observed that, ultimately, businesses are dependent on the external job market for the supply of suitable staff. It is the source of school-leavers and university graduates for junior posts and experienced people for senior or specialized positions. Even in conditions of high unemployment there are shortages of people with skills which are in demand. Countries such as Australia and Britain, for example, have a long record of failure to provide their young people with appropriate vocational training. If companies are unable to find staff or subcontractors with appropriate skills, their growth prospects and competitiveness are constrained. This situation may be so severe that companies are forced to relocate. Some multinationals have been forced to transfer operations from low-cost economies to high-wage countries, such as Germany, where skilled workers are available. Alternatively, businesses may compete for scarce skills through increased remuneration packages and benefits. Purcell (1989), for instance, sees star companies identified by the Boston Consulting matrix (discussed later in this chapter) as being prepared to pay above market rates to recruit and retain the best employees.

Economic changes since the mid-1970s have led to systematic responses in the attitudes and practices of employers. In his discussion of the flexible firm, Atkinson (1984) identifies a number of themes which underpin the employment plans of businesses in free-market countries:

- **Market stagnation.** Prolonged periods of recession and the increased competitiveness of world markets have produced a managerial obsession with the permanent reduction of unit employee costs.
- **Job loss.** Most large firms have undergone dramatic reductions in levels of employment. These reductions have been expensive in redundancy costs and have had significant negative effects on relations with remaining employees.
- **Uncertainty.** Despite continuous announcements of recovery, firms have been cautious about preparing for growth. In particular, they have been wary of a commitment to more full-time employees.
- **Technological change.** This is happening at an increasing pace and a reducing cost, requiring organizations – and their employees – to respond quickly by changing products, manufacturing methods and ways of working.
- **Working time.** Employers have maximized the value of employee time through restructuring work patterns to match periods of demand. This has led to a preference for part-time workers.

These factors have encouraged a move towards flexible jobs in flexible organizations.

Resourcing and the flexible organization

> The recruitment of employees with the required skills becomes a crucial responsibility and a major mechanism of control.
>
> (Blau and Schoenherr 1971: 347)

With high levels of unemployment, organizations in many countries have been able to dictate employment terms. As we observed in Chapter 3, there is a pronounced trend away from full-time work towards other job patterns. For example, at the time of writing, nine out of ten posts created in the UK are part time. We noted earlier that many businesses have distanced non-core activities – such as catering and cleaning – allocating them to external contractors. Similarly, technically specialized functions, for example the management of computer and telecommunications networks, have been subcontracted to specialist firms.

A modern flexible organization may adopt a structure along the lines of Handy's three-leaf 'shamrock' model (Handy 1989: 70):

- A **professional core** made up of managers, technicians, and qualified specialists.
- **Contractors** providing non-core activities and who are not direct employees of the organization.
- The **flexible labour force** composed of part-timers, temporary staff, consultants and contract staff performing tasks as and when required.

The allocation of work between the 'leaves' of the shamrock organization is generally decided at a senior level. The implications are considerable, often requiring main board approval, particularly for the employment of subcontractors. The decision to 'outsource' activities is usually taken on purely financial grounds, leaving people managers to clear up the resulting employee relations mess.

Resourcing strategies

Most large organizations employ human resource or personnel specialists to conduct, or at least coordinate, employee resourcing. This is a role which has long been regarded as part of the domain of personnel management. Personnel textbooks conventionally describe resourcing as a passive, technical procedure – a matching of available candidates to the requirements of the organization. In fact, successful recruitment must be proactive. Organizations can take one of three actions to fulfil their employee resourcing needs:

1 **Reallocate tasks** between employees, so that existing staff take on more or different work. This may be part of an organizational change programme, such as restructuring or reorganization. The emphasis is on flexible working practices, requiring multi-skilled workers and sophisticated assessment and development programmes.
2 **Reallocate people** from the internal employment market, through promotion or transfer between different departments. Traditionally, German and Japanese organizations have filled their supervisory and management posts from existing staff. Large Japanese organizations expect their potential managers to move between different functions during their careers. Japanese human resource managers, for instance, are likely to have worked in finance, production and marketing rather than specializing in 'personnel'.
3 **Recruit** new staff from the external job market. Countries in the free-market tradition have focused most of their resourcing activities on bringing in people from outside the organization. Employers have a choice between two types of recruitment:

- **Recruiting anybody and everybody.** Until comparatively recently, many workers in heavy industry were employed casually at the factory gate. In many parts of the world construction labourers and seasonal agricultural workers continue to be taken on in a casual fashion. With no commitment on either side, a rigid chain of command then rules. This approach predominates for employment at low-skill and low-wage levels. It is especially common in small low-technology companies.
- **Recruiting selectively.** Skilled and motivated workers are selected. These employees can be allowed to get on with the job with only broad guidelines or a policy framework to observe. This approach predominates in large organizations. The result has been the creation of an internal and external recruitment industry, including selection experts, recruitment consultants and headhunters.

External recruitment has the virtue of bringing in a wider range of experience but limits career opportunities for existing employees. It is predominantly a free-market approach to resourcing but even Japanese businesses have begun to recruit externally, particularly for scarce techno-logical skills such as computer programming. *Heddo-hantas* have become common in Japan, recruiting for small to medium-sized enterprises and foreign companies (Whitehill 1990: 129).

Types of resourcing strategy

Resourcing is a dynamic process, the movement of human resources through an organization. In terms of systems theory this can be represented as:

- input;
- throughput;
- output.

Businesses can assign people largely from existing staff or from the external job market. Companies which focus on internal supply are likely to view people as assets carrying long-term value, rather than as costs. This is in line with practice in social-market and Japanese organizations. It also reflects the spirit of the Harvard model of HRM discussed in Chapter 1. In essence the choice is between 'growing' or 'buying' (see key concept 7.2). 'Growing' is the central theme of human resource development discussed in Chapter 11. Needless to say, firms in free markets such as the UK and the USA have a tendency to 'buy' – and dispose of – employees as required.

Organizations can focus on internal or external job markets, or draw from both. Firms with an internal focus recruit at junior levels and 'grow' their employees into valuable assets through training, development and experience in the organization. Alternatively, companies can buy talent at a variety of levels from the external employment market. A mixed strategy offers a balance of continuity and commitment from long-term staff together with fresh ideas from imported 'new blood'.	**KEY CONCEPT** **7.2** *Grow or buy?*

Choices between 'growing' or 'buying' can be related to environmental conditions and organizational culture. In an early discussion of human resource strategy, Miles and Snow (1978) devised a typology based on the degree of risk taken by businesses in stable or unstable environments. They classified organizations as defenders, prospectors, analysers and reac-tors. A similar typology by Sonnenfeld *et al.* (1988) (shown in Table 7.1) uses slightly more dramatic terminology: clubs, baseball teams, fortresses and academies.

- **Defenders.** These are firms with small niche markets or narrow product ranges. As organizations they have an equally narrow focus, requiring stability and reliability. They need loyal employees with a long-term commitment. Staff enter at junior levels and are 'made' into worthwhile employees through extensive training and career development along largely functional routes. Incremental growth allows for new career opportunities within an internal job market grounded in a strong culture. Loyalty and commitment are encouraged through performance assessment based on behavioural compliance characteristics. Staff turnover is low, partly because employees are chained by organization-specific skills and a degree of institutionalization. This strategy is employed by 'clubs' in Sonnenfeld *et al.*'s (1988) classification.

- **Prospectors.** Innovative firms, moving in and out of markets to capitalize on opportunities and avoid competition. Top management consider themselves to be dynamic. Equating to Sonnenfeld *et al.*'s 'baseball teams', they are typical of sports and entertainment businesses. The instability of their marketplace requires constant flexibility and environmental scanning. In the eyes of 1970s and 1980s theorists, locked into the 'right person' recruitment models which we will discuss shortly, this could only be met by buying rather than making talent. Uncertainty does not allow for career systems, the focus being on recruitment from the external job market. New recruits have to be able to 'hit the ground running' (Rousseau 1995: 188). Rewards are high and geared to immediate results. However, commitment is low on both sides of the employment relationship: recruits are seen as 'passing through'. Learning is personal rather than organizational and knowledge leaves with the employee.

- **Analysers.** These firms are cautious innovators, waiting for prospectors to open up new markets before entering themselves. Analyser organizations are structured into stable and efficient production units with highly flexible and responsive marketing or service units. They emphasize quality and skill and equate to Sonnenfeld *et al.*'s 'academies'. As hybrids they take a mixed approach to making and buying employees: stable business units rely on internal promotion and development; flexible units buy in expertise as and when required.

- **Reactors.** These are 'fortresses' in Sonnenfeld *et al.*'s classification: failed defenders, analysers or prospectors, desperately attempting to survive. Their strategies are often incoherent, unable to 'make' employees but often 'buying' and selling. In their attempts to recover or instigate the 'turnaround' changes discussed in Chapter 6, the emphasis is likely to be on redundancies.

Human resource planning

For resourcing strategies to be implemented they must be translated into practical action. The strategic process can be organized logically – for example, following the decision sequence shown in Figure 7.1. For these decisions to be taken, information must be obtained, consequences gauged, political soundings taken and preferences assessed.

Table 7.1 Resourcing strategies

Type	Characteristics	Key HR function	Sectors
Academies	Active growers Low staff turnover Long-term service	Development	Office products Pharmaceuticals Electronics
Clubs	Passive growers Seniority Commitment Status Equal treatment	Retention or 'maintenance'	Public utilities Government Insurance Military
Baseball teams	Active buyers Staff identify with profession more than firm	Recruitment of star performers	Accounting Law Consulting Software Advertising
Fortresses	Cautious buyers Survival Cost cutting	Recruitment of generalists Redundancies	Publishing Textiles Retailing Hotels

Source: based on Sonnenfeld *et al.* (1988).

It is clear that many of these decisions are fundamental to an organization. If the implications are major, strategic decisions are taken at the centre of the business. The role of the human resource function is twofold:

- To participate in the decision process by providing information and opinion on each option, including:

  - redundancy or recruitment costs;
  - consequences on morale;
  - redeployment/outplacement opportunities;
  - availability of skilled staff within the organization;
  - availability of suitable people in the job market;
  - time constraints;
  - development/training needs/schedules;
  - management requirements.

  This forms part of the information collated from the organization as a whole.
- To support line managers dealing with the people consequences of implementing the decision. Information already gathered provides the basis for a human resource plan.

In other instances, decision-making has consequences of lesser significance to the business. Resourcing decisions taken at an operational level may lead from departmental expansion or cost-saving, transfer of activities, new product ranges and comparatively small changes in function. In practice, therefore, human resource planning has short-, medium-, and long-term aspects (see key concept 7.3).

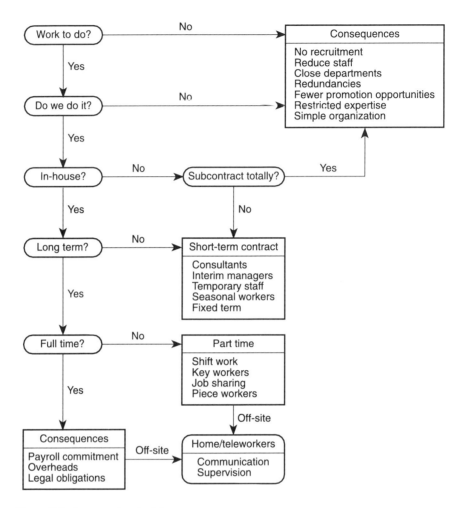

Figure 7.1 A resourcing decision sequence.

KEY CONCEPT 7.3 Human resource planning	A process which anticipates and maps out the consequences of business strategy on an organization's human resource requirements. This is reflected in planning of skill and competence needs as well as total headcounts.

Older texts refer to this topic as 'manpower planning'. (Presumably 'womanpower planning' was not much different!) Use of this quaint term has declined – but not disappeared – in favour of human resource planning (HRP). Some authors distinguish between manpower planning and HRP as distinct approaches (Hendry 1995: 190). Primarily a 'numbers game', manpower planning emphasized accurate personnel records and forecasting techniques (see key concept 7.4). It focused on questions such as:

- How many staff do we have/need?
- How are they distributed?
- What is the age profile?
- How many will leave in each of the next five years?
- How many will be required in one, five, ten years?

'A strategy for the acquisition, utilization, improvement and retention of an enterprise's human resources' (anonymous government publication cited in Pratt and Bennett 1989: 101.

KEY CONCEPT 7.4: *Manpower planning*

Some authors see little difference between HRP and manpower planning. For example Graham and Bennett define human resource planning as:

> an attempt to forecast how many and what kind of employees will be required in the future, and to what extent this demand is likely to be met. It involves the comparison of an organization's current human resources with likely future needs and, consequently, the establishment of programmes for hiring, training, redeploying and possibly discarding employees. Effective HRP should result in the right people doing the right things in the right place at precisely the right time.
>
> (Graham and Bennett 1992: 172)

The manpower planning approach regards the human resource manager as a personnel technician. Within this framework, the function of the human resource planner is to provide 'management' with the necessary advice with which to make decisions on issues such as:

- recruitment;
- avoiding redundancies;
- training – numbers and categories;
- management development;
- estimates of 'labour' costs;
- productivity bargaining;
- accommodation requirements.

Within this tradtion, Graham and Bennett envisage a long-term human resource plan as a detailed specification, by location, function and job category of the number of employees 'it is *practicable* to employ at various stages in the future' (1992: 175) (see Table 7.2). A plan should include:

- jobs which will come into being, be ceased, or changed;
- possibilities for redeployment and retraining;
- changes in management and supervision;
- training requirements;
- programmes for recruitment, redundancy and early retirement;
- implications for employee relations;
- a feedback mechanism to company objectives;
- methods for dealing with HR problems such as the inability to obtain sufficient technically skilled workers.

Table 7.2 Steps for long-term human resource planning

1 Create a company HRP group	This should include the main functional managers of the company, together with human resource specialists.
2 State the organization's human resource objectives	Within the context of the overall business objectives and considering: • capital equipment plans; • reorganization such as centralization or decentralization; • changes in products or in output; • marketing plans; • financial limitations.
3 Audit present utilization of human resources	Sometimes described as the 'internal manpower audit', detailing: • number of employees in various categories; • an estimate of employee turnover for each grade, analysing the effects of high or low turnover on performance; • amount of overtime worked; • assessment of performance and potential of current employees; • comparison of payment levels with local firms.
4 Assess the external environment	Placing the organization in its business context in terms of: • the recruitment position; • population trends; • local housing and transport plans; • national agreements dealing with conditions of work; • government policies in education, retirement, regional subsidies, and so on.
5 Assess potential supply of labour	'External manpower audit', considering: • local population movements (emigration and immigration); • recruitment and redundancy by other firms; • employing new work categories, e.g. part-time workers; • productivity improvements, working hours and practices.

Source: based on Graham and Bennett (1992).

Such a plan requires organization, belief in the process and detailed information. Not surprisingly, many organizations cannot meet these criteria. Tyson (1995: 77), reporting on a study of thirty large UK-based organizations, found that most had plans of three to five years' duration. Shorter-term plans were used by some retail firms which kept detail down to a year or so, whereas capital-intensive firms were more likely to favour long-term planning. Generally, managers were unhappy about five-year plans, regarding them as 'a constraint on business'. Tyson (1995: 80) identifies three distinct approaches to planning:

- **Formal, long-range planning**, creating a planning framework, usually expressed in financial terms with verbal commentaries. Notably, all the companies studied which used this approach consulted widely with interest groups.
- **Flexible strategies**, covering most of the organizations studied. Plans changed frequently in response to market changes. Plans were intentionally short term, often with minimal written detail.
- **Attributional strategies**, 'one step at a time'. Previous actions can be rationalized but, in truth, organizations using this approach are

cautious and are not really committed to any specific strategy. This can be compared with Mintzberg's concept of 'emergent strategies' (1994: 26) discussed in the previous chapter.

People as numbers

Generally, it is accepted that modern human resource planning should have a wider perspective, in tune with the philosophy of HRM, including 'softer' issues such as competence, commitment and career development. Modern human resource planning continues to use the 'hard' techniques of manpower planning but also includes a new focus on shaping values, beliefs and culture, anticipating strategy, market conditions and demographic change.

Nevertheless, in line with the tradition of formal, observable and 'objective' planning, numerical measurement and forecasting have been favoured over qualitative studies of opinion, attitude and motivation. 'Hard' data allows managers and planners to sit in their offices and wait for information. 'No need to go out and meet the troops, or the customers, to find out how the products get bought ... all that just wastes valuable time' (Mintzberg 1994: 258). The growth of information technology and management information systems has made numerical data readily available and possibly further discouraged collection of qualitative information. Numbers give a comforting feeling of unarguable objectivity and allow managers to detach themselves from shop-floor emotions. It is much easier to sack a number than a real human being.

Forecasting methods

Human resource planners have a choice of techniques available to them, for example:

- **Extrapolation.** This method assumes that the past is a reliable guide to the future. Various techniques are suitable for short- and medium-term forecasting, such as time series, trend analysis and measures of cyclical requirements. Since they rely on present knowledge and cannot take the unpredictable into account, forecasts are best in a stable environment. They tend to do little harm if kept pessimistic, but enthusiasm and political considerations often lead to overestimation. This can have expensive consequences.
- **Projected production/sales information.** As a normal part of the planning process, production, sales and marketing departments will prepare their own forecasts. Intelligent use of this data, taking the introduction of new technology and quality improvements into account, will provide an estimate of the quantity and nature of the human resources needed. Work study, managerial judgement and a certain amount of scepticism – particularly regarding sales forecasts – can be used to transform this information into employee requirements.
- **Employee analysis.** Modern computer packages offer extensive possibilities for modelling the total profile of an organization's human

resources. Employees can be classified in a variety of ways, such as function, department or grade. Age and length of service are important predictors of future availability. Skills levels and training or development needs can be compared with annual performance assessments.

- **Scenario building.** Scenarios are not strictly forecasts but speculations on the future. It is impossible to predict what will happen in twenty – or even five – years' time, but it is possible to describe some alternatives. Working through a variety of possible states can identify the uncertainties, help us gain an understanding on the main driving factors and produce a range of options. Given the dramatic changes and discontinuities experienced today, scenario building seems to be one of the most realistic and useful forms of planning. Instead of prescribing detailed plans, the process allows strategists to work through the consequences on resources and costs of different courses of action.

Employee turnover

In recent years managers have been preoccupied with reducing the size of the workforce, closing plants and encouraging people to leave. In times of economic growth the emphasis changes to retaining the people with required skills. Human resource planning has a role in anticipating wastage. In its 'manpower planning' days, it received considerable attention from planners for whom 'the statistical possibilities' were enormous (Pratt and Bennett 1989: 106). Turnover covers the whole input-output process from recruitment to dismissal or retirement and takes the consequences of promotion and transfer into account. Wastage deals only with leavers. Its importance lies in the freedom of employees to leave when they choose and hence its relative uncontrollable nature for employers. Early work by Rice, Hull and Trist (1950) identified three main phases of turnover:

1 **Induction crisis.** Some individuals leave shortly after joining an organization: uncommitted employees tend to leave in the first few months. Recent research appears to show that there are several kinds of induction crisis experienced in different ways in different organizations.
2 **Differential transit.** Some leave during the first year or so, when they conclude that the organization is an unsuitable career vehicle or source of income.
3 **Settled connection.** Some employees become long-term 'stayers'.

Despite the increase in flexible approaches to employment and the demise of the 'job for life' this pattern remains common. An Institute of Personnel and Development (IPD) survey of 211 British organizations found that around a quarter of workers leave their jobs in the first year (*Labour Turnover*, IPD, 1995). The highest rates of turnover, whether instigated by workers or management, are found among part-time employees. In 1994 turnover was 33 per cent for part-time manual workers and 31 per cent for non-manual part-time workers. This compared with 12 per cent for full-time manual workers and 14 per cent for full-time non-manual employees. Overall management and administrative grades had the lowest turnover rates (10 per cent).

The degree of wastage can be determined by a variety of turnover indices of varying sophistication. Three examples are:

1 The British Institute of Management (BIM) Index (annual labour turnover)

$$\frac{\text{Leavers in year}}{\text{Average number of staff in post that year}} \times 100 = \% \text{ wastage}$$

2 Cohort analysis, a survival curve is drawn of employees taken on at the same time to determine what happens to a group.
3 Census method, for example providing a histogram of the length of employee service.

'Soft' planning

HRM implies that planning has to go beyond the 'numbers game' into the softer areas of employee attitudes, behaviour and commitment. These aspects are critical to HR development, performance assessment and the management of change, which are considered in some depth in Chapters 6, 10 and 11. At this point, we can consider an outline of the process:

- **Where are we now?** Information needs to be gathered through some form of human resource audit. This can be linked to a conventional SWOT analysis of the organization's human capital:

  - **strengths** such as existing skills, individual expertise and unused talents;
  - **weaknesses**, including inadequate skills, talents which are missing in the workforce because they are too expensive, inflexible people and 'dead wood';
  - **opportunities**, such as experience that can be developed in existing staff and talent which can be bought from the external job market;
  - **threats**, including the risk of talent being lost to competitors.

- **Where do we want to be?** Essentially, what is needed is a clear strategic vision and a set of objectives.
- **What do we need to do?** For example, following the logical sequence in Figure 7.1 decisions must be made on the use of in-house or external staff (see Table 7.3).
- **Devise an action plan.**

Some kind of resource planning is used by as many as 60 per cent of large organizations but it has to be conceded that it is often done poorly. Ideally, it should be linked to corporate strategy but, as we saw in Chapter 6, corporate planners tend to ignore the human dimension.

Table 7.3 In-house and external human resources

In-house resources	Outsourcing
Management control	Legal contract
Long-term people	Focus on paying only for work you need
● can be developed	No extra pay/commitment
● build experience	Range of options, e.g.:
● understand organization	consultants
People are hassle	● variable expertise
Contractual arrangements	● expensive
● talent expensive	contingent workers
● overheads	● usually ex-managers
● large structure	● best for operational work
● hierarchy	homeworkers
● support systems	● lower level/specialist
People ambitious	● low overheads
● require advancement	● supervision issues
● can go elsewhere, taking knowledge	subcontracting

Resourcing information

Effective in-house resourcing requires accurate and comprehensive information. Strategies and human resource plans must be translated into actual jobs, and people found or developed to perform them. Some basic questions can be asked:

● What tasks are involved?
● What skills or competences are required to do the work?
● Are they to be found within the organization?
● If not, should extra people be recruited?

Researching the job

Conventionally, the first question is answered by a job analysis (key concept 7.5). Reminiscent of Taylor's techniques of 'scientific management', discussed in Chapter 1, it is a more or less detailed examination of the sub-tasks within an identified job. Jobs vary from the 'crystallized', such as manufacturing assembly where the job is precisely defined, to managerial and professional jobs, in which individuals have considerable freedom to vary their work (McCormick and Ilgen 1987: 38). The degree of freedom is determined partly by technology or personal expertise and partly by the organization. Job analysis is geared towards tasks which are already being done in some form and can be easily extrapolated from current activities.

Job analysis techniques vary from the rudimentary to the sophisticated. The latter require specialist skills and are more commonly used in the USA, where equal opportunities legislation is more stringent than in most countries. Long regarded as a somewhat tedious aspect of the personnel or work study function, job analysis has been highlighted as a valuable technique in ensuring compliance with anti-discrimination legislation in the USA. Conversely, the move towards flexible working has turned many organizations elsewhere away from closely defining jobs.

The simplest forms of job analysis are conducted by observing or interviewing existing jobholders and supervisors. Alternatively, the same people can produce a self-report according to an agreed format. Information is also available from records, 'experts', training materials, equipment descriptions and manuals. A basic six-step approach could be conducted as follows (Smith and Robertson 1993: 15):

1 Make use of relevant existing documents such as training manuals.
2 Ask the line manager responsible about the main purposes of the job, the tasks involved and the links with other people.
3 Ask the same questions of jobholders, preferably backed by a detailed activity record over a week or two.
4 Where possible, sit in and observe jobholders at work – preferably on more than one day and at different times.
5 Try to do the job yourself. (This is not possible if specialist machinery or training is required.)
6 Write the job description.

The job-related information produced by job analysis can be arranged according to a number of headings (see Table 7.4) to ensure that all relevant details are covered.

Table 7.4 A basic job analysis checklist

Job identification	Job title, department, grade or level
Relationships	Name or title of immediate boss; number and type(s) of staff jobholder is responsible for; links with other departments
Outputs	What are the end products or results of the job
Activities	The behaviours or actions of the worker in achieving these outputs
Performance	Required standards, agreed objectives
Individual requirements	Abilities, skills, experience, temperament, training, languages, etc.
Working conditions	The physical and social surroundings of the job, such as workspace, working hours, leave entitlement
Equipment	Computers, machine tools, vehicles, etc. used as an essential part of the job
Other information	Promotion outlets, training available, transfer opportunities

This method is cheap and relatively easy. However, more complex methods may be justified, such as:

- **Questionnaires**, which are generally purchased 'off the shelf' from specialist companies. Questionnaire techniques can provide a wealth of information but are often expensive and time-consuming. Examples include:

  - McCormick's **Position Analysis Questionnaire (PAQ)**. Worldwide, probably the best known. It includes 150 scales with benchmarks covering a variety of jobs (McCormick and Ilgen 1987: 44).
  - The **Work Profiling System (WPS)**. A modern, computerized and professionally packaged questionnaire system produced by Saville and Holdsworth (Smith *et al*. 1989: 18). This is made up of three overlapping tests, each consisting of 300–400 items. The package is analysed by computer to give a detailed job description and a profile of the ideal recruit.

- **The critical incidents technique**, which can provide a rich, qualitative perspective on a job. Incumbents are asked to describe a number of specific real-life incidents in which they participated. The most effective incidents are those which detail qualities required to do the job well.

Job analysis is not a value-free source of information. Employees are prone to:

- **exaggeration** – making jobs seem more demanding or complex than they really are;
- **omission** – humdrum tasks are forgotten in favour of less frequent but more interesting activities.

In contrast, information given by supervisors may lead to:

- **understatement** – jobs are portrayed as being easier and less complex than they are in reality.
- **misunderstanding** – frequently bosses do not know workers' jobs in any detail.

The various systems of job analysis also differ in the kind of information collected:

- **Job-oriented methods.** Detailed specifications of the tasks involved in specific jobs, for example 'spray chassis with anti-corrosive'. This approach produces accurate descriptions of individual tasks but it is difficult to extrapolate these to other jobs.
- **Worker-oriented methods.** More generalized accounts of required behaviour which can be compared with those employed in other jobs. Both the PAQ and WPS systems use this approach.
- **Competence-oriented methods.** Sometimes termed 'attribute'- or 'trait'-oriented approaches. Highly descriptive in terms of the skills, experience and personal qualities required, they require considerable skill on the part of the analyst in translating job content into compe-

tences. Case study 7.1 describes the use of competence criteria in retailing.

Arnold *et al.* advocate the use of more than one variety of job analysis to generate information for resourcing, job evaluation and training/development purposes (1991: 95).

The UK's largest retailers are among the most efficient in the world. They employ sophisticated management techniques in a number of areas including resourcing. Eight major groups – Marks & Spencer, Boots, CWS, the John Lewis Partnership, Kingfisher, Safeway, Sainsbury and Tesco – have formed the Consortium of Retail Training Companies (CORTCO). This organization promotes retailing as a career with opportunities in fields as diverse as computing, design, engineering, marketing, logistics, food technology, finance and surveying, as well as store management.

CASE 7.1 *Resourcing retail management*

Four core competences have been identified which are expected from applicants:

- self-confidence and personal strength;
- capacity for leadership and teamwork;
- planning and organizational abilities;
- analytical and problem-solving skills.

Evidence of leadership is held to be particularly important – for example being president of the student union, course representative or organizing a major social event. Their careers within these organizations are examined in Case 11.1, which discusses training and management.

(*Source*: Neil Buckley, 'Retailing' in *Career Choice*, FT Surveys, Financial Times 1995)

Discussion questions

1 Why do you think these four core competences are particularly important for retail organizations?
2 How would you rate yourself on these competences?

The job description

Whatever the degree of sophistication, the common outcome of job analysis is the job definition or description. In the past, job descriptions have been used as quasi-legal documents, with employees declaring their contents to be a definitive list of the tasks they were expected to perform: the 'not my job, guv' syndrome. Uncooperative employees would refuse to do anything which was not on the list and unions and employers would enter into trench warfare over any changes. Today, in a climate of change and flexibility, employers are reluctant to agree to a rigid list of tasks, preferring the employee to be ready to take on any required function. Job descriptions are out of date almost as soon as they are written and cannot be seen as documents to be adhered to rigidly. Conventionally, job descriptions detail information such as job titles, summaries of main functions and more detailed lists of activities within each job.

We will see later in the chapter that the 'flexible job description' has a significant role in modern selection strategies.

Researching people

Depending on the method used, job analysis provides a detailed description of the work to be performed but may not indicate the knowledge, skills or abilities needed to do it. The 'right person' model of resourcing advocates a **personnel specification** for this purpose. Personnel specifications represent 'the demands of the job translated into human terms' (Arnold *et al.* 1991: 95). Personnel specifications list 'essential' criteria which must be satisfied and other criteria which rule out certain people from being able to do the job. Competence analyses and sophisticated forms of worker-oriented job analysis, such as WPS, generate personnel specifications as part of the package. The step from job to person specification is never entirely objective, requiring inference or intuition. In fact, it is a wonderful opportunity to introduce discriminatory criteria which rule out particular groups (Ross and Schneider 1992: 150). Personnel specifications may be no more than blueprints for clones, a matter which will be explored further later in this chapter.

Checklists such as Rodger's Seven-Point Plan (Rodger 1953) have commonly been used for preparing personnel specifications. The desired qualities are categorized under seven headings:

1 Physical qualities, including speech and appearance.
2 Attainments – qualifications, membership of professional associations.
3 General intelligence.
4 Specific aptitudes, such as numerical ability.
5 Interests and hobbies.
6 Personality.
7 Domestic circumstances.

Slavish use of such a plan leads to evident danger. Items 1 and 7 could easily cause discriminatory choices and require rigorous and critical examination. As we shall see in the next chapter, further information is obtained by using selection techniques, including formal interviews, psychometric tests, assessment centres and biodata.

Matching people and jobs

Focusing on in-house resourcing, how can we make the best use of people? In practice, it is rarely possible to match perfectly the requirements of an individual job with the skills and abilities of the people available. Square pegs in round holes are not only bad for the organization; wrongly placed workers are also often unhappy and bored, or anxious about being out of their depth. In line with the three basic recruitment strategies outlined in Table 7.5, any mismatch between person and job can be resolved in one of the following ways:

- select the best qualified person for the job ('right person' approach);
- change job characteristics to fit the abilities of the people employed ('culture-fit' model);
- train people to perform more effectively (flexible person approach).

An organization may choose any one or a combination of these methods. However, all of them depend on the ability to identify and measure the characteristics necessary for successful job performance. At first sight this seems simple and obvious. However, a close examination reveals how complex this can be. People can perform a particular job successfully for varied and sometimes contrasting reasons. For example, a good manager may be personally well organized and able to clear mountains of paperwork quickly. Another manager may deal with similar tasks equally efficiently through skillful delegation. As such, it is the **totality of effectiveness** of the individual which matters rather than specific skills and abilities. Effectiveness also depends on context. Most jobs require an individual to work within a team where required skills or qualities can be spread between its members. In such a case it may not be necessary for every team member to possess all the qualities needed for effective performance.

Companies may be forced to review their strategies to take account of new market conditions or technological changes. After several years of sustained growth the British supermarket group Sainsbury faced competition from discounters. With 120,000 employees and a salary bill of £1.1 billion a year, the company decided to examine its human resource requirements. With the maxim of 'retail is detail' Sainsbury had achieved a reputation of high quality by ensuring that goods and procedures were extensively checked by staff. Management consultants were brought in to investigate the use of information technology in eliminating clerical and management tasks. Head-office functions were subjected to a 'business process re-engineering review'. Automatic reordering linked to electronic point of sale (EPOS) terminals eliminated the need for several management layers in stores and offices. This programme produced the possibility of reducing staff numbers overall, changed the roles of remaining staff and required a major revision in human resource planning.

Table 7.5 Recruitment strategies

Approach	Objective	Organization	HR emphasis
Suitability (right person for the job)	Get the job done	Traditional Hierarchical Fixed job categories	Job analysis HR planning Selection
Malleability (fit the culture)	Fit in with today's organization	Small core Strong culture Variable periphery	Appraisal Job training
Flexibility (employee for tomorrow)	Build a competitive organization	Flexible Lean	Performance Skills training Development

The right person?

Resourcing strategies should maintain the required number and quality of staff within an organization. They should also ensure suitability for its future development. There are two underlying and apparently contradictory approaches in common use (Haire 1959). The first methodology emphasizes the **right** (or best) **person for the job**. The individual is the variable element in the search; the job is fixed. This approach is associated with traditional western personnel management. People are sought with appropriate abilities and experience to perform the job with minimal training. It implies that individual jobs are relatively long term and unchanging and that people can be 'bought in' at any stage in their careers. Vacancies are filled from the internal or external employment market. When the job is no longer required, the incumbent is disposed of.

This model is conventionally described as 'best practice' in the UK and other free-market countries. Accordingly, most personnel or human resource management textbooks traditionally outline a 'prescriptive approach to recruitment based on a systematic analysis of the requirements of an individual job' (Wright and Storey 1994: 192). Almost invariably, the account focuses on a series of selection techniques, with limited discussion of the logic behind the resourcing process. There is rarely a suggestion that any other approach may be worth considering, although there may be references to the exotic practices of the Japanese in the obligatory 'international' section. Wright and Storey also rightly point out that 'best practice' only takes place in the largest organizations. Small and medium-sized enterprises generally recruit in an informal manner and rarely use sophisticated selection methods.

The 'right person' approach attempts to be 'objective'. It requires clear answers to questions such as:

- Is there a job to fill?
- If so, what tasks and responsibilities are involved?
- What qualities, skills or experience are required to perform the tasks?
- What process will identify these criteria best?

In essence, it is an attempt to find a seven-sided object to fit a seven-sided hole. It is a **discrimination** rather than a selection process: a matching technique which attempts to pin down the 'right' or 'best' applicant. By definition it excludes those people who are believed not to fit – a view of people as objects (Townley 1994: 94). Townley perceives an underlying belief that 'employees who are carefully and appropriately matched to their jobs are satisfied and productive' (1994: 94). Matching involves generating a taxonomy of qualities and skills (criteria) which are believed to be essential or desirable – including qualifications and experience. In turn, a matrix is constructed which ranks candidates in relation to the job criteria and imposes a decision point at which some people are accepted and others rejected. In the simplest case, this process can take place inside a selector's head; in the most complex, it involves elaborate selection techniques, multiple dimensions and rating scales, and requires a computer to calculate the resulting matrix. The 'right person' approach functions well under the following circumstances:

- when it is possible to define a job tightly;
- when the job is discrete and separable from other functions;
- when the job is best done by an individual with a specific range of skills.

Frequently, however, these criteria do not apply and jobs are identified for less rational reasons such as the following:

- we have **always** had a major accounts manager;
- department x **must** handle the task;
- people **like** it done in a particular way.

The 'right person' model is geared to static, self-satisfied organizations. It meets the needs of the 'job-box' model of organizational structure discussed in Chapter 4, where people come and go but the job continues indefinitely. It leads to positions being offered to people who match traditional criteria – the kind of people we have always had. It closes the appointments process to people who have traditionally been unsuccessful. In terms of equal opportunities this approach continues to disadvantage people from 'different' backgrounds and alternative outlooks. In essence it is a cloning process, resourcing a firm with more of the same people (see key concept 7.6). It eliminates any opportunity for the organization to be creative or experimental.

Cloning, or 'elective homogeneity', is the tendency for selectors to pick people like themselves, thereby reducing the breadth of skills and personalities in an organization. Simply matching the set of characteristics possessed by previous successful postholders, it is a safe, conservative way of filling jobs. As a low-risk but backward-looking approach it is unlikely to meet the future needs of the organization.	**KEY CONCEPT 7.6** *Cloning*

The second approach described by Haire focuses on **fitting the person to the organization**. Jobs are changed and reshaped to make the best use of individuals' skills within the organization. People are permanent but jobs can be varied. If more employees are required, a search is made for individuals who appear to have the personal qualities necessary to 'fit in' with the organization's culture. Personality is more important than technical skills in this context.

This method predominates in Japanese companies. The emphasis is on matching individuals to organizational culture rather than to organizational structure. Recruitment focuses on young people who can be socialized into the company's way of working. Recently western managers have taken an interest in this approach. It has been justified in terms of attracting creative and innovative employees. However, there is a distinction between creative and plastic minds. In reality, it is a means of hiring more potential clones who have the further 'advantages' of being young, cheap and easy to manage.

A third, more demanding, approach can provide a significant competitive advantage for organizations: recruiting **flexible employees**, prepared for future change and able to contribute rather than conform. Rather than aiming for rigid skills and ability profiles or malleable and gullible personalities, recruit people who are versatile and adaptable. This reflects a long-term strategy geared towards realizing talent for tomorrow's requirements and not simply meeting current needs or filling the organization with compliant clones. The emphasis is on diversity. Organizations should identify a range of individuals required for the future – including 'mavericks to buck the system' and not just 'conformist clones' (Armstrong 1992: 135). They will require training and development; they will not be docile and managing them may be difficult; but their potential is massively greater than that of any clone.

Taking this approach, some of the rhetoric of HRM must become reality. Instead of resourcing being viewed as a matter of recruiting individuals, it is seen as a means of adding to the total pool of competences in an organization's human capital (Sparrow 1994: 13). There is a genuine need for integration and coordination between resourcing strategies and people management processes such as assessment, development and reward. Creative people must be freed from overbearing control. They cannot be managed through compliance: commitment is the only 'glue' which can bind individual talents and innovation to organizational objectives. Fine words have to be translated into sincere action.

All options, including subcontracting, must be considered carefully before hiring new people. Case 7.2 outlines a 'keyworker' strategy undertaken by Burton. This form of flexibility offers long-term benefits but needs people who are ready for new demands and hence needs a detailed knowledge of individual jobs, people's capabilities and the range of work to be performed now and in the future.

CASE 7.2 **Job-splitting**	The Burton Group announced in 1993 that it would move away from full-time workers to a system which relied on 'key-time' employees. The Burton Group trades under a variety of retailing names in the UK, including Burton Menswear, Top Shop, Champion Sport and Debenhams. Key-time employees would work when demand required them. According to Keith Cameron, Burton Group Personnel Director, 'part time' carried a negative connotation:

> Key is a much stronger word and typifies exactly how we view these people. We need to make sure that key-timers are held in high regard, and so we had to bring them up to the level of full-timers.

In practice this meant that key-time staff who worked more than eight hours would have the same terms as full-timers, including pro rata sick and holiday pay, access to the company pension scheme and staff discounts.

Already major employers of part-time staff, the Burton Group quickly introduced schedules which increased the proportion of part-timers to 60 per cent. These changes were made to match staffing more closely to demand. Previously, staff would outnumber customers at 9.00 a.m. on a Monday, whereas customers would be queueing at inadequately staffed cash desks on Saturday afternoons. This simply followed the trend in retailing, where, for example, two-thirds of Sainsbury's 90,000 staff were part time, with an almost identical proportion of 60,000 employed by Marks & Spencer.

Burton's move caused controversy and aroused considerable anxiety amongst staff because of the implied threat to full-time jobs. Staff whose jobs had significantly changed and who could not accept the new conditions were offered redundancy terms.

USDAW, the shop workers' union, argued that keyworkers would not be able to give customers the same expert advice as full-time workers. Burton were also accused of attempting to cut costs by increasing the proportion of employees working less than sixteen hours a week, the threshold for National Insurance contributions. According to USDAW, a simultaneous elimination of paid tea breaks would cut the working week by 1.5 hours.

(*Source: The Independent*, 11 January 1993; *Personnel Management*, March 1993)

As we saw in Chapter 3, Burton's approach reflects increasingly flexible approaches to job patterns and a trend towards closer matching of human effort to demand.

Selectors and strategies

The 'right person' approach is entirely concerned with the individual, whereas the 'cultural fit' model is consistent with a focus on teamworking. In practice, the models are easily confused with each other and many selectors apply a mixture of both. Frequently, selectors believe they are using 'best practice' to find the person who meets the specified criteria. In fact, the person chosen is the one whose face fits. All too often resourcing emphasizes the selection of people who fit existing culture and practice at the expense of future needs.

Why does this occur? Employee resourcing involves risk and uncertainty. Above all, assessors want to avoid the consequences of picking the 'wrong' person. This may be for the valid reason that an unsuitable person will not perform to required standards. However, selectors are also aware of the consequences of an unfortunate choice rebounding directly on themselves (and their reputations). This encourages selectors to take 'safe' decisions minimizing risk of error. The individual clearly identified as a 'good bloke' by the organization and its senior managers becomes an attractive choice (Townley 1989).

The 'inbreeding' found at higher levels of management has been described as **organizational dry rot** (Smith 1991: 29). Poverty of ideas, stultified thinking and blinkered behaviour can be due to a narrow range of experience. It is imperative, therefore, that resourcing activities should increase the breadth of experience within an organization. To do this the interests of the organization should be divorced from those of any specific stakeholders, including those of its senior managers. However, resourcing costs money directly (e.g. advertising) and indirectly (the time occupied by comparatively well-paid people). As a consequence many organizations avoid the hassle and expense by taking a casual approach to one of the most critical aspects of people management.

Strategies for redundancy

Most of the discussion so far in this chapter has addressed human resource strategies relating to successful, growing companies. As we noted with reactor strategies, managers are also expected to implement redundancies and closures as a result of strategic decisions. Sir John Harvey Jones once observed that most companies refer to their workers as 'our greatest resource' but in practice do little to make them feel that way. We observed in earlier chapters that the workforce is one group of stakeholders amongst many, and within the free-market model of capitalism they are probably the weakest. Presenting a caring image to staff and the consuming public may have advantages but greater attention is paid to more powerful voices when action is required. Directors and financiers ensure that their interests are satisfied first – well before those of the employees. This reflects a **people-as-objects** rather than a **people-as-people** approach.

Handy argues that the concept of employees as assets is rarely treated with the same seriousness as football teams regard their players:

> in a football club, the players truthfully are human assets. They have a productive capacity, an earning power, that is potentially far greater than their cost. That cost has both a capital and a maintenance element. Rewards are proportionate to group performance, the asset has a finite life. There is no question of the organization assuming responsibility for the asset beyond the limits of its useful life, nor is there any stigma in the declaration that the asset has grown too old to be worth maintaining. The care and attention and protection given to key assets by leading clubs is of a different order of people maintenance than any known in industry. Training and development become vital, for if you can increase the productive potential of the asset, in a short time you not only have greater productivity, but also an appreciated asset in terms of capital value.
>
> (Handy 1993: 222)

He speculates whimsically that one day all businesses will require transfer fees for their best performers but concedes that this is unlikely.

Most job losses are due to age-old causes: business failures and cutting back on capacity in response to lower sales levels. Generally, the term 'redundancy' is losing its old stigma. In fact, a survey by Right Associates, in association with the IPM journal, found that out of 550 companies responding some 46 per cent used the term as a cover for dismissal on the grounds of incompetence (*Guardian*, 10 July 1992).

Planning for redundancies

There are some new features to job-cutting which are indicative of systematic changes in the way that human resource strategists view the process. Despite the emphasis on job security as a prerequisite for an effective human resource strategy, reality in free-market economies demands planning for redundancies. These may result from company failure, rationalization or reduction in demand for products and people. There are several terms for the process of losing a job, all with different connotations and nuances: being made redundant, 'letting you go', 'getting the sack', and so on. One currently fashionable euphemism is **deselection**. This implies that some form of systematic or thought-out procedure has been used to decide who will lose their jobs. Hendry (1995: 202) details a number of key issues:

- To what extent can overstaffing be corrected through natural wastage or redeployment?
- What agreements constrain the redundancy process. For example, 'last in, first out'?
- When should a redundancy programme be announced? How much consultation is required?
- How are redundancy entitlements to be calculated?
- Is it possible to have an entirely voluntary process? What restrictions should be placed on key staff leaving?
- Should the organization play an active role in outplacement?
- When will savings in salary and related items pay for the redundancy costs?

Large companies often employ portfolio management systems which view business units as growth, closure or disposal prospects. A classic, if simple, portfolio planning model is based on the Boston Consulting matrix shown in Figure 7.2. This offers a further typology for resourcing strategy:

- **Stars.** Profitable business units with a dominant market position, in which there are good prospects for employees with promotion opportunities and competitive salaries.
- **Cash cows.** Mature companies with a high market share but low growth rate. They produce a cash surplus as investment costs are low but profits are good, and they are secure but unchallenging for employees – promotions are only possible when staff leave or retire. The focus may be on managing a steady decline, squeezing as much profit out of the enterprise as possible. Salaries are comfortable until later stages when hard cost-cutting is required.

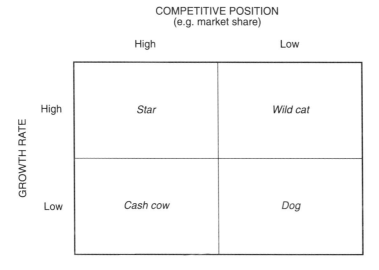

Figure 7.2 Boston Consulting Group portfolio planning matrix.

- **Wild cats.** New ventures with low market share but high growth rates. They are a risky environment for employees. If they are lucky, the group will invest and there will be considerable career opportunities and rapid promotion – provided they work for potential stars. Employees are expected to be flexible and the work can be exciting and fast-moving. If they are unlucky, they face closure or disposal to another organization. This type closely parallels the 'prospector' strategy discussed earlier.
- **Dogs.** Certain failures, with low growth, low share of the market and no strategic potential. The only hope for employees is sale to a more positive owner. Essentially, these are 'reactor' companies.

Companies using portfolio planning are likely to take decisions on purely financial grounds without regard to the welfare of employees. HRM in such organizations tends to be tough-minded, favouring employees in profitable business units. Those in less successful areas are likely to be disposed of unceremoniously.

Redundancy and retention

Managers in charge of redundancy programmes typically focus on target numbers, with little or no thought about the quality of the staff leaving the business. Retention strategies for key staff are even more important during periods of redundancy:

> It is the quality of the staff . . . not the quantity, which is the essential factor in downsizing. As we all know from experience, where there are programmes of voluntary redundancy, it is often the most skilled employees who go first because they are more marketable outside.
>
> (Thomson and Mabey 1994: 11)

An obsession with numbers leads to a haemorrhaging of valuable skills: years of work on building a strong competence base can be undone in a matter of weeks. Retention planning is discussed in greater detail later in this chapter.

International organizations and redundancies

Redundancy is governed by social legislation in most developed countries. The UK has some of the least restrictive laws. Nevertheless, organizations which do not anticipate legal requirements as a fundamental, and somewhat basic, part of HR strategy can expect the consequences. For example, the UK operations of the Leyland Daf truck-making company and official receivers Arthur Andersen were found to have made 2,400 employees unlawfully redundant because they failed to give ninety days notice. The workers were awarded £4 million compensation (*Personnel Management*, December 1993).

Businesses with operations in different countries must take their respective severance rules into account. For example, the oil giant Royal Dutch Shell decided in March 1995 to slim down corporate headquarters staff based in London and the Hague (*The Financial Times*, 14 November 1995);

1,200 jobs were to go out of 3,900, with intended savings of £190 million a year. The costs involved in redundancies in the two countries varied sharply, reflecting the marked difference between UK and Netherlands legislation on redundancies. The Netherlands is committed to the EU's Social Chapter and enforces significantly higher entitlements for both voluntary and compulsory redundancy. Accordingly, redundancies in the two capitals have widely different consequences. Whereas staff taking voluntary redundancy in the UK are given a lump sum based on years worked and final salary, Netherlands staff receive a further year's salary, with a minimum of £60,000. People made redundant compulsorily in the Hague are entitled to twelve months' full salary, 85 per cent of eight months' salary, and 70 per cent of a further four months'. This is equivalent to twenty-one months' salary in contrast to the six to nine months' to which London staff are entitled.

Although Shell cannot be accused of doing so, other – less scrupulous – organizations may well concentrate their redundancies in the country where severance costs are lowest.

Managers and professionals

Recent redundancies have affected managers and professionals more than ever before. Restructuring and delayering have meant redundancies for many experienced people in their forties and fifties. In the UK, executives in construction and financial services have been particularly affected. As a spin-off from the slump in building, the professionals – architects, surveyors and solicitors – who service the industry have suffered. Ironically, in terms of flexibility these are peripheral workers from personal choice. Newly qualified people in these areas have found it virtually impossible to get their first job. According to the Law Society, in the early 1990s most medium-sized legal firms reduced their staff numbers by about 15 per cent. The drop in membership income led to the society cutting its own headquarters staff by forty. Even accountants have been hit: the Institute of Chartered Accountants estimated about 3,000–4,000 redundancies amongst accountants in public practice during the period.

In *Thriving on Chaos*, Peters argues that most large companies are hopelessly overmanaged (1987: 355). Specifically, he considers that there are too many managers in too many layers – not that there are not enough indians, but that there are certainly too many chiefs. This overmanagement leads to inefficiency. He quotes a study by McKinsey & Company into thirty-eight advanced manufacturing technology systems. The study concludes that:

> The first step in accomplishing successful plant floor implementation of new manufacturing approaches is the clearing out of all the middle managers and support service layers that clog the wheels of change. These salaried people are often the real barriers to productivity improvement, not the hourly workers on the floor.

'Last in, first out' used to be a common rule. Nowadays, however, redundancies are much less likely to happen on this basis. Sectors such as banking have virtually abandoned the principle, although some, including the motor industry, still use it. Case 7.3 describes changes in the Hungarian Magyar

Hitel Bank. The changes advocated by Peters – specifically delayering – imply that companies are 'getting rid of dead wood' or 'winnowing out the poorer performers'. Current redundancy strategies seem to follow Peters' lines, aiming at keeping key skills and people with 'personal chemistry'.

CASE 7.3 **Magyar Hitel Bank**	The Magyar Hitel Bank (MHB) was a major force in Hungary's state-owned banking system. In 1994 it made a loss of 3 billion Forint and was also losing market share to foreign banks and the new private sector. In March 1995 a new Chief Executive, Zsigmond Jarai, arrived from the HongKong Shanghai Bank. Mr Jarai had extensive experience in Hungarian banking. He was given the minimum salary of 12,200 Forint and share options which would become profitable if he succeeded in improving the bank's situation.
	On his arrival, he found 171 directors or heads of department. According to Mr Jarai, 'I told them they were all sacked and that, in future, there would be only 45 directors and that they could all compete for the jobs. We rehired around 25.' In 1995 he implemented plans to cut the workforce from 4,200 to 3,100 and moved branches into smaller, cheaper buildings. New technology was introduced and lending manuals were drafted to reduce bad loans. The aim was to create Hungary's first indigenous electronic retail bank.
	(*Source*: adapted from *The Financial Times*, 21 November 1995, 'Executives purged', Virginia Marsh)

Recently, critics have argued that the cutting process has gone too far. As we have noted before, delayering or downsizing have led to 'dumbsizing' – a condition described by Hamer as 'corporate anorexia' (*The Financial Times*, 22 November 1995). Organizations have slimmed down to the point where they are denuded of the skills needed to grasp new opportunities and remaining staff are demoralized and overworked.

Summary

Employee resourcing is a wider issue than recruitment and selection. In this chapter we have discussed strategies for determining resourcing from either the internal or external employment markets. We considered a variety of models for resourcing strategies. We also discussed some approaches to human resource planning and the use made of information collected during the resourcing process. 'Best person', 'cultural fit' and flexibility perspectives were discussed, and examples drawn from British, French and Japanese approaches. Some of the limitations of job descriptions and personnel specifications were identified.

Further reading

Miles and Snow's typology is debated in Sonnenfeld, Peiperl and Kotter (1988) (reprinted in *Human Resource Strategies*, ed. Salaman, 1992). The planning process is discussed in Hendry (1995) *Human Resource Manage-*

ment: A Strategic Approach to Employment and Tyson (1995) *Human Resource Strategy.* Rothwell ('Human resource planning' in Storey, ed., 1995, *Human Resource Management: A Critical Text*) takes a fairly technical overview of the subject and also provides a useful attempt at explaining why HRP is a 'textbook' topic rather than widespread practice.

Review questions

1 How does employee resourcing relate to organizational strategy?
2 Describe in your own words what is meant by:

 - the 'right person' model;
 - culture fit;
 - the flexible employee.

 Which approach is most commonly used for employee resourcing in your locality?

3 Consider an organization of your choice and ask yourself the following questions:

 - Does it obtain its human resource requirements from existing staff where possible?
 - At what levels are people brought in from the external employment market?
 - Would it be beneficial to change these practices?

4 Distinguish between 'hard' and 'soft' human resource planning. Which is of greatest value to modern businesses?
5 Are resourcing decisions normally taken on a short-term operational basis or at a strategic level?
6 Are long-term resourcing strategies realistic?
7 To what degree are resourcing strategies constrained by the nature of the external employment market?
8 How has the concept of flexibility affected resource decisions?
9 What is the relationship between resourcing strategy, HR planning and job analysis?

Problems for discussion and analysis

1 Pribake manufacture biscuits ('cookies'). The company requires a steady stream of new product ideas, a small proportion of which will form a permanent element of its range. The board are considering a new appointment but cannot agree on the nature of the post. The Production Director feels that there is a need for an Operational Manager to look after chocolate-coated products. Conversely the Marketing Director wants an 'ideas' person to devise new products and enliven the company's range. The two cannot agree and the Managing Director has imposed a compromise. She has asked the Human Resource Manager to find an individual who can meet both requirements. After some

dispute they have produced a basic job definition along the following lines:

- **Job Title**: New Products Production Manager
- **Job Summary**: reporting at a high level with responsibity for development team and – possibly – maintenance staff. Overseeing manufacture of chocolate-coated range. Developing new product ideas and progressing through from trial to production stages.
- **Desirable qualities**: general management skills; able to manipulate technology effectively and realistically. If the successful candidate does not have direct knowledge of the actual machinery and techniques used in the company's factories, then s/he must have the ability to appraise systems and technology quickly.

After much discussion the HR manager has produced a list of additional competences which seem to meet the requirements of the post:

- Creativity – to develop marketable products which can be produced at a reasonable cost.
- Experience of, or familiarity with market research techniques and able to formulate research programmes and evaluate results.
- Ability to design and test product manufacturing processes.
- Familiarity with the properties and possibilities of available materials – for example what can and cannot be done with different kinds of chocolate.
- Familiarity with production line equipment including the ability to appraise production line speeds, error factors and quality improvements. New products must not pose insurmountable problems for production machinery or workforce.
- Versatility – the fewest development problems arise when products can be manufactured on existing equipment and made from simple and easily obtainable raw ingredients.
- Managerial skills to motivate and control the development team and ensure its effectiveness. A solitary genius will not work well in this environment.
- Ability to communicate persuasively with management and workforce, especially when products are trialled and inevitable teething problems occur. Also to communicate with senior management and marketing staff in promoting products within the company and in the marketplace.

The directors have also agreed on the following criteria:

- **Academic qualifications**: likely to be a graduate with a production or engineering speciality.
- **Ability**: above average. Strong in mechanical aptitude. High on creativity scores. High on verbal fluency. A flair for design.
- **Personality**: neither highly introverted nor extraverted. Good leadership and persuasion skills.
- **Experience**: there are significant elements of the job which seem to demand familiarity with this particular industry.

What deficiencies are apparent in the job description, competence list and additional selection criteria? How would you conduct the recruitment and selection exercise for this vacancy? What is the likelihood of finding a suitable candidate?

2 Everylang is a small, fast-growing translation bureau. It needs to keep tight control of its costs in a very competitive market. The owner considers that its success depends on quality, presentation, speed of work and the ability to provide translations to and from any language. Most of the work is from the main European languages and into English. The company employs twelve staff, the remaining work (over half) is farmed out to freelance translators who are paid only for the work they do. They deal with the office by a variety of means, including courier, post, fax and computer modems. It is sometimes difficult to get and maintain relationships with top-quality freelancers, especially those with good word-processing equipment and who are able to transfer work electronically.

Everylang has now grown to the point where the owner-manager is too busy with marketing, finance and developing new customers to be able to cope with the day-to-day running. You have been invited as an external consultant to advise on selecting an Office Manager for Everylang. It is apparent that the owner knows a great deal about the translation market but is inexpert in managing people. The owner is keen to promote a member of the existing staff, partly in order to improve motivation but mainly in order to keep costs down. Five have applied and you have been provided with a job summary on which to base your initial thoughts:

- **Title**: Office Manager.
- **Pay**: Translator salary + 30% + profit-related bonus and benefits.
- **Main purpose of the job**: day-to-day running of Everylang office, ensuring that incoming work is dealt with and returned to agreed standard of quality and delivery time.
- **Functions**: providing quotations for customers; dealing with enquiries by phone, post and fax; allocating work to full-time staff or freelancers; recording and progressing all incoming work, delivery on time and to the agreed quality; dealing with complaints; finding and monitoring new freelancers; completing personal computer records for billing and administration; dealing with any problems among staff.
- **Personnel specification**: none existing.

You are also given the applicants' details:

- **Helen**. Age 42. Five years with Everylang. No formal qualifications. Translates French and Spanish. Ex-secretary. Has been translating for almost twenty years and knows a large number of other translators. Very efficient, quick and accurate. She is keen on long legal translations and has developed a considerable knowledge of business law in French-speaking countries. Pleasant personality but a little short-tempered. She has a good working relationship with other staff members but tends to keep her distance and does not socialize with them. Likes to take a six-week holiday at her parents' home in France every summer. She has an arrangement with the owner to take this partly as unpaid leave.

- **John**. Age 36. Twelve years with Everylang. High-school qualifications in French and Italian. Also has a diploma in translating and interpreting in the same languages. A great language enthusiast, he is proud of his standard of work. He translates mostly from French, specializing in letters and product information. Takes a keen interest in the welfare of the other staff. They have a considerable regard for him, respecting his professionalism and his interest in them. Over the last year he has had arguments with the owner over policy and thinks the company is growing too fast. He believes that the ever-increasing pressure of work is leading to inadequate checking of translations. Personally, he is quite efficient but pays too much attention to small details. Has been thinking of going self-employed.

- **Jill**. Age 32. Three years with Everylang. Left school at the age of 16. Took evening classes in French for several years. Cheerful, chatty person who gets on well with customers. Not a particularly good translator but useful for short French translations needed quickly. Can understand Scandinavian languages quite well, particularly Norwegian – she worked in Norway as a Managing Director's personal secretary for two years. The other staff do not respect her as a translator and often patronize her. She copes well, brushing off their remarks and getting on with her job. She has applied for a number of other jobs recently – without success.

- **Francesca**. Age 26. Eighteen months with Everylang. Graduate in Spanish and Italian. Diploma in translating. Also speaks Portuguese. Undoubtedly the best translator in the office. She had considered becoming a language teacher but dropped out of the training programme after a year and joined Everylang. She is much younger than the other staff and relations are not particularly good. Gets on extremely well with major clients, who find her vivacious personality attractive to deal with. She gives customers a feeling of confidence in her abilities. Francesca sees Everylang as a long-term career job, is ambitious and enthusiastic about major expansion. At the moment, she is having major problems with her pre-school-aged child, who suffers from asthma. Sometimes she takes time off with little notice. She has promised the boss that her difficulties will be sorted out soon.

- **David**. Age 55. Three years with company. BA and MA in German Literature. Former export manager, made redundant from a major company. He translated on a freelance basis before joining Everylang. He is the only full-time German translator. A workaholic – he never seems to leave the office and is always ready to work overtime to complete a piece of work. He is regarded as bookish by the other staff. Sometimes David is extremely critical of other people's standard of work. He considers the qualifications of some of the other translators to be inadequate for the jobs they are doing. In general, he thinks that the owner is unimaginative and has failed to capitalize on non-European languages. He is very unhappy about his salary, which is much lower than his pay as export manager. However, he knows that he cannot cope with the uncertainties of being a freelancer.

The company does not have a performance assessment system.

What criteria would you employ in seeking the most suitable applicant? What methods would you use to obtain further information about these candidates? What are the likely advantages and disadvantages of promoting any one of these individuals?

8   Recruitment and selection

> This chapter examines current practices and decision-making in recruitment and selection. Selection methods are outlined and evaluated in terms of purpose and validity.

The very substantial volume of research in the areas of selection and appraisal is both a blessing and a curse.

(Murphy 1994: 58)

In Chapter 7 we discussed the 'why' of resourcing, evaluating strategies and plans which guide the process. We considered also the initial information-gathering from job analysis and the – sometimes unwise – strategies employed by selectors. This chapter follows on with an examination of the operational elements of resourcing, commonly termed recruitment and selection.

There is no shortage of material on these topics. Together with performance assessment, they are critical elements of effective people management. Not surprisingly, therefore, these aspects of employee resourcing have attracted a great deal of attention from human resource practitioners and occupational psychologists. Most textbook accounts are prescriptive, dealing with the subject in a 'do it like this . . .' fashion, almost invariably using an underlying 'right person for the job' resourcing model. However, since the early 1990s this approach has been challenged (Sparrow 1994: 15; Iles and Salaman 1995: 203). For example, Iles and Salaman argue that 'the limitation of the psychological and personnel-driven approaches to selection is that they are entirely, if understandably, concerned with improving the efficiency of the processes, and not with understanding their wider provenance and significance' (1995: 203).

As we noted in the last chapter, we cannot discuss how recruitment and selection take place without asking why certain techniques are used in preference to others. Within the HRM paradigm, they are not simply mechanisms for filling vacancies. Recruitment and redundancy can be viewed as key 'push' and 'pull' levers for organizational change. Recruitment and selection allow management to determine and gradually modify the behavioural characteristics and competences of the workforce. The fashion for teamworking, for example, has focused on people with a preference for working with others as opposed to the individualist 'stars' preferred by recruiters in the 1980s. Attention has switched from rigid lists of skills and abilities to broader-based competences. In general, as we noted in Chapter 7, there is a greater regard for personal flexibility and adaptability – a reorientation from present to future suitability.

We begin the chapter with a critical examination of the recruitment process, covering formal and informal approaches. We move on in the next section to consider the use made of information collected from candidates at the application stage from letters, CVs, application forms, biodata forms and references. Then we evaluate the effectiveness of various forms of interview before discussing other selection methods such as psychometric tests, work samples, assessment centres and graphology. The chapter concludes with a discussion of the merits of resourcing decisions.

Recruitment: marketing jobs

Following on from our discussion in Chapter 7, if resourcing strategy and planning have identified the need for new or additional work to be performed in-house, it is obviously necessary to make potential applicants aware of any vacancy. Essentially, this is a marketing process conventionally termed **recruitment**, which Lewis defines as 'the activity that generates a pool of applicants, who have the desire to be employed by an organization, from which those suitable can be selected' (1985: 29).

Potential candidates may come from an internal trawl of the organization, or from the external job market. The latter are reached through channels such as recruitment advertising, employment agencies, professional associations or word of mouth. We saw in Chapter 7 that organizations with a strong culture are likely to seek malleable new employees at school-leaving or graduate levels. More senior jobs are filled from the internal job market. When companies look for the 'right person', however, detailed personnel specifications may rule out internal candidates. In each case, the recruitment phase is critical since it determines the range of choice available to the selectors:

> The more effectively this stage is carried out the less important the actual selection of candidates becomes: if a firm can attract 20 high flyers for a job it hardly matters whether they choose amongst these high flyers with a pin, an interview or tests.
>
> (Smith *et al.* 1989: 24)

Internal recruitment marketing can take place by word of mouth, staff notices, newsletters and vacancy journals. Recruiting may be on a 'one-off' basis or linked to a development programme as discussed in Chapter 11. External recruitment marketing can include media advertisements, various public and private employment agencies, and headhunting. The role of the state varies, with some countries such as Italy requiring official notification to state employment agencies. As with other marketing campaigns the selection of appropriate channels, the creativity of vacancy presentation and the size of budget will determine success.

Informal recruiting

Cultural factors are important in determining the orientation between internal and external job markets. They also influence the nature of recruitment. Papalexandris (1991) compared multinational corporations operating in Greece and Greek-owned companies. She found that Greek employers preferred to recruit from among relatives, and friends of the owners or existing employees. Advertisements and agencies were used only when this failed to produce suitable candidates. Greek employers paid more attention to recommendations and previous experience than to qualifications such as degrees. In contrast, foreign-owned companies followed 'best practice' and focused on younger, inexperienced graduates attracted through agencies and advertisements. While acknowledging the usefulness of personal acquaintance and experience in providing information for the selection process, Papalexandris considers that Greek firms risk nepotism and depriving themselves of competent younger staff.

Formalized introduction schemes along similar lines occur in other countries, serving to perpetuate recruitment from pools of like-minded people. However, they have the benefit of supplying candidates who have a more realistic view of the organization, compared with people attracted by recruitment advertising. The former have gained their knowledge from the informal network, the latter from PR information. As a result, word-of-mouth applicants are likely to stay longer and be more suitable than recruits obtained by advertising. Word-of-mouth is discriminatory, since it restricts applications to established communities and excludes recently arrived minority groups who have not had time to become part of informal networks (Smith 1991: 31). Inevitably, people will recommend others from their own in-group even if they have no intention of discriminating.

Informal recruitment is common. A National Opinion Polls (NOP) survey (*The Independent*, 26 October 1995) found that, from a cross-section of the working population, jobs had been obtained in the following ways:

- 35 per cent through personal recommendation;
- 27 per cent through recruitment advertising;
- 13 per cent directly contacted by employer;
- 7 per cent from a job centre;
- 4 per cent recruitment agencies;
- 14 per cent unspecified.

At a senior level, headhunting has become a common, if not the predominant, method of recruitment. Otherwise known as executive search, headhunting is a system in which consultancies are used to locate supposedly 'outstanding' people. The marked absence of women and ethnic minorities in senior positions reveals this to be a further mechanism for cloning.

Formal recruiting

Equal opportunity demands equal access. This can only be achieved through public and open recruitment. However, recruitment marketing is expensive and time-consuming. For example, PA Consulting conducted a survey of ninety-one UK companies recruiting graduates (*Times Higher*, 21 January 1994). They recorded 318,988 applications for 3,372 vacancies in 1993. This averaged ninety-five applicants for every post, rising to 272 applications per vacancy for the major high-street and 'Blue Chip' companies. Organizations recruiting more than 100 graduates spent between £50,000 and £800,000 on recruitment programmes, with advertising taking a small proportion of the cost in comparison with stationery and travel. They averaged a remarkable 1,172 hours processing applications and arriving at a shortlist.

The effectiveness of recruitment is usually measured in terms of expediency: 'whether vacancies are filled with minimally qualified people at acceptable cost' or a sufficient number of applicants are attracted (Iles and Salaman 1995: 213). Rarely are the long-term consequences to the organization of cloned and barely adequate employees or the costs of recruitment taken into account. Doubts have also been expressed about the quality of people who are engaged in recruiting. Remarkably, the advertisements placed by recruitment agencies for their own staffing vacancies rarely ask for any knowledge of people management or selection techniques. Almost invariably they emphasize selling skills such as communication, dynamism and youth.

The likelihood of attracting 'suitable' applicants depends on the detail and specificity of the recruitment advertisement or literature. Key factors such as salary, job title, career and travel opportunities obviously influence response rates. As examples of marketing, considerable effort and money can be invested in the effectiveness of recruitment advertisements. However, employers do not wish to be swamped with applications from clearly unsuitable people. In some instances, honest job descriptions are designed to put off unwelcome applicants. For example, at Nissan UK job adverts emphasized the demanding nature of the work, clearly stating that (Wickens 1987: 178):

- the pace of work will be dictated by a moving production line and will be very demanding;
- work assignments will be carefully defined and will be repetitive.

A typical profile of satisfaction with various sources of recruitment is shown in Table 8.1. The survey showed that trade or professional journals attracted the most suitable candidates, whereas the local press showed the greatest cost-effectiveness. This is a poorly researched aspect of resourcing but it seems that employers are happier making a choice from an unexpectedly large pool of candidates than from a small pool generated by an unsuccessful recruitment campaign (Van Ours and Ridder 1992).

Specific journals or magazines are favoured for particular occupations, with employers and job-seekers gravitating towards the same titles on the same days. These change with time, dependent on the effectiveness of their

Table 8.1 Satisfaction with recruitment

Method	Satisfaction (1–5)
Internal	4.1
Local press	3.7
National press	3.5
Trade journals	3.2
Consultants	2.8
Agencies	2.7
Headhunters	2.5
Job centres	2.2
Professional registers	1.9

Note: A British Institute of Management/IPM study completed in 1980 compared ratings of satisfaction between various methods of recruitment available to employers and found the above levels of satisfaction with their effectiveness.

advertising sales departments, and good response rates require awareness of the state of play before placing any advertisements.

The approach to recruitment reflects cultural priorities. British recruitment marketing normally features salaries and benefits but French equivalents are vague in this respect, reflecting different approaches to rewards (Barsoux and Lawrence 1990: 47). UK companies base pay on job requirements; in France it depends on the candidate's qualifications. French advertisements define educational requirements in detail, sometimes indicating the number of years of study after the *baccalauréat* as the main heading. Specific *grandes écoles* may be requested. Management in France is regarded as an intellectual rather than an interpersonal matter. Hence recruitment is geared towards cleverness (Barsoux and Lawrence 1990: 47). Instead of the managerial buzzwords, such as 'dynamic', 'energetic' and 'high calibre', found in British advertisements, French equivalents seek out *les éléments les plus brillants*. The nuance is telling.

CASE 8.1
The job-seekers

Around the world, job-seekers find similar problems in gaining employment. They feel unfairly treated by insensitive employers. Unemployed people who are too young or too old, or come from unfavoured areas or disadavantaged groups are particularly susceptible to callous treatment. Two letters from different continents describe the treatment experienced by some job hunters.

First letter: 'Sad conclusions of job-seekers' (*Trinidad Guardian*)

The Editor: Kindly publish the following letter in your newspaper on our behalf.

Dear employers, we are a group of young and middle-aged persons from different social backgrounds and educational levels, ranging from CXC passes to university degrees, plus experience.

We recently compared notes as to our lack of success in obtaining employment over the past year, and have come up with the following conclusions and observations:

(1) On a number of occasions, the jobs advertised were 'filled', and the advertising and interviewing process was merely to fill a 'requirement'.

(2) Too many recruiters and interviewers use the opportunity of the interview to let us know how powerful they are, that they have the right to employ or not, to dehumanise, insult, embarrass, mentally abuse and to generally show us that we the unemployed are the lowest form of life on this earth.

(3) If you live in a depressed area, it is recommended that you use as your mailing address and point of contact the address of a friend or relative in a more respectable area.

Few invitations for interviews are sent out to Laventville or Maloney.

Popular Phrase

(4) Instead of the popular phrase, 'only suitable applicants will be acknowledge' (sic), we recommend that the statement 'only successful applicants will be acknowledged by dd/mm/yy' be used.

Please understand that it is extremely frustrating not knowing whether you are to be short-listed for an interview weeks after mailing out a letter.

(5) those of us who have been used during the interview process, tend, on the average, to relate our stories to at least eight other persons.

This means that the company whose employees were the abuser[s] receive negative public relations. In one case, a major account was moved from a bank. Take note, employers.

(6) Executive placement services are a waste of time. They play the 'skin' and 'club/lodge/contact' game.

Over the past year, not a single search company has even acknowledged any of the 11 letters which we all sent to them.

(7) The only success which we have had by way of employment were [sic] not through advertisement in the newspapers but by way of contact – someone knowing of the vacancy before it could be advertised. This to us is the saddest fact of all.

We, however, still are hopeful that we can obtain gainful employment.

THE GROUP OF ANXIOUS JOB-SEEKERS,
Maraval.

Second letter: 'Be more caring with job-seekers' (*Cape Times*)

I am an outplacement consultant specialising in assisting retrenched personnel. To those in positions of power over the unemployed may I remind you that the unemployed person, in many instances, could be your father, mother, brother, sister, friend or even yourself. Put systems in place to ensure that advertising response is dealt with in a pleasing and caring manner. It is dehumanising to have someone bark questions at you when your confidence is at a low ebb.

I understand the pressure of the job, having owned and run my own recruitment agency, and I know there are many chancers out there. However, if it were not for the chancers and the irritation attached, big business would not need your services.

I ask that companies looking for staff check up on the agencies they use by phoning in anonymously to check up on the treatment meted out to job-seekers. In my view, it leaves a lot to be desired.

What amazes me is the dignified way the unemployed people I work with handle themselves and the undignified response they very often receive from so-called human resource professionals.

Colleen Ingram
SOMERSET WEST

(*Sources: Trinidad Guardian*, 23 July 1992; *Cape Times* (Capetown, South Africa), 25 January 1996)

Targeting

In the UK, the recent massive increase in higher education has produced a consequent increase in the number of new graduates. British employers have begun to copy US organizations in targeting specific universities, courses and even lecturers. As we observed in Chapter 2, the pecking order favours 'old' universities, reflecting the prejudices of employers. A Glasgow consultancy, Yellowbrick Training and Development, indicated five 'insights' into targeting (*The Financial Times*, 25 October 1995; *Guardian*, 26 October 1995):

- Competition for the 'best' graduates requires employers to have a clear idea of what they mean by 'best'. Recruitment needs to send a strong, distinctive message to these people.
- There must be a move away from junior staff indiscriminately attracting as many applicants as possible to a more selective process involving senior management.
- Target key institutions and specific courses.
- Recruit whenever the needs of the business dictate, rather than to a fixed 'milkround' calendar.
- There will be a diminished role for glossy brochures. Instead, vacation and placement jobs will be used to provide 'two-way interviews'.

It is clear that many employers are likely to use this form of targeting to ring-fence jobs so that only specific groups are considered. Essentially, they discriminate against institutions where ethnic minorities and working-class people are more heavily represented.

Recruitment can be used to present a more positive, welcoming image to groups which are underrepresented, but to be successful this must be reinforced by similar initiatives further on in selection, induction and development mechanisms.

Researching candidates

Recruitment attracts a pool of applicants from whom successful candidates may be chosen. If a job analysis has been conducted, the **criteria** or competences which are deemed necessary have been identified. These may be well defined and focused on experience and skills, as in the 'right person' approach; or general and related to education, intellect and personality for the 'cultural fit' and 'flexible person' models. Since decision-making is based on these criteria, relevant information must be obtained from applicants. The initial response to a vacancy announcement can take a number of forms but each offers the opportunity for recruiters to obtain information on applicants and for applicants to gain an understanding of the job and the organization. The commonest responses requested are by telephone or letter. Telephone responses may be used for an exchange of information or as a means of eliciting an application form and literature describing the job and organization.

Application letters and CVs

Letters and CVs (or resumes) are typically used as initial applications. There is some variation between cultures. Generally, advertisements in France request a handwritten application letter, CV and photograph.

(Many French companies use graphologists in the selection process.) French CVs are shorter and more factual than the Anglo-Celtic model and include little or no personal information such as hobbies or sporting interests. Japanese recruiters expect an official family registry record, a physical examination report and letters of recommendation in addition to CV and photographs. The use of photographs arouses disquiet in countries where equal opportunities are a major issue since they imply that selection will be influenced by appearance and colour.

Job clubs and career advisers spend a great deal of time coaching job-seekers on the preparation of polished application letters and curriculum vitae. A study by Effective Resources (*Personnel Management*, October 1992) investigated the views of 231 agencies: 42 per cent of respondents favoured two-page CVs and 31 per cent preferred three pages; longer or shorter CVs were not regarded with favour. Half the respondents did not care whether or not the covering letter was typed, provided that it was legible. Coaching often results in a bland, standardized application which does not stand out amongst hundreds of others. Applicants might be best advised to try some cautious experimenting in layout, paper quality and typeface to achieve a more distinctive product.

Application forms

Both letters and CVs present a problem in a large recruitment programme: applicants may not provide all the relevant information and what there is will be presented in different ways. Comparison of applicants is easier if data is supplied in a standard form. Therefore, applicants who have replied to a job advertisement typically receive an application form (usually termed an 'application blank' in North America), asking often for information already supplied.

Candidates face a paradox with application forms. Because information is regimented into a particular order and restricted space, job-seekers may present very similar applications. As is the case with application letters, if candidates do not include details which distinguish them from the (hundreds of) others they stand little chance of being shortlisted. Conversely, if their responses are too unorthodox, the form immediately becomes a test of conventionality:

> Application forms are of doubtful benefit; they torment applicants rather than motivate them. They blunt any initiative in presentation. [. . .] inane questions such as: 'Describe yourself in one hundred words'. Or: 'What are your greatest achievements and failures?' [. . .] create sarcastic answers in the mind and false answers on paper. The curriculum vitae is a better tool; it is a chance for the applicant to sell him or her self. Its presentation and its content are also more useful and less boring to the member of staff who has to scrutinise them.
> (*The Sunday Times*, 8 August 1993)

An applicant's heart sinks when a carefully crafted CV appears to be ignored and a standard form arrives in the post. Hours are wasted completing forms which are not read because applicants are rejected on decision criteria, such as qualifications, which are not mentioned in the marketing process. However, an organization which does not use application forms has a major problem dealing with hundreds of letters and CVs. How are they to be analysed and compared? How is the choice of a shortlist to be made? Applicants will leave out crucial items of information, particularly when they are likely to have a negative impact. When and how is this information to be acquired? Interviews are expensive methods for filling in the gaps in a CV. Moreover, it is unfair to raise hopes, cause inconvenience and possibly expense for interviewees who are disqualified on the basis of information which could be picked up from an application form. Provided that they are not devised as medieval instruments of torture, short and pertinent application forms will continue to have a major role in recruitment.

Qualifications

We noted that educational qualifications are of major importance in some cultures, for example France and Japan. In other countries their value varies, depending on the level and nature of the vacancy. One study found that UK graduate recruiters relied primarily on educational qualifications as a selection criterion for shortlisting applicants, whereas skills and competences were sought at later stages in the selection process (*Personnel Management*, August 1992). In a different study, conducted for the Apex Trust, a survey of 2,500 employers found that educational qualifications rated only eleventh out of thirteen criteria for employers in the private sector, compared with tenth for trade qualifications. Public-sector employers rated them ninth and fifth, respectively. The most important qualities reported were honesty, positive attitude, timekeeping and motivation (*Personnel Management*, February 1991).

Biodata

Application forms and model CVs invariably include sections on experience, hobbies and other spare-time activities. Applicants frequently have serious difficulties in providing answers if they have fairly mundane interests. Does a passing interest in stamps and a small collection of CDs allow us to describe our hobbies as philately and music? Do holiday snapshots justify 'photography'. What went through a student's mind prior to writing 'I have recently travelled to Bolton' on her CV?

Traditionally, little use was made of this information. But it can be useful in discriminating between applicants who are similar in most other respects. In fact, with an increase in coaching on how to prepare CVs and answer conventional forms, applications have become more and more similar. Supposing an employer advertised for trainee customer service assistants. The response is likely to include numerous applications from school-leavers with insufficient qualifications to proceed into higher education. These applicants may seem much the same on paper, but some have greater initiative or people skills than others. Biodata (biographical data) forms have been developed to identify non-academic qualities such as these. Biodata consists of systematic information about hobbies, interests, and life history. The underlying rationale is described by Smith, Gregg and Andrews:

> Biodata methods are based on the assumption that *either* our characteristics are formed by the experiences we are subjected to in the course of our lives *or* our abilities cause us to select or become involved in certain types of life event. In either case, it follows that if we can accurately assess the events of a person's life, we can deduce something about their skills and abilities.
>
> (Smith *et al.* 1989: 54)

Biodata forms request detailed information of this kind, normally in the form of a multiple-choice questionnaire, covering the following areas:

- age, sex, place of birth, residence;
- family background, number of brothers and sisters, parental history;
- education, work experience;
- marital status, number of children;
- physical characteristics (weight, height) and medical history;
- hobbies and leisure interests;
- reading habits – newspapers, magazines, type and frequency of books read.

Questions items are largely factual or **hard** and could be checked with other sources if necessary. Other items are **soft** and include opinions, attitudes and feelings. It is also possible to collect the same data in a structured interview. Biodata is an expensive procedure to set up but cheap to administer, especially if the data can be entered on computer by optical scanning.

A typical biodata exercise takes the following sequence (Smith *et al.* 1989):

1 Job analysis identifies criteria for good performance.
2 A 'brainstorming' exercise generates relevant biodata items, such as 'interest in people', 'stability', 'imagination'.
3 Draft questionnaires are given to a large number – ideally over 300 – existing employees.
4 Replies are correlated with job performance. Items which correlate poorly or discriminate against particular groups should be discarded.
5 The revised questionnaire is then given to applicants.
6 Biodata items become out of date quickly. They should be rechecked every two years.

Biodata cannot be used in small organizations or for a 'one-off' job. A simplified version could be provided as a decision aid in such circumstances. This would entail interviewers collecting narrative personal histories and scoring the information against a previously determined scale. The main use of biodata is in the pre-selection of basic-level jobs such as apprentices or trainees. The logic is that if candidates are matched with existing staff, people with similar interests can be found who are likely to be suitable for the job. The greatest value of the technique is its ability to reduce staff turnover.

Biodata is specifically used to select people who are similar to those employed already. Although it is designed to eliminate unfairness, in a less obvious way it consolidates and makes 'scientific' an embedded practice which is prejudicial to the disadvantaged. Furnham reviews a number of studies comparing biodata with job performance and finds strong supporting evidence for its usefulness (1992: 231). He cites Russell *et al.* (1990), who examined the life details of 900 naval recruits and measured five biographical features:

- life problems and difficulties;
- aspects of task performance;
- work ethic/self-discipline;
- assistance from others;
- extraordinary goals or effort.

These were found to relate to other measures such as military performance rating. Furnham notes that factor analyses of biodata information relate to well-attested personality dimensions.

References

Virtually all employers request references as a matter of course, usually without any thought as to their purpose and value. Where a purpose is expressed, they tend to serve one or both of the following functions:

- To provide a factual check to maximize the probability of a truthful application.
- To provide evidence of character or ability.

The latter assumes that the referee is disinterested and capable of making a valid judgement, and is frequently misused. Candidates are most unlikely to offer referees who will write unfavourably. A classic study is frequently quoted to demonstrate the dubious value of the reference (Mosel and Goheen 1958). 1,000 applications for the US Civil Service were examined and it was found that:

- less than 1 per cent had poor references for ability or character;
- approximately 50 per cent were described as outstanding by the referees;
- the remaining references were satisfactory.

Moreover, when the work performance of successful candidates described by referees as being particularly suitable for the job was compared with that of those who were not, no difference was found between the two groups.

There is a growing and welcome trend for references to be simple factual checks rather than a source of 'evidence' for the selection process. There is also an issue regarding a referee's liability for the consequences of their comments.

Psychometric tests

Psychological tests have become commonplace. Psychometric means **measurement of the mind**. Psychometric tests purport to measure psychological characteristics, including personality, motivation, career interests, competences and intellectual abilities. Traditionally they take the form of pen and paper multiple-choice questionnaires but modern forms can also be presented on computer screens. Most tests require applicants to work through a large number of items in a given amount of time. Some ask candidates to choose between various alternatives, as in the following example:

● Which of the following best describes you?

  1 I never take time off from work because of illness.
  2 Sometimes I take time off work if I am very ill.
  3 I believe in taking care of myself. If I am ill, I stay at home

This kind of item is typical of personality and motivation tests. Other tests use pictures and geometrical shapes. Tests of number ability might offer a series of numbers and ask for the next two:

  2   4   8   16   ?   ?

This is a simple illustration – tests normally include items of increasing difficulty. The limited amount of time allowed ensures that few people can complete all items correctly.

Users argue that they provide valuable evidence which is not revealed by other methods. Additionally, there is a widespread belief that they are somehow objective, contrasting strongly with the subjectivity of interviewing. Candidates often feel that they may justifiably 'sell' themselves in an interview, creating an excessively favourable impression, whereas tests will magically reveal the truth. They give resourcing the semblance of scientific professionalism (Townley 1989).

Tests are based on the psychometric model (key concept 8.1) which 'assumes that there is an optimal set . . . of psychological characteristics for success at any human activity (in this instance, success at a particular job)' (Kline 1993: 374). Kline states that this is so obvious as to be banal. However, in our discussion of human resource planning we have seen that identifying such optimal sets is extremely difficult in practice. Specifically, job or personal specifications derived from traditional job analysis are backward-looking – they do not describe requirements for the future (Iles and Salaman 1995: 219). As we have seen, the traditional tightly prescribed 'job' is disappearing in favour of a more fluid, flexible role. Consequently, older notions of psychological 'dimensions' by which jobs and people are matched are being replaced by the more complex multidimensional concept of competences which will be discussed later in this chapter (see also chapters 10 and 11). Some of the advantages and disadvantages of tests are shown in Table 8.2.

| The dominant approach to selection in British and US textbooks. In its traditional form, it grounds the 'best person' model in psychological theory and testing. It embodies the use of refined techniques to achieve the best 'match' between job characteristics identified by formal job analysis and individual characteristics measured by psychological tests, structured interviews and other assessment methods. | **KEY CONCEPT 8.1** *The psychometric model* |

Table 8.2   Advantages and disadvantages of tests

Advantages	Disadvantages
Test results arc numerical, allowing direct comparison of applicants on the same criteria.	Responses can be faked on many tests to give a 'desirable' score. Some include 'lie detectors' to overcome this.
Tests provide 'hard' data which can be evaluated for their predictive usefulness in later years, i.e. compare predicted with actual performance.	Some people lack sufficient self-insight to give accurate responses.
Tests provide explicit and specific results unlike interviews and references which can be vague or 'coded'.	Tests are unreliable – temporary factors such as anxiety, headaches and illness can lead to variable results.
Tests measure substance rather than image.	Tests are invalid – many tests do not measure what they say they measure.
A battery of tests can cover a comprehensive range of abilities and personal qualities.	Tests are irrelevant – many tests do not measure qualities which are relevant to a specific organization, such as honesty and punctuality.
Tests are 'scientific' – empirically based with a grounding in theory. They are reliable, valid and discriminate between good, average and mediocre.	Tests require minimum literacy and a grasp of American jargon.
Tests provide a conceptual language to users, enhancing understanding of behaviour.	Good norms do not exist for most populations – comparison with white, middle-class, male US students has little practical value.
Empirical data from tests provide objective evidence to justify decisions.	Tests are unfair to anyone who is not a white, middle-class, male American because most have been constructed using them as a reference population.
Tests provide insights and explanations for behaviour. They can be used to justify individual rejections.	Freedom of information legislation opens 'objective' data to greater scope for challenge than vague, unrecorded interview data.
	Firms tend to use the same tests so that practice effects and knowledge of desirable answers can destroy their value.

Source: adapted from Furnham (1992).

Psychological testing has been used for different purposes in mainland Europe and North America, with the UK taking an intermediate view (Drenth 1978). The reasons for this are complex and reflect different traditions. The 'softer' European approach has relied on more descriptive, observational methods such as projective techniques and qualitative performance tests which draw on psychoanalytic theory. Conversely, the American approach has been dominated by behaviourist attitudes, emphasizing 'objectivity' and the quantitative use of data. This led to the development of a massive range of 'paper and pencil' tests suitable for individual or group use. Many European selection theorists have never been convinced of their merits. However, in recent years, the growth of a more systematic methodology has meant that the two approaches have converged to a considerable extent.

The use of psychometric tests has consistently increased. Mabey (1989), for example, found that 74 per cent of 101 companies employing over 2,000 staff used ability or aptitude tests; 59 per cent used personality tests. This compared to 62 per cent and 41 per cent, respectively, for 189 companies with fewer than 2,000 employees. Industrial Relations Services similarly found that 58 per cent of 173 UK employers surveyed used personality tests (see key concept 8.2) – half of these having introduced them in the previous two years (*Personnel Management*, July 1991). However, Storey (1994) reports a reduction in the use of personality tests in a survey of companies in Leicestershire.

Many lay people and psychologists believe that personality is a definite 'something' with a continuing existence at all stages of an individual's life and manifest in every situation that person encounters. Personality is generally expressed in terms of **types** or **traits**, and these form the basis of most personality tests used for resourcing and the documentation employed for many performance appraisal systems. An alternative approach is to regard personality as an artefact of a particular set of circumstances. In other words, the personality which appears to be an observer/tester depends on the meaning individuals give to a particular situation.	**KEY CONCEPT 8.2** *Personality*

In the public sector, the Local Government Management Board reported that over half of local authorities now use psychometric tests, with greater use of personality tests for senior appointments (*The Independent on Sunday*, 26 April 1992). The same study indicated that many tests were being adopted as a result of 'hard sell' techniques by consultancies and that monitoring of validity or effectiveness was scarcely ever undertaken.

A survey of over 700 students in 1990/91 by Kerr Brown Associates (*Personnel Management*, July 1991, February 1992) showed that 74 per cent had completed an aptitude test and 47 per cent a personality test during their job search. Of these only half had received any feedback. Remarkably, 40 per cent of those tested more than once were given the same test on more than one occasion. Some students received them on computer disk prior to initial interviews, thereby taking them outside controlled conditions. Almost half of those who took them undertook aptitude tests at or before the first interview stage, with 15 per cent also being given personality tests at that time. Many of the students believed that their chances of a second interview were affected by their performance in the tests. The tests seemed to be unpopular with students: only 2.8 per cent thought they allowed them to give the best presentation of their abilities, compared with 72 per cent who preferred interviews; 40 per cent thought the tests to be fair but 43 per cent considered that too much importance was attached to them.

Psychometric testing is particularly prevalent in Israel (*The Financial Times*, 8 March 1995). Ability tests are a feature of the university entrance system and recruitment for the air force. Software has been developed for a computerized psychometric system designed to rate candidates on the competences required by pilots.

Criticism of psychological testing

Increasing use has caused some disquiet amongst psychologists, particularly the proliferation of personality assessments (Bartram 1991). There are many available on the market which are promoted by people without adequate training and which make extravagant claims about their value and effectiveness. Many employers, including those with human resource specialists, do not have the ability to identify good and bad products. In an attempt to distinguish the trained from the untrained, the British Psychological Society has introduced a Certificate in Occupation Testing Competence.

Furnham (1992: 5) criticizes the underlying research which 'justifies' specific personality measures on a number of grounds:

- The choice of personality characteristics is often arbitrary and uninformed. Often they are historical relics, long abandoned and condemned by psychologists but still exploited as commercial products.
- Statistical analyses tend to be simple and naive, leading to more findings of significant differences than there are in reality. Usually, simple correlations are used – rather than 'robust and sensitive' multivariate statistics – when all the variables involved are multi-factorial.
- Most studies are exploratory, with no theoretical basis, and are not part of systematic programmes. As a result, they tend to be 'one-off', sometimes with interesting implications but no particular consequence.
- Organizational and social factors are often ignored – personality may not be the only relevant factor.

Blinkhorn and Johnson (*Personnel Management*, September 1991) criticize personality tests as predictors of job performance compared to ability and aptitude tests. They argue that their validity coefficients are often no better than chance. However, other specialists consider that personality tests are still valuable if they are used carefully and are not taken to be the main predictors. For example, conscientiousness is linked to job performance and extraversion scores are useful predictors for sales ability.

The greatest fault of personality tests is that candidates can lie. Individuals may score highly on extraversion because they are extraverts. Alternatively they can present themselves as outgoing because it is clear from the job description that selectors are seeking extraverts. It has also been argued that since tests are based on personality theory they cannot be interpreted without knowledge of the theory, in which most selectors are untrained. Another contentious issue is the effect of practice. If applicants are exposed to the same test on more than one occasion, they gain from the previous experience, often remembering answers.

Wood and Baron consider the effect of psychological tests in terms of 'adverse impact' on ethnic minority groups:

> 'Adverse impact' occurs when there is a significant disparity in test scores between ethnic groups, resulting in one group being disproportionately preferred over the other. The test is then said to have an adverse impact on the lower-scoring group.
>
> (Wood and Baron 1992)

They argue that the greater the degree of adverse impact, the more this has to be justified. Employers must be careful to test strictly for qualities which can be proven to be required for the job. Even when this can be demonstrated it remains important to find the method of measurement with the least adverse impact. A common problem is the effect of language proficiency on test performance. Typically, ethnic minority candidates are undergoing a selection procedure in the dominant community language, such as English, when they are stronger linguistically in another, such as Hindi or Italian. Their performance is masked by their comprehension of the questions and their ability to express their answers in a manner which is meaningful to the testers. Often, tests are time-limited. This is a reasonable gauge of mental speed for native speakers since their use of language is automatic. However, it is detrimental to people answering out of their native languages, since they need to translate at a conscious mental level. In effect the test becomes an assessment of 'proficiency in English' rather than a measure of its true objectives, such as 'problem-solving ability' or 'motivation'. The test has become unfair for anyone whose first language is not English.

In a case involving British Rail (BR) it was shown that in an analysis of 4,000 tests taken by potential drivers white people were twice as successful as ethnic minority candidates. Eight guards of Asian origin took BR to an industrial tribunal on the grounds that the tests were discriminatory. The verbal reasoning tests employed were not directly related to the job and were particularly difficult for people who spoke English as a second language. BR admitted that the tests had adverse impact on Asian workers and undertook to seek the advice of the Commission for Racial Equality in developing revised selection techniques.

Similarly, the Council for Legal Education (CLE) introduced a critical reasoning test for around 2,300 applicants to the English Bar's training school. The CLE had attempted to provide a test which was as fair as possible and it involved two firms of occupational psychologists and Birkbeck College of the University of London. However, the test was trialled on a group of existing students which included very few from ethnic minority groups. According to Makbool Javaid, Chair of the Society of Black Lawyers, it was felt that 'some of the questions would be difficult to answer for anyone who was not from a middle-class public school kind of background' (*The Times Higher*, 18 March 1994). The results produced a storm of protest and the tests were soon reconsidered. These reservations are widely known among human resource specialists and may explain Storey's (1994) report of a recent reduction in the use of personality tests.

Interviewing

The interview is a social ritual which is expected by all participants, including applicants. It is such a 'normal' feature of filling vacancies that candidates for a job would be extremely surprised not to be interviewed at least once.

Informal interviews

Many employers invite applicants for informal interviews prior to the main selection procedure. These interviews are useful for information exchange, particularly in the case of professionals (Breakwell 1990: 10). They provide the opportunity to discuss the full nature of the job, the working environment, prospects for further development and promotion. Candidates who decide that the job is not for them can elect to go no further. To avoid interviews degenerating into pointless chats, Breakwell emphasizes that both interviewer and applicant need to have checklists of essential points to cover. Interviewers should:

- Give a balanced picture of the job, including an honest account of its disadvantages together with a (larger) number of positive aspects. Honesty might seem dangerous but is best in the long run.
- Give a description of the organization in the same terms.
- Introduce the interviewee to other people in the department. This also allows interested parties to vet the applicant.

There seems to be some ambiguity as to whether informal interviews should be used as part of the pre-selection process by the employer rather than self-selection by the candidate. The crux of the issue depends on what interviewees have been told. If they have been led to believe that it is a truly informal information session they will not consider the process to be fair if they are subsequently told that they have not been shortlisted as a result.

Formal interviews

A survey of 173 UK employers by Industrial Relations Services (*Personnel Management*, July 1991) showed that despite the range of assessment methods available to them, 80 per cent regarded the formal selection interview as the most important source of evidence in making the final decision.

A selection interview can be defined neatly as a conversation with a purpose, but not infrequently the purpose is obscure to the point of invisibility. More often than not, purposeless chat would be nearer the mark. It is a form of social interaction in which the interviewer is engaged in active person perception of the interviewee (see key concept 8.3). From the interviewee's perspective 'one is managing a demonstration of knowledge or ability through a social vehicle, and one inevitably needs to attend to the social as well as the cognitive aspect of the interview' (Sternberg 1994: 181). In other words, the impression created depends as much on social factors as any demonstration of experience or expertise.

For many unskilled or semi-skilled jobs, the formal interview tends to be perfunctory and can be over in a few sentences. This is not necessarily a bad thing. For decades, the evidence has been that the more sophisticated and lengthy proceedings entered into by major organizations often have been no better in terms of outcome. According to Sternberg, 'Interviewers tend to prefer interviewees who are relaxed, who put the interviewers at ease, who are socially as well as verbally facile, and who have some degree of interpersonal sparkle' (1994: 182). In fact, the interview has attracted

> The perception of other people. Cues such as facial expression, posture, gesture, body movement, tone of voice, etc. are used to evaluate their current mood and overall personalities (McKenna 1994: 144). Each one of us has an **implicit personality theory** based on our experience, assumptions about people, beliefs and prejudices. The evidence of our senses is used to collect data about the perceived person and attribute characteristics to them according to our implicit theory.
>
> This is a simplification process and leads to a number of well-known errors of judgement, including:
>
> * **Logical error** – assuming that certain traits are always found together, e.g. if a person is described as 'objective' we tend to perceive them as 'cold'.
> * **Halo effect** – the tendency to perceive people as all 'good' or all 'bad'.
> * **Stereotyping** – seeing all members of a particular group, e.g., Africans, Scots, to have the same characteristics. Stereotyping leads to **prejudice**.

KEY CONCEPT 8.3
Person perception

severe criticism for a very long time. W. D. Scott is quoted as having said in 1915 that the selection interview is not a dependable selection method (C. Lewis 1985: 150). Since then the interview has been attacked on the grounds of its subjective nature, questionable validity and unreliability. E. C. Webster (1964) noted some significant findings:

* **First impressions** count. Interviewers make their minds up in the first few minutes, then seek evidence to support their opinion. A recent survey found that 74 per cent of interviewers made their decision on a candidate in the first five minutes (*The Times*, 23 April 1992).
* The candidate's **appearance** is the most significant factor, followed by information on the application form.
* **Unfavourable evidence** is valued more strongly than favourable evidence.
* The interviewer's **opinion** 'comes over' to the candidate during the interview and influences the candidate's further performance in an unfavourable or favourable direction.

Nevertheless, in a survey of sixty interviewers and ninety candidates in a 'milkround' exercise, 95 per cent of interviewers and 85 per cent of candidates considered interviews to be fair (*Personnel Management*, March 1992). Comparing panel with one-to-one interviews, 52 per cent of the interviewers said panel interviews were fairer, 35 per cent were unsure, and 13 per cent preferred one-to-one interviews. In contrast, nearly two-thirds of the candidates preferred one-to-one interviews, with only 13 per cent indicating a positive preference for the panel approach.

Evaluating methods

How do we judge the value or effectiveness of interviewing – or any other method of selection? Before going further it is useful to consider four basic requirements (Smith 1991: 32):

1 **Practicality.** Selection methods must be practical in a given situation, for

example cost, convenience and time available. Attitudes of employers and candidates to the methods are also relevant. In Case 8.2 we can see that Toyota considered recruitment of a new workforce to be important enough to justify a lengthy selection procedure.

2 **Sensitivity.** The ability of a method to distinguish one candidate from another is important. Interviews may rank a number of candidates fairly closely, whereas tests may give a wide range of scores. Toyota addressed this problem by using a number of different methods, including biodata, interviews, tests and work samples. (Work samples will be discussed later in this chapter.)

3 **Reliability.** How consistent are the results? Conventionally, there are three forms of reliability measure:

- **Comparison over time.** If a method is used on the same group of candidates on different days, are the scores likely to be similar? This is sometimes called test-retest or intra-rater reliability.
- **Inter-rater reliability.** If two or more assessors are involved, how much agreement is there between them?
- **Internal consistency.** If several items in a test or procedure are meant to measure the same characteristic, such as sociability, how close are the ratings?

4 **Validity.** Does the method achieve its purpose in distinguishing the most suitable applicants from the others? Three measures of validity are available:

- **Face validity.** Does the method appear to be measuring what it is supposed to measure? This is important since it is essential that candidates believe that they have been fairly treated. Disappointed applicants frequently complain about apparently irrelevant interview questions or test items. For example, one selection test includes the question 'Do you like tall women?' Whether or not this has deep psychological significance, its appearance is enough to bring derision on the test. In Case 8.2 we see that Toyota made certain that interview questions were directed strictly at job-related issues.
- **Construct validity.** To what extent does the method measure a particular construct or human quality such as commitment?
- **Predictive validity.** How well does the method predict the suitability of a successful candidate?

Reliability and validity are expressed as correlational coefficients where perfection is represented by 1.0 and pure chance is shown by 0. Establishing the validity of a particular procedure logically requires the employer to take on a large number of applicants, good and bad, and then compare their job performance with that predicted by the selection method. This kind of **predictive validity study** is impractical in most circumstances. The fact that we never know how the people we did not select might have performed is sometimes termed 'the one that got away' problem.

Research shows that similar results can be obtained by a method termed **concurrent study**, where selection methods are employed on existing employees at the same time as the selection procedure is taking place.

Performance of existing employees is then correlated with prediction scores of the selection method. Again, however, this is rarely done, partly because accurate performance measures are difficult to obtain for many jobs.

Fairness is a further requirement: specifically, it is important that candidates perceive the process to be fair. As we see in the Toyota illustration, good candidates are more likely to accept an offer if they consider that the procedure has been fair, effective and considerate. Moreover, candidates must receive full and accurate description of the job and their prospects in the company. Misleading impressions can lead to wastage sooner rather than later as the new recruit realizes that expectations and reality do not match. This is particularly the case with young employees, for example graduates, who tend not to have clear 'vocational maturity' or awareness of their own skills and career needs (Herriot and Fletcher 1990).

CASE 8.2
Toyota in Europe

In common with several other major Japanese car manufacturers, Toyota has established a production facility in Europe. By 1994 it had spent nearly £1 billion on its factories in Britain and development facilities in Brussels. Production in 1995 was forecast to be 90,000 cars with a workforce of 1,950. The cars included 80 per cent local content, derived from 200 European suppliers. In the long term Toyota aims to employ 3,000 staff producing 200,000 cars at its factory in Burnaston, Derbyshire, UK. Its resourcing practices were typical of Japanese transplant ventures. The first 1,100 staff included just seventy-eight Japanese, over 90 per cent of the employees being locals living within 35 miles of the factory. The average employee was male, aged around 30 and had no experience of car production. Workers were called 'team members' and had typically gone through a six- to seven-month recruitment process. According to Bryan Jackson, Director of Human Resources, 'We want people who can work as a team and who have ideas for improvements and can demonstrate an ability to learn' (reported in the *Guardian*, 17 December 1992). The resourcing procedure included:

- A five-page application form with biodata items 'designed to test commitment'. These included questions about personal values and achievements.
- A three-hour 'testing and orientation phase'. This was a series of tests to measure numerical skills, attitudes and learning ability. They included a Video-Interactive Test of Learning, which asked candidates to give responses to a number of situations.
- Then came the interview phase. Bryan Jackson explained that:

> We didn't want the traditional 20–minute interview, and the you-go-to-the-same-football-match-as-me-so-you-must-be-okay line. Instead candidates received a 'targeted behavioural interview' which consisted of 75 minutes of questions on situations they had experienced. Their decisions were assessed on the basis that 'It's well known that past behaviour is a good predictor of future behaviour'.
>
> (*Guardian*, 17 December 1992)

- Having survived this far, candidates were then given a work sample: six hours on a simulated production line making wheel trims or fuel filters under realistic conditions.
- The final hurdles were a further (one-hour) interview, two references and a medical.

Prior to the first car being manufactured, 400 production staff were employed from over 20,000 applicants for the 39-hour-a-week, £13,000-a-year jobs.

The British workers had achieved quality standards comparable with those of the company's Japanese plants. However, Japanese factories made further productivity gains in reaction to the recession. European manufacturing was not expected to be profitable until production had reached 130,000–140,000 vehicles a year.

(*Source: Guardian*, 17 December 1992)

Interviews revisited

Recently there has been a revision of opinion concerning the value of interviews (Smith *et al*. 1989: 209). Earlier research findings were based on small samples. The use of **meta-analytic** techniques allows the combination of statistics from a number of small studies to give much larger samples. For example, Weisner and Cronshaw (1988) combined validity coefficients from 150 studies and concluded that interviews can be more valid than suspected. In fact, their validity depends on the **type of interview**. Traditional or unstructured interviews comprise the vast majority and are generally no more than cosy chats. Their validity was found to be 0.2 (very poor), whereas structured interviews, especially those based on job analysis, were found to be significantly better, with a validity of 0.63.

Structured interviews are conducted to a format – rather than a script – and focus questioning on the job rather than on irrelevant incidentals such as holidays and golf. Two standard methods are:

- **Criterion-referenced** interviews, based on job analysis with a set of questions geared to experience and skill for interviewers to **choose** from.
- **Situational interviews**, based on the Critical Incidents technique. A reasonable number (typically twenty) of real-life work incidents are obtained from jobholders or their supervisors. Possible ways of dealing with these situations are outlined and rated as suitable or unsuitable, frequently on a points system. These situations are presented to candidates as hypothetical problems and responses evaluated against predetermined ratings.

To be effective, an interview must be more than a friendly chat. The greater the degree of planning beforehand, the greater the likelihood of a high degree of validity as a selection tool. The function of the interview is to obtain predictive evidence regarding a candidate's likely performance on specific criteria. The questioning style can be linked to the kind of evidence required and may take one of three principal routes:

- **(Hypothetical) problem-solving questioning**, in which the candidate is presented with situations to evaluate or solve and which can be expected to test the candidate's abilities in a number of respects, e.g. intellect, grasp of information, problem-solving ability, lateral thinking, practicality, creativity, etc.
- **Behavioural (past) event questioning**, which assumes that previous handling of situations and problems predicts an individual's future

performance in similar circumstances. In Case 8.2 we saw that Toyota used 75–minute interviews of this kind as part of their selection procedure for new workers.

- **Patterned behavioural event (life) questioning**, which attempts to identify an individual's career or life strategy, establishing how rational and sensible changes in that person's life have been and drawing conclusions about stability, seriousness of application and likely motivation. The 'culture fit' approach emphasizes this perspective. For example, Japanese companies such as Toyota are more interested in personality than technical skill. They look for a personal philosophy which fits the corporate culture (Whitehill 1990). They seek stable employees who:

  - have no signs of restlessness;
  - are able to work as part of a group;
  - have no unconventional political or social beliefs.

Not surprisingly, as we saw in Case 8.2, Toyota supported interview information with a biodata test focused on establishing the likely degree of commitment from prospective recruits.

Other approaches which have ethical considerations to take into account include the following:

- **Stress interviewing**, where the candidate is pressurized, sometimes aggressively. The justification is that the job is pressurized and therefore it is important to establish how the candidate is likely to perform under stressful circumstances. One study asked interviewers if they ever deliberately put candidates under stress in interviews to see how they would cope (*Personnel Management*, March 1992). The findings were disturbing, with 13 per cent saying they often did, 27 per cent saying sometimes, and 27 per cent rarely.
- **Sweet and sour** interviews, where interviewers take completely different approaches, one pleasant, one unpleasant, in an attempt to gain a wider range of responses from the candidate.

Preparation for interviews

Training for interviewers stresses a number of factors conducive to making a good impression on the candidate. The interviewer should ensure that relevant information (application forms etc.) is read beforehand – it is surprising how many interviewers are found to be reading such material for the first time **during** the interview. The interview should take place in an appropriate environment – a quiet room without interruptions, with comfortable but business-like furniture and so on. The candidate should be put at ease as much as possible.

A major change in recent years has been the improvement in applicants' interview techniques. Redundant staff are commonly given the opportunity of outplacement counselling, which normally includes advice on CV preparation and coaching in interview technique. Managers who are rarely involved in selection, perhaps only conducting interviews once or twice a year, are at a disadvantage against trained applicants. Interview coaching is similar in principle to training politicians for television appearances. Astute trainees can learn how to mask insincerity and to promise the earth with apparent conviction.

Against trained interviewers, the most useful tactic for applicants is to become familiar with the company they are applying for. This requires research on the company's history, products or services and its reported strategy. Knowledge of the industry or sector in which it operates is also valuable. This information should not be acquired by pestering the recruitment section on the telephone. Given the number of applications to advertised vacancies at present, this is likely to be unwise. Whether or not any direct questions are asked on these subjects, applicants who have researched the territory will be able to form their responses in a way which makes it clear that they have done so.

Interview techniques

There are significant variations in the way employers conduct interviews. The most common method is the **singleton** interview, when the candidate's fate is determined by one session with a single interviewer. For obvious reasons, this method is likely to be regarded as unfair by interviewees who are not selected. There is no check or record of bias on the part of the interviewer, who may have made a judgement on a complete whim.

A longstanding method which attempts to overcome this problem is the **panel** or **board** interview, involving a number of interviewers. Typically, two or three people ask questions in turn. A classic format involves an **operational** interviewer, usually a line manager from the department offering the job, and a **personnel** interviewer, normally from the personnel department. There may be an additional chairperson. Each asks questions appropriate to their areas of expertise, the operational assessor asking task-related questions and the personnel assessor investigating career aspiration and motivation. The board is sometimes much larger: there are instances of as many as seven or nine interviewers.

Superficially, the panel interview is judged to be fairer since all questioning takes place in a public arena and candidates' responses are heard by all parties. It also offers the candidate a more varied range of questions, expanding the evidence available to the assessors. As a consequence, personal bias should have less effect. However, the situation is likely to be more stressful for candidates. There are also opportunities for organizational politics to enter the situation, especially when the procedure is an internal selection.

A further variant is the **sequential** method, with two or more interviews but with the candidate only being expected to face one interviewer at a time. This method carries most of the advantages of singleton and panel interviews with fewer of the disadvantages.

It is possible to use **group** interviews in certain circumstances. We will see later in this chapter that they are useful within assessment centre programmes as information sessions.

As with many other aspects of selection, interviewing has been formalized and packaged into training programmes available for both selectors and candidates. Untrained assessors are likely to conduct interviews in an unstructured way. Interview training is a useful component of management training, an issue considered in more depth in Chapter 11. The best training programmes encourage people to become aware of their body language and questioning styles, helping them to develop interview techniques which open up fresh areas of evidence. Many junior managers and job-club participants have had the opportunity to see themselves 'in action' on video taking part in mock interviews. Initially demoralizing (for most), this is an invaluable method of providing feedback.

Packaged training methods have led to a certain sameness, however, and seasoned job applicants and interviewers now enter into formalized duals where each participant is aware of the underlying dynamics. Typically, interviewers are taught to:

- Ask **open** not closed questions to elicit the maximum information. Questions beginning with **how**, **what**, **why**, **when** reduce the frequency of yes/no answers and force candidates to think about their replies.
- Provide **supportive** body language which suggests interest in what the candidate is saying without indicating approval or disapproval.
- Use questioning styles such as the use of **funnelling**. Here the interviewer asks a succession of **how**, **what**, **why** questions on the same subject in an attempt to achieve a depth of evidence.
- Consider factual or **hypothetical** questions, such as 'How would you go about setting up a telephone system for a remote island in the Pacific?' Provided that the interviewee is not a qualified telecommunications engineer, an applicant for a totally unconnected job will have to think hard to provide a full, imaginative but practical answer.

Tom Peters dismissed this 'quick analysis' technique as honouring glibness (syndicated article, *The Independent on Sunday*, 8 May 1994). Many interviewers have strong opinions on what they are looking for and how they should set about it. Peters held that 'interviews should be the centrepiece of a respectful courting process' foregoing 'pop quizzes and sadistic questioning rituals'. Arguing that the past was the only guide to future performance, he set out an interviewing programme in typical guru style:

1 **Put the candidate's resume under a microscope.** Pull an applicant's CV apart, following up experiences and achievements:

- remember that 'the kid who went through college without participating in extracurricular activities – without **leading** those activities – is not likely to be a tiger on the job';
- scrutinize college grades;
- make an extensive check of references, previous work samples and work commendations ('employee of the month certificates or their equivalents').

2 **Look for a legacy.** Good performance in the past is not enough – how did they make their previous jobs better and different?

3 **Examine their turn-ons.** Talk about the applicant's 'peak experiences at work or school'. Apparently, 'what a person brags about is a key to future job performance'. Essentially, is the candidate a solo performer or a team worker?

4 **Seek deviance, defiance and adventure.** Has the applicant broken with convention and done something in an unusual way, for example by taking time out from education and travelling the world? 'Curiosity and productive kinkiness in the past will raise the odds of getting more of the same in the future.'

5 **Pursue animal energy.** If the 'spirit and zest' of the candidate exhaust you by the end of the interview, 'hire that one on the spot'.

6 **Trust your gut.** Ignoring interview nervousness, is the applicant 'the kind of person you would like to hang around with'?

Work samples

Interviews suffer from a basic problem: they obtain answers from candidates which, in effect, are unverifiable claims. When asked what they would do in a particular situation it is only natural for candidates to give the answer which they feel the interviewer wants to hear. There is no guarantee that a candidate would actually behave in that way in a real situation. In addition, it is common for candidates to exaggerate their abilities or experience and play down their inadequacies.

The work-sample technique attempts to overcome this problem by asking candidates to take on **mini-jobs** in a selection situation. As we saw in Case 8.2, properly designed work samples capture key elements of a real job. As such, they are realistic rather than hypothetical or abstract and should include features of the context in which the job functions. Work samples have shown some of the highest validity scores compared to other selection methods (Smith *et al*. 1989: 70). They are comparatively easy to organize and even the smallest of companies could employ the simpler forms, such as the following:

- a typing test for jobs requiring keyboard skills;
- bricklaying;
- role-playing;
- group decisions;
- presentations;
- reports.

The most sophisticated of work-sample procedures include 'in-basket tests', sometimes called 'in-tray exercises'. These are normally used for managerial jobs. Candidates are given a typical in-tray containing a selection of material such as letters to be answered, reports to be analysed, items to be prioritized, etc. They are given instructions on what to do and a time limit. Standard scoring methods are available. Work samples are often used as part of an assessment centre programme.

Assessment centres

Recent surveys indicate increasing use of assessment centres, especially by large companies. They have been heavily researched in recent years, with the emphasis on their reliabilty and predictive validity. They show up well in comparison with most other forms of selection or assessment such as interviews and personality tests. Meta-analyses indicate much more respectable validity coefficients for assessment centres in predicting managerial success than with any other method. However, as we will discuss shortly, their use is not entirely without difficulties.

Assessment centres are procedures and not necessarily places. They function on the principle that no individual method of selection is particularly good and no individual assessor is infallible. Accordingly, they use multiple methods and several assessors in structured programmes which attempt to minimize the inadequacies of each method and cancel out the prejudices of individual selectors. Inevitably, assessment centres are a very expensive method of selection. However, cheaper methods are focused towards past or present performance. This may be adequate where applicants are being assessed for jobs which are broadly similar to their current or previous work. When this is not the case, and applicants are being considered for more stretching tasks, they fail to provide the evidence as to how candidates are likely to perform. Most management promotions come into this category. Good managers need to demonstrate knowledge, skills and abilities which may not have been required at lower levels. How can we identify these characteristics? Assessment centres are particularly useful in this respect because they are focused on **potential**. They bring taxing problems and challenges to candidates in a situation which allows systematic observation and measurement of their performance.

The origins of the assessment centre lie in the violent history of the twentieth century and the need for officer selection. Originally devised by the German army in the 1930s, assessment centre techniques were soon taken up in other countries. The British War Office Selection Board subjected candidates to a three- or four-day assessment geared to evaluate leadership and organizational abilities. This included exercises in which intending officers had to negotiate obstacles such as rivers with a motley collection of squaddies and an assortment of ropes, planks and oil drums. They also included lengthy interviews and long written reports.

Some modern assessment centres with an 'outward bound' inclination continue to include such exercises, but most consist of group discussions, psychometric tests, interviews and exercises such as 'in basket' work samples and presentations. The underlying intention is to measure applicants on the competences which are deemed to be appropriate to the job. Simulations in the assessment centre are designed to bring out the behaviour which demonstrates possession of these competences. The intention is not to estimate current ability but to predict future performance, possibly at higher management levels.

After the Second World War the method spread to the public sector and then to industry. The first industrial application was at the American Telephone and Telegraph Company (AT&T). Their experience had a major influence on subsequent use elsewhere following a number of studies in which employees were compared with initial assessment centre evaluations. These studies showed a significant correlation between the evaluations and subsequent work performance (Smith *et al.* 1989). The model form of assessment centre is an expensive process:

> A typical assessment centre involves six participants and lasts from one to three days. As participants go through the simulations they are observed by assessors (usually three) who are specially trained in observing and evaluating behaviour. Assessors observe different participants in each simulation and take notes on special observation forms. Then, after the simulations are completed, assessors spend one or more days sharing their observations and reaching agreement on evaluations of participants. Their final assessment, contained in a summary report for each participant, gives a detailed account of participants' strengths and development needs as well as an evaluation of overall potential for success in the 'target' position.
>
> (Byham 1984: 55)

Table 8.3 shows the seven conditions which classically characterize assessment centres.

Problems with assessment centres

Whether or not it is costed in financial terms, the impact on management time is considerable. Managers may appreciate the value of high-quality selection procedures, but will be reluctant to devote so much time. Additionally, the traditional process is group-based and is unusable in situations where only one or two candidates are being considered.

The effectiveness of an assessment centre depends upon its design and

Table 8.3 Classic characteristics of assessment centres

1 A number of assessment techniques must be used, of which at least one must be a **simulation**. Simulations could take the shape of work samples, group exercises and in-baskets. Simulations are designed to bring out behaviours which are related to dimensions of performance on the actual job in question.

2 There must be **multiple trained assessors**.

3 Ratings must be **pooled** between assessors and assessment techniques in order to provide a judgement on selection, training or development programme.

4 Overall assessment of behaviour has to take place at a different time from the observation of behaviour.

5 Simulation exercises must be pre-developed to elicit a number of desired behaviours. They must be tested in advance to ensure that the results are relevant to the organization and that they are reliable and objective.

6 All dimensions, qualities, attributes or characteristics to be measured by the assessment centre must be determined by some form of job analysis.

7 The assessment techniques used must be designed to provide evidence for the evaluation of these dimensions.

Source: based on Blanksby and Iles (1990).

the anticipation of problems. Common design faults have been well documented (Dulewicz 1991: 50):

- The criteria for measurement are too woolly. Often, the competences on which candidates are being assessed are very **poorly defined** and not expressed in behavioural terms which can be measured.
- The competences are not mutually exclusive and **overlap** each other. Candidates are rewarded or penalized twice, depending on their strength in a particular area.
- Criteria are tied to the **past**, rather than being forward-looking.
- Exercises are **badly designed** and do not relate to experiences which are likely to occur within the organization. Alternatively, and perhaps because of this, they do not relate to the assessment criteria.
- Assessment centres contain a wide range of procedures, from group exercises to psychometric tests. Results from these procedures take a variety of forms. Integrating the results is **complex**, particularly when combining evidence on single competences from a number of procedures. Poor technical design at this stage will lead to misleading findings.
- Poor assessor training. Line managers are unlikely to be good assessors unless they have been trained to avoid pitfalls such as 'halos and horns'. Also they require guidance on the range and skew of their assessments. Assessors need to be consistent in how they pitch their ratings, avoiding overleniency or severity.
- Poor pre-selection and briefing of candidates has the consequence that some candidates flounder from the beginning of the programme. Others become hostile towards a procedure which appears to them to be unfair or disorganized.
- Poor programming, leaving both assessors and candidates unsure of what they are supposed to be doing. They may be allotted too little or too much time at different points in the assessment.
- Inadequate handling of the programme events due to lack of coordination or commitment.
- Inadequate (or non-existent) **follow-up** may occur in the form of badly handled feedback counselling or inaction on assessors' recommendations.
- Poor evaluation of candidates' experience and assessors' performance on the programme.

Dulewicz (1991: 50) considered that there were three broad phases which accounted for most of these difficulties:

- programme design;
- selection and training of assessors;
- effective follow-up action.

He attributed many of the shortcomings to inexperience. Assessment centres are involved and complex. Good design is dependent on the knowledge and skills to design and develop what is a 'highly precise and sophisticated tool'.

Graphology

Graphology, or handwriting analysis, has a long history on the mainland of Europe. It originated in Italy in the early seventeenth century and was further refined in France and Germany, where it is used widely. The essence of graphology is that analysts claim to be able to describe an individual's personality from a sample of their handwriting. Their theoretical base is that of trait psychology, which holds that personality has a number of fixed dimensions which are relatively unchangeable and do not depend on the situation. This is not to say that people do not change; indeed many graphologists believe their strongest asset to be the identification of neurotic or stress-related conditions which may be transient. Some graphologists also claim to be able to detect such characteristics as alcohol problems, homosexuality and dishonesty. The British company S. G. Warburg has used graphology in selection for a long time:

> The recent candidate interviewed for a junior job in Warburg's computer department provided an excellent CV, and seemed able and confident in the course of two interviews. His handwriting sample, however, was abnormally cramped. The lines were crooked and the letters spidery and badly squashed. At best, it seemed the writing of an ill-educated child. But Mrs Nezos [graphologist] thought otherwise. For an employer like Warburg, the prospect of hiring a drug addict is too frightening to contemplate. The man was turned down for the job.
>
> (*The Independent on Sunday*, 20 October 1991)

Evidently, the graphologist believed that spidery, squashed writing indicated drug addiction!

Handwriting analysis is routine and highly regarded in many continental European countries but is generally regarded with disdain in the UK. Moss (1992) reports high levels of use in France, including in large companies such as St Goberin, Elf Aquitaine, Crédit Lyonnais and Peugeot. In Switzerland, Crédit Suisse, Sandoz and most banks and insurance companies use graphology. Curtis Casewit, an American graphologist, claimed that West Germany had as many graphologists as dental surgeons in 1980 (*The Economist*, 16 June 1990). To a degree, it also has a following in the USA.

In the UK there has been a marked resistance to its use, especially among psychologists. Moss (1992) attributes this to a lack of tradition in the UK. Recently, however, there has been a considerable upsurge of interest, fuelled partly by publicity from consultants but also by dissatisfaction with results of more traditional methods of selection. The British Institute of Graphology claimed that handwriting assessments on up to 8,000 candidates a year were being commissioned by prospective employers in the UK, indicating that the secret use of graphology was greater than public statements admitted (*The Independent*, 4 March 1991). Additionally, membership of the institute has risen from 170 to 300 in three years, indicating an increase in activity.

Cox and Tapsell (1991) compared analyses by graphologists and non-graphologists of fifty handwriting samples provided by managers on a training course. When assessment centre results were compared with the handwriting analyses, they found that the graphologists did slightly worse than the non-graphologists in rating the candidates. Moreover, the two graphologists failed to agree with each other!

The different attitudes towards graphology were highlighted in Shackleton and Newell's (1991) comparison of selection methods in the UK and France. They extended the methodology of an earlier UK study by Robertson and Makin (1986), comparing responses from companies in the Times Top 1000 list and similar French firms in *Les 200 Premiers Groupes des Échos* (see Table 8.4). Apart from the use of graphology, other differences are apparent on the two sides of the channel. Unlike British firms, French companies rarely use multiple-interviewer panel or board interviews but do use the sequential system. Whereas references continue to be considered in many UK decisions (but less so than in 1986), they are used only as factual checks in most large French companies. Tests tend to be used by the larger companies and exclusively so in France.

Resourcing decisions

> In seeking employment, much depends upon the applicant's manner and dress; if he is rude and ungainly, and expresses himself in an awkward manner, an employer will at once conceive a prejudice against him, and curtly decline the proffer of his services. But if, on the other hand, he is pleasing in his manners and dress, he will not only be engaged to fill a vacancy, but will sometimes be taken into the establishment, although no vacancy exists. Applicants for employment should also be scrupulously neat in their attire, and clean in their persons; for an employer naturally argues that a person who is careless of himself will be equally so about about his business.
>
> *(The Dictionary of Daily Wants, 1859)*

Selection is a decision-making activity, 'the psychological calculation of suitability' (Townley 1994: 94). If the recruitment process is open, selection decision-making normally takes place in a series of stages. Recruitment marketing may attract hundreds – sometimes thousands – of responses. The first decision stage is termed pre-selection. Its purpose is to reduce applications to a manageable number, with the emphasis on **rejection** rather than selection. Evidence is gathered from letters, CVs, application

Table 8.4 Comparison of British and French methods

Method	UK (%)	France (%)
Application forms	93	98
Interviews	93	94
More than one interview	60	92
References	74	11
Cognitive tests	70	50
Handwriting	2.6	77
Biodata	19	4
Assessment centre	59	19

Source: Shackleton and Newell (1991).

forms, and possibly biodata or screening tests. Large Japanese employers administer formal entrance examinations (Whitehill 1990). Regardless of the methods used, the intention is to arrive at a comparatively small number – the **short-list** – of apparently well-suited applicants.

Preselection is open to considerable abuse and plays a major role in the cloning process. Frequently decisions are made on arbitrary grounds, ranging from the absurd – use of the 'wrong' colour of ink, for example – to the discriminatory, excluding particular groups such as women, ethnic minorities, graduates from other than specific schools or universities, and people over a certain age. Preselection offers those so inclined an ideal opportunity to reject unwanted candidates without having to give detailed reasons. Unless the organization has an equal opportunities monitoring system, with each application logged, categorized and tracked throughout the selection procedure, this a glaring loophole, allowing hidden and illegal discrimination to take place. It is common for two identical applications to be treated differently if one is sent with an obvious ethnic minority name and the other is evidently from the majority population. Herriot notes the irony that pre-selection and initial interview result in rejection of the largest proportion of candidates and yet these stages are the least valid and reliable (Herriot and Fletcher 1990).

After pre-selection screening, surviving applicants meet the formal decision-making procedure termed selection. In the 'best person' model, selection is a matching process, where an applicant's qualities are compared with criteria deemed necessary for the job, when the measurement of the former is extremely difficult and evidence for the latter is a matter of opinion. In contrast, 'culture fit' focuses on personality and compatibility with existing staff. In Japan, attention is given to such matters as political views, family background and personal finances. These would not be relevant for the average western company (Whitehill 1990). We have noted that these two models are frequently confused and decision-making is a matter of identifying the 'ideal' or clone candidate, a process rationalized by talk of 'fitting in'.

Sophisticated selection methods are not common in small companies, most of which continue to depend on informal methods for selection decisions – typically references and one or two interviews. In contrast, large organizations have adopted a range of methods to aid decision-making. However, Table 8.5 indicates that some methods are considerably better than others. This is especially true for employment categories, such as blue-collar workers, where it had not previously applied (Townley 1989). The trend is most obvious in Japanese- (as we saw in the Toyota case study) and US-owned firms but it is also apparent in UK and other European companies. Regardless of the resourcing model employed, procedures have become more elaborate. At Mazda in Michigan USA, for example, the process involved several weeks' assessment and included application forms, aptitude tests, personal interviews, group problem-solving and simulated work exercises. These were designed to weed out 'druggies, rowdies, unionists'. Selection emphasized team-working behavioural traits rather than technical skills, and successful candidates had an average age

Table 8.5 Comparative validities

Validity range	Methods	Rating
0.4–0.5 +	Work sample tests Ability tests	good to excellent
0.3–0.39	Biodata Assessment centres Structured interviews (or higher)	acceptable
Less than 0.3	Personality tests Typical interviews References Graphology	poor
Chance (0)	Astrology	

Source: adapted from Smith *et al.* (1991).

of 31, little or no factory experience and were overwhelmingly (70 per cent) male.

Townley argues that this has not resulted from the increasing professionalization of human resource specialists. Neither is it a reaction to the difficult task of selecting from the large number of applicants attracted by any job advertisement during an economic recession. She attributes the trend to the increasing prevalence of HRM, with its emphasis on the 'attitudinal and behavioural characteristics of employees' (Townley 1989: 92). Guest (1992) observes that the 'excellence literature', authored by Tom Peters and others, together with accounts of Japanese management methods, has focused the minds of many western managers on the importance of recruitment, selection and socialization of employees. This leads to an interest in factors which can be assessed by a range of technical methods such as psychometric tests. In recent years their use has increased in Europe, particularly in the UK, whereas equal opportunities legislation has forced a different approach in the USA.

So, confining our discussion to 'best person' and 'culture fit' models for the moment, is selection best conducted subjectively or objectively? Smith and Robertson (1993: 255) compare the two approaches:

- **Clinical**, or subjective. Just as a doctor diagnoses a medical condition on the basis of perceived sympoms, an 'expert' or experienced person reviews information on candidates. Choice is based on the expert's experience and expertise.
- **Actuarial.** This is comparable to calculating an insurance premium. Various factors are quantified and put into a weighted equation. For example, experience may be given twice the value of educational qualifications. The candidate scoring the highest number of points is selected.

They conclude that the actuarial approach is better than the clinical method, but not to a very major extent.

Flexible employees for the future must come from a diverse background.

Poor selection decisions are frequently the result of confusing essential competences with trivial characteristics associated with good performance. These associations arise from past-focused rather than forward-looking resourcing criteria. This is the essence of cloning, a key issue in our next chapter, on the management of diversity.

Summary

In free-market countries the personnel profession has adopted a 'best practice' model which fits the prevailing business ideology. This model prescribes a quest for the 'right (best) person for the job'. To achieve this goal, criteria are used to rate prospective applicants by means of selection techniques, including biographical data, interviews, psychometric tests, group exercises, simulated work samples and even handwriting analysis. The most definitive form of selection is likely to take place within the context of assessment centres, which involve several assessors and a variety of selection techniques. The 'best person' or psychometric model has achieved the status of orthodoxy in free-market countries. Elsewhere different models of resourcing apply. For example, in Japan there is a greater concern with personality and background than presumed ability. Recruits are sought who will 'fit in' with the culture of the corporation, who will be content to build a career within the organization, who will absorb the goals of the organization.

Further reading

Smith and Robertson (1993) provide a definitive outline of recruitment and selection, based on the psychometric model, in *The Theory and Practice of Systematic Personnel Selection* (2nd edition). More recent critiques of this approach are given, first, from a competence perspective by Sparrow in Anderson and Herriot (eds) (1994) *Assessment and Selection in Organizations: Methods and Practice for Recruitment and Appraisal*, First Update and Supplement 1994; second, from a 'social process' viewpoint by Iles and Salaman in Storey (ed.) (1995) *Human Resource Management: A Critical Text*.

Review questions

1 Are selection methods objective?
2 Discuss the advantages and disadvantages of the following:

- structured and unstructured interviews;
- assessment centres;
- psychometric tests.

3 What criteria can be used to judge the effectiveness of selection methods? Define 'validity' and 'reliability' in your own words.
4 Evaluate the role of the line manager in the resourcing process.

5 What are the major differences between the French and British approaches to resourcing?

6 Is it possible to guarantee equality of opportunity in a resourcing process?

Problems for discussion and analysis

1 The general manager of Saveplenty Stores has been interviewing applicants for sales and management jobs for twenty-three years. She believes that she can identify good and bad candidates by chatting to them for ten minutes. You have been placed in her department as a graduate trainee and have been given the task of organizing recruitment for a new superstore. How would you do this and what role should the general manager play?

2 You are a human resource specialist with a large software company. The company has agreed to set up a joint venture in Paris with a major French computer manufacturer. The venture will adapt and distribute US/UK software in French-speaking countries. Being fluent in French, you have been chosen as HR Manager. Most of the other senior staff are longstanding managers from the French company. Your first task is to recruit approximately sixty junior managers and technical staff. The procedures and choices have to involve your French colleagues. How would you conduct the exercise and what difficulties would you expect?

9

Managing diversity

This chapter considers how opportunities are constrained to the detriment of individuals and organizations. We examine how businesses and their managers can maximize human capital.

People are different. They vary in gender, culture, race, social and psychological characteristics. Attitudes towards these differences can be negative or positive, depending upon individual perspectives and prejudices. In earlier chapters we identified the tendency to form like-minded 'in-groups', to favour members of one's own group and for those in authority to recruit people like themselves. The consequences can be seen in a lack of opportunity for women, ethnic minorities, the disabled, the middle-aged and other disadvantaged sections of the community. The best jobs are ring-fenced and barriers are placed to prevent the progress of people from such groups.

However, as members of organizations it is difficult to challenge the often subconscious actions and elaborately entrenched justifications for unfairness. Not least, this is because discrimination and prejudice are expressions of power and the expression of power entails the ability to prevent, inhibit or punish critical comment. Yet, if people are the key assets of a business it is important to realize the maximum benefit from their human capital. True competitive advantage requires the best from everyone – without restrictions; it demands a prejudice-free and inclusive attitude towards actual and potential employees.

In reality, this has to be viewed as an ideal since discriminatory and non-inclusive behaviours have a deep psychological basis. Research shows that prejudice is difficult to remove. For example, if someone is prejudiced against a particular group, meeting someone with positive qualities from that group does not dispel the prejudice:

> the prejudiced person is capable of rationalising the situation in such a way as to conclude that the person he or she met is unique in some respects, and is unlike the stereotype. [. . .] For example, an anti-Semite will not be swayed in

his or her view of Jews by evidence of their charitable behaviour, nor will those who have a deep prejudice against black people be persuaded by coming in contact with intelligent and industrious people in this group.
(McKenna 1994: 260)

Nevertheless equality of opportunity is an objective worth striving for. It can be addressed at all levels: governments have a role to play through legislation to prevent discrimination; organizations need to focus on the management of diversity, making the most of a wide pool of talent; strategists should consider equal opportunity policies, targeting and positive development of underrepresented groups; people managers can monitor their activities and increase awareness to minimize discrimination.

In this chapter we will address some key questions:

- Why should we encourage diversity in human resources?
- What are the function and value of formal legislation and equal opportunity policies?
- Why do people from certain backgrounds figure so prominently at the upper levels of virtually all professions?

We begin by placing the topic in its environmental context, examining the economic, cultural and ethical justifications for equality of opportunity. Then we move on to consider how organizations can develop strategies to maximize the use of diverse kinds of employee. The remainder of the chapter examines specific forms of discrimination, including gender, ethnicity and age discrimination, and also discusses harassment and the problems associated with employing ex-offenders.

The environment and opportunity

Anthony Jay is reputed to have said that 'success is when preparation meets opportunity'. Preparation depends on personal effort but opportunity is linked to social factors such as economic conditions, education and other people. Effectively, society determines who is given opportunity and who is not through the process of discrimination. Overt prejudice is comparatively easy to observe but the true nature of unfairness lies in the way opportunity has been institutionalized within society. The status quo is constructed to benefit certain types of individual from particular backgrounds or those who are able to adapt most easily to its requirements. Typically, this has denied opportunity to women and minority groups.

Most countries have a concentration of particular social groups at the top of their institutions. Others are found further down. As a consequence, skills and abilities are not used to the full – a situation which is detrimental to society as a whole. However, the advantaged are unlikely to admit that their positions come from privilege rather than competence. For them, change is not a priority. An example can be seen in India, where government attempts to assist disadvantaged castes have met with violent protests by the privileged. Other instances are readily found in developing African states where paid employment is scarce. Managers are under pressure to offer jobs to people from their family or tribe (Akinnusi 1991). This is a form of **particularism** (see key concept 9.1).

KEY CONCEPT 9.1 *Particularism*	Discrimination favouring particular groups and individuals over others. It derives from a reliance on personal relationships such as ethnic origin, religion or tribal community. It contrasts with **universalism**, in which personal relationships are ignored and emphasis is on other criteria such as qualifications, expertise and ability to do the job.

Particularism leads to discrimination. Worldwide, this mechanism can be extended to include a number of forms, including discrimination on the grounds of the following:

- **Age** – arbitrary age boundaries excluding younger and older workers.
- **Disability** – discriminating against people with special needs.
- **Gender** – limiting certain types of jobs to either males or females.
- **Ethnic origin** – preference for particular racial, linguistic or religious communities.
- **Background** – often seen as cliques – networks of people from similar backgrounds – reserving the best jobs for themselves. In addition, people with socially undesirable backgrounds, such as ex-offenders, are actively discriminated against.
- **Nepotism** – common in small companies which rely heavily on family members.

Many countries use legislation to reduce such discrimination, for example in areas such as equal pay, race and disability. The effectiveness of such legislation is seen in the proportion of disadvantaged groups achieving responsible positions. This tends to be disappointing. We will see that, in most parts of the world, the presence of women and people from ethnic minority groups becomes increasingly rare towards the top of most organizations and some groups, such as the disabled and the over fifties, are conspicuously absent from many firms.

Legislation can take a number of forms:

- **Positive action.** Measures to prevent discrimination by insisting on, for example, non-discriminatory recruitment procedures, training programmes and pay rates. This does not include any preferential treatment for disadvantaged groups. UK legislation takes this approach.
- **Affirmative action** or positive discrimination. A longstanding approach in the USA, designed to advantage the disadvantaged, including women, African-Americans and Hispanics. Laws only applied to the public sector and its suppliers. This approach has come under severe criticism in the 1990s from white, middle-class males, who argue that laws intended to encourage equality are unfair to them. It is illegal to use positive discrimination in the UK.
- **Targeting.** Quotas for the employment of particular groups have been enforced in the USA. In Europe quota systems commonly apply to the disabled and, in a few countries, other groups such as ex-servicemen,

but enforcement is not usually strict. Quotas are generally illegal in the UK and in 1995 the European Court ruled against quotas for women employees as a form of sex discrimination against men. However, voluntary targets can be set and monitored within individual organizations provided they do not conflict with equal opportunities legislation.

More widely, it should be emphasized that legislation is only effective if institutions and individuals charged with its implementation are themselves committed to the concept of equal opportunity.

Education and meritocracy

Education plays a key role in causing and, potentially, curing institutionalized discrimination in advanced countries. As early as the nineteenth century, the sociologist Weber held that people should be promoted solely on the basis of relevant qualifications. He proposed this condition in order to overcome the nepotism and patronage which prevailed in the public and private sectors at that time. Since then qualifications have become significant, if not essential, requirements for a successful career.

The importance of education for personal advancement is best illustrated in France, where a clear and simple equation exists between management success and intellect. Intellect is taken to be the possession of the right qualifications from the right educational institutions. In France, not only is admission to one's first job dependent on educational attainment, but attendance at a *grande école* eases the path right to the top:

> L'Ex*pansion* surveyed how the French business community viewed graduates of every one of the top *grandes écoles*. Among the shortcomings cited, graduates of Polytechnique were considered to be too elitist, those of Centrale unimaginative, those of HEC over-ambitious and those of l'ENA too theoretical. This educational type-casting tendency is reinforced by a fairly rigid pecking order in salaries. The market value of new graduates is closely tied to the intellectual reputation of their alma mater.
>
> (*The Times*, 16 January 1992)

The right qualification admits a recruit to a much higher entry level than would otherwise be the case. Thereafter, *grandes écoles* diplomas do not compensate for lack of effort but they make promotion considerably easier (Barsoux and Lawrence 1990: 58). As an employee rises in the organization, technical ability becomes less important than the 'social' skills required to delegate, resolve conflicts and motivate staff. At the higher levels:

> the effects of attending the 'right' school come to fruition, as some individuals move from line jobs into positions of power that put a premium on such qualities as distinguished appearance, good manners, tact and good taste. Emphasis on social competence tends to favour the products of the *grandes écoles* who possess the necessary self-confidence and social wherewithal. So while companies ostensibly drop educational credentials as a means of selection, they replace them with credentials which elevate members of the same population.
>
> (Barsoux and Lawrence 1990: 58)

Whereas in some countries – Germany, for example – training is seen as the key to effective performance, the French are inclined to view intellectual quality as the most important factor. Accordingly, French education is highly selective, emphasizing the production of 'high-flyers' who will be given early responsibility in their business careers. They produce managers with an analytical perspective in which every business issue is seen as an intellectual problem (as shown in Table 9.1). People rejected by this process have poor prospects compared with the USA, for instance, where – in theory – anyone can get to the top.

Barsoux and Lawrence observe that the French have identified a class of top business people: *cadres*. The word 'cadre' has a meaning beyond 'manager', entailing considerable prestige and an apparent homogeneity of lifestyle and attitudes. They are targeted by advertisers who regard them as high-spending consumers with taste and style. Cadres lie at the centre of an intellectual pecking order, with the principal success route being via school physics and engineering, through the *grandes écoles* and then into the major industries. As a consequence, industry is dominated by technologists. Second-ranking students may take Business Studies, Finance or Behavioural Sciences at universities and other less prestigious educational establishments, proceeding to lower-status areas sectors such as retailing.

Reflecting these status differentiations, traditional French organizations have been divided into rigidly defined social levels (Poirson 1993):

1 Senior executives (*cadres supérieurs*).
2 Junior and middle management (*cadres*).
3 ETAM – administrative, technical and supervisory staff (*baccalauréat* plus two years' technical studies).
4 Workers (Non-*baccalauréat*).

Potentially, French education offers a route to the top on grounds of merit. In practice, there is a strong bias towards the children of existing cadres and government employees who understand the system and its requirements.

In this respect it is not unlike the British educational system. A survey reported in *The Economist* (19 December 1992), found that two-thirds of top jobs surveyed were occupied by public-school men, with over 50 per cent being from Oxford and Cambridge. This represents virtually no change since the mid-1970s. Of the others, 27 per cent came from the most prestigious institutions, such as top Scottish universities, leaving only 11 per cent without higher education. We can attribute this partly to clone-seeking selection and promotion procedures. For example, major companies tend to visit the same narrow range of universities for annual recruitment and headhunters tend to assume their clients have conservative requirements.

Table 9.1 Grandes écoles education and management skills

Strengths	Weaknesses
Strong capacity for formulating problems	Interpersonal communication
Marked aptitude for reasoning through data given in figures	Capacity for managing people
Good capacity for planning	Capacity for implementing strategy

Source: after Barsoux and Lawrence (1990) and Poirson (1993).

Education fails to deliver true meritocracy for a number of reasons, for example:

- **Life chances** are not taken into account. People from privileged backgrounds have a greater opportunity to achieve acceptable qualifications. They have parents who understand the system and, if necessary, can purchase private education. It is infinitely easier for a student with affluent, supportive parents to obtain good grades than it is for those having to work to support themselves and perhaps children or relatives.
- **Second chances** are discouraged or have reduced effectiveness. Educators, particularly university academics, have achieved their status by passing exams and acquiring degrees. Their personal status and function is legitimized by the belief that clearing these hurdles is indicative of underlying intellect and personal worth. They offer limited sympathy and understanding for people who fail examinations at any stage – unless there are overt causes such as illness. In fact, failure can occur because of a whole range of non-intellectual reasons: domestic, financial or motivational. The critical timespan for education leading to paper qualifications (age 14–21) coincides with the transition from childhood to adult life – a traumatic maturational period for many. However, people who attempt to recover the situation at a later – more stable – age find the way littered with innumerable obstacles.
- **Snobbery and class.** Regardless of the consequences of social circumstances and maturational crises, as we have seen, possession of a 'good' degree from a 'good' university is viewed generally as evidence of intrinsic virtue, allowing entry to a range of powerful in-groups. However, in-groups have an unpleasant side to them: prejudice against outsiders. For example, the development of mass higher education in the UK has produced a great deal of snobbish disquiet in certain circles.

Worse, a number of major employers now confine their recruitment to a restricted number of older universities where they can continue to find really worthy candidates – people just like themselves. A study by Brown and Scase (reported ahead of publication in the *Guardian*, 20 November 1996) indicates that the privilege accorded to Oxbridge graduates has been reinforced since British polytechnics were converted into universities. Prestigious employers, including investment banks and law firms, continue to obtain their recruits from elite sources. In line with our discussion in previous chapters, this is a low-risk selection strategy from the employers's perspective.

The meritocratic ideal

People in developed – and many developing – countries no longer 'know their place' in society. Those who have a vested interest in preserving plum jobs for a select elite are facing overwhelming opposition from a generation whose career aspirations and expectation of equitable treatment by employers would have been unthinkable a few decades ago. However, there is some way to go before a universal meritocracy prevails (see key concept 9.2). This is exemplified in an extract from a review of a television programme, *The John Bull Business*, shown on the United Kingdom BBC2 channel:

> The City was long a preserve in which what mattered was not *what* you knew but *who* you'd been to school with. Big Bang was supposed to have changed all that and much was made at the time of the new, thrusting, yuppie meritocracy that would leave the old buffers swinging from lampposts by their old school ties.
>
> All bullshit, of course, this being Britain. Here is Grand Old Buffer Lord Rothschild (RIP) talking to Bernard Levin about his City career: 'Rothschild's bank invited me to go in there. That was very lucky for me indeed.' This was enough to wake even Mr Levin. 'You say Rothschild's bank invited you as though you were called Smith,' said he, incredulously, 'but you are called Rothschild after all. It's not all that surprising, is it?'
>
> 'Aahm', harrumphed the GOB in his best pompous ass voice, 'I think in the modern world less attention is paid to the name Rothschild, whether it's in a bank or anywhere else, and I think that's as it should be. So I went in and I was a stranger there – I didn't understand the language at all – and there came a moment when they said to me, "We'd like you to be chairman." And so I said "OK".' No wonder the Japanese are astonished by the City.
>
> (John Naughton, 'No gnus is bad gnus', *The Observer*, 30 August 1992)

KEY CONCEPT 9.2 Meritocracy	Meritocratic procedures aim to make judgements on the basis of evidence of competence such as examination results or the achievement of targets. We have noted already that educational achievement is not simply a matter of merit. Evidence of merit is invariably contaminated by social factors and life chances. A meritocratic but socially fair system should:

- take aggregate outcomes into account – in other words, if the process does not produce a balanced proportion of gender, ethnic origin and so on, then it is unfair;
- take life chances into account;
- require organizations to institutionalize the representation of specific groups within their key decision processes – including selection and promotion.

In practice, the number and range of disadvantaged groups is so huge that true fairness is a difficult objective to achieve. Well-meaning advocates can find themselves embroiled in endless verbal battles over the subtle nuances and implications of the concept. We turn next to its practical consequences on people management at the organizational level.

Diversity and the organization

> Fairness, justice, or whatever you call it – it's essential and most companies don't have it. Everybody must be judged on his performance, not on his looks or his manners or his personality or who he knows or is related to.
>
> (Townsend 1970: 59)

Why should business organizations and their managers offer equal opportunities to a diverse range of employees? Two fundamental perspectives are identifiable which can be related to different models of HRM (Goss 1994: 156):

- **Human capital.** 'Artificially' blocking the progress of any group results in less than optimal use of an organization's human capital. Discrimination is irrational since it limits the resource value of employees. This view is compatible with 'hard', or free-market HRM, discussed in Chapters 1 and 2.
- **Social justice.** A moral or ethical interest in social equality, compatible with 'soft' or social-market HRM. Economic benefits are secondary to this social duty.

Goss sees the human capital perspective as fluctuating and opportunistic: a shallow commitment 'capable of being adopted or abandoned, in line with legal or economic expediency' (1994: 156). It is also narrow, restricted to legal requirements and short-term employment market conditions. This contrasts with the more principled social justice viewpoint, which embodies a deeper and wider commitment, extending beyond minimum legal requirements.

Organizations benefit from a deep, principled commitment to equality of opportunity because it leads to (Ross and Schneider 1992):

- a diverse workforce which enriches ideas and perspectives within an organization;
- imaginative ideas to assist total quality management;
- recruitment or promotion of the most talented people;
- an environment which encourages them to stay;
- improved motivation and commitment which raises productivity;
- reduced wastage and recruitment costs which increase profitability.

In recent years the UK Equal Opportunities Commission has argued strongly for the human capital approach, pointing, in particular, to the waste of women's abilities. However, some commentators contend that whereas this is valid for the economy as a whole, equal opportunity practices may be a significant expense rather than a benefit for individual firms.

All businesses operate within the national or supranational legislation governing equal opportunities in a specific country. As we noted earlier, the USA has required a number of employers to take measures of **positive discrimination**, typically requiring them to fill quotas from underrepresented sections of the community. To do so, recruitment criteria such as qualification or skill requirements may be relaxed for members of those groups. This is an attempt to achieve the equal-share level of opportunity outlined in Straw's model (detailed in Table 9.2).

Alternatively, **positive action** may be required or undertaken voluntarily by governments or employers. Under-represented groups are assisted and encouraged to participate in training and development initiatives, support groups and mentoring schemes. This requires that organizations are aware of their disadvantaged employees and the jobs they are doing, so that the problem of **occupational segregation** can be tackled (see key concept 9.3). People from disadvantaged groups, if they are employed at all, tend to be confined to 'boring jobs with no prospects' in the secondary sector (Molander and Winterton 1994: 96). Curiously, for example, whereas black and

Table 9.2 Levels of opportunity

Level	Opportunities	Barriers
1 Equal chance	Everyone has the same chance, e.g. the right to apply for vacancies; be considered for a position.	Formal or informal barriers, e.g. employers may ignore applications from people living in ethnic minority areas.
2 Equal access	Disadvantaged groups are not barred from entry into organizations but may be confined to lower levels of work.	Institutional barriers, e.g. appraisal methods which favour certain groups, or promotion requirements – such as mobility – which effectively bar many married women.
3 Equal share	Access is free. Representation achieved at all levels. Legislation may require quotas for disadvantaged groups, e.g. the disabled.	Only those lawful, justifiable and necessary, e.g. specific-language speakers to work with ethnic groups.

Source: based on Straw (1989).

Asian people are comparatively well represented in the television industry, it is thought that fewer than thirty of Britain's 5,000 long-term contract journalists are from ethnic minorities (*The Independent*, 25 April 1995). A decade ago the same criticisms were made of television companies but a number of equal opportunity initiatives have gone some way to redressing the situation.

KEY CONCEPT 9.3 *Occupational segregation*	Disproportionate representation of particular groups in specific sectors, job-types or levels of responsibility. Horizontal segregation places men and women, for example, in different jobs, such as chambermaids (women) and porters (men). Vertical segregation places one group in better-paid positions than another group, so that men are better represented at managerial levels while women are concentrated in lower, adminstrative jobs.

Strategies for diversity

Many organizations have adopted **equal opportunities policies** – statements of commitment to fair human resource management. However, equal opportunities policies are notoriously ineffective, often no more than fine words decorating office walls, designed to appease politically vociferous activists and soothe consciences. They disturb vested interests too rarely. The obstacles to creating a diversified workforce are embedded in organizational culture – particularly the subculture at the top. A serious equal opportunity policy requires (Molander and Winterton 1994: 102):

- Allocation of overall responsibility to a specific senior executive.
- Agreement of the policy with employee representatives.
- Effective communication of the policy to all employees.
- An accurate survey of existing employees in terms of gender, ethnic origin, disability, etc. and the nature and status of their jobs.

- An audit of human resource practices and their implications on equal opportunities.
- Setting equal opportunity objectives within the human resource strategy.
- Resources, such as training and development capabilities, to back up these objectives.

This approach can be incorporated within an integrated framework termed the **management of diversity** (outlined in key concept 9.4). The pitfalls in the process are evident. A 1995 report (*Targeting Potential Discrimination*) produced by the UK Equal Opportunities Commission detailed findings from 2,000 companies and showed that over two-thirds did not collect information about the gender and ethnicity of their employees. Auditing HR systems is also problematic.

The management of diversity goes beyond equal opportunity. Instead of merely allowing a greater range of people the opportunity to 'fit in' or to be an honorary 'large, white male', the concept of diversity embodies the belief that people should be valued for their differences and variety. Diversity is perceived to enrich an organization's human capital. Whereas equal opportunity focuses on various disadvantaged groups, the management of diversity is about individuals. It entails a minimization of cloning in selection and promotion procedures and a model of resourcing aimed at finding flexible employees.

KEY CONCEPT 9.4
Management of diversity

However, the main difficulties arise from cost and lack of commitment, exemplified by **tokenism** - the employment or promotion of isolated individuals to represent their gender or colour. This is no more than an inadequate sop to equal opportunities: 'We have done as much as we need to – we have a disabled person in the office.' **Paternalism** is a related attitude, where discriminatory decisions are taken for the 'benefit' of particular groups, as illustrated in Case 9.1.

In an attempt to eliminate any liability for toxic damage to unborn children, American Cyanamid decided in January 1978 to remove all women of childbearing age from contact with any chemical which, in the company's opinion, carried a risk. In effect, the company banned all women aged between 16 and 50 from production areas at its Willow Island, West Virginia, plant. The only exception was for women who could prove they had been surgically sterilized or accepted such a sterilization at the company's expense. Five women accepted this offer.

The other women in the plant were offered only lower-paid jobs. Thirteen women and a union representative took legal action which was eventually settled out of court. In addition, the Occupational Safety and Health Administration (OSHA) cited American Cyanamid for violating a clause in the OSHA Act of 1970 which required employers to provide employees with a place of work which was free from recognized hazards. However, this was defeated by a summary legal judgement. This decision was confirmed by the OSHA's Health Safety Review Commission, which considered that the hazards which required sterilization for foetal protection were not cognizable under the OSHA Act. A further appeal by the Oil,

CASE 9.1
American Cyanamid

Chemical and Atomic Workers' Union to the District of Columbia Circuit Court of Appeals failed to overturn the judgement.

(*Source*: Dorothy Nelkin and Laurence Tancredi (1989), *Dangerous Diagnostics*.)

Discussion questions

1 Was the company right to take the action it did?

2 If not, how should the company have dealt with the problem?

Case 9.1 is a rather horrific example of heavy-handed action to 'protect' staff but it illustrates how people strategies can sometimes lose any sense of humanity.

In South Africa affirmative action programmes have shown relatively promising results (South African *Sunday Times*, 21 January 1996). A survey by FSA-Contact showed a massive majority of firms with affirmative action programmes. Only 5 per cent had a quota system but nevertheless their activities had led to an improvement in the proportion of senior positions filled by black managers from 2.5 per cent in 1994 to 9.5 per cent in 1995.

In the UK effective equal opportunity strategies have focused largely on women. Some organizations, such as the British Broadcasting Corporation (BBC), have a policy of improving the representation of women in management and professional positions. To this end the BBC set 1996 as a target year when women were expected to hold 30 per cent of senior management and 40 per cent of middle management posts. In the Netherlands, by comparison, women already held 40 per cent of comparable positions in the television station VPRO by 1992, compared with 12 per cent of senior executives and 24 per cent of senior producers and middle managers in the BBC that year (*Guardian*, 20 November 1992).

In a more general attempt to bring skilled women back to the workplace, tax concessions for workplace childcare were introduced in 1990 in the UK. However, there was a slow uptake as many companies were struggling or actively shedding staff. By 1992 there were only 425 workplace nurseries, providing 12,000 places (*The Observer*, 8 August 1993). The estimated demand exceeds a third of a million. A number of employers entered into 'partnership provision', teaming up to provide joint facilities for their staff. The biggest provider, the UK's Midland Bank, has arrangements with public-sector employers who provide accommodation while the bank puts up most of the capital: 114 creches account for 830 places; originally the bank had planned for 300 creches but the recession led to a change in policy. Before the scheme a mere 30 per cent of experienced staff returned to work after maternity leave, increasing to 80 per cent when the creche facilities became available.

Childcare facilities, equal and minimum pay, pregnancy and parental leave, pensions and part-time workers' rights all affect women more than men. Changes in the business environment can result in a hardening of attitudes towards employees. During the recession of the 1980s and 1990s, employers lost enthusiasm for radical changes in these areas, with no incentive from labour shortage to drive developments. Equal opportunities may well have taken a step backwards in this period.

By the mid-1990s, however, companies which had withstood recession took a different view. The British retailer Boots, announcing an expansion programme which would add a further 200 units to its existing 1,100, strengthened policies which would encourage women workers. Its 51,000 staff already included 45,000 women and the number in management and supervisory positions had doubled in five years (*Guardian*, 30 August 1994). However, this still represented only 25 per cent of store managers (compared with 18 per cent in 1991) and 15 per cent of head-office managers (an increase of 4.5 per cent since 1991). The proportion of women returning after maternity leave had increased from 7 to around 50 per cent in the preceding five years and Boots were training six childminders for the Nottingham area, where the company was based. The company also increased its flexible working arrangements, updated its equal opportunities policy and introduced a new code on sexual harrassment.

The management of diversity is a natural consequence of human resource strategies which focus on flexible working arrangements. Part-time work and, especially, homeworking are particularly attractive to some women and disabled employees.

Gender and sexual discrimination

Many countries, including all members of the EU, have sex discrimination and equal pay legislation. However, informal psychological and organizational barriers continue to bar the progress of women. In 1993, for instance, although forming almost half the workforce in the UK, women earned just 79 per cent of average male earnings. Whereas women's participation in the employment market has increased rapidly, in most countries their share of senior jobs is still low. Again in 1993, the UK National Management Salary Survey showed that women made up 13 per cent of 'senior staff' – the lowest level of responsibility – and a mere 1 per cent of chief executives. Among directors of large companies, only 3 per cent are women. The processes of occupational segregation and **sex-typing** of jobs continue to be prevalent, so that women are concentrated at the base of most organizational hierarchies in jobs which are less prestigious and lower paid than those favoured by men.

Internationally, the United Nations concludes that women are facing a global **glass ceiling** (key concept 9.5) and that 'in no society do women enjoy the same opportunities as men' (*The Financial Times*, 11 December 1995). In developing countries women represent under one-seventh of administrators and managers. In the most developed country, the USA, the Glass Ceiling Commission states that between 95 and 97 per cent of senior managers in the country's biggest corporations are men. According to Robert Young, Director General of the Institute of Management, 'men are the prime barrier to women in management. Despite some progress, old fashioned sexist attitudes are still common and represent a real, not an imagined, barrier.' Helena Kennedy, a prominent lawyer and one of Britain's few women QCs, commented:

> What we have to fight is the idea that access to these jobs is based on merit and it will only be a matter of time before women break through. What it is actually based on is men choosing people who are like themselves. It's all about cloning. That's why it's so hard to make the breakthrough and that's why it has to be consciously tackled.
>
> (*The Independent*, 19 December 1992)

KEY CONCEPT 9.5

The glass ceiling

The term 'glass ceiling' describes the process by which women are barred from promotion by means of an invisible barrier. This involves a number of factors, including attitudes of people in power and the inflexible processes and requirements geared to the cloning process which ensures that 'men of a certain sort' will generally succeed. In the USA the term is also used to describe the barrier which prevents progress for other disadvantaged groups, for example ethnic minorities.

Employer prejudices explain some of the difficulties which women experience. They include beliefs that women should be at home; should only work for pin money; are unreliable because of domestic commitments; cannot take responsibility; are not mobile. In fact, the majority of women's earnings are a significant and often essential contribution to the household earnings. Moreover, at a management level Scase and Goffee (1990) found that in a survey of six major British corporations the women managers were better qualified than their male counterparts and only 55 per cent of the women were married, compared with 93 per cent of men. Of the women, only four in ten had children.

Central to many employers' attitudes is a belief in the Victorian model of the family, where the woman stayed at home looking after the children and the man went out to work. As we saw in Chapter 3, this pattern has become uncommon in much of the developed world. Dual-career and one-parent families, equal parenting and the dismantling of lifelong career structures have eroded the distinction between male and female roles. Regional figures for 1995 show that female workers outnumber males in no fewer than twenty-five English and Welsh counties and Scottish regions. Yet attitudes have not caught up with reality: a CPM Field Marketing survey found that 47 per cent of male respondents thought that mothers should not work (*Personnel Today*, 28 July 1992: 2).

Within Europe, unions have pressed for greater comparability between the rights of women and men parents. A framework agreement offers both parents the right to three months' unpaid leave within the first eight years of a child's life. Individual governments can determine whether some of this leave should be paid – Nordic governments have had similar arrangements in place for some time. Despite the UK's opt-out from the Maastricht Social Chapter, it is likely that many British multinationals will concede the same benefits.

Gender differences

A further contributor to the problem is our perception of gender differences, real or imagined (see key concept 9.6). There are differences between men and women, other than the physical, but there is little agreement as to what they are. For example, Bevan and Thompson (1992) found evidence that men and women rated working behaviour differently:

- Males tended to favour and aspire towards qualities which were essentially **individualistic** and **competitive**, such as intelligence, dynamism, energy and assertiveness.
- Women stressed qualities of a more **cooperative** and **consensual** nature: thoughtfulness, flexibility, perceptiveness and honesty.

They concluded that since male managers are prevalent, females are disadvantaged by being evaluated against male standards of behaviour. This has been described as the 'male-as-norm syndrome' (Wilson 1995: 3). Given similar jobs and appraisal ratings, men are more likely to be offered training or promotion. Also, women are more likely to **underestimate** their own skill levels and therefore inhibit their own progress. However, not all women meekly accept the male order (see Case 9.2).

All human societies divide themselves into two social categories called 'female' and 'male'. Each category is defined on the basis of varying cultural assumptions about the attributes, beliefs and behaviours expected from males and females. The gender of any individual depends on a complex combination of genetic, body, psychological and social elements, none of which is free from possible ambiguity or anomaly (Helman 1990). Traditionally, sexual differences have been used to justify male-dominated societies in which women have been given inferior and secondary roles in their working lives.

KEY CONCEPT 9.6 *Gender*

Some deal with the situation by playing the game according to male rules. In a study of Greek organizations employing both female and male managers, Bourantas and Papalexandris (1990) found no difference between leadership styles. Their explanation was that women were imitating male patterns of behaviour in order to achieve success. This approach attracts mixed and complex reactions, particularly from other women. For instance, Margaret Thatcher, former UK Prime Minister, sometimes regarded as being a better man than most men, was an object of some fascination:

> Mrs Thatcher has acted out a role which is forbidden to women within conventional notions of femininity, revelling in power, dominating, 'handbagging' and humiliating men, a role which can be incorporated and allowed within the 'nanny' image, under the cover of rectitude. A common reaction from women is often mixed, a combination of a recognition that Mrs Thatcher has done little or nothing for her own sex, and of an admiration, sometimes unreserved, for the way in which she has shown rather conspicuously and publicly that women are not weak and indecisive, nor deficient in stamina and guts.
>
> (Webster 1990: 2)

Margaret Thatcher saw toughness, practicality and the ability to cope as being particularly **female** qualities (Webster 1990: 51). Nevertheless, she surrounded herself with a Cabinet of men and did little to benefit other women politicians. Thatcher appears to have been an exception in trying to assert her views over others. In general, women are more likely to regard themselves as **enablers** of other people, seeing themselves as opening up information to employees, building up the confidence of their staff and encouraging them to develop and use their skills. The development of women managers is discussed in Chapter 11.

There is no denying, of course, not only that men and women are sometimes different in their approach but that this may sometimes lead to conflict. Indeed, as we see in Case 9.2, a woman who speaks her mind may suffer the consequences.

CASE 9.2
Four Ms . . .
plus two

In August 1995 Janet Street-Porter, head of the new cable channel Live TV, made a celebrated speech at the Edinburgh Television Festival in which she said:

> A terminal blight has hit the British TV industry nipping fun in the bud, stunting our growth and severely restricting our development. This blight is management – the dreaded four Ms: male, middle-class, middle-aged and mediocre.

Previously, there had been some reports of disagreement with two other Ms, Kelvin McKenzie and David Montgomery, directors of the parent Mirror Group TV. Live TV's audience levels were extremely low. During Ms Street-Porter's absence on holiday Mr McKenzie purchased the television rights for the early stages of the Rugby League World Cup for transmission – programming which was outside Ms Street-Porter's concept of the channel. Within a month she had left Live TV.

Discussion question
In as much as anyone can tell, do you think Ms Porter's job would have been safe if she had not made her speech at the Edinburgh Television Festival?

It is clear that much of the debate about male and female behaviour revolves around sexual stereotyping, which has a significant cultural basis. Hofstede argues that, within any society, there is a men's culture which is different from the women's culture (1994: 16). This difference may explain why traditional gender roles are so difficult to change.

Sexual harassment

Some aspects of male culture are distinctly unattractive – even to many men. From school to shop floor, locker room to office, the culture of masculinity expresses itself in 'jokes' revolving around three stereotypes of sexuality (Mills and Murgatroyd 1991: 78):

- The ideal or **real man** syndrome – toughness, football and so on.
- Definitions of males as **not-females**.
- The normality of **heterosexuality**.

In traditionally all-male factories, workshops and warehouses, joking is reinforced by sexually explicit, homophobic or racist language, swearing, pictures of nude women (where they have not been banned), sexual bragging and suggestive horseplay. This serves to create an immensely threatening atmosphere for women and others, discouraging any attempt to enter this 'man's world'. In office and managerial environments these elements are less evident but sexual harassment – ranging from unwelcome comments on appearance to physical advances – remains common. Canadian surveys show that as many as 70 per cent of women have been sexually harassed at some time during their working lives (Moynahan 1993).

Sexual harassment is a difficult topic for managers to deal with, since it involves personal relationships and the individual interpretations of those involved (see key concept 9.7). The issue has often been trivialized or ignored in a 'conspiracy of silence'. In a survey of top British companies, Davidson and Earnshaw (1991) found that only 64.8 per cent of respondents regarded it as a serious management issue. Given that this was based on a response rate of only 22 per cent from their sample, this finding probably overestimates management concern.

| Definitions vary considerably but most are agreed that it is sexual attention which is unwanted, repeated and affects a woman's work performance or expectations from her job. However, it is possible for one incident to be sufficiently severe to be regarded as harassment. It differs from sexual banter or flirting since it is one-way; it does not have the involvement and acceptance of both parties. In the USA the Equal Employment Opportunity Commission has extended the definition of sexual harassment to include a range of actions which lead to a 'hostile work environment'. This definition includes unwelcome touching, joking, teasing, innuendos, slurs, and the display of sexually explicit materials. | **KEY CONCEPT** **9.7** *Sexual* *harassment* |

Few cases develop into formal complaints or tribunal cases but the consequences on morale are severe, with victims frequently leaving to escape harassment. The effects on victims can include nervousness and depression. In the work context, this affects concentration and productivity and increases the likelihood of absenteeism (Wright and Bean 1993). The effects can spill over into the home, possibly leading to the break-up of relationships.

Employers have a moral duty to protect staff from sexual harassment. In general, if employers tolerate sexual harassment they convey the impression that one gender does not deserve respect; they are prepared to sacrifice motivation and commitment; they must accept the consequences on efficiency. Organizations can deal with sexual harassment by (Moynahan 1993):

- surveying the organization to determine the extent of sexual harassment;
- writing and circulating a strongly worded policy indicating possible disciplinary action;
- providing an effective reporting mechanism, protecting the rights of accusers and the accused;
- using packaged workshops, which help to define harassment and prevent 'misunderstandings';

- providing assertiveness training, appropriate for women working in jobs which have traditionally been regarded as male, which encourages the ability to provide verbal or even written feedback to unwanted behaviour – the ability to say 'no' firmly and at an early stage is particularly effective;
- providing gender-awareness training to emphasize different perceptions of teasing and 'harmless fun' between men and women.

Increasingly, employing organizations are liable to legal action for sexual harassment by one employee against another.

Gender and the law

Husbands (1992) found that nine industrialized countries (from a sample of twenty-three) had statutes which specifically mentioned sexual harassment and several others had recognized it and defined it by judicial decision (see Table 9.3). In most other countries it is included by implication within measures to cover unfair dismissal, misconduct or criminal behaviour.

Legal definitions of sexual harassment fall into one of two types:

- **Quid pro quo.** A narrow, traditional definition of sexual harassment as a demand by a person in power, for example a supervisor, for sexual favours from a subordinate in return for a job, pay increase, promotion, transfer or other benefit.
- **Hostile environment.** A wider definition, including unwelcome sexual advances which have the effect of creating a hostile, intimidating, abusive or offensive working environment.

Australia, Canada, New Zealand, Switzerland, the UK and the USA have endorsed both definitions, either by statute or judicial decision. Other countries, including most members of the EU, have depended on the quid pro quo definition. In the USA damages in excess of $100,000 have been granted. In other countries, most awards have been less than US$10,000.

Table 9.3 Legislation covering sexual harassment

Statute	*Judicial recognition*
Australia (federal level, most states)	Australia (one state)
Belgium	Canada (federal level and some provinces)
Canada (federal level, number of provinces)	Ireland
France	Switzerland
Germany (Berlin)	United Kingdom
New Zealand	United States (federal level and some states)
Spain	
Sweden	
United States (several states)	

Source: based on Husbands (1992).

Generally, legislation to promote gender equality is complex and varied, with a wide divergence in different countries. In the UK, the principal legislation is found in: the Equal Pay Act of 1970, providing for equal pay for comparable work; and the Sex Discrimination Act of 1975, which makes discrimination against women or men (including discrimination on the grounds of marital status) illegal in the working situation. Subsequent UK and EU legislation has generally improved women's rights in the area of pregnancy and maternity. The Equal Opportunities Commission (EOC) was established under the Sex Discrimination Act of 1975 with powers to monitor implementation of the Sex Discrimination and Equal Pay Acts. Case 9.3 details an action by the EOC in which an employer discriminated unlawfully against men.

CASE 9.3
Dan Air

In the mid-1980s, Dan Air carried 1 million passengers a year on its scheduled services. It was also the UK's largest charter airline. To cope with the holiday season, its 470 permanent cabin staff were augmented by another 450 for the summer. The Equal Opportunities Commission was alerted to this situation as none of these was male. In 1985 Dan Air's representatives argued that this policy was justified by the Health and Safety at Work Act (1974) because they were worried about the threat of AIDS. Their legal counsel made a number of observations (summarized in the EOC's formal investigation report):

- AIDS largely affected homosexual men.
- Up to 30 per cent of men attracted to cabin work were homosexual.
- Cabin crew tend to be sexually promiscuous.
- AIDS is mainly transmitted by sexual intercourse.
- AIDS is also transmitted by blood and saliva. Cabin staff could pass it to passengers if they cut themselves.

Despite a claim that expert medical evidence would be given to support this case, none followed.

During a visit to Dan Air's offices in 1986, the EOC discovered that the airline did not advertise for cabin staff but recruited from direct applicants. On average, 400 applications were received from women and forty from men each month. Male telephone applicants were discouraged and men were never interviewed. However, no man was told that males were not employed as cabin crew. Instead, men were advised that the posts were filled and they should reapply in the future.

Dan Air claimed that as many as thirty cabin staff cut themselves each day, but the accident book recorded just sixteen cases of cuts or grazes in 1985. Their belief in the proportion of men attracted to cabin work and their general promiscuity seemed to be based on prejudice rather than fact. Medical experts concluded that there was no risk to passengers and crew. The EOC found that Dan Air's case was groundless and issued a non-discrimination notice which the company did not contest.

(*Source*: Simon Garfield (1994), *The End of Innocence: Britain in the Time of AIDS*, Faber and Faber.)

Discussion question
Does this case demonstrate ignorance of medical matters or social injustice?

It has become common for men to make complaints of unfairness because of their gender. In fact, the number of male complaints to industrial tribunals has exceded those from women. Paradoxically, assertive males are using legislation intended to increase women's participation at work to further their own interests.

Old boys, new girls

> Women feel that what matters is how well they do their work; men, that what matters is how well they play the game. At senior levels, what matters most is playing the game.
> (George New, quoted in *The Independent on Sunday*, 8 November 1992)

Old boys' networks are a principal factor in preserving male privileges at work. These networks are informal and frequently invisible. They date from school and university and are reinforced by semi-social activities such as playing golf. Men devote far more time than women to such networking activities and are more likely than women to get jobs through personal contacts. Many of these jobs were unadvertised.

When women attempt to network among male colleagues, they are viewed as aggressive or sexually provocative: 'males seem to perceive friendliness from females as seduction' (Wilson 1995: 232). The alternative is to create networks of their own. For example, in the UK, groups such as Women in Shell, Women in Banking and the City Women's Network foster the careers of their members through job referrals, advice, contacts and support. Senior women managers in education formed a Through the Glass Ceiling group in 1990.

The progress of female recruits is monitored by comparatively few organizations in Britain. However, a positive indication was that by the end of 1995 almost 300 of the UK's largest organizations, employing more than a quarter of British employees, had signed up to Opportunity 2000. Members are required to audit the positions currently occupied by women and set ambitious targets. Opportunity 2000 promotes childcare facilities, equal and minimum pay, pregnancy and parental leave, pensions and part-time workers' rights. As a result, in comparison with the low figures prevalent throughout the rest of industry, 16 per cent of directorships and 32 per cent of management jobs in these companies were held by women.

Disability

Disabled people are amongst the most disadvantaged. In 1986 the European Commission estimated that 10 per cent of the Community's population had some form of disability. This amounted to 27 million people. A recommendation was adopted in the same year which encouraged member states to 'take all appropriate measures to promote fair opportunities for disabled people in the field of employment and vocational training'. However, there is no general legislation against discrimination on the grounds of disability. Quota systems for the employment of disabled people have largely been ineffective because of inadequate supervision by governments.

Also, where social legislation for the disabled is weak, companies have found it comparatively easy to argue that they cannot provide suitable access or facilities to meet their needs.

Some individual countries outside the EU, including Canada and the USA, have initiated their own legislation. After decades of ineffectual quotas, the UK was the first country in the European Union to introduce a Disability Discrimination Act, in 1995. This makes it illegal for businesses to discriminate against disabled people as employees or customers. In 1995 there were 3.8 million people of working age in the UK alone with some form of disability. Under 30 per cent of disabled adults in the UK are in full-time jobs. The disabled have also been targeted disproportionately for voluntary redundancies.

The Act requires all businesses employing more than twenty people to make 'reasonable adjustments' to shops, offices and factories, where administrative or physical barriers have led to discrimination against disabled people. The government estimated that, on average, this would cost less than £200 per employee. This compares with US research which shows that their tougher legislation can be accommodated for under $1,000 dollars per person in the majority of cases (*The Financial Times*, 6 November 1995).

The introduction of the Act did not take place without criticism. Many disability groups and businesses have argued that it is too vague and does not give clear guidelines. For example, whereas it makes direct discrimination against the disabled illegal, this does not apply to people with 'substantial impairments'. The legislation is policed by a weak but complex system of monitoring bodies, including the National Disability Council and the National Advisory Council on the Employment of People with Disabilities. Firmer legislation has been refused by the government, largely on the grounds of cost.

Ethnic discrimination

For historical reasons, most countries have populations with different ethnic origins. Typically these are highlighted by colour or religious differences. There are around 13 million black and other 'visible minority' residents in the European Union. Few countries have true equality between these groups – in fact, many are stateless, with no rights at all. Worldwide, race discrimination legislation remains comparatively rare. In the EU, for example, only the UK and the Netherlands have appropriate laws. The original Treaty of Rome does not mention the issue. In the UK, there are different priorities between Britain and Northern Ireland, the former having legislation against racial discrimination, the latter banning religious discrimination. For example, during 1994 62 per cent of black men in London between the ages of 16 and 24 were unemployed – three times the rate for young white men. The same survey found that over one-third of black men of working age in London, and one-fifth of black women, were out of work.

In common with women and the disabled, members of ethnic minorities are rarely found among the senior executives of large companies. This can be linked to the frequent ineffectiveness of equal opportunities policies. A Commission for Racial Equality survey (*Guardian*, 25 February 1995) of the largest 168 companies in Britain found that 88 per cent had issued statements committing themselves to racial equality. However, just 45 per cent had a serious plan to implement racial equality.

Racism

Racism is usually equated with hostility and prejudice. The media encourages this simplistic picture by linking it to the racial abuse and violent behaviour of neofascist parties. Their members' antics are a product of frustration with their own inadequacies – projected onto a visible minority. In general, however, fascists have little power and influence and the perception of racism as obvious prejudicial opinions and attitudes obscures subtler, more insidious forms of discrimination (Sivanandan 1991). Racism cannot be reduced to 'human nature and individual fallibility' which leave the state, politics, and 'major structural aspects of contemporary life out of focus' (Husband 1991: 50).

Howitt and Owusu-Bempah point to a 'new racism', characterized as 'being a far more complex and subtle form of racism which, superficially, lacks the traditional emotive denigration of black people' (1990: 397). They conclude that 'seeing racism solely as a form of interpersonal antagonism not only sanitizes it, but prevents us from defining ourselves as racist if we do not *feel* racial hatred' (1990: 397). Hence stereotypes appear which are not seen as 'prejudiced':

> Asian women are seen as 'passive' or 'hysterical' or subject to oppressive practices within the family; there is the stereotype of the strong dominant Afro-Caribbean woman as the head of the household; and the description of the over-aggressive African woman.
>
> (Sayal 1990: 24)

The problem is not so much racial discrimination as **racial disadvantage**. This arises from the inability of the liberal-minded middle classes to perceive the structural advantages which contribute to their own success. Dominelli argues that:

> it is the subtle presence of racism in our normal activities, coupled with our failure to make the connections between the personal, institutional and cultural levels of racism which make it so hard for white people to recognise its existence in their particular behaviour and combat it effectively.
>
> (Dominelli 1992: 165)

Ben-Tovim *et al.* (1992) criticize the ideology of 'colour blindness', since it:

- fails to appreciate the pervasiveness of racism;
- confuses racism with urban deprivation and class inequality;
- is conveniently compatible with a range of political opinions;
- accommodates the 'universalistic ideologies and practices of public administration';
- denies racism purely as overt and deliberate discrimination.

They note some rationalizations for ignoring other forms of racism: that raising the question of racism is divisive; that the problems of the ethnic minorities are the same as those of the white population, or the working class, the inner cities, and so on.

Braham *et al.* (1992: 106) suggest that widening our definition of discrimination to include indirect or 'institutional' racism gives a much better understanding of the barriers faced by ethnic minorities (see key concept 9.8). Institutional racism is virtually unrecognized in commercial organizations but it is an extremely contentious issue in the public sector – for instance in the areas of social work and housing. At one extreme there are those obsessed with race issues, ignoring other forms of disadvantage; at the other, those who consider that 'there is no such thing as institutional racism and that those who say there is are totalitarian monsters, running amok, reducing nice white people to tears' (Alibhai-Brown, *The Independent*, 11 August 1993). Braham *et al.* (1992) caution that it is important to acknowledge the wide range of practices involved – some much more obvious than others. Rejecting the proposition that all institutions are uniformly racist, they argue that 'the kind of procedures . . . that disadvantage black people *also* disadvantage other groups'. We noted in Chapter 8 that the process of cloning is focused on replicating the people in power rather than discriminating against any particular group.

Institutionalized racism is an indirect and largely invisible process which can be compared with cloning and the glass ceiling. It is a term encompassing the – often unintentional – barriers and selection/promotion procedures which serve to disadvantage members of ethnic minority groups.   **KEY CONCEPT 9.8** *Institutionalized racism*

The British Civil Service is a good illustration of the existence and strength of institutionalized disadvantage. A Cabinet Office report in 1995 concluded that it was a bastion of the white, male middle classes, making it difficult for ethnic minorities to progress into its upper reaches. The report concluded that the main barriers to career development were:

● Prejudice and/or ignorance among line managers.
● A lack of confidence in themselves among ethnic minority staff.

These barriers were derived from attitudinal or cultural stereotypes which limited expectations and opportunities on both sides.

Race and ethnicity legislation

Legislation against discrimination has an important bearing on human resource management in countries such as the USA and the UK, but virtually none in others. The British Race Relations Act 1976 defined two forms of racial discrimination (*The Commission for Racial Equality: An Introduction*):

● **Direct discrimination.** This occurs when someone is treated less favourably than another because of his or her colour, race, nationality (including citizenship), or ethnic or national origins.

- **Indirect discrimination.** This is when a requirement or condition which applies equally to everyone has unequal and detrimental impact on a particular racial group, and cannot be justified irrespective of colour, race, nationality or ethnic or national origins.

Among the predominantly Anglo-Celtic countries, the UK is alone in not having an affirmative action policy. In Canada and New Zealand, for example, it is theoretically possible to enforce targets for the recruitment of particular groups. Within the UK the Commission for Racial Equality (CRE) is able to:

- give advice to people who feel they have been discriminated against, attempt to reach a settlement between parties such as employers and employees, and also provide legal representation in a court or industrial tribunal;
- take action against discriminatory advertisements and in situations where people have been instructed or pressurized to discriminate on racial grounds;
- investigate organizations which have been accused of racial discrimination – if it is shown that discrimination has occurred, the CRE is empowered to issue a non-discrimination notice which the organization is required to observe.

The CRE provides employers with guidance on their responsibilities under the Act and offers advice on equal opportunities and fair employment. This includes an employment code which has been approved by Parliament. It does not have the force of law but failure to follow its recommendations can be used in an industrial tribunal. In a wider European context, according to the CRE:

> Neither the Treaty of Rome nor the European Convention on Human Rights provides explicit protection from racial discrimination. Furthermore, the protection afforded by the domestic legislation of other European countries is very limited. This means that, while people coming to Britain have the protection of the Race Relations Act, those going to other European countries from here will find far fewer legal safeguards. The CRE's concern is that there should be a rapid improvement in protection from racial discrimination across Europe, and that the Race Relations act should not suffer dilution in any future attempts to harmonise laws across the Community.
>
> (*The Commission for Racial Equality: An Introduction*)

Religious discrimination

On 1 January 1990 the Fair Employment (Northern Ireland) Act 1989 came into force. The new legislation builds on the previous 1976 Act, designed to promote equal opportunities for religious groups. This is the most radical equal opportunities legislation in the United Kingdom, going further in most respects than the Race Relations Act in Great Britain (Lustgarten and

Edwards 1992: 284). It follows North American, rather than British, practice in requiring affirmative action.

All public-sector agencies and those private sector employers with more than twenty-five employees are required to ensure that its HR practices do not discriminate unfairly against any religious group. They must also register with the Fair Employment Commission (FEC) and file returns which show numbers and percentages of Protestants and Roman Catholics at each level of responsibility within the organization. If the FEC finds that the employer does not have a reasonable balance of religious groups it can require a company to revise its practices. The FEC can ask for goals and timetables for training, encouraging applications from an underrepresented group, and negotiating redundancy schemes which help to preserve or gain fair representation. The Act is reinforced with over twenty criminal offences, which can be used in cases of non-compliance, leading to fines and economic sanctions.

Ageism

Discrimination on the grounds of age is prevalent but often unrecognized. Some countries such as Canada, France, New Zealand and the USA have legislated against ageism. In other countries employers are allowed to specify age ranges for job applications. For example, in the UK Heasman found that 30 per cent of advertisements carried discriminatory references against older workers (1993: 28). Half of these advertisements specified a maximum age limit of 35. Other advertisements use terminology such as 'youthful' and 'dynamic' which carries an implicit messsage that older workers are not welcome to apply.

The absence of legislation in the UK can be attributed to a comparative lack of interest amongst organizations such as the Institute of Personnel and Development and the Confederation of British Industry. These organizations have preferred self-regulation and promoting raised awareness to counter ageism. Such voluntary methods did not work in relation to race and gender and there is no reason to assume that they will with respect to age discrimination. However, critics point out that the proportion of men over the age of 50 employed in the UK is broadly similar to that in the USA, where legislation has been in force since 1967.

Ageism has become newsworthy in the UK, with a Private Member's Bill tabled to legislate against it in 1996. A quick survey of British newspaper job adverts at the time of writing shows that references to age seem to be far fewer than the 30 per cent found by Heasman, perhaps in anticipation of this. Many of Britain's largest companies, including Marks & Spencer and SmithKline Beecham, have elected to extend equal opportunity polices to cover ageism.

Curiously, the European Commission has been a major culprit – putting firm age limits in its vacancy announcements, for example in two advertisements in the *Guardian* (5 April 1994) and a number of other newspapers for 'Advanced Broadcasting Services'. The first, COM/R/A/118, Commission Career A4, appeared to be the more senior of the jobs, requiring a 'university degree in a relevant field with at least 15 years of post-graduate experience'. Taking 21 as the earliest graduation age produces a minimum age of 36. The second age delimiter was the condition that 'candidates must have been born after 06/05/1943' making the oldest candidates 51 on the closing date for applications. Hence the advertisement had an effective age 'window' of 36–51. The more junior posts (COM/R/A/108, Career A8/A5) asked for three years' post-degree experience and stated: 'candidates must have been born after 06.05.1958'. The age window was therefore 24–36. After the caveat 'The age limit may be waived for: temporary agents of the European Community Institutions, compulsory military service, education of children and physical handicap', the advertisements ended with the statement (in bold): 'The Commission's policy is to ensure equal opportunities for men and women.'

There is a common view amongst employers that people over 45 are not worth recruiting, promoting or training. This is against a demographic trend where – in developed countries – the group of over-45s covers one-third of the workforce. The proportion will continue to increase into the next century. Common stereotypes about older workers include the following:

- that they are slow to learn;
- that they are unwilling to accept and adapt to new technology;
- that they lack enthusiasm for training.

However, research shows that older workers:

- are more reliable and conscientious;
- are more loyal and committed to staying with their organization;
- have greater interpersonal skills;
- work harder and more effectively;
- show equal levels of productivity to younger staff.

Older workers are less effective at work which requires heavy physical activity or the continuous, rapid processing of information. Conversely, they are better than younger people at jobs requiring accuracy and reliability, and the use of knowledge.

Older workers often do not portray the kind of image that many younger managers subscribe to. For the company to appear smart and modern, a youthful customer-facing workforce is preferred. Extensive downsizing in organizations throughout the western world has concentrated on early retirements. The result is that many companies are entirely staffed by people under 50 – with the exception of senior managers.

Ex-offenders

Obtaining a job is particularly difficult also for ex-offenders. They have a number of specific difficulties over and above employer prejudices. For a variety of reasons they tend to show the following:

- unrealistic and **negative expectations** leading to underachievement, such as restricting applications to manual jobs;

- **Poor motivation** from a variety of causes, including past failure experiences;
- **Learning difficulties** or unhoned skills;
- General **ignorance** of the employment market.

An Apex Trust survey of 2,500 employers in England and Wales (*Personnel Management*, February 1991) indicated that, out of thirteen selection criteria, employers rate honesty as the most important quality. Also, they are only prepared to take on the long-term unemployed – a category including many ex-offenders – if they have basic skills training. This is held to be much more important in employers' estimation than the formal qualifications which many training agencies set out to provide. Only a small minority of employers, 15 per cent in the public sector and 3 per cent in the private sector, completely ruled out employing ex-offenders; sex-offenders caused the greatest difficulty. Sixty per cent of public sector and 82 per cent of private sector employers reported satisfaction with ex-offenders they had taken on.

Probation Services in some parts of the UK have introduced special schemes to encourage higher levels of employment amongst people leaving prison. The Probation Service in South Glamorgan has linked employers, prisons and other agencies in the Forum for Offender Employment, which has generated initiatives which either tailor services to address the special needs of ex-offenders or encourage greater knowledge amongst agencies and prospective employers. Seventy-five per cent of South Glamorgan clients were without work; 90 per cent were long-term unemployed before the schemes commenced. The initiatives included:

- A one-week pre-release course for offenders completing prison terms. This included CV preparation, interview practice, advice on training opportunities and, perhaps most importantly, advice on how and when to reveal information on past convictions.
- Secondment to the Probation Service of two employment specialists with knowledge of the employment market and recruitment processes and the ability to use this knowledge in counselling clients.
- A job conference involving large local employers.
- A Job Club specifically for ex-offenders.

Early results showed a positive trend, with forty ex-offenders placed in jobs.

Summary

Equality of opportunity is a matter of both social justice and sound economic sense. Traditionally, women, ethnic minority groups and the disabled have been disadvantaged, but with high rates of unemployment older workers and ex-offenders have been badly affected. Granting opportunity is beneficial to organizational effectiveness as well as personal success. The strategic management of diversity leads to a wider range of ideas and abilities, offering greater scope for innovation and competitive performance in the future.

Further reading

It seems that one can search in vain for a reasonable (or, indeed, any) treatment of this subject in most 'academic' HRM texts. Goss's (1994) *Principles of Human Resource Management* is an honourable exception, providing some theoretical insights into key issues. Torrington and Hall's (1995) *Personnel Management: HRM in Action* (3rd edition) provides a largely legalistic but useful interpretation. Wilson's (1995) *Organizational Behaviour and Gender* is a refreshing reappraisal of many fundamental issues where women have traditionally been sidelined. Flanders's (1994) *Breakthrough: The Career Woman's Guide to Shattering the Glass Ceiling* provides a detailed manual on to how to cope with traditional male bastions. The literature on ethnic minority employment and racism is extensive, whereas disability, ageism and the difficulties of ex-offenders are not so well covered. Braham *et al.* (eds) (1992) *Racism and Antiracism* includes chapters from a number of contributors who take their subject matter into wider considerations of equal opportunities, including the merits of legislation.

Review questions

1 Distinguish between equal opportunities and the management of diversity. How is it possible to justify either in a commercial organization?
2 Is positive discrimination an effective method for ensuring equal opportunities?
3 Discuss the attitudes of young people towards older workers. At what age should people cease paid employment?
4 What are the limitations on the employment of the disabled? What can be done to improve the situation?
5 Should women and men play an equal role at work?
6 Outline the differences between racial prejudice and institutional racism. Do other groups experience institutional barriers?
7 How would you design a positive action programme for ex-offenders?

Problems for discussion and analysis

1 The borough of Kenwood is situated on the outskirts of a large city. It is predominantly populated by white, middle-class people and is considered reasonably affluent by comparison with its inner city neighbours. Just under 20 per cent of residents are over pensionable age, of whom 7 per cent are over 75 years of age. The vast majority continue to live in their own homes, an increasing proportion living alone. The ageing population has significant resource implications for the local authority.
   The social services department is responsible for the home help ser-

vice, which comprises three full-time managers and a team of forty part-time women workers. In addition to providing practical help and social support to their elderly clients, they are often the first people to be alerted to a deterioration in a person's situation. They are a crucial element in enabling people to stay in their own homes, saving the local authority enormous sums of money. However, their status does not reflect their true importance to the community and the section is regularly scrutinized for potential budget cuts.

The local authority has an equal opportunities policy which 'strives towards the elimination of discrimination within the workplace'. The social services department noted that the few black staff recruited were in low-paid or insecure posts and tended not to stay long. To try to prevent the policy remaining no more than a piece of paper, it was decided that an equal opportunities monitoring committee should be set up. This has met quarterly for the last three years and comprises staff representing all grades within social services, plus representatives from the main personnel department and two co-opted councillors. It is seen as undesirable to have such a group entirely made up of white representatives, so the few black staff available are under constant pressure to volunteer for membership.

One exception to the tendency of black staff to stay no more than a few months is Mary, a middle-aged black woman who has worked for the local authority for seventeen years, always as a home help. She is a tolerant person who likes the flexibility of the work. She has regularly encountered clients whose questions and comments are inadvertently offensive and insensitive but has said little to her managers. However, having been allocated to a couple whose racism is overt and sustained, Mary made a complaint to her harassed line manager, who sympathized and reallocated a white home help to the couple concerned. Mary got on with her job without further comment. Over the next few weeks the manager thought about her own response, felt it had been inadequate, and referred the incident to the equal opportunities monitoring committee.

The reaction of group members was diverse. Some of the comments were as follows:

- What do you expect? Old people are always unreasonable about everything.
- They may well be suffering from dementia, if so, they can't be held responsible.
- Living in this area, they're probably not used to black people and don't know how to react.
- Would Mary like any further action?
- We did all we could in practical terms; we can't withdraw the service from them.
- The line manager should have visited and confronted them.
- Oh dear, how awful.
- Has this sort of thing happened before, do we know?

- Black staff are particularly discriminated against and should receive appropriate support.

The final response came from one of two black members. He proposed a Black Workers' Support Group, open to anybody working for the local authority who defined themselves as black. The group would meet every two months within paid working time. The existence and purpose of the group would be made known to other colleagues, who would be asked to demonstrate support by enabling participants to attend. Benefits to the local authority might accrue from being seen to be implementing its own equal opportunities policy and potentially retaining staff, who would feel less isolated and marginalized.

The majority of group members had considerable reservations about this proposal although most did not say so openly. While most doubts centred on the impact on overstretched departments and the possible adverse reaction of colleagues asked to cover extra duties, one of the councillors was more direct: 'Where exactly will this end? In no time at all we'll be expected to pay for part-time workers' support groups, Irish workers' support groups, etc., etc.' The proposal was referred to the senior managers' meeting for further consideration. There was more support within this forum, but it was felt that the Black Workers' Support Group should be chaired by a senior manager. Black staff pointed out that the group would not work if it operated on such hierarchical terms and, in any event, all managers of the grade proposed were white. Managers' expectation that they would receive copies of the minutes of each meeting met with a similar response. While they were uneasy with their lack of control, senior managers felt it would be more controversial to refuse permission. The Black Workers' Support Group went ahead and the local authority began to receive enquiries about the scheme from outside the organization and praise for its initiative. With significant cuts proposed to the home help service in the next financial year, and with school-age children to care for, Mary has felt too busy to attend.

How effective is the equal opportunities policy in Kenwood? Did Mary's supervisor take the right decision? What is the value of the Black Workers' Support Group?

2 Most people think Frank is a nice guy. He is a good networker, knows everyone in the company and is always the first to buy a round of drinks at any social event. He is married, has three children and an attractive house in a very expensive area. He is the Senior Accounts Controller in the Purchasing Contracts department and is thought to run a very efficient department. For several years he had a relationship with Margaret from Government Sales. This broke up in a somewhat emotional fashion last December when he finally told her that he had no intention of leaving his wife.

Audrey, the Government Sales Co-ordinator, has come to see you regarding some stories that are being told in her department. It seems that Margaret has been telling people that Frank is not entirely honest. She has claimed that he has been taking bribes from contractors, accepting cash, holidays and improvements for his house in return for signing contracts. Margaret has not said this in Audrey's presence because Audrey is a rather straitlaced person who has always made it clear that she disapproved of the relationship. Audrey and Margaret do not get on very well as a result.

You are the General Manager responsible for these departments. How would you proceed?

10

Performance management

> This chapter considers how employee performance can be evaluated and fostered. Assessment and reward strategies are related to concepts of effective working behaviour.

In Chapter 8 we looked at how the performance of potential recruits can be predicted from evidence collected during selection procedures. This was followed by an examination of the difficulties encountered in any attempt to ensure equal opportunities and to overcome the powerful socio-cultural mechanisms which promote the interests of privileged in-groups. In this chapter we extend our debate to the evaluation of current employee performance.

Performance assessment has a long history based on comparative judgements of human worth. In the early part of the nineteenth century, for example, Robert Owen used coloured wooden cubes, hung above work stations, to indicate the performance of individual employees at his New Lanark cotton mills in Scotland. Various merit ratings were represented by different coloured cubes, which were changed to indicate improvement or decline in employee performance (Heilbroner 1953; cited in Murphy and Cleveland 1995: 3).

Like the employee selection techniques described in Chapter 8, modern performance assessment developed from sophisticated rating systems designed by work psychologists for military use during the two World Wars. By the 1950s such methods had been adopted by most large US business organizations, spreading worldwide thereafter. Initially, performance assessment was used to provide information for promotions, salary increases and discipline. More recently performance measurement has had wider purposes:

- Identifying and enhancing desirable or effective work behaviour.
- Reinforcing this behaviour by linking rewards to measured performance.

- Developing desired competences and building human capital within organizations.

Enthusiasts for performance assessment argue that it serves a key integrating role within an organization's human resource processes. First, it provides a checking mechanism for resourcing policies and procedures, evaluating the quality of recruits and hence the underlying decision-making process. Second, it monitors employee's commitment and the relevance of their working behaviour to business objectives. Third, it provides a rationale for an organization's pay policies. Taken at face value, these intentions seem entirely compatible with an integrated and strategic approach to human resource management. In reality, however, the definition and measurement of good performance is a controversial matter, involving fundamental issues of motivation, assessment and reward.

All aspects of performance management arouse controversy, especially appraisals and performance-related pay. Critics point to weaknesses in the methodology and basic philosophy of these two areas. Employees are often dissatisfied with the methods of performance management systems and managers are frequently reluctant to engage in the process because of its confrontational nature. At a deeper level, it can be argued that if true commitment exists performance management is superfluous. In too many organizations it enforces the compliance of an unhappy workforce.

Despite its problematic reputation, the use of performance assessment has been reinforced through the increasing prevalence of performance-related pay (PRP). As we will see later in this chapter, this is based on an oversimplified view of work motivation. Employers, consultants and right-wing politicians remain wedded to PRP schemes despite considerable evidence against their effectiveness as motivators.

Within HRM literature there is some ambiguity as to whether reward should play a supporting role, a view implicit in the Harvard model of HRM, or, conversely, **drive** organizational performance – an opinion which finds greater favour amongst exponents of hard HRM (Kessler 1995: 254).

In this chapter we set out to debate these issues and to search for answers to questions such as:

- What criteria should be applied to distinguish 'good' from less acceptable performance?
- Which are the most appropriate techniques for measuring performance?
- How can performance management be used to reinforce an organization's human resource strategies?
- How can true competence be identified in jobs which allow a considerable degree of impression management?
- Does performance management really encourage desirable work behaviour?

We begin with a discussion of the environmental factors which have led to the widespread use of performance assessment techniques. These include legislation, the demands of technological change, increasing flexibility and diversification, and changes in workforce composition. We

proceed to look at the way in which organizations favour certain stereotypes of good performance. The next section evaluates the decision-
making underlying the adoption of performance assessment strategies.
Finally we discuss the activities involved in assessment such as appraisal
and counselling.

The environmental context

> The effects of context variables on appraisal processes and outcomes have
> been the object of speculation but have not been empirically examined in the
> detail that these effects warrant. We believe that context is the key to under-
> standing appraisal in organizations.
>
> (Murphy and Cleveland 1995: 407)

The business environment exercises both a direct and an indirect influence
on the conduct of performance assessment. Whereas legislation has specific
consequences, particularly in the USA, most environmental factors have a
diffuse and often unrealized effect on assessment and pay structures. It is
likely that different individuals – and organizations – will respond in
varying ways to these factors. Some will be highly sensitive to possible
legal implications, practice elsewhere and the state of the job market; others
will be virtually immune to these influences. The main environmental
factors identified as having a contextual influence on performance management are outlined below.

Business culture

At a national level, culture affects performance management through socio-
political traditions and attitudes which determine whether assessment is
acceptable, and to what degree. Cultural norms dictate 'acceptable' standards of performance and the management methods by which they are
assured. For example, in a number of Asian societies, the employment
relationship is a matter of honour, and obligations are regarded as morally,
rather than contractually, binding between the two parties. In a situation
where people are automatically expected to do the job as agreed, the role of
performance assessment is questionable.

Conversely, as we saw in Chapter 5, 'commitment' in western organizations is rarely a 'hearts and minds' phenomenon and this is exemplified
in the policing nature of performance management. It is a modern version
of scientific management in which the detail of work is supervised in a
sometimes overbearing way. Within English-speaking countries, performance-related pay encapsulates a fusion of the Protestant work ethic (key
concept 10.1) and free-market ideology: work is virtuous and virtue
should be rewarded generously. It fits particularly well with the free-
market ideology of right-wing politics. As an instance, between 1986
and 1996 the UK government granted tax relief in respect of the profit-
related element in profit-based PRP schemes (Armstrong 1995: 154). The
declared intent was to foster a stronger identification with the employing
organization.

> The belief that work is virtuous in itself. Work can be defined as 'an activity directed to valued goals beyond enjoyment of the activity itself' (Warr 1987: 5). Hard work is to be admired and leisure is equated with laziness. Spare time is perceived as evil: 'the devil makes work for idle hands.' In some societies the work ethic became a fundamental religious principle, the Puritans and Calvinists holding it to be such a virtue that Max Weber termed it the Protestant work ethic. Nineteenth-century factory owners used the principle to justify eleven- and twelve-hour days. The concept is sometimes extended to include the virtue of frugality as against waste. It justifies regarding the poor as sinful, since success and ambition are virtuous and wealth is a sign of God's favour.
>
> **KEY CONCEPT 10.1**
> *The work ethic*

Legislation

In free-market economies the employment relationship between workers and employing organizations is seen as a contractual matter. This relationship is expressed in formal or legalistic statements of obligation between the two, such as written employment contracts, job descriptions and performance objectives. Performance measurement has the purpose of ensuring that the employee fulfils the contract.

Performance measurement has become a sensitive legal issue in the USA because of possible consequences on equal opportunities (Murphy and Cleveland 1995: 11). Since the 1970s, assessments have been regarded as tests and are subject to guidelines enforced by the Equal Employment Opportunities Commission. Employers taking personnel decisions on the basis of performance assessment have to be mindful of possible legal action on one of two grounds:

- Validity or accuracy of assessment ratings as predictors of future performance and promotion potential.
- Validity or accuracy of ratings as measures of past behaviour.

This legislation is specific to the USA, but all human resource managers have to be mindful of possible breaches of equal opportunities legislation in their own countries.

General economic conditions

Prevailing attitudes towards employees and, in turn, their response to performance assessment are considerably affected by issues such as unemployment. In line with our discussion in Chapter 3, growth and shrinkage in the job market is conventionally believed to be followed by changes in the behaviour of workers and employers. At times of high unemployment, workers are thought to be concerned about losing their jobs and hence more conscientious and tolerant of strict management. When suitable employees are scarce, managers must be cautious – unflattering assessments can trigger an employee's move to another organization.

The relationship between the economy and assessment is circular and complex. Performance management is justified by organizational efficiency, and the overall efficiency of organizations in a country is crucial for its economic well-being. Income generated by effective, as opposed to inefficient, performance encourages economic wealth. Performance management has become the chosen western instrument to drive out ineffective activity. It incorporates both stick and carrot: the first in terms of sanction, criticism or discipline; the latter in the form of praise or cash.

Industry sector

Methods of performance management vary considerably between different industrial sectors, partly as a matter of the nature of the work involved, tradition and fashion. Sales-dominated industries such as financial services tend to have clear individual or team objectives which can be translated readily into performance targets. Performance-related pay is common in this sector and commission-only contracts are not unusual. In other sectors objectives are more diffuse and difficult to measure, so that PRP is not easily justified.

Technological change

Computer networking is likely to have a dramatic effect on the nature of supervision, and hence performance assessment (Murphy and Cleveland 1995: 408). In Chapter 4 we observed that modern organizations can extend beyond their formal physical boundaries by means of networked systems. Work can be done at a distance by travelling executives, overseas affiliates or telecommuters working from home. This raises intriguing issues for performance management. For instance, how does a manager assess the performance of a homeworker when there is little or no personal contact between the two?

Technology has the power to provide extensive statistics, such as the time an individual spends logged on to a system, the number of key strokes and the volume of output, but does this information provide a meaningful measure of job performance? If the employee's task involves elements of creativity, accuracy and thoroughness, how can these be assessed? If managers become dependent on 'objective' measures of work, they may be forced to bring their personal assessments into line 'even if they know that the workers who spend the most time at their desks may not be the best performers' (Murphy and Cleveland 1995: 408).

Advanced technology requires expert users. It is common for managers not to possess the same level of expertise as their subordinates. Such managers are not qualified to assess their performance and, moreover, subordinates are well aware of the fact. In these cases supervisors have neither the competence nor the credibility necessary for effective performance management.

Flexibility and diversification

As we have already seen, in the 1980s and early 1990s the traditional nature of the employment relationship in free-market countries changed, moving the balance of power firmly in favour of employers. We noted in Chapter 7 that job descriptions have disappeared, or at least have been diluted, so that employees can be asked to do virtually anything required by the organization. Conversely, performance criteria have been more tightly defined, typically expressed in the form of demanding objectives: forever-moving goalposts. Performance assessment has become the crucial means of monitoring this relationship.

Employee relations

Performance management is a means of enhancing managerial control, particularly through individual performance-related pay schemes. In Chapter 12 we will observe that the individualization of pay diminishes or neutralizes the role of collective bargaining. The purpose and influence of trade unions is undermined, reducing both their effectiveness and their attractiveness as an alternative focus for employee commitment.

Workforce composition

Largely forgotten in the controversy over PRP, the other main function of performance assessment is the identification of individual strengths and weaknesses. As we will see in Chapter 11, the latter can be targeted for improvement through training and development. Strengths may indicate a potential star performer worthy of a management career route and promotion. Assessment employed to determine development needs ultimately serves to increase a nation's human capital.

Less positively, demographics and a history of unequal opportunities affect the conduct of assessment, since they largely determine who assesses whom. For example, in countries such as the UK it is likely that performance assessments are largely carried out by white, male managers, whereas the people they assess are probably of mixed gender and ethnic origin. this is one of a series of organizational issues which we consider further in the next section.

The organization and effective performance

How do organizations decide which performance criteria should be measured? How do they differentiate between a good, average or indifferent employee? In our discussion of organizational HRM in Chapter 4 we observed that organizations take many forms. No matter how an organization is structured, its output is the product of an interaction between different employees, departments, divisions and so on. Frequently it is difficult to determine whose performance has been critical, or most significant, to the completion of a particular task. Current trends towards networking and team-based projects make individual performance even harder to gauge. Offe (1985) once stated that identifying an individual's contribution to meeting an organization's goals is like listening to the sound of one hand clapping. Yet some people are singled out as key performers. On what basis?

It is arguable that they may not be outstandingly good performers in an absolute sense but rather simply the people who conform most closely to the organization's norms. Each organization defines effective performance in its own terms: being a 'good' manager in one organization is not the same as being good in another (Gunz 1990). Company cultures and management styles vary, and effective performance often translates as conformity to the house style. According to Gunz (see Figure 10.1), organizations differ greatly, so that the contexts in which managers operate vary considerably. This leads to different ideas about effective management – so that some companies emphasize, for example, engineering quality, others financial performance or market dominance. In each case people find it comparatively easy to recognize good management but may find it hard to say why. This leads to certain types of people being promoted. As these people are seen to succeed everyone else draws their own conclusions about what it takes to get ahead. This closes the loop, reinforcing the dominant image of effectiveness:

> the figure suggests that promotion patterns in a firm will be resistant to change because of the model's closed loop. The system is remaking itself in its own image, something organisational managers are usually aware of even if they do not always admit it openly.
>
> (Gunz 1990: 3)

This is consistent with evidence from a large number of studies reviewed by Campbell *et al.* (1970), who found that judgements of managerial effectiveness or *good*ness are actually measures of personal success. When people are asked to identify a good manager, they do so on the basis of an individual's promotion record, salary, global ranking of success and so on. Often the identification of promotable staff is devolved to individual managers. They tend to favour subordinates of two types:

- those who are reliable – that is, they do things in the way the managers would;
- those who have skills which the manager does not possess.

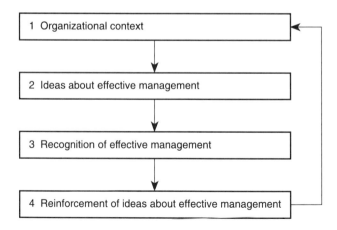

Figure 10.1 The renewal of managerial structures.
Source: Gunz (1990).

Most of all, as we have noted already in previous discussions of the cloning process, they favour employees who are similar to themselves.

Morgan draws parallels between organizations and political systems in that both vary from autocracy to the democratic decision-making seen in some voluntary organizations (1986: 144). He attributes a major role in determining successful performance to political processes such as conflict, power-play and intrigue.

The 'right' image

Following this line of logic, it is clear that any performance assessment system is vulnerable to the cloning process. Without thought, performance management can drive out diversity. It is also open to manipulation by employees who can identify the qualities necessary to 'get on' in a particular organization.

For example, there is evidence that appearance affects success. Two American studies (NBER working papers reported in *The Economist*, 11 December 1993) found that women judged to be overweight or under-weight earned less than their average counterparts. In contrast, slightly overweight men earned more than the average. However, both men and women who were judged to be more attractive than average earned an average of 5 per cent more than plainer people. Appearance can be changed to some extent but behaviour can be finetuned to meet the organization's expectations. The latter can be termed 'impression management' (see key concept 10.2).

Image is created as part of one's idea of one's own identity. It is a product of individual and social elements, constantly shaped and reshaped to fit the expected behaviours of the current role. In other words, people act. An image can be learned or acquired through training, a deliberate process called impression management.

KEY CONCEPT 10.2
Impression management

Impression management

Every organization has its cultural symbols and rites: standards of dress and personal appearance, time-keeping, participation in semi-social activities. We choose to conform or not. We may pretend to be enthusiastic, agree with management opinions, or even take up golf for networking rather than sporting reasons. Such behaviour can be described as 'manipulating the impression others gain about us' (Hinton 1993: 23). The archetypal example is the selection or promotion interview, where most of us make a special effort with appearance and manner to achieve a favourable impression. This is easy to sustain for 20–40 minutes, but not necessarily convincing. Long-term success requires a consistent and believable image sustained over a considerable period.

The most significant quality required for selection to top jobs is the ability to create a good impression (Miller and Hanson 1991). The key feature of a well-honed image is that it gives the impression that applicants have qualities they do not possess: a false portrayal of abilities, disguising the lack of true competences behind socially valued characteristics.

Control of one's public image depends on self-awareness. Degrees of self-awareness vary. Some people are invariably 'themselves', whereas others are acutely sensitive to the impression they convey and modify their behaviour constantly. For example, salespeople are much more likely to succeed if they can 'finetune' the impression made on customers. Snyder (1974) attributed this to **self-monitoring**. Good salespeople are high self-monitors, responding quickly to customers' reactions. Low self-monitors make little effort to modify their behaviour, even in an employment interview. Hinton (1993) points to skilled politicians who change their message depending on the audience and are thereby perceived as being 'in-touch with the people'. Bill Clinton was seen to do this extensively during his campaign for the American presidency, sometimes making contradictory statements to different audiences and portraying himself as a liberal or a conservative as required.

Some images derive from the role models around us: successful people in the company or media stars. In the UK – particularly in England – the class structure, education system and institutions such as the civil service and the City serve to create and promote specific images. The French *'cadre'* system, described in Chapter 9, can be analysed in similar terms. In Chapter 7 we noted the condition described by Smith as 'organizational dry rot' (1991: 29). Picking people like ourselves to join our in-group is symptomatic of this condition at a national or institutional level. Too many organizations are dominated by identikit clones with similar images and ideas and whose concept of talent-spotting is finding more of the same.

Influencers

Miller and Hanson note that our ability to recognize real ability 'is contaminated by what we have come to call *the smile factor'* – closely related to the halo effect described in Chapter 8. The one-to-one interview is the most susceptible, but at assessment centres 'the fish-bowl setting gives influencers/impressers space to perform' (1990: 55). A classic example is the excellent salesman who fails to perform well after promotion to sales manager. Time and time again the different requirements of the two jobs are ignored. Miller and Hanson studied four groups of widely different US executives and people deemed to have 'high potential' by their organizations. They describe their results as, 'to put it mildly, alarming. These organizations seeking leaders for major responsibilities were apparently confusing demonstrated leadership with some of the behavioural characteristics which some leaders exhibit' (1990: 55). They found that all the people studied were particularly good at influencing others. They communicated well and were able to get other people to accept their ideas. They were generally sensitive and articulate, able to listen as well as talk. However, few had the motivation and the ability to manage or exercise leadership. They termed the majority **influencers**, people who wanted 'to have an

impact on others but who did not want continuing or complete responsibility for the performance of others' (1990: 55). They were natural coaches
and facilitators but reluctant to confront staff over missed deadlines or
other forms of poor performance.

Admitting that influencers are likely to be bright and analytical, Miller
and Hanson consider them to be too aware of the complexities inherent in
any situation. They lack the confidence to take one direction as opposed to
any other and therefore cannot be proactive or take risks. Further, because
they are not aware in detail of the activities of their staff, they are unable to
monitor changes effectively. Leaders are able to take tough decisions, can
handle ambiguity and give direction. Miller and Hanson concluded that as
many as eight out of ten people promoted into executive positions are
influencers rather than leaders: 'most of the people running these organizations are not leaders; they only look as though they are' (1990: 56).

There is nothing new in saying that 'real self' and 'outward image' are
different constructions and that success is probably more dependent on the
latter than the former. However, it is worth stressing that organizations do
not benefit from this process. Images are distracting and misleading. Promotion on the basis of image does not produce employees capable of doing
the job to an internationally competitive standard. Performance assessments tend to value image qualities: apparent self-confidence, the ability
to talk charismatically, etc. Indeed, **charisma** – the essential characteristic of
the successful double-glazing salesman – is much admired and respected in
a leader (see key concept 10.3):

> in business and management periodicals the term is employed a great deal in
> the context of discussions of certain prominent figures. In such discussions,
> the term is often employed to describe someone who is flamboyant, who is a
> powerful speaker, and who can persuade others of the importance of his or
> her message. The non-charismatic leader, by contrast, is often depicted as a
> lacklustre, ineffectual individual.
>
> (Bryman 1992: 22)

Weber regarded charisma as one of three sources of authority (the other two being **rationality** and **tradition**), portraying it as a magical and hypnotic force based on direct personal contact. In modern life charisma is often fake – a product of carefully orchestrated mass communications.	**KEY CONCEPT** **10.3** *Charisma*

Charismatics are perceived as having the power to transform organizations, as having a mission and as being able to inspire awe and obedience.
They can also be lethal: a poison-pill for the ultimate wellbeing of any
organization, as instanced by DeLorean, Harvey Goldsmith, Robert
Maxwell and many others. Yet, like particularly dim lemmings, people
managers – from personnel officers to boards of directors – will opt for
the charismatic in preference to the non-charismatic.

It can be argued that at senior levels managers need to be figureheads and
spokespersons for their organizations. For these roles the required fluency,
credibility and general communicating skills are those of a charismatic

person. Indeed there may be a case for such a role to be entirely that of figurehead, not requiring any substantive abilities beyond those required for that role. A monarch, for example, can serve as a figurehead without executive power, allowing a prime minister to administer and direct. However, the tendency to overvalue charismatic skills has repeatedly led to foolish choices for 'number one' in large and small organizations. A further danger for performance assessment lies in the tendency to use cloning criteria at junior levels which are only relevant for people at the top of the organization.

Image can be construed as a decorative edifice built on the foundation of substance (real competence). An image which satisfies an audience does not necessarily preclude ability. Curiously, failure does not seem to dent common belief in the value of charisma. Similarly, the success of people with image and substance is commonly attributed to charisma – reinforcing a belief in its necessity. Countering this process is difficult, as can be seen from Case 10.1. It requires a recognition by senior managers that they may have succeeded by cultivating successful images rather than by being the best available. Their organizations need assessment methods which are immune to this process: techniques to identify substance or necessary competences, rather than the obscuring irrelevances of a polished image (key concept 10.4).

KEY CONCEPT 10.4 *Substance v. image*	**Substance** can be defined as that body of competences, knowledge and experience required to fulfil a particular function. **Image** is the **apparent** totality of such knowledge and abilities as outwardly presented by an individual or group.

Langtry and Langtry compare two extreme management types which are oversimplified but identifiable within most organizations (*The Independent*, 3 November 1991). I stands for image or 'me', O equals objective or 'others':

- **I-managers** maintain a high profile, speak well at meetings and are particularly effective at interviews. They are good networkers and make a point of getting to know the right people. They develop a good 'veneer', deliberately projecting a positive and confident image. Effective self-publicists, they make sure that everyone knows how hard they work and how successful they are. They are skilled careerists, and with sufficient emphasis and repetition they ensure that myth becomes reality.
- **O-managers** do not indulge in such elaborate charades. Innovative and supportive, they are quietly hardworking, getting on with the job as efficiently as possible. They only come to the attention of senior management when they challenge simplistic ideas which the I-manager enthusiastically adopts. The tendency is for their work to be ignored in favour of the I-manager's claims and for their criticism to be interpreted as negative. Their fatal mistake is to assume that recognition will follow a job well done. Usually the I-manager goes streaking past them up the career ladder.

Obviously, this delightful typology divides managers too sharply into two simple categories but it captures the essence of the problem. Another perspective comes from examining the outcome of a process which places far too many ineffectual people in managerial positions. This is illustrated in Case 10.1, where a British project designed to bring UK parts manufacturers up to Japanese standards highlighted poor leadership skills as a major obstacle. The UK managers may have had a considerable degree of charisma but this did not translate into action.

In the UK, the Department of Trade and Industry sponsored a two-year 'Learning from Japan' project. The £450,000 project put twelve 'second-tier' vehicle component businesses in contact with Japanese companies in the UK and Japan. The twelve businesses were typical of 3,000 similar firms making parts for around fifty larger 'first-tier' companies which deliver to car manufacturers. Most second-tier companies have poor quality control in comparison with their Japanese counterparts, typically producing 100 defective parts for every one made by a Japanese company. The Learning from Japan project showed that the fault lay with management. According to the Project Director, Betty Thayer from Andersen Consulting:

CASE 10.1
Learning from Japan

> I've not been to a UK factory where the people on the shop floor are incapable of doing what needs to be done (to match the Japanese), but I've met a lot of (UK) managers who are incapable of leading.

'Leading' is not a magical charismatic quality exercised by someone in a remote office. Japanese managers focus on the shop floor, control production processes carefully and pay great attention to detail. In a modern interpretation of scientific management, workers are taught to follow a proven procedure exactly. Standard procedures, completed over and over again, reduce the likelihood of defects. Production workers can suggest further improvements which lead to productivity and quality improvements, each small-scale change adding to efficiency and cutting costs. British workers have shown some resistance to such exacting procedures. For example, John Pearson of Stadium, one of the participating companies, commented that:

> On plastics moulding machines in the UK you have a tradition of operators twiddling with the controls and following their own procedures to make a specific part. There's a certain amount of resentment when you try to get them all to follow a standardised approach.

Stadium works closely with Nissan and Toyota and has learned a great deal from its customers. From a low base, the company has improved its productivity by 50 per cent in five years. However, there is still some way to go – productivity remains at half the level of Japanese suppliers.

(*Source*: based on *The Financial Times*, 6 November 1995, 'Skills of parts chiefs criticised: Ways of the East help progress in Hartlepool', P. Marsh.)

Discussion question
How do British managers need to change in order to change British workers?

Assessment and organizational change

The conduct of performance management is affected also by the success of the organization. Assessors and the assessed may vary their standards depending on their perception of the organization's overall performance, career prospects and, consequently, their feelings of security and optimism. The emotional background to assessment can be directly affected by the prevailing culture of the organization. Attempts to develop a strong, cohe sive culture encourage closer agreement between raters on the standards they expect.

As we observed in Chapters 4 and 6, delayering and downsizing have had the effect of increasing the ratio of staff to managers throughout the western business world. As a consequence, managers have a greater number of assessments to conduct on people they know less about. Widespread structural changes in large organizations also bring new combinations of people together with little knowledge of each other – but perhaps fewer longstanding prejudices.

Intriguingly, managers' routes to power appear to have a direct effect on the way they assess subordinates:

> Attribution theory suggests that raters who have risen through the ranks will have a distorted perception of how well they performed in the job (they will readily recall good performance and will discount poor performance), which may lead to unrealistically high standards.
>
> (Murphy and Cleveland 1995: 415)

On the other hand, managers look after their own and assess their own staff generously. It is well known that performance ratings tend to the positive, with more people being judged as good performers than one would expect from a normal population. This is termed **rater inflation**. It happens generally, but is particularly evident when assessors rate employees they have themselves previously promoted or selected.

Why does this happen? Most explanations are couched in terms of organizational politics:

- **Preserving morale.** A positive performance assessment – whether or not it is deserved – is an act of praise. It offers an opportunity for a manager to say 'thank you' and 'well done', boosting morale and commitment. It engenders good working relationships between managers and subordinates. It maintains a cosy atmosphere.
- **Avoiding confrontation.** Conversely, a critical assessment is likely to have the opposite effects.
- **Maintaining management's image.** If managers rate staff poorly there is an implication that they make bad selection decisions and run poor-quality departments. This can have unfortunate consequences on their own performance ratings.

From a psychological perspective, it can be argued that managers develop a bonding or personal working relationship with their favoured staff, which inevitably leads to biased assessments of their performance. The organization's human resource strategies should be focused, in part at least, on overcoming this problem. In the next section we consider the strategic choices which are open to us.

Performance strategies

> Organizations face a critical paradox. No other management tool is more critical to productivity than effective performance appraisals, yet they can actually impair employees' performance.
>
> (English 1991: 55)

As we observed at the beginning of this chapter, performance assessment or appraisal has been in use for a considerable period, particularly for management and sub-management grades in large corporations. The range of jobs covered by performance assessment is steadily increasing, but there remain areas of employment where performance measurement does not yet feature and there is a great deal of conflict over its introduction.

From a strategic perspective, the process of assessment is an exercise in management power and control (see key concept 10.5). It is a method by which an enterprise can evaluate its employees and feed back the organization's views to them. Furthermore, evaluation can be linked to 'stick and carrot' measures in the form of:

- Critical comment indicating the firm's disapproval.
- Incentives to reward and encourage 'good' performance in the form of enhanced pay and promotion prospects.

We saw in Chapter 1 that **behavioural consistency** is a major focus for models of HRM which hold that business competitiveness is improved by enhancing employee attitudes, behaviour and commitment. To do so, it is imperative that the organization has effective methods of communicating its standards or norms of behaviour. Assessors and the assessed may have entirely different perceptions of both the reasons for performance appraisal and the criteria for judgement. Proponents argue that performance management should be:

> a process or set of processes for establishing shared understanding about what *is* to be achieved, and of managing and developing people in a way which increases the probability that it *will* be achieved in the short and longer term.
>
> (M. Armstrong 1992: 163)

Performance management strategies are particularly concerned with workforce **motivation** or, more accurately, management belief in the factors which lead to employee effort and commitment.

Motivation and performance

As we observed in Chapter 3, a considerable body of literature exists on the relationship between motivation and work performance. Theories range from the simplistic rational 'economic man' concepts underlying scientific management – implying that workers are only interested in money – to complex 'expectancy ' theories which explain motivation in terms of a calculus of conflicting needs. Morgan (1986: 149) points to the diverse range of interests which people bring to the workplace:

- **Task interests** – focused on the job being performed so that, for example, someone in sales is committed to selling, enjoys dealing with customers and takes pride in being able to clinch a sale.

- **Career interests** – aspirations and visions of one's future, which may or may not include the current job.

These are complemented by **extramural interests** which incorporate leisure pursuits and domestic relationships. They cannot be divorced from work, since they compete for an individual's time and psychological or physical effort. Performance management strategies must take account of people as whole beings, with work forming just a part of their lives.

Achievers and non-achievers

A number of researchers have attempted to identify the important factors leading to successful performance by comparing recognized high achievers with average performers. This method focuses on distinguishing key psychological differences between people in the two groups. However, as Furnham notes: 'it cannot be assumed that these factors *caused* the success, indeed they may have been a *consequence* of success' (1990: 30). Factors such as confidence and knowledge of a particular area may have been present at an early stage in a person's career or, alternatively, developed as that career became successful. For example, Charles Handy uses the term **helicopter view** to describe the broad strategic grasp of business expected from senior managers. They are unlikely to have achieved this perspective without wide experience at lower levels.

Reviewing some of the vast selection of books on the rich and famous, Furnham finds consistent themes such as:

- **Perseverance** – tenacity, single-minded determination and concentration.
- **Ability** – especially in creating and exploiting opportunities.
- **Contacts** – knowing the right people.
- **Self-reliance** – striving for independence.
- **Thinking big** – but taking modest risks.
- **Time management** – making the best use of time and planning progress.

The weakness in these studies lies in their essentially retrospective and descriptive nature. They do not set out to test the hypothesis that individuals setting out on a career with a particular set of personality characteristics will be more successful than average. Nevertheless, Furnham finds that certain values, which he describes as PWE (the Protestant work ethic), recur, providing 'some evidence for the fact that specific PWE values – namely tenacity, perseverance, autonomy, independence, and hard work – are to be found in financially successful individuals and companies alike' (1990: 31).

Locus of control

Performance management is based on the underlying belief that managers can influence behaviour and therefore that rationality is the basis of human action. Unfortunately, the available psychological evidence suggests that this is not the case. Research shows that people vary significantly in their reactions to the persuasion or coercion of others, depending on their perception of the ability they have to control their own lives. At one extreme, some individuals will believe that what happens in their lives is the consequence of their own decisions, abilities and behaviour. These people are judged to have an **expectancy of internal control**. There is evidence that individuals who have an expectancy of internal control ('internals') are better performers and tend to occupy most of the higher level jobs (Andrisani and Nestel 1976). Internals take more notice of the feedback provided by performance management but do so according to their own agenda. If good performance produces appropriate rewards, they will deliver more of the same. If it does not, they are likely to devote their internal strengths to finding another job. On the other hand, externals see little connection between their own performance and eventual success. When criticized for below-average work they will attribute their failure to causes outside themselves and the disapproval of the appraiser to personal dislike.

At the other extreme are individuals who attribute events to fate, to God, to luck or to more powerful people. They consider life to be outside their personal remit and are permanent victims of chance or the wishes of others. They are said to have an **expectancy of external control** (Furnham 1990: 42). People with an expectancy of external control will be more compliant at the surface level, following instructions from supervisors and fitting social expectations. 'Following orders' they will fit neatly into bureaucratic structures but will demonstrate little initiative.

Are you in charge of life . . . or is life in charge of you? Most people have times when the former is true, and other times when the progress of life is firmly out of their hands. Some are permanently in one camp or the other. It is clear that being in charge of one's own life, career and circumstances leads to feelings of wellbeing and confidence and equates with successful and happy times. This is true **empowerment**. However, it is doubtful whether performance management is entirely compatible with this state. In the next section we elaborate on how organizations can place performance assessment within a wider framework of human resource management.

Performance management systems

Amongst the ten principles of HRM discussed in Chapter 1 and elsewhere we placed consistency, coordination and control. These strategic aspects of performance assessment are exemplified in the integration of appraisal and performance-related pay processes within performance management systems. M. Armstrong (1992: 162) sees the functions of such systems as:

- reinforcing the organization's values and norms;
- integrating individual objectives with those of the organization;
- allowing individuals to express their views on the job;
- providing the means for managers and staff to share their expectations of performance.

A major British survey of public- and private-sector organizations showed that 20 per cent claimed to have such a system; 65 per cent had some kind of performance management process; whereas 15 per cent stated that they had no policy (Bevan and Thompson 1992). The survey showed no consistency in approach or understanding of the concept of performance management. Bevan and Thompson found two contradictory strategic themes for performance management:

- **Reward-driven integration**, emphasising performance-related pay (PRP) based on short-term targets with a consequent undervaluing of any other human resource activities.
- **Development-driven integration**, using appraisals to provide information for developing an organization's people geared for long-term objectives, in line with our discussion in the next chapter. When in existence, PRP is complementary to this.

They concluded that the first theme was dominant in the UK, serving to reinforce the prevalent cashflow-driven short-termism of British managers.

Management by objectives (MBO)

The origins of strategic performance management can be traced to the concept of management by objectives. This is a technique to establish individual performance objectives which are tangible, measurable and verifiable. Individual objectives are derived or cascaded from organizational goals. Top managers agree their own specific objectives, ones compatible with the organization's goals but restricted to their own areas of responsibility. Subordinates do the same at each lower level, forming an interlocked and coherent hierarchy of performance targets. Hence, management by objectives lies within the strategic way of thinking which forms a key element in HRM (see Table 10.1). MBO encompasses four main stages:

1 **Goal-setting.** This is the heart of the MBO process. Goals are specific and desired results to be achieved within an agreed period of time. They must represent real progress. They should be:

- challenging, stretching the individual beyond comfortable performance;
- attainable, realistic within cost and resource constraints;
- measurable, specific, quantifiable and verifiable – objectives are best set in numerical terms such as 'increased sales by x thousand', 'reduced staff by y per cent';
- relevant – directly related to the person's job and consistent with overall organizational objectives.

Alternatively, goals are sometimes set against the acronym SMART:

- S – Specific or Stretching
- M – Measurable
- A – Agreed or Achievable
- R – Realistic
- T – Time-bounded

Table 10.1 The MBO Process

Essential elements	Key stages
Goal-setting	1 Establish long-range strategic objectives
	2 Formulate specific overall organizational goals
	3 Agree departmental objectives
	4 Set individual performance targets
Action planning	5 Draw up action plans
Self-control	6 Implement and take corrective action
Periodic reviews	7 Review performance against objectives
	8 Appraise overall performance, reinforce appropriate behaviour and strengthen motivation through: • management development • reward • career and HR planning

2 **Action planning.** Goals or performance targets are the 'ends' of the MBO process; action plans are the 'means'. They require individual employees to ask themselves what, who, when, where and how an objective can be achieved.

3 **Self-control.** MBO is a self-driven process, with each person participating in setting their own goals and action plans. This results in greater commitment to their own objectives and an improved understanding of the process. Each person is expected to control their own behaviour in order to achieve performance targets. In return it is essential that they are given sufficient information and feedback to gauge their progress.

4 **Periodic reviews.** It is not sufficient to review progress at the end of the MBO process. Individuals must be provided with an opportunity to check their performance at regular intervals so that obstacles can be identified. Reviews should take a positive coaching approach rather than critical approach.

MBO pre-dates human resource management and derives from a period when strategic thinking and the integration of organizational objectives were being emphasized by management writers. Since then, the development of HRM has maintained the focus on strategy and integration. This has been reinforced by the fashion for performance-related pay, fostered by the prevalent belief that reward should be firmly tied to results. Whereas MBO concentrated on individual management of one's own performance, the spread of PRP is underpinned by the use of assessment systems to manage the individual.

Prescriptions for performance management systems

Bevan and Thompson (1992) describe a model performance management system as follows:

- The organization has a shared vision of its objectives or a mission statement, which is communicated to its employees.
- There are individual performance management targets, related to unit and wider organizational objectives.
- There is a regular formal review of progress towards achieving the targets.
- There is a review process which identifies training, development and reward outcomes.
- The whole process is itself evaluated, feeding back through changes and improvements.

Rather as in the MBO approach, the central features of such a system are an **objective-setting** process and a **formal appraisal** system. Typically, the performance management system is owned and implemented by line managers. The role of human resource specialists is to aid and advise line managers on the development of the system. In a slightly different approach, English (1991) argues for a 'rational' system of performance management, which should have the following characteristics:

- There is a clear statement of what is to be achieved by the organization.
- Individual and group responsibilities support the organization's goals.
- All performance is measured and assessed in terms of those responsibilities and goals.
- All rewards are based on employee performance.
- Organizational structure, processes, resources and authority systems are designed to optimize the performance of all employees.
- There is an ongoing effort to create and guide appropriate organizational goals and to seek newer, more appropriate goals.

Many organizations consider that they have a performance management system along these lines. Often they often do not, because one or more of the following conditions is missing:

- Agreement among all critical parties on what is to be performed.
- An effective way to measure desired performance.
- A reward system tied directly to performance.
- An environment conducive to successful performance.
- A communication programme to gain understanding, acceptance and commitment to the system.
- A performance-based organizational culture.

Case 10.2 outlines an attempt to introduce a performance management system related to police pay. The structure of British police remuneration has taken on a labyrinthine complexity over the years, including shift working, overtime, tied housing, lifetime contracts, pension rules, disciplinary procedures, rank structure and payment. The intricacy of these arrangements meant that no matter how keenly the service wanted to reward and encourage good performance there were always good reasons why things should be left as they were. The senior ranks tried to improve efficiency within these constraints but their new policy initiatives simply highlighted the inflexibility and generated considerable frustration. On some occasions the initiatives led to insensitive management practices which did not allow a reasonable quality of working life for the lower ranks. The rising crime rate and tight budgets have neutralized the effect of most efficiency measures, and the public impression is that police performance has got steadily worse.

Police forces in the UK are organized on a regional basis, each force being headed by a Chief Constable. It is not surprising that the police pay structure bears little resemblance to conventional business forms. Nevertheless the perceived culture of restrictive practices and inertia attracted the attention of a government convinced of the virtues of performance-related pay. They wanted a system based on market principles which would encourage the management ranks to develop and motivate their subordinates, promoting those who showed initiative.

CASE 10.2
Police pay

Sir Patrick Sheehy, Chairman of BAT Industries, was given the task of recommending changes in line with government expectations. The Sheehy Report recommended the lowering of pay for new recruits, abolition of overtime, fixed-term contracts for those promoted beyond Police Constable and introduction of performance-related pay for senior ranks. Pay would vary between postings, with less money for those regarded as being less demanding. Chief Constables would be assessed on a number of performance indicators, which would also allow forces to be arranged in league tables. It was believed that this would enhance local efficiency, but doubts were soon raised based on the history of performance measurement, knowledge about human motivation and the impact of PRP on output in private-sector organizations. For example, Barrie Irving, director of the Police Foundation, commented, 'Still, trying to make sense of policymakers' determination to control organisational performance from the top has always been a nice little earner for management consultants and no doubt the same will be true in this instance.'

Sheehy recommended changing rank structure and rewards to make policing 'on the beat' more attractive as a career and to cut bureaucracy and a top-heavy management hierarchy. By cutting out inspectors and superintendents, it was argued, more officers could be employed at the sharp end. However, as had been identified by Egon Bittner in the USA twenty-five years earlier, there is no practical definition of the tasks of a police officer – and if there were, it would be virtually impossible to check that the tasks had been done. The function of policing is highly varied, often ad hoc and dependent on inspiration for success rather than on a rigid industrial-type process.

Police officers argued that lengthy inquiries into serious crimes and crime prevention measures would not be rewarded whereas arrests for trivial crimes would. Sheehy claimed that only the lazy or inefficient had anything to fear from the recommendations but did not endear himself to police officers by describing the 21,000 who attended a Police Federation rally as an 'unrepresentative minority'. In fact, they were almost half the off-duty police in the country at that time.

Few of the Sheehy recommendations were introduced.

(*Source*: *Guardian*, 3 July 1993, Barrie Irving: 'Handcuffed and facing the trials of Hercules'.)

Discussion questions
1 Was opposition to the Sheehy report based on rational argument?
2 Is it possible to assess the quantity and quality of police work accurately?

Reward management

Reward or **compensation** management is an aspect of HRM which focuses pay and other benefits on the achievement of objectives. Typically, it incorporates other changes in pay administration and policy, including:

- decentralization of responsibility for setting pay levels;
- uniform appraisal schemes;
- flexible working practices;
- performance-related pay.

Traditional payment systems fall into one of two categories or include elements of both:

- **Set wages or salaries.** Fixed payments which may be on an age, responsibility or seniority scale. Historically, most 'office'-type jobs have been paid in this way.
- **Payment by results.** Payment based on the quantity or quality of work. This includes piecework for manual labour. As we noted earlier, payment by results is common in sales and financial services. The catering industry is also heavily geared towards direct payment from satisfied customers through gratuities (tips) or service charges.

Both methods are relatively straightforward if there are clearly understood scales or methods of work measurement. However, many commentators have severely criticized the apparently chaotic and disorganized nature of pay management between the 1950s and 1980s. In recent years there has been an attempt to remedy this situation. As we saw with the case of police pay, the fashion has been towards the development of performance-related pay schemes which are related to assessments of performance through individual employee appraisal.

For instance, during 1992/93 in the UK, Industrial Relations Services found that the proportion of pay settlements based at least partly on individual performance assessments had increased from 14.5 per cent to 20 per cent over the previous year. This was the standard method in certain industries, such as finance and information technology, and it had become common for managers and administrative staff in the public sector, and in chemical and engineering industries.

Pay is a sensitive issue. Most employers have been cautious with the introduction of PRP. Often it is applied to senior managers first, then extended to other employees. Usually, it has been an 'add-on' to normal pay. Rarely does it replace the existing pay scheme completely. More commonly, PRP has (ACAS 1990):

- formed part or (rarely) all of the general pay increase;
- been used to extend pay above scale maxima for employees with high levels of performance;
- replaced increases previously paid on the basis of age, or length of service.

Such caution is due to the complexity and sensitivity of performance-related pay in the context of employee relations. People take pay scales seriously. Negotiating and justifying radical changes to a pay structure can be difficult and time-consuming. It is sensible to do this in a gradual way, commencing with senior managers who are more likely to be committed to demanding performance objectives. Even if they are not so committed, it gives experience of the advantages and disadvantages of performance-related pay. It also gives pay administrators experience of pay schemes which are more complicated to operate than traditional methods.

The basis of performance-related pay systems

What is performance-related pay for? According to Brading and Wright, 'Pay is one of the strongest communicators of how much an organization values the contribution, of an individual or group' (1990). Simplistically, it seems only fair that people should be paid according to their contribution and a number of studies indicate that most people in business agree with this. In a classic experiment, Fossum and Fitch (1985) asked three groups of subjects – students, line managers and compensation managers – to make decisions on pay increases for hypothetical people, taking into account factors such as seniority, budget constraints and cost of living. All three groups gave far more importance to performance and contribution than other factors. Research into the attitudes of corporate boards and chief executive officers, among others, have all produced similar findings.

Theoretically, appraisal-related pay schemes can benefit both employers and employees. By emphasizing the importance of efficiency and effective job performance, employers can benefit from higher productivity. Higher pay can be targeted at the 'better' performers, encouraging them to stay with the company and continue to perform to a high standard. Good employees benefit from extra pay in return for extra quality of performance. According to this view, properly directed pay can reinforce appropriate behaviour. According to this view, well-designed PRP schemes can focus effort on organizational targets and encourage a results-based culture. However, these links must be justified and real if they are not to demoralize other members of the workforce. This is particularly important in relation to senior management, as can be seen in the case of British Gas (see Case 10.3 below). Accusations of 'fat cat' behaviour can also seriously affect stock market views of a company's organization.

CASE 10.3
British Gas

In 1994 the remuneration committee of British Gas recommended pay increases from 11 to 75 per cent for directors earning £200,000 or more. A new structure replaced a complex system which overemphasized share options and bonuses. This included a pay package worth £475,000 for its Chief Executive, Cedric Brown. This placed Mr Brown on about twenty times the earnings of the average British Gas employee – a ratio typical of British companies. This compared with differentials of five to eight in Japanese companies.

Facing a House of Commons committee, Cedric Brown argued that he was paid much less than many other chief executives of large British companies. In the USA a smaller utility company paid its CEO ten times as much. Indeed his pay could be regarded as modest when compared with a total payout of $203 million to Michael Eisner, Chairman of Walt

Disney, in 1993. Mr Brown's remuneration was justified on the grounds that it was 'the rate for the job' and that it would take this kind of salary to attract top international managers. However, Mr Brown had never worked for any company other than British Gas, had apparently been happy on lower pay in the past, and there was no indication that he was about to be headhunted by anyone else.

Public criticism was fuelled by the fact that 25,000 British Gas workers were in the process of losing their jobs. Redundancies and relocations were making their mark on employee morale and commitment. The changes also included the closure of half its showrooms. The remaining retail outlets would concentrate on appliance sales. They would no longer accept payment for gas bills, offer advice or accept service complaints. The Gas Consumer Council complained about this reduction in customer service, especially given an increase of 19 per cent in complaints over the previous year.

As part of this process, another executive was reported as being offered a bonus of £36,000 on top of his salary of £120,000 for pushing through changes in the work and pay scales of retail workers. The 2,600 workers were being asked to take pay cuts from their average £13,000-a-year salaries, along with reductions in holiday entitlements.

The attendant publicity about 'fat cats' dogged Mr Brown for the subsequent two years. As a symbol, angry shareholders brought a pig named Cedric into the Annual General Meeting and fed it from a trough. Mr Brown suffered further criticism when it was revealed that British Gas had tied itself to a number of supply deals at inflated prices. In 1996 the continued existence of British Gas as an independent entity seemed uncertain. Mr Brown announced his retirement – with a pension of £250,000 a year.

Discussion questions

1 Was criticism of Mr Brown reasonable?
2 Were the various payments made to Mr Brown fair

   - to him?
   - to British Gas employees?

Performance-related pay can be related to the performance assessment of the individual, group (team), department or company. There are several systems in common use, which can be put into one of two categories:

1 Appraisal-related pay schemes

   - Merit pay, paid as part of a person's annual increase on the basis of an overall performance appraisal. This method has a long track record and is commonly regarded as an effective motivator. However, it is frequently undermined by budget restrictions, when the merit element is often set too low to motivate.

     There are also instances when the payment is used as a *market supplement* to retain individuals who have skills for which there is demand but whose performance is not particularly meritorious. For example, competition for merchant bankers with particular skills has led to telephone number bonuses in the City of London. For example, it was claimed that Deutsche Morgan Grenfell had drafted a job offer which included a guaranteed first year bonus of £350,000 – on top of a basic salary of just £120,000 (*The Observer*,

9 June 1996). However, it is known that breaking the clear link between appraised performance and payment of PRP reduces the overall effectiveness of PRP as a motivator for other employees (ACAS, 1990).

- Individual incentives, given as unconsolidated (one-off) payments or gifts such as holidays, golf sets or vouchers.

2 Collective performance schemes

- Bonuses, paid to all staff in an organization, department or team. In common with all collective performance rewards, they are designed to reinforce corporate identity and performance. The John Lewis retail firm paid out a total of £57 million in 1995 to its 35,000 partner employees in the form of bonuses equivalent to 15 per cent of each person's salary. In 1996 the jeans manufacturers Levi Strauss proposed a payout of a year's salary to each permanent employee at the end of 2001, provided they had worked at least three years and the company reached its objective of a $7.6 billion a year cash flow (*The Independent*, 14 June 1996).

- Profit-related pay, schemes in which employees are allocated a payment equivalent to an agreed proportion of the organization's profits. As we have noted already, profit-related pay has been encouraged in the UK through tax incentives for schemes registered with the Inland Revenue.

- Option schemes. Executive share option schemes are particularly prevalent in the USA but have also become common elsewhere (see Case 10.4). They allow senior managers to benefit from the continued success of the organization through the purchase of shares at designated dates in the future at a fixed price. The more successful the company – and therefore the greater the likely increase in share value – the higher the reward to the executive. This is seen as an important incentive to motivate people who can dramatically affect the prosperity and even survival of the business.

  Employee share option schemes apply to less senior staff and tend to be considerably less generous than executive schemes. Generally, a sum is allocated from company profits and used for share purchase for employees. Save As You Earn (SAYE) option schemes may also be registered with the taxation authorities. These allow staff to save a proportion of their salary via the pay administration process and accumulated for a fixed period. This may be paid to them at the end of that time, with a bonus equivalent to the interest which could have been earned in a savings account. Alternatively, and more beneficially, the sum plus bonus can be used to purchase shares at the price prevailing at the start of the scheme. Preferential tax arrangements have been made for shares held in trust for a fixed period.

Case study 10.4 illustrates the use of some of these techniques to pay senior employees.

CASE 10.4
Top people's
pay at BP

BP believes in good competitive pay for good competitive results. In setting the senior team's remuneration the Compensation Committee takes into account a number of factors in addition to individual performance, notably pay in comparable companies and the fact that BP operates internationally. We will not, therefore, set remuneration at levels which are blatantly uncompetitive with overseas comparators and so risk straining the loyalty of staff who are potentially very mobile.

(Lord Ashburton, 'Chairman's letter', *BP Summary Financial Statement 1994*)

According to the 1994 *Summary Financial Statement*, the reward strategy for BP's most senior executives is based on three principles:

- Reward should have a strong performance focus and be linked to business results and to the creation of shareholder value.
- Base salary should be balanced with short-term and long-term incentives.
- Reward should be related to competitive practice in both the oil and non-oil sectors of the relevant employment markets.

The Chairman argued that the package had been constructed to meet the principle that 'reward should reflect performance, over both the short and long term'. At the time, the scheme applied to eighty-seven senior executives and included the following three elements:

- **Base salary.** This is within the market-related range for the executive's home country, and is reviewed annually to reflect competitive practice, individual and business performance, general economic factors and the global nature of the business. With increasing seniority, the proportion of base salary decreases and the following two variable elements increase.
- An **annual performance bonus.** This is a cash payment for achieving collective and individual targets specified in annual performance contracts. These include both financial and non-financial targets.
- The **long-term performance plan (LTPP).** The Compensation Committee has the discretion to award shares to executives if certain long-term targets are met. The relevant performance measure is BP's shareholder return relative to competitors' during the performance period. The competitor group comprises Amoco, Atlantic Richfield (Arco), Chevron, Exxon, Mobil, Shell Transport and Trading, and Texaco. Maximum awards are made only if BP's performance is better than all seven of these competitors. Minimum awards are made if BP exceeds the performance of at least two competitors. The plan also requires that senior executives make a substantial personal investment in shares at the beginning of the period. This is intended to ensure a closer alignment of executives' interests with those of their shareholders.

(*Source*: BP *Summary Financial Statement* 1994)

Discussion questions

1 Do you consider that BP's reward package really motivates senior employees?
2 In what ways does the package align employees' interests with those of shareholders?

Flavour of the (last) month?

Kanter observes that whenever any US organization comes up with a 'new' pay scheme a merit element is involved (1989: 233). For example, in 1985 General Motors switched to a merit system for 15,000 employees, extending this to a further 110,000 in 1986. Uvalic (1991) found that most Northern European countries in the EU – including Germany, France and the Netherlands – were favourably inclined towards PRP and that discussion of the issue was common.

The spread of PRP into the state sector has been more recent. The UK Conservative government encouraged performance-related pay in preference to industry-wide pay scales. PRP has also been a prominent feature of the attempt to commercialize practices in the public services, intended as a key factor in encouraging business-like behaviour amongst managers.

The earliest use of PRP in the British Civil Service dates back to an experiment in 1985 affecting a range of senior grades (principal to under-secretary). The scheme involved payment of a minimum £500 unconsolidated bonus paid as a one-off lump sum to no more than one-fifth of eligible staff. The exercise drew a range of comments but it was decided to extend the scheme to most other grades, including non-management staff. Ironically, the Review Body on Top Salaries, which covers judges, permanent secretaries, senior military officers and diplomats, felt that PRP was unsuitable for politically sensitive posts.

Performance-related pay was introduced for the 800 National Health Service general managers in 1986 based on annual objectives, individual performance reviews and financial rewards where the achievement of objectives could be clearly demonstrated (Murlis 1987). For general managers, the process relied on an appraisal procedure called the 'individual performance review' (IPR). The system had the following characteristics:

- The method was objectives-based, stated wherever possible in quantifiable terms.
- Appraisals were conducted on the 'parent–grandparent' system. Unit general managers would be assessed by the district general manager, with the chair of the regional health authority acting as 'grandparent'.
- Managers were rated in one of five bands. 'Grandparents' had final responsibility and were required to ensure that no more than 20 per cent received the highest rating level and 40 per cent the next.
- An individual at the highest level 'consistently exceeds short-term levels of performance and makes excellent progress towards long-term goals', justifying a salary increase of 3–4 per cent a year, up to a maximum of 20 per cent over five years.
- At the lowest level, an individual 'meets few short-term objectives and makes little or no progress towards long-term goals', receiving no increase at all.

Performance-related pay has also been a major feature of the managerial transformation of former state-owned industries which have been privatized. Thames Water was privatized in 1989 but began preparing for the process three or four years earlier. The introduction of pay schemes based on performance rather than national wage bargaining started in 1988. By 1992 PRP had been extended to 50 per cent of Thames Water staff. Performance-related pay was seen as one element in the process of culture change, the other features being the introduction of a management development scheme, recruiting people from outside the organization, and the improvement of internal communication.

> If you kept your nose clean, and did not get noticed, you did well. Now we are encouraging people to use their initiative, to push out boundaries, to do more than they are asked to increase productivity. The trick is to reward those who perform above average and to be seen to be doing so.
>
> (Richard Marshall, Group Personnel Director, Thames Water; quoted in *The Independent on Sunday*, 15 November 1992)

London Electricity, a privatized utility company, started PRP with senior management then applied it to industrial grades, including meter readers and joiners. Meter readers were paid for the number of readings they achieved. Those who achieved the best performance did so by working outside normal hours in order to find customers at home.

Criticisms of performance-related pay

There is a widespread opinion among senior managers that PRP must be a good thing – but the evidence for its effectiveness is not overwhelming. Indeed, the search for a positive relationship between PRP and good performance has been described as being like 'looking for the Holy Grail' (Fletcher and Williams 1992). As one variable in a complex situation, it is not surprising that a connection cannot be proven.

However, research does indicate that most employees are unhappy with PRP. The main criticisms address:

- **Fairness.** As we can see from the exercise in Case 10.5, the concept of 'fairness' is problematic and open to interpretation. Some employers have gone to elaborate lengths in an attempt to make their system appear fair. This may involve sampling the work of lower-level workers, listening in on phone calls, examining files, checking through a proportion of completed work. The Bank of America has been cited as spending over $1 million a year and employing twenty people to monitor 3,500 credit card workers for their merit scheme. Not surprisingly, such attempts at 'fairness' have not been entirely popular amongst employees. The system seems to be distinctly Orwellian: 'big brother is watching you.'
- **Managerial judgement.** The process is dependent on skilled line managers. As we have observed, for various reasons managers feel under pressure to rate their staff as above average. As Kanter says, 'far from freeing the energies of employees to seek ways to improve their performance, subjectively based merit pay systems throw them back on the mercy of their bosses' (1989: 235). Typically, such systems are cynically regarded by employees and attacked by unions as being open to abuse and favouritism. They can also result in a rash of high marks by supervisors who feel exposed to the wrath of their employees. Relationships between managers and employees are often uncomfortable, and this process tends to charge that relationship with even more emotion.
- **The value of the reward.** Many senior managers seem more concerned with managing the pay bill than motivating staff, so that PRP is often budget- not performance-led. A common compaint is that the merit element is too small as a percentage of the whole – commonly 3–10 per

cent. This is not enough for it to be a motivator for improved performance. The solution is obvious at one level: increase the merit element to a significantly motivating level such as 15–25 per cent. But this only serves to highlight the difficulty in making a judgement on who gets an increase and being seen to be fair about it. Most employers have not felt confident enough about the process to go beyond a token percentage level.

- **The relationship with company performance**. Fletcher and Williams (1992) could find no correlation between company performance and PRP. PRP schemes were used by both high- and low-performance businesses.
- **Demotivation.** PRP benefits 20 per cent of employees at the expense of 80 per cent. Consequently it demotivates far more people than it enourages.
- **PRP and flexibility.** It increases the likelihood of flexibility and management power. Not surprisingly, PRP has attracted hostility from many unions as collective bargaining is sidestepped. Intriguingly, however, PRP schemes have largely been focused on core – in other words, relatively permanent, well-paid, non-manual – staff, rather than peripheral, often lower-paid and less skilled workers (Kessler 1995: 469).
- **Conflict with the team philosophy.** The obsession with individually based performance pay conflicts with HRM's emphasis on teams.

Employee dissatisfaction was highlighted in an internal review of a performance assessment and payment system covering 68,000 Inland Revenue employees (*The Independent*, 5 April 1994). The inquiry surveyed 800 staff and found considerable dissatisfaction, concluding that the performance system was acting as a demotivator for most staff. As well as the familiar complaint that merit payments were too low to provide any incentive, a number of further criticisms of the operation of the system were listed:

- Employees found themselves on a treadmill which was continually being speeded up – the goalposts were being moved as targets moved ever upwards.
- Employees were being assessed by managers who did not know them.
- Performance-related pay for junior employees was restricted by 'budgetary constraints' but this limitation did not seem to apply to senior officials.
- Objectives were often imposed rather than negotiated.
- Subjective criteria led to disagreements on the quality of performance, leading to a perception of unfairness.
- Individual targets were not compatible with team performance.

The reduction in the inflation rate to low single figures has further reduced the perceived effectiveness of incentives. Merit payments of 2–3 per cent are not seen as much reward for exceptional performance. Indeed such payments may be viewed as insulting. Performance systems established in a high-inflation period have proven to be a financial embarrassment to some companies. British Telecom scrapped a system for junior and middle managers on the grounds that managers were being overpaid in comparison with equivalents in other firms. Consolidated performance pay was restricted to the top 10 per cent in 1994, with one-off bonuses being paid to most.

CASE 10.5 *Fairness*	Scenario 1: a photocopying shop has one employee who has worked in the shop for six months and earns $9 per hour. Business continues to be satisfactory, but a factory in the area has closed and unemployment has increased. Other small firms have now hired reliable workers working at $7 an hour to perform jobs similar to those done by the photocopying shop employee. The owner of the photocopying shop reduces the employee's wage to $7. Is it fair to cut the worker's wage from $9 to $7 an hour? Compare your decision with scenario 2.
	Scenario 2: a house painter employs two assistants and pays them $9 per hour. The painter decides to change his business and go into lawn mowing, where the going wage is lower. He tells the current workers that he will keep them on if they want to work, but will only pay them $7 per hour. Is this employer being fair?
	Kahneman *et al.* (1986) found that around 85 per cent of respondents said that the employer was unfair in scenario 1, whereas the response was virtually the reverse for the second scenario. It appears that the change in the nature of the business was seen as a fundamental alteration in the framework of 'fairness'.

The assessment process

> Appraisal is seen as essentially an exercise in personal power. It elevates the role of the supervisor by emphasising individualism and obscuring the social nature of work.
>
> (Storey 1989: 14)

In this final section we consider performance assessment as an activity. Traditionally, performance assessment uses a rating system known as appraisal (key concept 10.5). In most companies it is a matter of something being done to the employee rather than a process in which the employee plays a valued and important part. Assessments are generally an annual exercise, although some organizations may undertake them more frequently, perhaps every six months, especially with new entrants or recent promotees. For lower-grade employees, some companies are content with an assessment every two years.

KEY CONCEPT 10.5 *Appraisals*	Performance assessment is one of the many people management techniques which 'classify and order individuals hierarchically' (Townley 1994: 33). Appraisals rate individuals on quasi-objective criteria or standards deemed to be relevant to performance. Traditional appraisals rated individuals on a list of qualities, primarily work-related attitudes and personality traits. Modern assessment is often focused on competences.

Appraisal and conformity

Appraisals tend to be formalized. In many organizations they take the shape of preprinted forms and typed instructions prepared for the appraising manager or supervisor. Dates of completion and return are fixed and the whole process is monitored and administered by the personnel or HR department. Theoretically, appraisals can be completed in a number of ways:

- **Self-assessment.** Individuals assess themselves against rating criteria or targeted objectives.
- **Peer assessment.** Fellow team members, departmental colleagues or selected individuals with whom an employee has working interaction provide assessments.
- **Line management.** The employee's immediate supervisor(s) provide the assessment. Alternatively, other line managers may be involved.
- **Upward appraisal.** Managers are appraised by their staff.

In 98 per cent of cases, the appraiser is the immediate supervisor or line manager with, usually, further comments or countersignature provided by the supervisor's own manager. This has been described as the 'father and grandfather' system – appropriate terms, given the essentially paternalistic nature of the process.

Long (1986) found that most appraisals are now shown to employees, with 92 per cent being shown the completed form; 83 per cent of companies allowed employees to record their opinions if they disagreed with the assessment. This move to 'openness' is to be welcomed but it is worth considering exactly what the term actually means, given that appraisal is inevitably linked to the encouragement of behavioural consistency. Appraisal is a procedure designed to encourage conformity to the standards, norms or image required by the person completing the assessment. The focus is on the kind of behaviour the company culture requires, discouraging any behaviour which does not fit. This is consistent with the tendency for appraisals to be conducted as a subjective assessment of personality characteristics rather than as an objective measure of achievement (Philp 1990).

Appraisal normally requires rating on a series of categories. Management and lower-level appraisals are commonly conducted in different ways. Management assessments tend to feature results-oriented criteria, typically against objectives agreed at the beginning of the year. Non-managerial appraisals are more likely to be **trait-ratings**, which is to say that, no matter what the questions may ask overtly, they are actually rating the employee on behavioural or personality criteria. In essence, they are no more than crude personality questionnaires. This remains the case if the criteria are couched in terms of job-related qualities:

> Received wisdom is now that the appraiser judges the work not the person, with trait-rating being replaced by appraisals which identify and measure some aspect of performance. This, however, introduces the problem of defining and measuring performance, whether this should include, for example, skill, knowledge, potential and overall 'worth', etc., and the relative weight which should be attached to behaviour or results.
>
> (Townley 1994: 43)

According to Philp:

> The disadvantages of this approach are numerous. For instance, the terms themselves are extremely ambiguous and it is unlikely that any group of managers would share exactly the same interpretation of any of them. Any appraisal using such words would be extremely subjective and, as a result, totally unfair.
>
> Also, because assessment in these terms deals with the individual rather than with the results they produce for the organization, it is very difficult to communicate with the individual involved. The person being appraised is likely to see any critical assessment of this type as a personal attack. The factors deal with the emotive areas closely concerned with personality, and the majority of people will tend to react defensively.
>
> (Philp 1990: 5)

There is not unanimous agreement on this point. English states that 'A performance appraisal should evaluate traits as well as skills. Because an employee's facility in working with others can be critical, it's important to assess attitude, communication skills, leadership, appearance, and other relevant qualities'.

Despite the fact that most assessors are completely unqualified to make judgements on anyone's personality, even in the most general of terms, the traditional appraisal form asks for a numerical rating on a scale of 1–4 or 1–7 (from excellent to appalling) (see Figure 10.2). Additionally, more detail is asked for in the form of supplementary written comments, which could range from one word such as 'good' to a paragraph or more of detailed criticism and/or praise. Moreover, there are usually an overall rating, which may be tied to promotability, and a section to indicate areas for development or training. Finally, there are normally sections for comments by the person being appraised, possibly in the form of notes of a counselling interview and comments by the appraising manager's own supervisor.

The document is usually signed by all the contributors and forms part of the company's personnel records. It can be used for promotion boards, training and management development programmes. What happens if an employee disagrees with the assessment? Despite its critical consequences for promotion prospects and perhaps remuneration, only half of all organizations allow any form of appeal.

To appreciate some of the points made in this section more fully, it would be useful for you to photocopy Figure 10.2 and complete an assessment on someone well known to you – or even yourself!

The counselling interview

Having tested the manager's talents as untrained psychologist, the next part of the process expects the manager to be a qualified counsellor! This takes the form of a face-to-face dialogue between (normally) the appraising manager and the appraisee, although it is sometimes done by the countersigning manager. The whole process is designed to focus the power of the organization on a direct and individual basis. However, it is also clear that the scope for conflict and avoiding conflict by various means are considerable.

Many, perhaps most, managers are reluctant to engage in the appraisal

J. SMITH & CO. ANNUAL PERFORMANCE ASSESSMENT

This document should be completed by the responsible line manager and returned to the Human Resource department by..

Name of appraisee:

Job title:

Department:

Name of manager completing assessment:

	A	B	C	D	E	F
1 KNOWLEDGE & EXPERTISE	I___I___I___I___I___I___I

Comments:

	A	B	C	D	E	F
2 ATTITUDE TO WORK	I___I___I___I___I___I___I

Comments:

---

3 **RESULTS**

A B C D E F

|___|___|___|___|___|___|

Comments:

---

4 **INTERPERSONAL SKILLS**

A B C D E F

|___|___|___|___|___|___|

Comments:

---

5 **WRITTEN AND VERBAL COMMUNICATION**

WRITTEN

A B C D E F

|___|___|___|___|___|___|

Comments:

VERBAL

A B C D E F

|___|___|___|___|___|___|

Comments:

---

6 **NUMERICAL & DATA SKILLS**

A B C D E F

|___|___|___|___|___|___|

Comments:

                                        A   B   C   D   E   F
7 **OVERALL RATING** |___|___|___|___|___|___|

   Comments:

NOTES ON COUNSELLING INTERVIEW

   Manager's signature.............................

   Date..............................

APPRAISEE'S COMMENTS

   Appraisee's signature.............................

   Date..............................

SENIOR MANAGER'S COMMENTS

   Senior manager's signature.............................

   Date..............................

Figure 10.2   A simple appraisal form.

process, first, because it is difficult to criticize someone's performance honestly, knowing that the appraisee will read the comments. Potentially, the whole exercise is confrontational, and many counselling interviews have turned sour because of carelessly worded appraisals. Most people find criticism difficult to accept, and registering a point with an employee without causing offence requires high diplomatic skills.

The process is dependent on the personality and management style of the appraising manager. Some managers will be blunt and perhaps brutal in their approach. As a consequence, they may not produce any improvement in behaviour but rather sullen resentment and a reduction in quality of performance. Others will regard the whole exercise as something to be avoided. As we noted earlier, the result will be rater inflation: an assessment which is overgenerous or, at best, neutral in order to avoid conflict. The process also depends to a great extent on the quality of the appraising manager. If that individual is not particularly capable, the evaluation of the subordinate may well be inaccurate or misleading and may blight the person's career.

It can be argued there is an increasing tendency to focus on marginal performers in the light of harsh economic conditions. Companies consider that they are unable to carry inefficient employees and the assessment procedure offers a source of data which will support dismissals. In theory, performance appraisal provides documentary evidence of inefficiency which would be hard to refute. In practice, rater inflation often undermines the process, providing generous appraisals for questionable performances.

Objectivity and subjectivity in assessment

As we have seen, some of the key issues of performance management revolve around questions of fairness, judgement and interpretation of both results and behaviour. Serious attempts have been made to address these areas. Performance assessment focuses on one or more of the following criteria:

1 **Results.** In line with MBO and similar objectives-based systems, employees are rated on their achievements, expressed as well-defined, personal or organizational targets. For example, a sales person may be given the objective of $x thousand worth of sales in the year. How this is achieved is not the subject of assessment. As we have already observed, objectives are easier to define for some jobs than others. This approach can be complicated by the use of a 'moving target'.
2 **Processes.** In this case the emphasis is not on measurable results but on **how** the outcomes are achieved. It can be argued that compliance with quality procedures – or, alternatively, provision of a particular level of service – is an example of a process assessment. However, if these are measurable in some way, they can be translated into results, for example the proportion of defective items or the number of complaints.
3 **Behaviour.** Weaker and less objective assessments – which are probably the most common – focus on employee behaviour which is only tangentially connected with either achieved results or work processes. A

favourite approach for managers incapable of seeing the 'wood from the trees', they allow ample opportunity to dwell on personal prejudices over appearance, dress and manner. Such assessments provide a direct feeder mechanism into culture-bound and organizationally unhealthy practices designed to increase conformity and eliminate diversity. A number of large organizations have countered this tendency by using:

- **behaviourally anchored scales (BARS).** These are relatively expensive techniques to maintain, requiring 'experts' to develop rating scales anchored to real-life behaviour through critical incidents. However, they force appraisers to make comparatively objective judgements, placing individual behaviour in the context of the organization as a whole, rather than on inadequate personality categorizations. They are less usable in situations where new technology or procedural changes require frequent updating of scales.
- **behavioural observation scales (BOS).** These are constructed in a similar way to BARS, but assessors are required to list the frequency of occurrence of particular behaviours within a particular period, rather than make comparative judgements of better or worse performance.

Recently there has been a trend towards performance management systems which assess **competences**. We concluded in Chapter 8 that competences are behavioural constructs or 'dimensions' of desirable abilities. Defining a set of competences appropriate to a particular job requires knowledge of the required skills and abilities and the long-term strategy of the organization. They can be determined through interviews and questionnaires with relevant people or workshops dedicated to the purpose. We will consider this topic further in the next chapter within the context of development.

Summary

HRM is associated with sophisticated and intensive performance assessment, typically involving performance-related pay. The assessment of performance can be beneficial to personal development. We considered performance management as an integrated system. Theoretical descriptions of such systems emphasize their value to the link between individual employee performance and the achievement of strategic goals. However, there are philosophical issues of what precisely represents 'good' performance, and further technical problems of measurement. This has led to an unhappy marriage of uncertain appraisal techniques with an ideological enthusiasm for performance pay. Free market organizations are particularly concerned with performance-related pay as a motivating factor, but this trend appears to be ideological rather than rational. Current evidence shows that performance-related pay demotivates more people than it motivates. We completed the chapter with a critique of appraisal methods and a discussion of recent attempts to objectify their use.

Further reading

Perry Hinton's (1993) *The Psychology of Interpersonal Perception* is a very readable introduction to the considerable body of psychological studies on how we perceive other people. The ACAS advisory booklet *Appraisal Related Pay* (1990) provides a useful guide to best practice for the introduction and conduct of performance related pay schemes. Murphy and Cleveland's (1995) *Understanding Performance Appraisal: Social, Organizational, and Goal-based Perspectives* is a thorough review of assessment from an applied psychology perspective, detailing much of the findings on rater error and inflation.

Review questions

1 Do organizations prefer conformists?
2 Should males and females be assessed differently?
3 Discuss the view that performance appraisals are unnecessary.
4 Explain the following terms:

- behavioural consistency;
- competences.

5 Compare and contrast Bevan and Thompson's (1992) textbook model of performance management with English's (1991) rational model.
6 Discuss the ways in which externals and internals react to performance assessment.
7 'A fair day's work for a fair day's pay.' How can a company's pay system be designed to meet this criterion?
8 Outline the arguments for and against the use of performance-related pay.
9 Define 'rater inflation'. What are its causes and implications?
10 Is it possible for appraisals to be objective?

Problems for discussion and analysis

1 The Consumer Relations department has been the source of considerable difficulties for you this year in your role as General Manager. The Manager, Jean Davis, her assistant Lyndon Greaves, and the six staff are involved in a constant battle with Sales. First, they say that the number of complaints has gone up substantially. Jean says that customers seem far more ready to find fault with deliveries than ever before. She blames the salesforce for errors in order-taking. She has become aggressive in the way she deals with Sales and has accused you of ignoring the problem. Lyndon is more reasonable but says that his people are grossly overworked. They have developed a backlog in clearing customers' letters and phone calls, and sick leave has increased.

Conversely, the Sales department is working better than ever before. They have a new PRP system in place, based on targets for orders taken by each person. The field salesforce have embraced PRP enthusiastically, with orders 20 per cent up on last year. Most have received generous bonuses. The board are very pleased with this and have asked you to extend PRP to other departments, including Consumer Relations. However, Jean and Lyndon are very negative about the idea, demanding to know how they are likely to be assessed when they are behind on their targets.

What is your analysis of the situation and how would you deal with it?

2　International Holidays is a travel agency group. The company has forty-three shop units, each employing between four and eight front-office staff. Each unit has a manager. The company has been suffering from low trading levels in recent years. The situation has not been helped by the devaluation of the currency, which has made foreign travel more expensive. The Managing Director has asked you to set up a Performance Management System to improve the motivation of the staff. How would you do this? What difficulties would you expect in ensuring that the system achieved its objectives?

11

Developing people

> This chapter evaluates human resource development as an investment in people and considers training and career planning in flexible organizations.

Business page pundits argue that industrialized states must move away from low-technology products with poor margins which can be produced more cheaply in low-wage countries. Similarly, developing countries aiming to join the ranks of the advanced nations must acquire a capacity for producing sophisticated products and services. High-technology products require long-term research, expensive and sophisticated production equipment and precise quality procedures. Above all, they require skilled human resources capable of performing effectively in this environment.

At the organizational level, enterprises need people with appropriate skills, abilities and experience. These qualities can be **bought** from outside the organization through recruitment, consultancy and subcontracting, or **grown** by training and developing existing employees. This chapter focuses on the second approach. The strategic choice between buying and growing is made on the basis of cost-effectiveness, urgency of requirement, and the need to motivate staff.

Political, cultural and historical elements also influence the decision. Organizations with an internal job market orientation, for example most large German and Japanese companies, have made a practice of growing their own talent, taking employees on at the apprentice or graduate stage but rarely thereafter. Conversely, business in free-market countries such as the UK focus on the external employment market, invest little in developing their own people and looking outside for expertise when needed.

Throughout this book we have distinguished HRM from previous models of people management by its emphasis on the integration of an organization's people policies and activities. Investment in employee skills to support the needs of advanced technology is a prime example of this approach. Financially obsessed managers in free-market countries have preferred cost-cutting to investment in people or new technology. More-over, there has been a chronic failure to understand the link between the two: investment in new equipment has been viewed as worthwhile only if it leads to a cut in employee costs. Managers in Australia and the UK have been wedded to a penny-pinching mentality, avoiding the kind of high technology which requires expensive, skilled workers. Their counterparts in Singapore and Korea have invested more readily in new machine tools in order to increase output and profitability, frequently taking on extra staff to meet demand.

Systematic human resource development (HRD) (see key concept 11.1) maximizes the human capital of an organization, devoting time, money and thought to improving the pool of essential competences among its staff. It has a general impact on business performance by enhancing product knowledge and service expertise. HRD emphasizes people as people rather than numbers. In Table 11.1 we can see that HRD motivates staff, drawing on their talents and demonstrating that they are valued by the organization. It is also claimed that it empowers staff, allowing individuals to take a measure of control over their own careers and develop life patterns which offer increased opportunity and satisfaction.

Human resource development (HRD) is a strategic approach to investing in human capital. It draws on other human resource processes, including resourcing and performance assessment to identify actual and potential talent. HRD provides a framework for self-development, training programmes and career progression to meet an organization's future skill requirements.

KEY CONCEPT 11.1
Human resource development

What is the relationship between development and training? The two terms are sometimes used to mean the same. However, Goss (1994: 62) observes that they are often regarded as mutually exclusive activities. He attributes this to the hierarchical nature of most organizations, in which

Table 11.1   The principal elements of human resource development

- Effective resourcing, induction and deployment of high-quality people.
- Identification and improvement of skills and motivation amongst existing and longer-serving employees.
- Regular job analysis in relation to organizational objectives and individual skills.
- Review of the use of technology and its use in replacing routine tasks.
- Performance management and assessment through identification of key tasks.
- A focus on skills and general abilities rather than paper qualifications.
- Training needs identification.
- Provision of training programmes to improve current performance and support career development.
- Provision of opportunities for personal growth and self-development.
- Assistance to people to manage their own careers.
- Encouragement of the acceptance of change as normal and as an opportunity.

Source: adapted from Thomson and Mabey (1994).

training is something done to lower-level workers whereas development is a process experienced by managers – hence 'management development'. As Goss rightly points out, this approach is incompatible with the central principles of HRM, which hold that all employees are assets whose competences need to be developed. According to Hendry, 'Increasingly, we are getting away from the divisive notion that managers are "developed" while the shopfloor are merely "trained". The principles of adult learning apply to each' (1995: 366). It is appropriate, therefore, to regard training as an integral aspect of HRD.

Following our Business in Context model, this chapter examines human resource development at a number of levels. We begin with a consideration of the environmental issues which encourage or discourage training and development in various countries. We go on to consider organizational factors, paying particular attention to the fashionable concept of the 'learning organization'. The next section addresses strategic decisions, focusing on planned development programmes for managers and whether or not women should be treated as a special case. Finally we examine key aspects of HRD as an activity, encompassing issues such as the merits of in-house or outsourced training and the evaluation and costing of training programmes.

HRD at the environmental level

In Chapter 2 we introduced the idea of human capital – investing in people as national or organizational assets. Human capital development in the form of education and skills training can be an effective response to constraints imposed on the employment market. Specific skills may be in short supply – even during periods of considerable unemployment – and technological developments outdate some skills and require entirely different competences.

There is a considerable variation between education and training levels in different countries. For example, technology and production have long been regarded as high-status activities in Germany. Success in these areas demands a high level of technical training amongst the workforce. As a consequence, German businesses place a higher value on technical merit than, say, those in the UK. Ironically, training systems in the two countries are similar, depending on a mixture of academic education and vocational courses – unlike in France, Japan and the USA, where there is a greater concentration on full-time education (Stevens and Walsh 1991: 31). Significantly, however, there is a markedly greater commitment to training in Germany with levels of participation and achievement which have no comparison in the UK.

Whereas the British apprentice system has been more or less dismantled, it remains intact in Germany: 50 per cent of German school-leavers (compared with a mere 17 per cent in the UK) participate in apprenticeship schemes covering over 300 occupations. The consequences are evident. Throughout the 1980s British industry was subjected to a withering series of criticisms. A good illustration is a comparison of UK and German kitchen and metal plants which showed that in the UK (Steedman and Wagner 1987):

- less modern technology was in use;
- there were frequent breakdowns;
- there were long repair times;
- there was a low level of technical competence.

German companies had a staggering 60 per cent higher rate of productivity. Underlying this was a dramatic contrast in levels of managerial expectation and participation in training. In Germany 90 per cent of employees had completed a minimum of three years' craft training; in the UK the equivalent figure was only 10 per cent. Even more worrying was the fact that the British managers surveyed seemed unconcerned. Supported by their higher technical skills, it is scarcely surprising that German companies dominated the high-value, quality end of the market while British companies concentrated on cheaper, low-profit products.

Similar criticisms could still be levelled against British industry in the 1990s. According to Stevens and Walsh:

> It has been argued that a significant fraction of the British labour force is in danger of becoming trapped in a low-skills, low-quality equilibrium with low initial education and poor skills leading to low productivity and a predominantly low-quality market orientation of the companies they work for. Dependency upon low-cost competitive strategies in much of British industry undermines the demand for higher skills.
>
> (Stevens and Walsh 1991: 25)

Industrial sectors vary, some being considerably better than others. In 1994 a National Institute of Economic and Social Research survey evaluated high-level skills in the engineering and chemical industries in Britain and Germany and the resulting effect on industrial competitiveness. Researchers identified a relationship between the much greater employment of technically proficient postgraduates in German engineering firms and the superior levels of innovation in products and processes. British engineering firms were dismissed as technical 'followers', content with their products and blind to the value of research and development. In contrast, UK chemical companies employed a similar level of PhD graduates to their German counterparts, providing a 'virtuous circle' of high-quality postgraduates and employer demand.

A Barclays Bank report (*Bridging the Skills Gap*, 1994) indicated that 69 per cent of small businesses surveyed believed training to be important – but only 23 per cent had invested in training during their first three years of trading. Small business owners rely heavily on their previous employment experience. Unfortunately, this revealed that just 19 per cent had any sales or marketing skills. Even fewer – 14 per cent – could claim financial expertise. It is likely that many business failures in the early years of trading could be prevented with adequate training.

In 1996 a skills audit completed as part of a competitiveness White Paper commissioned by the Deputy Prime Minister, Michael Heseltine, showed that British standards of education and vocational training had still not improved (*Guardian*, 14 June 1996). The White Paper, optimistically entitled

Creating the Enterprise Centre of Europe, focused on the country's comparatively poor levels of numeracy and literacy amongst school leavers: 30 per cent of 16- to 17-year-olds were judged to be inadequate in numeracy; 21 per cent in oral communication. More generally, 32 per cent were regarded as having a poor business ethic.

Again and again, British firms report 'skill shortages', even in periods of high unemployment, leading to a reliance on overtime, subcontracting (often overseas) or a containment of growth – instead of creating jobs as in the USA. Significant blame is attached to the inadequacies of the British education system, with its focus on cultivating an academic elite as opposed to developing numeracy and communication skills throughout the population. We noted in Chapter 2 that the recent explosion in higher education and the establishment of vocational qualification targets may eventually lead to improvements. Currently, however, it is estimated that those organizations in British industry who do train their staff are paying upto £10 billion a year to make up for the past deficiencies of the education system (*Financial Times Guide to Business in the Community*, 1995).

British companies are not alone in devoting considerable resources to 'remedial' programmes. The Australian Association of Graduate Employers surveyed 150 of the largest public- and private-sector employers in the country, asking them about 5,000 graduates recruited in the previous three years (*The Times Higher*, 25 February 1994). Their criticisms of new graduates echoed those of British school-leavers, including:

- lack of basic knowledge of grammar, sentence structure and spelling;
- inability to explain ideas clearly in writing or speech;
- inability of many to write or speak clearly 'in a business sense'.

Employers stated that their deficiencies had been noted during the selection process but these faults were so common that they had to be accepted in order to fill vacancies. Academics were criticized for setting a standard for students based on their own use of jargon and their inability to express themselves lucidly in simple English. Employers had to compensate by providing communication courses.

Vocational education and training

Table 11.2 illustrates the relatively poor vocational base in the UK during the 1980s compared with its near neighbours. The early 1990s actually showed a reduction in job-related training: from 15.4 per cent of workers to 14.9 per cent (3.16 million workers) reporting that they had received such training. In the same period, the Employment Gazette found a disappointing response from young people on various government-sponsored schemes such as Youth Training and employment training and trade apprenticeships. Almost 200,000 young people on these schemes were not aware of having been given job-related training.

Against the backdrop of gloom, however, CBI figures indicated a more positive attitude among medium-sized and large companies, those employing 200–5,000 people. These businesses were planning to increase spending on training. However, bad though the British training performance may be,

Table 11.2 Vocational education (percentage of workforce)

	Britain (1988)	Germany (West) (1987)	Netherlands (1989)	France (1988)
University degree	10	11	8	7
Technician diploma	7	7	19	7
Craft diploma	20	56	38	33
No qualification	63	26	35	53

Source: *National Institute Economic Review*, May 1992.

it has been argued that the real situation is not quite so dire (Stevens and Walsh 1991: 36). Whereas the level of technical qualification in the UK appears to be very low, the reported training activities of organizations is much higher. This discrepancy can be explained by the historical absence of recognized basic and intermediate-level vocational certification. It may be that the employment market contains many individuals with usable skills but they have no means of proving their worth to employers.

In fact, the reluctance of many British employers to engage in training can probably be pinned down to two things:

- The short-term, cost-based approach to all management activities. In this case, demand for a quick and obvious benefit from training expenditure.
- The difficulty of proving the connection between training and improved efficiency.

Hendry argues that the connection has never been proven:

> One of the things which gets in the way is the fallacy, promoted by the Employment Department among others, that the benefits of training can somehow be demonstrated on the bottom-line. As a rhetorical device, it may encourage employers to train by saying 'training pays', but no one has ever satisfactorily demonstrated this.
>
> (Hendry 1995: 364)

We will expand further on this issue later in this chapter. The development of National Vocational Qualifications (NVQs), and their Scottish equivalents (SVQs), which certificate defined levels of technical competence, may eventually redress the problem. As an illustration, Case 11.1 describes aspects of the Scottish system. The scheme uses five levels of achievement from 'shop-floor' to managerial standard.

Scottish Vocational Qualifications (SVQs) cover all aspects of work from traditional craft jobs to management level activities. Based on the same standards as the NVQs offered in the other parts of the UK, they are work-based and aim to demonstrate that people can carry out particular tasks competently. Individuals can learn at their own speed and are then assessed on the job.

SVQs in management have been developed by the National Forum for Management Education and Development (NFMED). The qualifications are awarded by SCOTVEC

CASE 11.1
Vocational training in Scotland: SVQs

in conjunction with other bodies such as the Institute for Personnel and Development, the Marine and Engineering Training Association and the Open University, as well as NFMED.

For example, the level 3 SVQ demonstrates supervisory competences, whereas the level 4 qualification is aimed at managerial standards. Candidates awarded level 3 must demonstrate the ability to:

- maintain services and operations which meet quality standards;
- contribute to the proper use of resources;
- contribute to the training and development of employees, including themselves;
- help to plan, organize and evaluate work.

The more demanding level 4 SVQ requires evidence of skills in:

- improving service or product operations;
- contributing to organizational change;
- recruitment and selection.

It also requires candidates to demonstrate that they are capable of playing an influential part in:

- allocating and evaluating work;
- creating and enhancing effective working relationships;
- exchanging information for problem-solving and decision-making.

The advanced, level 5 SVQ is aimed at experienced senior managers.

(*Source*: adapted from *The Scotsman*, 17 May 1996.)

Goss (1994: 70) observes a contradictory feature in the initiative. On the one hand the emphasis is on outcomes, specifically overt behavioural features of doing a job, giving a narrow focus to the training involved. On the other hand, the opportunity to progress through a sequence of levels is a strong developmental feature. NVQs and SVQs are the end-product of a government initiative to provide a national framework for training activities. In 1993 the UK government introduced the Modern Apprenticeship scheme to provide 16- and 17-year-olds with the opportunity to train for NVQ/SVQs up to level 3 (equivalent to two A levels). However, progress in gaining the interest of employers appears to be slow. In particular, there has been considerable reluctance among smaller companies to participate in the scheme or recognize the value of the qualifications.

A further initiative sponsored by the British government is the Investor in People award, given when an assessor appointed by the Training and Executive Council (TEC) (Local Enterprise Council in Scotland) is satisfied on four national standards:

- There is public commitment from the top of the organization to develop all employees to achieve the business objectives.
- The organization regularly reviews the training and development needs of all employees.

- The organization takes action to train and develop individuals on recruitment throughout their employment.
- The organization evaluates the investment in training and development to assess achievement and improve effectiveness.

This particular scheme is aimed at tying training and development to business strategy (Goss 1994: 70). Achieving the award requires substantial commitment from an organization. It involves a considerable degree of planning, assessment and documentation in support of an application. Again, however, progress has been slow. For example, a major survey in Leicestershire indicated that few employers in the county were familiar with either this programme or a third government programme, the Management Charter Initiative (MCI) (Storey *et al.* 1994). The latter takes the NVQ/SVQ framework further to provide management qualifications at four levels: supervisory, certificate (first-line management), diploma (middle management) and masters (senior management). The MCI scheme has focused on generic competences, considered later in this chapter.

Discussion of training and development in the media and management literature tends to become idealistic and evangelical. In reality, many employers take an extremely hard-nosed attitude towards the topic – particularly, as we have seen, in countries such as the UK with a notoriously short-termist view of business. Employer reluctance to embark on training young recruits to can be attributed to one or more of the following (Stevens and Walsh 1991: 37):

- **Poaching.** Some employers train while others do not. The non-trainers are likely to poach trained workers from those who train. Development requires trainees to acquire general skills as well as skills specific to the training company. Employers are reluctant to offer general skills training for fear of poaching. According to Stevens and Walsh:

  > firms may be unwilling to invest in the development of their employees because they are unable to be sure that they, rather than some other employer, may enjoy the benefits of such investment [. . .] investment in training, once completed, is embodied in the individual, and as such is not under the direct control of the firm undertaking the investment.

  Whereas UK firms are afraid of 'free-riders', their German counterparts see themselves as having a responsibility to contribute to the common good. Along with the activities and support of government, this attitude maintains a high level of training in Germany. Elsewhere – in France, Japan and the USA, for instance – the poaching problem is less evident since the training of young people takes place largely within the formal education system. Most of the burden and costs is placed upon the trainees.

- **Cost.** Young trainees anticipate higher wages in comparison to recruits for semi-skilled jobs. The reduction in the numbers of young people coming onto the employment market has increased competition and wages for higher-calibre trainees. Also, people are paid when training but do not produce anything and occupy the time of trainers, who are not managing or supervising during this period. The differential between young trainees and experienced workers is much less in Britain than it is in Germany. In terms of basic pay, trainees are paid twice as much as their German counterparts in the three years after leaving formal education. Consistent with their lack of interest in the subject, British companies seem not to value expertise as much as German firms.

- **Individual lack of interest.** We saw in Chapter 2 that human capital theory predicts that the young are more likely to choose training than the old because their indirect costs are lower than those of older workers. It also predicts that there should be a direct relationship between additional training and increased income. The perception of young workers in the UK is that there is no direct link: the skill differential may be small or non-existent. They also see that promotions are not based on qualifications. It is known that qualifications are mainly used as filters in the recruitment process (see Chapter 8). Their value comes a long way behind previous job performance and the selectors' perceptions of their potential. Hence young British workers do not see vocational training as being worthwhile. In Australia, an attempt has been made to tie vocational qualifications directly to pay, resulting in a stimulation of training levels.

- **Weak links between training and performance.** Training does not have strategic importance for many companies in the UK, partly, as we have noted, because of the difficulty of proving the connection between training and improved performance. By contrast, training is fundamental to the business culture in Germany and Japan. The British problem may be compounded by the delegation of training to personnel specialists or line managers without strategic direction at board level. Lower-level employees are even less likely to be aware of competitor practices than their senior managers.

The situation is not static, however, and concern has been expressed in a number of countries about the appropriateness of national skill bases for the future. German business has expressed increasing disquiet at the gulf between the needs of industry and the nature of university training. Business has regarded the non-vocational prejudice of traditional universities with scepticism (*The Times Higher*, 28 January 1994) and some companies have turned to sponsoring private university courses in an attempt to provide suitable courses. Mobil Oil and twenty German companies funded a recently opened college, the Nordakademie at Pinneberg near Hamburg, and reported fifteen applications for each place. Such colleges concentrate on intensive programmes geared to business themes, including marketing, computing and human resource management, completed in a much shorter timespan than traditional university qualifications. The practicality of such courses has facilitated rapid promotion for many students within major German companies. At this point it is appropriate to examine organizational issues in more detail.

HRD and the organization

In this section we see that organizational priorities have changed in recent years. The focus has moved from piecemeal training activities to more systematic human resource development. In fact, many businesses have reoriented themselves away from training individual employees towards becoming 'learning organizations', with the emphasis on continuous learning. For example, Whipp (1992: 45, 52) argues that one of the critical ways in which HRM can improve an organization's competitiveness is through its impact on the 'knowledge base' of the business:

> The role of knowledge is paramount in the way an HRM approach can help create competitive advantage. That knowledge has both technical and social components. What becomes critical is the extent to which a company's knowledge base matches changing competitive conditions through learning.
> (Whipp 1992: 53)

Competitive advantage comes from the development of an organization's human capital: a learning experience for employees and the organization as a whole (see key concept 11.2). For some time, this learning experience was encapsulated within a particular model of training: a comparatively straightforward, organized function which depended heavily on planning. The systematic training model pervaded organizations so thoroughly as to be accepted as the received wisdom. In the UK this was encouraged by the Industrial Training Boards established in the 1960s. Depending on a series of logical steps it normally involved the following (Sloman 1994):

- a training policy;
- a method for identifying training needs;
- the formulation of training objectives;
- the development of a training plan;
- the implementation of a planned training programme;
- validation, evaluation and review of training.

Learning consists of a relatively permanent change of behaviour as a result of past experience. Learning is taken to mean more than acquiring knowledge. It encompasses the way in which outmoded values and techniques are shed in favour of new ones. At an organizational level this requires a collective process of change in its shared worldview, including perceptions of the company and its market.	**KEY CONCEPT 11.2** *Learning*

The systematic training model assumed an organizational environment based on slow change, hierarchical lines of authority and clear requirements. It was a logical series of steps centred on the use of an objective **training needs analysis**. Normally, this would take the shape of an empirical exercise to identify current needs while bringing in the organization's objectives for consideration. It provided a framework within which the trainer could ensure a thorough and 'professional' job was done. However, it required a methodical and time-consuming series of activities which do not fit in so well with modern organizations.

Today's organizations are constantly changing and have much looser systems of control than the companies of the 1960s (Sloman 1994). The systematic training model does not incorporate a link with development and other human resource initiatives and, consequently, offers an inadequate framework for modern trainers. For example, structural changes require the movement of people from activities whose human resource requirements are shrinking to those which are growing. The skills required are those appropriate to the new work area. It is wasteful in both human and budgetary terms to have to dismiss people in one function while simultaneously hiring new people in another.

Whether or not an organization is growing, there is a need to develop skilled people for the future to replace those who are promoted or leave the company. Consistent with human resource strategy, succession planning links development to career structures and promotion policies. It must also take individual career plans and intentions into account. Typically, such a programme is linked to the human resource plans of the company, reflecting its anticipated needs in the relatively long term. Good employers take this seriously.

As an illustration, Siemens continued taking on one-third more electrical engineering graduates than it could justify during the early 1990s in order to protect its future innovation prospects. Before the recession Siemens recruited an average of 3,000 a year but the poor level of business brought considerable cost-cutting – including cuts to the jobs of existing employees. In order to meet anticipated needs Siemens offered full-time contracts to 300 graduates and part-time (19–25-hour) contracts to a further 600 (*The Independent on Sunday*, 30 January 1994). The latter could begin developing their expertise, combined with further academic training, with a strong chance of being offered full-time posts as the economy recovered.

From training to development

Following the argument in the previous section, it becomes clear that with its incorporation into HRD training has become a complex topic, with a significant shift in emphasis and importance from the systematic training model. Trainers experience a conflict between two contrasting trends (Sloman 1993). On the one hand, organizations are demanding higher levels of training to meet their skill needs, linking training to strategic initiatives such as total quality management (TQM), culture change and customer care. But this centralizing trend contrasts with a decentralizing approach to the delivery of the training. There have been changes in responsibility in line with the growth of HRM, delayering and divisionalization. Increasingly, training is seen as the province of line managers, with specialist trainers being used as an internal consultancy resource.

The new approach requires an effective communication system between the strategic decision-makers, line managers and specialist trainers. Together, these changes have made the traditional model of training management obsolete. Sloman (1994) poses some questions which are vexing training managers:

- It is accepted that training should be closely linked with business strategy. But what does this mean in practice? How should this be done?
- How should training relate to corporate culture?
- How important a breakthrough are competences?
- Should the training manager be operating as an internal consultant? If so, what does this mean in practice?
- Should the company be attempting to become a learning organization, and if so, how?

The strategic link with competitiveness means that HRD has become more important, but there have been pressures on training budgets. Critical eyes have looked at training departments in search of firm evidence of their ability to deliver.

In an attempt to identify a new model for training, Sloman interviewed thirteen major UK organizations and conducted a postal survey of a further twenty-two. They had all won National Training Awards between 1989 and 1991. These companies were assumed to be at the 'leading edge of training practice'. Of these, twelve primary respondents and twenty postal respondents had a written training plan. These plans were commonly integrated with wider organizational change initiatives. Six of the interviewed companies made direct reference to a link with quality programmes such as TQM and BS5750 (a major British quality standard). Other than for new recruits, training focuses on development, updating and retraining but also has a wider agenda within organizations. According to Rainbird and Maguire (1993), 'it also includes activities which are more closely linked to developing employees relationships with colleagues, legitimising new working practices and changing company culture' (1993).

Sloman found that many of his surveyed companies had introduced the following initiatives:

- Regular training reports to the board with a frequency ranging from monthly to annually – the organizations reporting most frequently emphasized a need to supply high-quality management information and to obtain high-level endorsement of training activities.
- Wider dissemination of training information throughout the organization.
- Feedback from line managers on the relevance and impact of training.
- The development of line managers to make them capable of training, including 'facilitator training' and 'training the trainer' courses.

The emphasis on decentralizing training has caused difficulties for trainers. As with many others in the former personnel-related area, they are seen more as facilitators and agents of change than as instructors. Trainers have experienced considerable uncertainty. They are more involved with strategic decision-makers but often have an unclear career path ahead of them. In many cases they have become managers of externally sourced training, providing advice and acting as internal consultants.

The idea of regarding training as an internal consultancy has attracted considerable support. It has an obvious appeal for organizations which divide functions into 'buyers' and 'sellers' and provide an internal accounting system which allocates training costs to budget-holders. Separate training centres can be accurately costed and their value established.

There are some unsatisfactory aspects, however. If an organization employs external consultants to provide a service such as training it can do so on the basis of single transactions. If these prove to be unsatisfactory, the purchaser has the option of changing to a different supplier. In other than the largest organizations, the buyer of an internal consultancy's services does not have this freedom. Additionally, the emphasis on 'independence' sits uncomfortably alongside current management thought, which places responsibility for all human resource activities with line managers. Some businesses have rationalized these conflicts by taking a new perspective, regarding themselves as 'learning organizations'.

The learning organization

In recent years the idea of the learning organization has 'captured the imagination of trainers and others' (McKenna 1994: 210). As we can see from key concept 11.3, this is a view that organizations have to go beyond sporadic training into a permanent state of learning in order to survive in today's business environment. The characteristics of a learning organization are detailed in Table 11.3. Garvin (1993) highlights three key areas:

- **Meaning.** A learning organization has the ability to create, acquire and transfer knowledge. It can modify behaviour to accommodate new knowledge and insights.
- **Management.** The organization shows evidence of learning from others, systematic problem-solving, experimentation and internal transfer of information, for example by job rotation.
- **Measurement.** The organization possesses mechanisms which assess the rate and level of learning. By taking practical aspects of its key functions, such as quality and innovation, managers can ensure that gains are made from the learning process within an acceptable timescale.

KEY CONCEPT 11.3
Learning organizations

A learning organization is not simply an organization which carries out extensive training but rather an organization 'which facilitates the learning of all its members and continuously transforms itself' (Pedler *et al.* 1989). A learning organization is one which lives and breathes knowledge acquisition and skill development – the ultimate extension of 'learning on the job'.

It is evident that many of the virtuous aspects of 'learning organizations', such as extensive job rotation, mirror practices commonly found in large Japanese corporations. The concept has been much trumpeted, but one can justifiably ask if such idealistic objectives can be met in a harsh, competitive

Table 11.3 Criteria for a learning organization

---

1 The formation of **organizational policy and strategy**, and its implementation, evaluation and improvement are consciously structured as a learning process.

2 There is wide **participation and identification** in the debate over policy and strategy. Differences are recognized, disagreements aired and conflicts tolerated and worked with in order to reach decisions.

3 **Management systems** for accounting, budgeting and reporting are organized to assist in learning from the consequences of decisions.

4 **Information systems** should 'informate' as well as automate. They should allow staff to question operating assumptions and seek information for individual and collective learning about the organization's goals, norms and processes.

5 **Information on expectations** and **feedback on satisfaction** should be exchanged by individuals and work units at all levels to assist learning.

6 Employees with external links – such as sales representatives and delivery agents – act as **environmental scanners**, feeding information back to other staff.

7 There is a deliberate attempt to share information and learn jointly with **significant others** outside the organization, such as key customers and suppliers.

8 The organization's **culture and management style** encourage experimentation, and learning and development from successes and failures.

9 Everyone has **access to resources** and **facilities for self-development**.

Source: adapted from Pedler *et al.* (1989).

business environment. Critics argue that the concept may be unrealistic and sometimes counterproductive. Sloman concludes that the goals of the model are so remote from most trainers' reality that:

> Bluntly, it asks from most managers too great a leap of faith and does not describe situations they can recognize. Indeed, the very phrase 'learning organization' could be regarded as unhelpful; it is firmly 'trainer-speak' and does not carry a high likelihood of achieving resonance with a hard-bitten manager who is struggling to achieve short-term financial targets.
>
> (Sloman 1994)

Perhaps the most striking proof that most companies are **not** learning organizations comes from the very existence of training courses. Firms may decide that they require particular sets of behaviours to retain their competitiveness. They may choose to achieve those behaviours by means of training courses. Doing so indicates that the processes which should create and support those behaviours is missing within those organizations.

On the other hand, managers and others learn a great deal on the job – whether or not they are in a 'learning organization'. They learn how their organization works, how to survive within it, and how to get things done. This informal education within the organization may conflict with learning from formal courses:

> The problem thus is not that managers won't learn, or that they resist learning but that they have learnt too much and too well. They have 'learnt the ropes' and these lessons about how their organization works may obstruct their openness to further learning.
>
> (Salaman and Butler 1994: 38)

Development programmes

Whether it takes place within a learning – or non-learning – organization, the fundamental principle of human resource development is that it goes further than piecemeal training. In this section we go on to examine the organizational and personal decision-making which lead to systematic, planned HRD programmes. We focus on key aspects such as induction, fostering star performers and management development. We discuss the part played by individuals in their own development, examine the role of mentors and question whether women and men should be offered separate development programmes.

Where does HRD fit into the human resource strategy of an organization? It should be part of a planned and systematic process in which:

- **Competences** are identified by a performance management system.
- These are matched with **needs** specified by the human resource strategy.
- **Gaps** are addressed by the development programme.

Within an HRD programme, training is geared towards planned development rather than being an isolated activity unconnected to the organization's objectives. In fact, HRD programmes can use a combination of organized patterns of experience as well as formal training. It can be an empowering process which provides the following (M. Armstrong 1992: 152):

- A **signal** that the organization believes its employees are important.
- The **motivation** to achieve the skills required by the organization and the consequent reward.
- **Commitment** to the organization from an understanding of its values and learning how to uphold them.
- **Identification** with the company through a clearer understanding of its aims and policies.
- **Two-way communication** between managers and staff as a byproduct of workshops and other training activities.
- **Need satisfaction**, since being selected for training fulfils a need for achievement and recognition in itself.
- **Job enrichment**, coming from the additional skills obtained from training programmes which can be applied to other aspects of their work.
- **Change management**, as education and training provide people with the understanding and confidence to cope with change.

These elements are readily communicated to employees when they first join an organization through the induction process.

Induction

Development starts with the effective induction of new employees – the period of training which takes place immediately on recruitment. Notionally, induction programmes are intended to help newcomers adjust to the job, the people they will work with, and wider aspects of the organization's structure and culture. However, in reality comparatively few employees are provided with this treatment. Looking after newcomers tends to receive low priority in a busy environment but in Case 11.2 we can see that matters are improving for graduate recruits in competitive industries such as retailing.

Unfortunately, joiners are commonly 'thrown in at the deep end'. Finding themselves in a strange environment and told to get on with it, they are easily forgotten. Raw recruits are left feeling anxious and vulnerable, forced to make sense of new surroundings and learn correct procedures the hard way. Many managers regard this approach with favour: after all, this was how they learned to cope and get to grips with the business. It is regarded as a test of competence, of machismo, of the ability to survive in a demanding environment. This can be a valuable 'growth' experience, but there is a considerable risk of individuals becoming disillusioned, leaving or developing bad habits.

As we noted in earlier chapters, there is a well-known 'induction crisis', in which a proportion of new recruits leave within the first few weeks. Effective recruitment and selection take time and cost money. Careless handling of new recruits can render this easily into waste. It is a questionable way of dealing with a significant investment. In the same way as young seedlings and transplanted cuttings are the most vulnerable plants a gardener has to look after, newcomers and promotees are the employees at greatest risk of disillusion and failure. New plants attract pests and diseases: they do not have the tough outer layers, deep roots and ability to survive which more mature plants have developed. In the same way, problems and difficulties loom large for the newcomer to the business. Most people experience some anxiety during this period. Newcomers will worry about their ability to fit in, their competence to do the job, and the impression they are creating in the eyes of their bosses and colleagues.

The casual western approach to induction contrasts sharply with Japanese practice. New employees in large Japanese companies receive intensive and prolonged induction training. For example, at Toyota a typical apprentice (secondary-school leaver aged 18) devotes the first two to four months of employment to learning the Toyota Production System. This includes:

- the intricacies of *kaizen* – continuous job improvement;
- *kanban* – a card system which conveys information between factory and suppliers.

After this training, the trainee is ready to start on production. There is additional on-the-job training on a slightly slower than usual production line. This is also the opportunity for the trainee to absorb the 'fighting minds' mentality. This is the ability to withstand the pressure of the full-speed production line in a motivated, positive manner. The pressure is formidable, requiring total and unflagging concentration. The induction programme emphasizes teamwork: fundamentally, it is a process of **socialization**.

Some overseas subsidiaries have sent new recruits to parent factories in

Japan, and they have returned as converts to Japanese practices with 'modelled behaviour patterns'. Intensive induction programmes are designed to produce loyal employees through a process dominated by personality 'development', imbuing workers with the company's history and purpose and thereby fusing the individual and the organization.

Similar advanced practices are used in the west, especially for management trainees. Case 11.2 illustrates the situation in advanced retailing companies.

CASE 11.2
Retail
management

Retailing has been transformed in recent years, with major supermarket and other chains adopting increasingly sophisticated methods such as 'just-in-time' ordering and information technology. We saw in Case 7.3 that their resourcing requirements have become exacting in order to provide the calibre of graduates necessary to provide future managers. We noted that the CORTCO consortium in the UK, comprising Boots, CWS, Kingfisher (B&Q, Comet and Woolworths), the John Lewis Partnership, Marks & Spencer, Safeway, Sainsbury and Tesco, has focused on the promotion of graduate careers.

Newly qualified graduates are paid £15,000–£16,000 a year and are quickly given responsibility. Progress can be fast, so that after just eighteen months in Marks & Spencer a recruit can be responsible for a store with an annual turnover of £7–8 million a year. After the same time with Safeway a graduate might be in charge of four managers and fifty staff.

At Aldi, the food discounting chain, prospects can be even better. Starting on £26,000 a year, promising graduates receive nine months of intensive training in order to become district managers responsible for between five and seven stores. From this they can go on to oversee fifty stores as regional managers or become specialists in finance, distribution or purchasing. However, these jobs are restricted to graduates who can quickly demonstrate the right analytical and people skills and are able to deal with problems quickly and flexibly.

(*Source*: based on *The Independent*, 6 June 1996, 'Retail begins to sell itself', Philip Schofield.)

Discussion questions
1 What kind of training would benefit graduate recruits in their first few months with a major retailer?
2 How is it possible to distinguish potential high-flyers at that stage?

Star performers

As can be seen from the case of Aldi, demand is intense for people with the right combination of skills for a particular industry. The market for talented staff, or **gold-collar workers**, is becoming international, and the ability to recruit, develop and keep them 'provides a significant and sustainable competitive advantage . . . chief executives ignore this at their peril' (Sadler and Milner 1993). Four categories of potential star performers can be highlighted:

●   Highly trained **specialists** – found in large numbers in high-technology industries such as computing, or those with intensive research and development such as pharmaceuticals. In the case of retailing, finance, distribution and administration are highlighted specialist areas.

- Good **managers** and **leaders** – such as retail group managers.
- **Sales** and **marketing** people – who are able to acquire business.
- **Hybrids** – individuals with the potential to cross over from a specialism, such as human resources, into general management.

Development programmes must provide these individuals with the following:

- A sense of mission, providing a more satisfying cause than just pay and security.
- An organizational structure which encourages rather than stifles creativity.
- A performance management system which identifies and rewards talented individuals, giving them opportunities to develop their skills through challenging work.
- A clear statement of the link between strategic objectives and the desire of talented people to excel.

Sadler and Milner identify just a few companies, such as NatWest Bank, Unilever, ICL and Motorola, which, they believe, demonstrate best practice. **Mentor** relationships have been found to be highly effective (see key concept 11.4). Kram (1983) found that mentors offered specific benefits in two main areas:

- **Career support**: sponsoring individuals for high-profile, challenging or stretching tasks; coaching in appropriate techniques; protecting the trainee from unfair treatment.
- **Psycho-social support**: offering acceptance of anxieties and concerns, counselling from the basis of dealing with similar experiences, providing a role model and friendship within the organization.

Mentors are established managers who can provide support, help and advice to more junior members of staff. A mentor should not be a direct line manager, but should have an understanding of the employee's job. Ideally, mentor and junior should have the same gender and ethnic background, so that advice is based on similar life experiences. **KEY CONCEPT 11.4** *Mentoring*

Thomson and Mabey (1994: 60) consider that successful mentors should be seven to ten years (or, perhaps, more) older than the individuals they are mentoring. The age gap should allow mentors to reflect on their own careers and work experience and to be able to give considered responses (Thomson and Mabey 1994: 61):

- Meeting with a mentor, typically on a monthly basis, encourages an individual to collect his or her thoughts and structure the learning experience by talking those thoughts through with the mentor.
- Mentors can help to clarify an individual's thinking by questioning and challenging.

- In order to be successful, mentors must have the ability to listen well and to probe into shallow thinking.
- The primary role of a mentor is not to advise – although this can occur – but to provide feedback and information on recent developments in the organization.

Mentors can help build the individual's self-confidence in what may initially seem an unfriendly and perplexing environment. Self-confidence is a key requirement for empowerment, the ability to take one's own decisions.

Empowerment and HRD

The notion of empowerment has become increasingly popular in both North America and Europe. It is particularly relevant in the context of human resource development. There is nothing new in the notion that decision-making should be delegated as low down the organization as possible, and that individuals should take responsibility for their own work, but empowerment has significant implications for the career structures and work behaviour of employees. Empowerment is often presented as something provided for the benefit of employees. In fact, its use is driven by financial considerations deriving from two issues:

- **Downsizing.** Slimmer companies typically have fewer management layers. The consequence is that the remaining managers are not available for day-to-day decisions – they **must** be taken by lower-level employees.
- **Speed of response.** In an increasingly competitive market, customers expect fast, authoritative decisions on price availablity. There is no time for staff to refer to 'the manager'.

In this environment there is a need for confident, speedy decision-making based on a high degree of product expertise. Moreover, in return for empowerment, employees must accept that career opportunities have diminished. Much of the ladder has disappeared and vertical promotion is only available to the few star performers. HRD in this case is focused on building resilient people who are able to gain rewards from existing jobs. Their future lies in 'horizontal promotion', regular moves between different jobs on a similar level.

Specifically, development programmes require an emphasis on decision-making and customer-handling skills together with in-depth product and service knowledge. In the absence of managerial backup it is necessary for empowered staff to have a wide understanding of the organization's functions and goals. They must be able to function well in circumstances for which procedures are not specified and which have no detailed prescriptive rules, and must be flexible and proactive enough to make events happen.

It is evident, therefore, that empowered businesses cannot work with the same personalities – including management – as those found in hierarchical organizations. Neither is there scope for rigid specialists in narrow fields of work. Not surprisingly, workers in these organizations must resemble those in Japanese companies, where supervisors have typically managed as many as a hundred individuals. They must be generalists with a broad perspective of their role in the organization. Empowerment is especially significant in fostering an individual employee's self-development.

Self-development

Development is the responsibility of the individual as well as the organization. Career success requires self-control, self-knowledge, systematic career evaluation and frequent role change. Selecting a career path depends on factors such as the following:

- **Self-awareness** – being able accurately to assess one's own skills, abilities and interests.
- **Ambition** – self-esteem, confidence and motivation.
- **Opportunity** – education, experience and social contacts.

People develop their lives and become distinctive persons through an interaction of three processes: genetic inheritance, life events and self-creation (Glover 1988). These are so intertwined that we may be unable to attribute a particular event to any one of them. Genetic inheritance determines many of our physical and mental capabilities. Hence the opportunity to succeed in education or business is constrained, to some extent, by inherited factors outside our control. Even health and the duration of our lives is subject in part to genetic determination.

Our lives also depend heavily on accident or chance, since the process of living is predominantly an unsystematic series of incidents. We choose to apply for specific jobs or particular universities because they meet our needs at a specific point in time. These decisions produce unanticipated side-effects. For example, later we might find ourselves living in a specific location and engaged in projects we would never have contemplated if we had not taken that job or gone to that university.

However, there are major components of life which are controlled by our own actions, leaving scope for intention and direction. The more we plan and take action, the greater the control we have over our lives. To a degree, we shape our own selves by imagining the kind of person we want to be: perhaps being more successful, being respected, or being seen as kind or helpful. When we take actions which contribute to the achievement of these goals we are involved in a process of self-creation. Few of us have a systematic **life plan**, but rather a loosely organized collection of sometimes minor aims. Most people have restricted opportunities, so that self-creation is a matter of taking account of reality and adjusting to what is possible. A checklist such as that shown in Table 11.4 can be useful for this purpose.

Work is a major area in which self-creation can take place Table 11.5 describes a likely development programme for new managers. According to Glover, the search for an imagined self explains much of our working behaviour. Self-creation is not necessarily a fully conscious activity, and people are inevitably constrained in achieving their goals. Some jobs crush any opportunity for advance, forcing people into behaviour which gives a false impression of the personalities they are, or want to be. The apparently

Table 11.4 Individual development checklist

---

1 What is the best way to spend my time?

2 Who else could do my work?

3 What am I improving and why?

4 What do I feel strongly about?

5 What are my special strengths and weaknesses?

6 What am I doing to increase my effectiveness?

7 What are the likely benefits and risks of achieving my objectives?

8 What have I learned in the last month?

9 What motivates me most?

10 How many of my objectives do I achieve on time?

11 What is my action plan for one month, one year, five years?

Source: based on Margerison (1991).

unsympathetic social security clerk, for instance, may be a creation of the framework of rules within which that individual must operate. The rules of the job mask any warmth or caring.

Organizations may use customer care programmes to train people in a form of impression management, producing staff who are groomed and dressed in a certain way and use approved body language and facial expressions. This veneer of humanity may be beneficial to some and certainly improves the organization's image, but the end-result is a constraint on true self-expression. We have to be careful that the organization does not take over our true selves. In fact, developing one's self is a learning and a recognition process. Work may teach us about a lifestyle that we do not want:

> We are lucky if work brings out in us things we did not know we had. But we can also discover things about ourselves in a less satisfying way. We take a job because it is well paid, or because others find it interesting, and then find we are stifled by it. Parts of us are denied expression. ('It was not really me', we

Table 11.5 A development programme for new managers

---

1 Obtain an accurate assessment of individuals' skills and abilities.

2 Reflect their strengths, weaknesses and preferences by giving individual responsibility.

3 Set target job(s) and timeframe(s).

4 Give challenging tasks early on.

5 Assign role models.

6 Provide objective feedback.

7 Ensure accurate and realistic expectations.

8 Give individuals experience of a variety of functions.

9 Ensure that everyone is committed, including top management.

10 Allow periodic evaluation and redirection of career plans.

Source: based on London and Stumpf (1984).

say afterwards.) Relationships lead to the same kind of self-discovery: in some we flourish and in some we are stifled.

(Glover 1988: 136)

Self-creation can be a **conservative** process when we are satisfied with our achievements. It is transformed into self-preservation when we can no longer imagine further development but see only risks and threats. The emphasis for middle-ranking executives may be the retention of their current status or standard of living. This produces a need to secure their jobs and defend them from change, blocking the advance of others and stifling development of the organization.

Management development

The main focus of HRD for many organizations lies in management development. In principle anyone can become a manager, and many do so without any formal training or development. However, graduates typically aim for formally designated management trainee positions which promise a structured development programme and steady progression through the management ranks. General management traineeships are rare; most are functionally based and applicants join functions such as marketing, production or human resources. So Mobil, for example, has no fewer than eighteen possible entry points and British Telecom has traineeships in up to fifteen business units (Guha 1995).

The trend has been away from long induction periods and work-shadowing towards immediate 'real' jobs in which trainees perform useful activities, often with management responsibilities. Traditionally, trainees remain in particular functions for fixed periods of time – perhaps six months, a year or longer. Of late, competence-driven development programmes have required trainees to achieve a certain standard before moving on.

Storey justifiably observes that 'the panoply of HRM technology is seen in its fullest form in the management of managers' (1995: 7). General management capabilities are developed in various ways. Companies such as Mars, Proctor & Gamble and Unilever have highly structured programmes. Others are more individually based or informal. Training may also involve academic study. For example, Unilever trainees study for a management diploma with the Henley Business School (Guha 1995). Vicere and Freeman (1990) identified the use of a range of different management development methods in a study of 150 major US companies (see Table 11.6). At this point it is useful to consider the role of management education.

Management and professional education

Many development programmes involve formal business education, including diplomas, business degrees and, above all, the Master's in Business Administration (MBA). MBA programmes have emphasized rational decision-making and a top-down strategic approach to business. It is worth noting, as we observed in Chapter 1, that introduction on to the Harvard

Table 11.6   Development methods

Method	Use (%)
Job rotation	72
External executive programme	48
In-company development programme	47
Taskforces/projects	32
On-the-job training	28
Coaching/mentoring	26
Performance feedback	6
Teaching/consulting colleagues	1

Source: based on Vicere and Freeman (1990).

MBA was crucial to the growth of HRM. In 1990 American business schools alone awarded 75,000 MBAs 'of widely varying quality' (*The Economist*, 2 March 1991).

In the 1980s MBA graduates could guarantee substantial salary increases and the likelihood of 'fast-track' careers. More recently their prospects have become less assured. Employers have questioned the quality of the product they receive for premium salaries. Harold Leavitt expresses the opinion that 'business schools transform well-proportioned young men and women . . . into critters with lopsided brains, icy hearts and shrunken souls' (quoted in *The Economist*, 2 March 1991). A 1990 report commissioned by the US Graduate Management Admission Council (GMAC), quoted in the same feature, concludes:

> The curricula of business schools have recently concentrated far more on the building of elegant, abstract models that seek to unify the world economic system than on the development of frameworks to help students understand the messy, concrete reality of international business. Yet this reality seems certain to prevail in a world in which tomorrow's problems are much more difficult to predict, with the only certainty being that they will be different from today's problems.
>
> (*The Economist*, 2 March 1991)

Such criticisms have encouraged a number of business schools to revise the content of MBA courses and the way in which they are taught, focusing on programmes which are custom-designed to meet the requirements of individual companies.

Nevertheless, academic courses can stretch the boundaries of managers' experience, exposing them to a wide range of concepts, theories and ideas they would never come across otherwise. They also provide students with the means to understand and communicate with people in different business specialisms. McKenna argues that academic and experiential learning should 'coexist and complement each other for the betterment of the provision of management education and learning' (1994: 210). Between them, formal education and experiential learning can be used to build the combination of skills, knowledge and abilities – the management competences – necessary for effective managerial performance.

An excellent example of this approach is provided by the car manu-facturing giant Ford (*The Times Higher*, 3 November 1995). Worldwide, 5,000 employees are engaged in part-time study for bachelor's, master's and PhD degrees. In Britain alone the company has increased the number of employees studying part-time for degrees from sixty in 1992 to 1,100 in 1995. Additionally, 250 individuals are sponsored by the Employee Development and Assistance Programme, a joint union–management arrangement. A further 120 students are sponsored by the company on sandwich engineering and business courses.

Developing management competences

Earlier in this chapter we raised the issue of competences in relation to the Management Charter Initiative. What are management competences? There are two main perspectives on the skills necessary for management:

- **'One best way.'** The **generic** approach assumes that there is a range of competences or portable techniques which can be learned and used in a variety of organizational settings.
- **'It depends.'** The **contingency** view holds that running an organization efficiently requires competences or methods unique to that enterprise. This approach emphasizes common sense, experience, rule-of-thumb techniques and wisdom. It acknowledges the complexity of the business environment. It also recognizes that what has worked once in a particular situation is likely to work again.

Taking the former approach, in the 1970s the American Management Association (AMA) initiated a major study of management competences. Two thousand successful managers were studied over a five-year period with the intention of identifying generic – common – competences from actual job performance. The research identified thirty statistically significant competences, of which eighteen were generic and could be regarded as essential for all successful managers (Boyatzis 1982). The remainder were related to organizational requirements or individual management styles. The generic competences could be placed in four groups: intellectual, entrepreneurial, socio-emotional and interpersonal, the largest group. These are elaborated in Table 11.7.

As part of the introduction of a business-style management structure, the UK National Health Service has undergone radical changes since the 1980s. In particular, there was a move to general as opposed to functional and professional management. General managers were responsible for the achievement of service objectives and were accountable for performance. General managers were expected to develop a new culture and would require a different set of competences from their predecessors. Regional health authorities set about determining these competences and finding appropriate people for the new jobs. Case 11.3 is an example of a competence-based development programme designed to meet the needs of one health authority.

Table 11.7   Generic management competences

Intellectual competences	Logical thought – being able to think in a logical and organized manner.
	Conceptualization – being able to relate apparently unconnected events into a meaningful pattern.
	Diagnostic use of concepts – being able to use theories or models, or to develop new ones if required.
Entrepreneurial competences	Effective use of resources – planning and organizing, with an image of efficiency and achievement.
	Proactive initiation – taking effective action rather than merely responding to events.
Socio-emotional competences	Self-control – an ability to suppress impulses and control personal reactions. This requires self-discipline and a capacity to place organizational requirements above individual needs.
	Spontaneity – free, unconstrained self-expression.
	Conceptual objectivity – impartiality and the preservation of emotional distance; the ability to balance opposing points of view.
	Accurate self-assessment – a realistic appraisal of one's own strengths and weaknesses.
	Stamina and adaptability – the 'stickability' or resilience required to cope with long hours, and the flexibility to deal with the unexpected and the vagaries of different period.
Interpersonal competences	Self-confidence – showing that, as 'natural leaders', they know what they are doing.
	Developing others – coaching, counselling, mentoring and being part of a team.
	Impact – being able to influence others.
	Use of unilateral power – being able to take the leadership role.
	Use of socialized power – negotiating and alliance-building, using team roles.
	Use of oral communications – being able to communicate clearly and persuasively.
	Positive regard – valuing other people, being able to delegate and allowing employees to perform.
	Managing group processes – fostering and developing commitment and team spirit.

**CASE 11.3
Competence-
based
development**

The South East Thames Regional Health Authority (SETRHA) was responsible for providing services to 3.2 million people in the south-east of England. It employed 73,000 staff of whom around 15 per cent were in management grades. The Human Resources Department had to arrive at a set of competences with the agreement of senior managers already in place. Existing managers were employed in a wide variety of jobs and there were no clear models of general management within the public sector. The HR Department gained the public support of the Regional General Manager to implement a process based on a sample of thirty managers within the region. Using trained interviewers employing the Critical Incidence technique, Repertory Grid Analysis and expert panels, they identified the following competences:

1 **People orientation**: promotes team working and cooperation; takes others' interests and views fully into account; supports and enables staff to achieve their objectives; and manages in an open manner, establishing good relationships with a wide range of staff.

2 **Personal skills**:

- communication skills:
    - (i) oral – expresses complex issues succinctly. Spoken communication is clear, confident, enthusiastic and appropriate for audience.
    - (ii) written – expresses complex issues succinctly. Written communication is clear, concise, well researched, grammatically correct and appropriate for audience.
- interpersonal skills – shows listening and empathy skills; recognizes threads, identifies lines of agreement and keeps order; negotiates sensitively, keeping in mind key objectives and outcomes; consults and takes account of a wide range of opinion.

3 **Persuasion/influence** – is able to influence people and 'win the day'; persuades people to accept and implement controversial decisions; assists others to see issues in a wider context.

4 **Leadership** – takes control and manages a situation; draws on strengths and weaknesses of others; acts as a catalyst, giving direction and energy to learn; gives clear instructions.

5 **Persistence in goal achievement** – is hardworking, accepts responsibility and follows through issues to completion; routinely meets tight deadlines; is willing to confront difficult issues with energy to resolve them; accepts organizational goals and shows high level of personal commitment; continues to pursue goals despite setbacks.

6 **Consistency under pressure** – accepts pressure and always meets deadlines; keeps sense of humour and resilience; remains accessible to staff.

7 **Creative resource management** – thinks independently and has original ideas; finds entrepreneurial solutions but recognizes organizational culture; manages creatively in a crisis; uses budgets creatively, thus enabling achievement of goals; is able to respond to shifting priorities by changing use of resources.

8 **Priority and objective-setting** – sets clear priorities; recognizes implications of priorities for organization and staff; delegates and monitors progress towards objectives; takes short-term action in light of major objectives.

9 **Problem analysis** – is able to grasp a complex problem quickly; uses information and analysis effectively to identify options; considers solutions to problems that are entrepreneurial and new, and appreciates possible outcomes; tackles difficult as well as easy problems.

10 **Planning and organization** – thinks ahead and plans practical actions to achieve objectives; recognizes needs and takes action to meet them; ensures staff are aware of and pursuing plans.

11 **Decision-making** – makes quick decisions without unnecessary consultation or delay, recognizing where further information/support is necessary; recognizes the implications of decisions for long-term goals; is willing to make unpopular decisions if necessary.

(*Source*: taken from Perkins, David and Snapes, Tony (1992), 'Developing the best managers?' in Vickerstaff, Sarah (1992), *Human Resource Management in Europe*, Chapman & Hall.)

Discussion questions
1 To what extent do the competences identified above overlap with the AMA's list of generic management competences?
2 The Health Authority management expended considerable time and effort in arriving at their list of competences. To what degree did this process produce better conclusions than a short commonsense exercise would have done?
3 Do Health Service managers need to demonstrate all these competences in order to do their jobs well?

This competence analysis was used as the basis for 48–hour, residential Career Development Workshops, including an assessment centre process and a subsequent career development programme. Participants were given feedback on their performance within the workshop. The aim was to identify individuals with the potential for general management. This process was used to identify competence requirements in a specific business culture. How do we address similar issues in a global context?

Developing the international manager

As we saw in Chapters 2 and 5, the growth of international trade demands managers who are able to function effectively in a range of countries and cultures. Rothwell (1992) concludes that international managers have the following development needs:

- proficiency in their existing task or business specialism;
- language training;
- experience of living and working abroad;
- cultural awareness and interpersonal skills;
- knowledge and information.

Increasing numbers of business courses are adopting an international focus. Many incorporate periods of study and work experience overseas. Organizations have the opportunity to recruit trainees with this background. Within the European Union, the European Community Action Scheme for the Mobility of Students (ERASMUS) was adopted in 1987. This set out to increase the proportion of students spending some of their study time in a partner country from 2 to 10 per cent within five years. A credit system was initiated in the following year to allow students to gain credits towards their final qualification. A number of institutions have adopted joint qualifications with partners in the EU, allowing students to gain two qualifications as part of their programme.

It can be argued that there is no substitute for a period of work abroad since this undoubtedly promotes cultural awareness and knowledge of overseas circumstances. Employees may have been to the target country on a previous vacation and the knowledge gained during a fairly relaxed holiday may be more extensive than from a rushed business trip. That prior experience can be built upon. A traditional – and unashamedly sexist – approach was outlined by Noonan:

the man is the key to achieving the objectives. Before selecting and sending out a man to an alien culture, the exporter owes it to him fully to research local conditions, including salary structures, taxation, schooling and medical facilities, fringe benefits, and to ensure that the selected branch manager has the independence of personality to survive the inevitable trials and frustrations that will be encountered, especially in the formative year. The family circumstances of the individual may have a strong bearing on his ability to perform. If he is married, then his wife will need to be equally independent in order to cope with the periods when he will be travelling within the region and with the other frustrations of living in a city where all the home comforts may not be so readily available, or where the climate may present its own adverse reactions.

(Noonan 1985: 229)

Cable & Wireless, the telecommunications company, recognized that the international nature of their organization required a rather more sophisticated approach to the development of managers capable of working in more than one country. Case 11.4 outlines their practice in the mid-1990s.

CASE 11.4
Cable & Wireless

Cable & Wireless has been described as 'a relic of empire' which has become a significant force in worldwide telecommunications since its privatization. In 1994 a total of 41,348 employees worked in more than fifty countries, including 8,041 in the Caribbean, 16,042 in Hong Kong and 10,086 in the United Kingdom. The operating companies functioned within a 'federation' and encouraged the transfer of ideas and experience. Staff were exchanged between countries as diverse as the United States and Russia, France and Japan, Hong Kong and Jamaica, St Vincent and the Falkland Islands. According to James Ross, former Chief Executive:

> one of our main priorities is to release the skills of our employees, organizing them in such a way as to achieve extraordinary things. The federation helps towards this end as new structures and processes make it easier to deploy our people wherever their skills are needed. The result is a vigorous transfer and exchange of knowledge and ideas that not only keeps the Group competitive but opens up new opportunities for employees.
>
> (*Cable & Wireless Report and Accounts 1994*)

To assist in this process a new £28 million training centre was opened in Coventry with seventy teaching staff. Cable & Wireless's Human Resources team also offered a comprehensive programme of advice and help, including:

1 A Global Opportunities brochure for employees interested in working abroad.
2 An Assignment Programme detailing short-term placements.
3 A Global Moves document aimed at business units to assist them in forming their local policies for importing or exporting skills.
4 Personal International Briefing packs giving specific information on:

- terms and conditions;
- information on host countries;
- suggestions for minimizing domestic upheaval;
- renting and moving house;
- education for children;
- refocusing the spouse's career.

Such assistance is regarded as essential to give employees confidence and attract and retain them against competition from other global companies.

(*Source: Cable & Wireless Report and Accounts 1994.*)

Discussion questions

1 What benefits are there for the employees and employers in moving employees between countries?

2 To what extent has Cable & Wireless properly prepared its employees for these career moves?

3 Is the process fair to the partners of these employees?

In contrast to Cable & Wireless, many companies do little more than ship staff to another country for a period of immersion: an international form of the 'sink or swim' approach to induction. The cost of this experience may be more than economic, with severe stress imposed on employees and their families. There is much more to be gained from following Cable & Wireless' practice of adequate preparation, providing support during the experience and debriefing on return to help employees come to terms with their learning.

Developing senior managers

Where do senior managers come from? A Guardian research project (James Nicholson and Vassilis Karatzas, reported in the *Guardian*, 24 April 1993) examined the careers of chief executives in Europe's largest companies. They found a marked contrast between those in British companies and those in the rest of Europe. Not a single British chief executive was found with a production or engineering background: BOC, RTZ, GEC and BTR, for example, were all run by people with financial training; BP, Wellcome, National Power and ICI were managed by chief executives with marketing or general management backgrounds. Conversely, German companies such as Hoechst, Mercedes, VW and Bayer were controlled by people with engineering or science qualifications and careers in production. Only one major German company, BASF, was found with a finance specialist in charge. A similar picture was found in Switzerland and France.

A study by consultants Heidrick and Struggles International (*Guardian Europe*, 16 March 1993) found that most French senior managers were *grandes écoles* graduates, and a surprisingly large number (45 per cent) had been state employees at some point. Few British or German managers (8 per cent) have had experience of state organizations. This difference reflects the much greater interventionist tradition of government in France. Typically, French managers have been trained to be ambitious, intellectually alert and original. They will have been expected to obtain rapid promotion, to have good connections and to have varied their jobs. German managers are more likely to have worked their way upwards in one company, slowly gaining experience and becoming adept at production and efficiency. In all of these countries, as we saw in Chapter 9, it is evident that women are conspicuous by their absence in the higher ranks of management. Can this situation be corrected through human resource development programmes?

Developing women

The low numbers of women in management have produced a case for special consideration to be given to the development needs of female managers. For example, the provision of career breaks, refresher training, job-sharing and extended childcare facilities can make a considerable difference in career progress. Hammond (1993) identifies three critical stages in women managers' careers:

- joining organizations;
- establishing competence in management jobs;
- strategies to progress up the management ladder into more senior jobs.

According to Hammond, in comparison to men, women learn more from others and from facing up to hardships. Conversely, men say they gain more from assignments, but it seems that men tend to be given more challenging assignments.

Specific HRD programmes can be set for women focusing on greater self-awareness, appreciation of career opportunities and encouragement to manage their own careers. This kind of programme boosts confidence. It is equally valuable for young trainees and mature returners. Hammond considers that women make outstanding developers. They appear to have more 'attending' skills than men – the ability to work on and care about several tasks simultaneously. However, there are few senior women managers to act as role models.

Development programmes involving seminars or attendance on women-only courses allow many female managers to compare notes, discuss issues in common and make sense of advancement in what is primarily a male world. Sharing experiences openly and honestly appears to be easier for women than men. Men tend to find it difficult to avoid competing, and this leads to exaggeration, denial and an unwillingness to open themselves to criticism. Accordingly, women can gain more from the sharing experience than men. Hammond stresses that they may also bring in life issues outside the immediate work scenario, which men tend to ignore.

HRD as an activity

In the final segment of this chapter we examine HRD at the activity level, focusing on the training and experiential processes which make up development programmes. We examine the continuing role of training needs analysis and the value of formal training as opposed to experiential 'action learning', and consider similar issues in the context of leadership development. The chapter concludes with a discussion of how training activities can be evaluated in terms of cost-effectiveness and quality.

What should be the aim of HRD activities? Vickerstaff argues that:

> well-trained employees make better products, serve the customer more effectively, and are likely to have more ideas about how to change the process and the product to improve quality and efficiency. However, the benefits of a well-

trained workforce can only be realised if the training effort is properly managed.

(Vickerstaff 1992: 132)

Organizations can be described as 'upskillers' or 'de-skillers' (Ashton and Felstead 1995: 242). The latter use a scientific management approach to simplify job requirements, remove the opportunity for initiative and reduce employees to a near-robotic state. Training (if it exists) in such cases becomes no more than rote learning of procedures. However, Ashton and Felstead (1995: 243) found optimistic evidence that in many British industrial sectors there are widespread reports of an increase in job skill requirements. In many instances, increased skill demands are linked to flexibility, increasing the importance of training attached to multi-skilling and job enlargement. Training and development activities are reaching sophisticated levels in many countries. As an illustration, Case 11.5 indicates expectations of training professionals in South Africa.

CASE 11.5
The top training position in South Africa

Woodburn Management Selection advertised a position for a person able to 'develop and implement world class, leading edge performance improvement training and development strategy and practices' for a client company in the Gauteng area. The successful individual was expected to be aged 28 or over with degree-level education and a minimum of five years' training experience, including at least two years in a 'progressive, leading edge training and development environment'. This individual would have 'excellent knowledge on the Theory of Learning, the training industry and team behaviour understanding, as well as general business acumen'. The successful candidate would report to the General Manager: Human Resources. The key areas of activity would include:

- developing and implementing Training and Development strategy;
- managing a world-class learning centre;
- designing, developing and implementing training materials (internal and external);
- evaluating, validating and monitoring training processes;
- conducting training needs analyses;
- managing budgets, reports and staff.

Applicants were expected to be 'assertive, have well-developed communication and interpersonal skills, and the ability to interface effectively across cultural lines. Applicant were also required to be 'able to see the big picture, think globally and be good idea generators'.

(*Source:* South African *Sunday Times*, 'Business Times' section, 28 January 1996.)

Customer demands are driving training for service and product quality, but this is generally focused on 'core' staff with career structures rather than part-time and temporary employees. However, the latter tend to be highly visible to customers, particularly in retailing. Studies in this sector and in the hotel and catering industry indicate that, in contrast to the management trainees discussed in Case 11.2, most staff receive induction training, some customer care instruction and little else (Rainbird and Maguire 1993).

In addition, we need to distinguish between the training needs of the individual and those of the organization. Personal and corporate objectives must be reconciled. Individual employees frequently look for wide-ranging courses which will help them in promotion. They will look to develop transferable skills which are seen as valuable by other employers. In contrast, local management are more interested in training which improves performance on their present jobs, leading to improved output quality and productivity. In other words, employees seek training which will make them more marketable, whereas organizations prefer training which makes employees more productive. Taking the organizational viewpoint, Nowack (1991) distinguished between these two types of criterion as follows:

- **Training needs**: when the employer wants the employee trained for tasks or behaviours which the business considers important and in which the employee's proficiency is inadequate;
- **Training wants**: when employees desire training for tasks and behaviours in which they are not proficient but which the organization considers unimportant.

Nowack considers the first pupose of a training needs analysis to be to 'weed out' the wants. Rainbird and Maguire (1993) found evidence that the balance lies predominantly with the management agenda, with training focused on organizational rather than individual development. While increasing thought is being given to management and professional development, this does not seem to be the case with sub-management grades. Their training appears to be heavily biased towards job- and company-specific skills.

A decision must also be taken on whether to conduct training in-house or to employ outside means. As we can see from Case 11.5, modern training specialists have to manage both. If the choice is made for in-house training, should it be by means of a course or on-the-job? We need to ask the following questions (Fowler 1991):

- What **knowledge** do employees need to perform their jobs well? This includes detailed job-specific knowledge, such as product information, and broader knowledge, for example about who is responsible for marketing literature in the organization.
- What **skills** or **competences** are needed, and to what level? Employees must be able to turn basic knowledge into good performance. Skills can be developed through direct tuition, coaching, planned experience or work simulations.
- What **attitude** characteristics do we need? Interest, commitment and enthusiasm are always important, but there may be a need for employees to develop a particular type or set of attitudes focused on, for example, customer service.

The starting-point for any development programme is a clear measurement of individual aptitudes and experience. Ideally, individual employees should be developed from where they are now, with their own particular requirements being addressed. Different people will benefit from different kinds of training even when performing the same job. If the organization is clear on the level of knowledge, skill or attitude required, development can be geared towards correcting individual shortfalls in meeting these standards. The measurement will normally be provided by the following means:

- Through the **performance appraisal** process, which should identify each employee's personal training needs as agreed by the individual's supervisor. Sloman (1993) found this to be the primary source of information among his surveyed companies.
- If there is no formal appraisal system, from an examination of each individual's **productivity** and quality of output. This method is commonly used in production and manual work.
- By employing **assessment centres** for development purposes. These are normally used for employees seen to have potential for advancement, and workers are assessed in similar ways to those used by the centres for selection. Information is obtained from group exercises, job simulations and psychometric tests.
- By giving **checklists** or **questionnaires** to individual employees and their supervisors with training requirements in mind.
- Through **succession plans** indicating the likely next generation of managers and their training shortfall.
- By integrating various methods to form a **skills audit** of the company.

The assessment should be considered in terms of immediate training and long-range development, and a balanced plan should be produced. Ironically, employees who have the most extensive education and higher qualification levels appear to have the greatest access to and participation in continuing training (Rainbird and Maguire 1993). There is also evidence to show that part-time and manual workers are particularly disadvantaged, along with employees in small private firms.

Nowack (1991) proposes a nine-step model for a training needs exercise:

1 Preparing a **job profile**. Jobs for which training is required need to be identified clearly. The job profile is based on between twelve and fifteen dimensions, or job requirements, within which groups of behaviours can be classified. The number of dimensions depends on factors such as:

- what the job involves;
- its complexity;
- the skills required for effective performance.

Information is obtained from **subject-matter experts** – people who have detailed knowledge of the job(s) being considered. These include workers currently performing that work, their supervisors and others involved with the input or output to and from those jobs. Information comes from individual interviews, focus groups and survey techniques. Focus groups, for example, discuss the skills deemed important to each job and list them in dimensional categories within the following broad areas:

- necessary technical knowledge and experience;
- communication skills;
- decision-making or problem-solving;

- administrative skills;
- management skills.

Each group indicates how important they feel each dimension is to a particular job – from 'very' to 'not' important. They are also asked to estimate the likely frequency of occurrence of each dimension in terms of 'several times a day/week/month/year'. The lists are compared and integrated to form a definitive job profile.

2 Preparing a **training needs questionnaire**. This is a critical part of the process. Targeted towards particular jobs or job levels in the organization, it is addressed to the people performing the jobs and their immediate supervisors. It includes questions aimed at obtaining three categories of information:

- **attitudinal**, describing employees' feelings about their work, their perception of organizational procedures and policies, pay, career, management and environment;
- **dimensional**, summarizing views on the job dimensions in terms of their importance and employees' proficiency (expressed on a 1–5 scale);
- **demographic**, containing questions relevant to employees' time within the organization.

3 **Administering** the questionnaire. A decision must be taken on the size of sample required to complete the questionnaire. This will depend on the resources available and the number of people involved in target jobs. In a relatively small organization the questionnaire can be directed to all relevant employees; in larger organizations, where hundreds of people may be performing similar tasks, a sample will be more appropriate. The target audience should offer alternative perspectives on specific jobs, for example by asking workers and their immediate supervisors to evaluate the workers' jobs. The questionnaire should be accompanied by a covering letter giving details of:

- the purpose of the exercise;
- how and when to return the questionnaire;
- the exercise's voluntary, anonymous and confidential nature.

Standard methods can be adopted to increase the percentage of questionnaires returned, such as offering incentives (prize draw, restaurant vouchers, etc.).

4 **Analysing responses.** Returned questionnaires are statistically analysed, preferably by means of a computerized package. A simple mathematical method can indicate the most crucial training needs: each respondent's measure of **importance (I)** is multiplied by the equivalent rating for **proficiency (P)** for every dimension. The resulting **(IxP)** scores can be utilized in a variety of ways. For example, mean scores can be compared across dimensions for a specific group or between groups. Alternatively, supervisors' ratings can be compared with employees' judgements of themselves. It is useful also to compare different departments and to check for differences between new and experienced employees.

5 **Interpreting the results.** Nowack suggests that three follow-up questions should be addressed:

- Is there some commonality between the highest-ranked training needs?
- What is the explanation for any differences between supervisor and employee assessments?
- Is there a reason for differences between groups of employees, e.g. senior and junior workers?

Different levels of employee will inevitably have different perceptions of the importance of particular development needs. Workers on the shop floor may be particularly concerned with day-to-day matters such as dealing with complaining customers effectively or working a particular machine. Managers may be more interested in longer-term, strategic requirements such as filling in stock returns accurately and understanding the fine differences between product categories in order to identify trends. These differences have to be evaluated logically.

6 Organizing **follow-up focus groups**. The interpretation of questionnaire results will identify a need for further clarification. This is best provided by small focus groups, which can consist of workers, managers or a mix. They can review IxP scores and offer further explanation. Groups should provide a final executive summary, which will be useful for managers and trainees.

7 Obtaining **feedback**. The feedback of results to managers and respondents is an essential part of the exercise. Planning and presentation of results is crucial for further progress and as a record of the process for future use.

8 Determining **development objectives**. The goal is to produce an objective for each dimension identified from the questionnaire and follow-up exercises. These should be tied to an explicit statement of the competences required for effective performance of the jobs in question. Each training need must be categorized as:

- imparting **knowledge**;
- changing **attitudes**;
- modifying **behaviour**.

Once this is done, the criteria for successful training can be established. For example, if delegation skills are a training need, what behaviour needs to be established by the trainee?

9 Setting up a **pilot training programme**.

Training methods

Training managers are presented with an ever-increasing range of learning methods. Traditionally, they have been divided into two categories:

- **On-the-job training**, including demonstrations of equipment and procedures, instruction manuals and PC-based training packages.

- **Off-the-job training**, such as group briefings, projects and formal courses.

Off-the-job training can be in-house, taking place within the organization, or external, for example at a local college or university.

Revans (1972) argued that classroom-based management education is not adequate (see Table 11.8). He devised a systematic, experiential or **Action Learning** programme based on job exchanges which place managers in unfamiliar situations and ask them to take on challenging tasks. The programme has the following requirements:

- The tasks must be based on **real** work projects.
- Projects must be **owned** and defined by senior managers and be important to the future of the organization.
- The process is an **investment** requiring a real return on cost.
- Managers must work in **groups**, learning from each other and crossing boundaries between functions and departments.
- Projects must go beyond analysis – they should require real **action** and change.
- **Content** (programmed knowledge) and **process** (questions/methods) of change should be studied.
- There must be **public commitment** from participants to action/report.

Revans's ideas are consistent with the principles of the learning organization discussed earlier in this chapter. The emphasis lies with learning rather than training and with meeting the changing needs of an organization in a competitive world. His approach is also mirrored in many current programmes aimed at developing leaders.

Leadership development

> I would argue that more leaders have been made by accident, circumstance, sheer grit, or will than have been made by all the leadership courses put together.
>
> (Warren Bennis 1990)

Table 11.8 Comparison of training and Action Learning

Traditional	Action Learning
Individual-based	Group-based
Knowledge emphasis	Skills emphasis
Input-orientated	Output-orientated
Classroom-based	Work-based
Passive	Active
Memory tested	Competence tested
Focus on past	Focus on present and future
Standard cases	Real cases
One-way	Interactive
Teacher-led	Student-led

Source: based on Margerison (1991).

The skills of leadership have attracted management theorists and trainers alike. Whereas good leaders are comparatively easy to recognize when they are in positions of authority, developing people to achieve the necessary qualities is not so easy. Just as the nature of leadership is not fully understood, the appropriate methods of training and leadership are a matter of controversy. At the same time, leadership training is a lucrative area for training consultants, and management gurus have been ready to produce packaged methods. According to Crofts, elective as opposed to despotic leadership 'is all about influence, persuasion and motivation – about making people **want** to do things your way' (1991).

It is arguable that many supposed 'leadership' courses are actually teaching management skills rather than those of leadership. A typical leadership course focuses on:

- Identifying the **nature of leadership** and the form of leadership which the individual trainee wishes to adopt. This incorporates a range of options from being able to give orders (to 'boss') to a more inspirational form.
- Promoting **self-awareness**, the identification of those leadership skills which individuals feel themselves to be lacking.
- Giving a general boost in **self-confidence**.

The focus in each case depends on factors such as the following:

- Participants' level of **seniority**. It would be counterproductive to encourage a junior manager to adopt the manner and style appropriate to a managing director.
- The organizational **culture** in which trainees have to operate. Authoritarian forms of leadership would be disastrous in a participative business.
- Trainees' **personalities**. People vary in their degree of assertiveness and sensitivity and need to develop a leadership style which fits naturally with their personality characteristics. It is easier to develop abilities which already exist in an embryonic form than to attempt to change an individual's whole character. The latter is probably impossible.

Part of the programme would involve team exercises requiring the solution of a hypothetical problem.

Many courses have taken on an 'outward bound' element. These use sport or other outdoor physical activities that require skill as a vehicle for experiential learning. Such programmes claim to develop management skills such as leadership, teamwork, communication, problem-solving, change management and the ability to cope with stress. However, much of this learning does not translate naturally to the office. There have also been lasting physical and psychological effects of a negative kind – particularly with older, unfit participants.

Perhaps a more positive approach comes from involvement in corporate community initiatives (*Financial Times Guide to Business in the Community, 1995*). Delayered and slimmed-down organizations offer reduced opportunities for promotion and, hence, for development at lower levels of management, but at the same time demand greater 'soft skills' – teamwork, listening, negotiating, influencing and general communication – from their employees. Community projects offer the scope for these skills to be honed and tested in 'power without authority' organizations. The UK's Business in the Community (BITC) has originated a number of schemes, for example:

- 100-hour development assignments;
- career-change 'transitional' secondments;
- 'business on board' – trusteeships with voluntary-sector groups.

Seconded and voluntary participants have found that they learn from each other, break down barriers and increase their team skills.

Evaluating and costing training

Sloman (1993) found that organizations were placing increasing importance on training effectiveness and value for money. More than half of his surveyed companies evaluated every training event and many others were examining ways of doing so. Virtually all respondents had training budgets, but practice on decentralizing these varied widely. Many training budgets were held by line managers, with a charging mechanism for training activities organized by training departments. One respondent (Sony Manufacturing) abandoned this practice because 'training was not high on people's agenda' and departmental budget spends were not being analysed properly. Other sources indicate a wider problem. For example, of 200 organizations which were 'committed to training', attending conferences held by the UK Industrial Society, only 10 per cent had an evaluation system in place (van de Vliet 1993).

Given the lack of evaluation in practice, what methods could trainers use? The most obvious are 'happy-sheets' or questionnaires handed-out to participants on completion of a training course. These are forms which ask trainees to rate the presentation and usefulness of the course and invite comments. The inherent flaws of this approach are well known (P. Lewis 1991):

- They are usually completed in the euphoric period at the end of the course when trainees are relieved to have survived, when they are looking forward to going home, and when pressure and stress have been lifted. At this point in time the world has taken on a comfortable, rosy glow.
- A personal relationship has been developed with the trainers, so criticism is toned down to avoid upsetting them.
- Most of all, the evaluation concentrates on the wrong issues. Often cursory attention is paid to the value of the training experience to the trainees, their future job performance and hence the organization. Instead, forms are likely to concentrate on the overall enjoyability of the course and the quality of the environment in which it took place. According to McKenna 'It is known for trainees to be throughly satisfied with a programme merely because the instructor or trainer did a good job entertaining them' (1994: 212). Happy-sheets are excellent for comments on the comfort of hotel accommodation, speed and service

in the restaurant and the stuffiness of seminar rooms. Usually they tell us little about the cost-effectiveness of the programme.

The evaluation of training has attracted considerable attention (Crittan 1993). A number of models exist, of which Hamblin's (1974) is perhaps the best known. Hamblin stratified training into five levels which could be evaluated independently:

- **Level 1**: the reactions of trainees during training to the trainer, other trainees and external factors.
- **Level 2**: learning achieved during training, assuming basic aptitude and receptiveness on the part of the trainee.
- **Level 3**: job behaviour in the work environment at the end of the training period.
- **Level 4**: the overall effects on the organization.
- **Level 5**: ultimate values – factors such as business survival, profit, the welfare of interested parties and social/political welfare.

However, the fact that such models exist has not led many organizations to use them! Hendry echoes some astute criticisms of evaluation:

> The whole notion of evaluation is based on training as a discrete event – namely the training course – and justifying the substantial visible costs associated with off-the-job courses and full-time training staff. Take these away, as Hamblin (1974) and Crittan (1993) have observed, and the rationale and pressure for evaluation largely collapses. Evaluation of training events was always a fallacy as long as it ignored the equally important process of practice back on the job which ensures that training transfers.
>
> (Hendry 1995: 366)

McCormick and Ilgen conclude that the state of affairs in evaluation is 'abysmal', with few training programmes having been evaluated and those that have leaving 'much to be desired in terms of experimental rigour' (1987: 231). In practice, Hendry (1995: 364) argues that the most progressive firms use a mixture of 'hard' and 'soft' criteria:

- **'Hard' evaluation criteria**: short-term improvements in measurable performance, such as individual productivity and quality adherence.
- **'Soft' criteria**: indirect benefits from intermediate human resource goals, including reduction in staff turnover, promotability and flexibility.

Summary

Competitiveness demands a diverse workforce and up-to-date skills. The free-market belief in 'buying in' skill has proven inadequate, even in times of high unemployment. HRD allows people managers to be proactive, focusing on employees as investments for the organization. One of the great strategic contributions of HRM lies in the planning of skill availability in advance of need. Development programmes involve more than training. They begin with the induction and integration of new employees. They require constant accurate assessment, counselling and personal challenge.

Development also involves the socialization of employees to fit the cultural requirements of the company. A much-publicized modern approach places development within the learning organization. HRD focuses strongly on management development. Career plans, performance objective-setting and training programmes are more often directed at managers than lower-level employees. With the integration of training activities into human resource development programmes, trainers are particularly concerned with the merits of formal as opposed to experiential training, cost-effectiveness and quality.

Further reading

The psychology of learning and memory and their relationship to training can be found in a number of general textbooks. For example, McKenna (1994) links theory and practice together well in *Business Psychology & Organisational Behaviour*. From the managerial perspective, *Managing Learning*, edited by Mabey and Iles (1994), contains a wide-ranging selection of articles from recent years and is a valuable compendium of theoretical insights and research findings in this area. Ashton and Felstead's (1995) critique of 'Training and Development' in *Human Resource Management: A Critical Text*, edited by Storey (1995), provides a good overview. Margerison's (1991) *Making Management Development Work* provides a systematic approach to the subject, with useful tips for both organizations and individuals.

Review questions

1 Consider an organization of your choice.

- Does this organization offer systematic development?
- Does it aim to develop employee skills as a long-term strategy?

2 How is human resource development distinguished from training?
3 What is a training needs analysis? How would you conduct an analysis for a small retail company?
4 How has the concept of career development changed in recent years? What are the implications of the reduction in management layers in many large organizations for an individual's career aspirations?
5 Outline the essential differences between Action Learning and formal training.
6 Discuss the argument that women should be treated differently from men on HRD programmes.
7 Using the individual development checklist, outline your own developmental strengths and weaknesses.
8 Draw up your personal career plan for the next five years.

Problem for discussion and analysis

Lisa was a recent recruit. The Personnel Manager was very pleased to have taken her on as her assessment centre results were outstanding. She was a graduate in Mechanical Engineering and apparently keen to apply her university training within the organization, a medium-sized manufacturer of aluminium products.

Previous female graduate recruits had received a brief induction period, involving visits to all departments, and then been placed in marketing or personnel jobs. None had risen beyond the junior management grades; higher posts seemed to be reserved for men promoted from Production and Finance. The board had decided that the company's attitude towards women was old-fashioned and preventing them from making the best use of their human resources. Lisa provided the opportunity to do something positive about the problem. With the support of the MD, the Personnel Manager set out to offer Lisa a development programme which would give her the opportunity to achieve a senior management post within a reasonable period.

Tina Johnson was a determined and thorough Personnel Manager. In her late forties and without much in the way of academic qualifications herself, she was aware that many bright young recruits were going to university before taking their first job. She was also in touch with the greater expectations of young people qualified to this level. She found that they were unhappy with the idea of several years at a junior level before being offered a seriously demanding job.

Lisa did not seem to be any different to the other graduates taken on by the company. Outside the male-dominated production and service areas, there were many female graduates at the lower management levels. Lisa had been with the company for three months and had completed the 'grand tour' which was the company's induction programme.

Tina decided to conduct a development interview with Lisa. Tina began by asking her how she felt about the company so far.

'It isn't quite what I expected,' said Lisa. She seemed ill at ease and nervous.

'Oh, in what way?' asked Tina in a friendly but quizzical tone.

'Well, I suppose I was expecting to use my university training from the beginning rather than being shown around places like Marketing and Distribution,' Lisa answered in a very apologetic way.

Tina decided to persist: 'Yes, but we think it's important for you to have a proper induction programme so that you get a basic understanding of the way the company operates. We invest a lot of time and money in our new recruits, three months is a long time to spend just on induction, you know.'

Lisa continued to look doubtful, and clearly wasn't convinced: 'I just don't think I learned very much, that's all.'

'Why was that?' asked Tina, sensing that she had a problem she had not anticipated.

Lisa took some time composing her answer. It was clear that she was fumbling for words which would allow her to express her opinion without upsetting the Personnel Manager. 'I really wanted to show people that I know a lot about mechanical engineering, but nobody seems interested. Besides, several people told me that I would probably end up in Marketing anyway. Most women do, don't they? Or Personnel, and I'm definitely not interested in that.' She emphasized 'personnel' with a grimace.

After the development interview Lisa wrote a letter couched in hostile terms, accusing the company of misleading her and having no idea of how to use graduates. She had been offered a scholarship to study for a PhD at an American university and had accepted it. She would be leaving the company in a month's time.

How would you have designed Lisa's development programme? What resistance would you have reasonably expected and how would you have overcome it?

12

Employee relations

This chapter discusses the nature of employee relations within the HRM framework and examines the roles of trade unions, arbitration and legislation.

In this chapter we examine the mechanisms by which organizations and workers communicate and resolve conflict within the employment relationship. Why 'employee' rather than 'industrial' relations? The latter has acquired a negative connotation, one associated with conflict between trade unions and employers and which conveys a picture of acrimonious strikes and lock-outs (Blyton and Turnbull 1994: 7). The term 'employee relations' avoids such preconceptions and also serves to widen the scope of the topic to encompass flexible and cooperative relationships between individuals and organizations (key concept 12.1). As with much of the terminology associated with HRM, the newer term is broader in perspective and indicates a more proactive approach.

KEY CONCEPT 12.1 *Employee relations*	Employee relations is not confined to unionized collective bargaining but encompasses all employment relationships. It goes beyond the negotiation of pay and benefits to include the conduct of the power relationship between employee and employer.

In earlier chapters we observed that HRM is generally associated with a move from collectivist employee relations – stressing union–employer bargaining arrangements – towards individual-based negotiation, reinforced by personal contracts and performance-based pay systems. The change has not been total in those countries where HRM has been influential and is certainly not universal. In reality, collective negotiation and representation remain common.

The common perception also relates to an outmoded picture – a

Thatcherite world, which is being replaced in the UK, at least, by a more conventional European model. EU legislation is steadily bringing British companies into line with the attitudes of the social-market, differentiating them from their US cousins. This is exemplified by the requirement that all large multinational companies operating in more than one EU country must have Europe-wide works councils, ensuring an enhanced role for collective representation in the twenty-first century.

The employment relationship also encapsulates different cultural assumptions about the roles, entitlements and obligations of these stakeholders. Accordingly, national employment systems are heavily influenced by their ideological and cultural traditions. We noted in Chapter 2 that businesses operate within varied legal frameworks, reflecting underlying ideological beliefs about the rights of employers and employees. As an example, we shall see later in this chapter that German companies operate within a social market which places great importance on a balanced relationship between employee and employer. German business culture also emphasizes regulation. Hence the German job market is based on detailed legislation, formalized consultation procedures and protected employee rights. Conversely, legislation in free-market countries tends to leave employee consultation to local arrangements and provides little employee protection. Paradoxically, countries such as Canada, the UK and the USA have a history of more advanced equal opportunities legislation than Germany, specifically for ethnicity, reflecting their multicultural nature.

We begin this chapter at the environmental level with an evaluation of the role of collective bargaining in different business cultures, ranging from the free market in the USA and UK, through the social market represented by Germany, to Japan as an example of Asian-Pacific approaches. We move on to consider the organizational context and discuss both management and employee strategies. The chapter concludes with an overview of employee relations as an activity. Specifically, we focus on discipline, the role of various forms of industrial tribunal, the negotiating process and the resolution of conflict.

Collectivization and confrontation

This section considers the problematic concept of the employment relationship. Regarded by neo-classical economists (see Chapter 3) as an exchange of labour for pay, it is also a power relationship in which the employer has the formal authority to direct effort towards specific goals, whereas the employee can – informally – frustrate the achievements of those objectives. The employment relationship goes beyond money to include a number of secondary issues, discussed in the same chapter, such as working conditions, the length of the working day, vacation time, freedom to arrange one's work, and measures of participation.

Through **collectivization**, workers could band together to protect their mutual interests. From the late nineteenth century, trade unions have fought for improved conditions for their members. The first unions were formed for defensive purposes – often in response to cuts in wages, refusing to implement change without payment and setting the scene for future accusations of intransigence.

Unions have been described as a mixture of movement and organization (Flanders 1970). On the one hand, they met workers' individual needs: protecting them from exploitation; negotiating improved wages and conditions; developing career prospects. On the other, unions had a wider, collective purpose which often extended to a political role. Workers were expected to subordinate personal advantage to the greater interests of the membership as a whole. In this respect, trade unions offered an alternative focus for employee commitment and a power base which clashed with the prerogatives of management.

> modern societies have developed a whole range of *labour market institutions*, ranging from social custom and moral codes to labour law and collective agreements, that is, the outcome of collective bargaining at an aggregate level which lies above the private level between employer and employee.
>
> (Van Ruysseveldt *et al.* 1995: 2)

The history of trade unionism varies from one country to another in terms of the following:

- **Business sector**, focusing on job conditions within an industry or specific company. Initially, unions in most countries organized around specific **crafts** such as boiler-making; this pattern remained dominant in the UK until the late twentieth century. In contrast, German trade unions have represented all the workers in a specific **industry** since 1945 (see Table 12.1).
- **Ideology**, extending their role beyond the workplace and influencing social and political change to the advantage of their members. Many unions were instrumental in the creation of political parties, such as Labour in Australia and Britain. Employee relations have been a battleground for ideology, local disputes being played out as skirmishes in a much larger war. In the USA, for example, the prevailing business culture of scientific management and Fordism created a particular trade union response and an irreconcilable conflict between the interests of 'capital' and 'labour' (see Table 12.2). Remarkably, the view from the 1920s expressed in Table 12.2 remains typical of many US organizations today. In fact, most American management writers ignore trade unionism, taking a unitarist (see key concept 12.2) rather than pluralist or collective viewpoint (Guest 1992). Beaumont (1992) argues that this perspective is reflected in a considerable reduction in US union membership and collective bargaining in recent decades. American HRM literature also emphasizes individual relationships and marginalizes trade unions (Blyton and Turnbull 1994). Unions have been viewed as restricting the nation's competitive position and protecting insiders (those with jobs) at the expense of those without. However, Van Ruysseveldt *et al.* (1995: 2) contend that 'no modern society has ever accepted a purely individualistic determination of the employment relationship'.

Table 12.1 Categories of trade unions

Craft unions	Recruiting members from a distinct trade or occupations, historically linked to an apprenticeship system. Originally such unions aimed to preserve jobs within the craft exclusively for their members. Technological change has blurred and sometimes eliminated the craft skills, and unions have survived by changing their membership boundaries to incorporate other areas.
Industrial unions	For example the National Union of Mineworkers in Britain, IG Metall in Germany. These are the dominant form in Germany but slow to develop in the UK. They aim to represent all employees in a particular industry regardless of their type of work.
General unions	Broad-ranging unions representing a variety of industries and job types, with little restriction on potential membership. Some are so extensive that they have been termed 'super-unions'.
Occupational unions	Recruiting members within a particular occupation or group such as teachers, police or firefighters.
White-collar unions	Concentrating on non-manual occupations such as banking.

Source: adapted from McIlwee and Roberts (1991).
Note: No classification system provides an 'ideal' description of union types.

Table 12.2 Assumptions of confrontational industrial relations

1 Workers' and employers' interests are generally opposed. Employers:
   - want the highest output at least cost;
   - try to lower wages, increase hours, speed up workers;
   - try to remove the least efficient workers;
   - maintain the worst possible working conditions;
   - discharge workers when possible;
   - replace expensive, skilled workers with cheaper, low-skilled employees;
   - reduce numbers through automation;

   Conversely, unions:
   - attempt to obtain continuous employment;
   - seek the highest wage rates;
   - look for the best working conditions.

2 Effort and increased output produce lower wages. Employers prefer to reduce prices to increase market share, rather than passing on productivity benefits to workers as higher wages.

3 Wages depend on the relative bargaining strengths of employers and workers.

4 Employers' bargaining strength is always greater than the workers'.

5 Employers' full bargaining strength will be exerted against individuals.

6 Individual bargaining produces competition between workers. This tends to lower wages to the level accepted by the weakest bargaining worker.

7 This applies during employment as well as recruitment. If workers speed up in response to bonuses, there is competition between workers.

Source: Hoxie (1923).

KEY CONCEPT 12.2
Unitarism v. pluralism

The unitarist view is implicit in American models of HRM. It holds that the interests of employees and the firm should be the same. Pluralism, on the other hand, recognizes that every organization is composed of different interests which are not balanced. Pluralists accept that conflict is natural and are concerned with the means by which it can be managed.

Kanter describes the tradition of American management as being firmly rooted in paranoia:

> One of the lessons America's mythologized cowboys supposedly learned in the rough-and-tumble days of the American frontier was that paranoia was smart psychology. You couldn't trust anybody. They were all out to get you, and they would steal from you as soon as your back was turned.
>
> (Kanter 1989: 117)

'Self-reliance' became the motto of the country. Everything outside one's own control was treated as an adversary and a potential enemy and had to be dominated. This applied as much to trade unions as it did to competitors. Elsewhere in the democratic world, such an extreme position was unusual. Nevertheless, it cannot be assumed (by benign unitarists, for example) that there is a common agenda between employers and the employed which can be 'managed'. There is an inevitable, if latent, tension between the two (Blyton and Turnbull 1994: 4).

Historically, unions attempted to replace all individual bargaining with **collective bargaining** (see key concept 12.3) in order to increase employee bargaining power and counter employers' attempts to create competition between workers. This required solidarity between union members. Union goals were to obtain standardized wages and conditions at the best possible level. In contrast, employers have preferred to deal with employees on an **individual** basis.

KEY CONCEPT 12.3
Collective bargaining

Collective bargaining takes place between employers and trade unions under the following circumstances:

- when employees are members of trade unions which undertake to negotiate on their behalf in matters such as pay, working conditions, other benefits, and work allocation;
- when employers recognize trade unions and their officials as legitimate bargaining agents.

Braverman (1974) regarded the weakness of workers in the employment relationship as an inevitable consequence of the role of management. He concluded that managers owed a responsibility to the market, over and above their duties to shareholders and employees. If managers did not deliver continually increasing levels of productivity and efficiency, then their businesses would not survive. The workforce held the key to survival through their creativity, imagination and problem-solving abilities. However, these same qualities could be used to resist manager's aspirations for change.

Employees were human beings with their own objectives which frequently differed from management goals. Under the nineteenth-century craft-based system of production individual employees held a considerable degree of power through their possession of knowledge. Very often managers had no idea what workers were doing. The value of scientific management and Fordism lay in their ability to de-skill jobs and remove knowledge, and hence bargaining power, from the workforce. Braverman's original analysis has been criticized for oversimplifying the nature of skill since most workers were unskilled or semi-skilled at best. Fordism led to a relative standardization of the employment relationship throughout the developed world until around 1980, with the following characteristics (Van Ruysseveldt *et al.* 1995: 2):

- permanent, full-time jobs;
- wage increases on the basis of experience and training;
- extra payments for inconvenient or anti-social arrangements, such as weekend working;
- regular working hours and a clearly defined working week;
- paid holidays;
- the right to collective representation and a degree of consultation on changes of working practices.

Trade unions conducted negotiations with employers within this framework. This form of employee relations was associated with vertical and horizontal division of labour, hierarchical management and close supervision of work. However, since the mid-1970s – as has been made evident in this book – this pattern of working life has disintegrated under the pressures of competition from newly developing countries and the arrival of flexibility. In consequence, the 'traditional' role of trade unions has been undermined.

Union activity was focused on people within the internal employment market. New working practices, on the other hand, may reduce the core workforce within the internal market to small and sometimes insignificant numbers. Moreover, in line with our discussion in Chapters 3 and 4, jobs may be on relatively short-term, or part-time contracts. Variable working hours have become a valuable source of flexibility. Extended opening hours have offered employers the opportunity to generate more money from the same equipment and accommodation.

Further, the reduction in workforce numbers has mainly affected older workers – the unions' traditional constituency. For a variety of reasons, employers have preferred younger workers who have been shielded from, and sometimes denied access to, trade union organization. As a consequence union membership has declined in many countries – in the UK by as much as a half .

Van Ruysseveldt *et al.* (1995: 7) argue that the 'classic' analytical and theoretical frameworks for studying employee relations reflect the times in which they were conceived and do not provide a satisfactory perspective for today. The shift in the nature of the employment relationship, introduction of flexible working practices and elimination of large, homogeneous workforces have been so significant that any pre-1980s perspective becomes simply a historical curiosity. As we shall see in the next section, the world – particularly the UK – has moved on.

Employee relations in the UK

Why should we single out the UK as an illustration of transformed employee relations? Most of the readers of this book will be far too young to know that the British were once notorious for industrial disputes and walkouts. In fact, they were daily occurrences in the 1960s and 1970s, such that industrial relations was perceived as a 'problem' which brought down governments. Weak management and intransigent unions produced industrial chaos, manifested by low productivity, hostility towards change and highly publicized disputes, fundamentally weakening the UK as an economic power.

The reputation of British personnel managers was not enhanced during this period. When HRM came on to the scene in the 1980s, personnel management had become bogged down in a form of industrial relations characterized by 'firefighting' – undermining any claim to being strategic or proactive (Hendry 1995: 12). By this time, personnel management had moved away from its neutral balancing role between employees and management. It had become a frontline activity in defence of the organization. Strikes, pay deals and overtime needs were largely dealt with in an ad-hoc piecemeal fashion with little sign of any strategy. In a context of industrial warfare, long-term thinking was displaced by short-term coping.

Hendry also attributes the lack of strategy to personnel managers' preference for dealing with industrial relations in an informal and personal manner (1995: 13). Their knowledge of the personalities involved on the management and union sides and their willingness to engage in 'off-the-record' discussions and make compromise deals all depended on a quick-witted ability to clinch agreement on the spur of the moment. There was no place for long-term strategy – 'manpower tactics' were the prevailing practice (Atkinson 1984) .

The situation changed dramatically during the 1980s and 1990s. Recessions, New Right politics, restrictive legislation on industrial action (see Chapter 2, Table 2.6) and massive restructuring in many organizations considerably reduced the power and role of unions. They also led to the downfall of the industrial relations 'industry'. Instead:

- Detailed obligations between employer and employee were replaced by informal commitments.
- Job descriptions became flexible.
- Job demarcations diminished in the face of flexible working practices.

Consequently, the new employee relations extend beyond collective bargaining – or, rather, two-sided warfare – to include non-unionized organizations, where dialogue may be between employers and individual employees and alternative negotiating structures exist. Hendry reflects on the perspectives of people in the 'industrial relations orthodoxy' who see a 'persistent weakening of employee power within organizations through the substitution of individualized systems for collective ones' (1995: 49). The development of corporate cultures also offends their confrontational instincts and is perceived virtually as a top management plot. HRM is implicated as an anti-union philosophy (Guest 1989: 44) which:

- can be aggressively anti-union, advocating the withdrawal of recognition from existing unions;
- can produce more generous rewards through individual pay deals, making unions seem unnecessary;
- can neutralize or control unions through close attention to their activities by means of single-union agreements, no-strike clauses and pendulum arbitration – these can be reinforced with careful recruitment, socialization, communications, team working and so on.

Such tactics are theoretically plausible. However, it is difficult to find instances of HRM being responsible for these developments. Rather, HRM tends to coincide with such actions. If anything, it comes into play when dealing with the subsequent mending of fences (Hendry 1995: 51).

Employees and managers frequently have different goals. Governments have also taken sides. For example, Prime Minister Margaret Thatcher crippled British trade unions in the 1980s. Recent management literature assumes that the worldwide balance of power has swung to employers. This is described by some as a 'new realism' among both managers and employees. Strikes virtually disappeared from the scene in countries such as Britain. In the UK in the early 1970s nearly 13 million days a year were lost through industrial action. In the 1980s this dropped to an average of just over 7 million days a year. In 1995 the comparable figure was just 440,000. Similarly, as we saw in Chapter 2, Case 2.2, there has been a substantial reduction in days lost because of strikes in South Africa. In both countries strikes have been largely restricted to the public sector and have been responses to government attempts to contain public spending. The private sector, meanwhile, has contained industrial action by means of tactics such as:

- elaborate communications techniques;
- career development;
- quality circles;
- performance-related pay;
- non-union status.

For instance, Caterpillar UK, the British subsidiary of Caterpillar Inc. – a major manufacturer of earth-moving equipment – considered it worthwhile to offer a financial inducement to its workers to give up collective bargaining rights (*Guardian*, 15 January 1994). As part of a two-year deal, most of its 1,000 employees were offered £500 each to give up trade union recognition and join a staff association. Unions were surprised by the move and linked it to Caterpillar's decision to create a European-wide works council.

In the UK the transformation in employee relations was hailed as a major shift in the industrial climate. David Hunt, then Conservative Employment Secretary, wrote:

> Britain has seen a dramatic improvement in industrial relations in the last 10 years. Our strike rate is lower than Germany's. The number of working days lost throught strikes was down from over 29 million in 1979 to 0.6 million last year. [. . .] Trade unions now operate in the same sort of market as most other organizations: one in which people are free to decide whether or not to join. If trade unions offer services which people want and for which they are prepared to pay, they will attract and retain membership. Union membership has, however, fallen in each year since 1979. [. . .] Membership, which at its peak in 1979 stood at 13.3 million, had dropped to 9 million by 1993. [. . .] I see signs that some forward-looking unions are recognising . . . reality. They are abandoning posturing and political manoeuvring and are concentrating on how to help their members.
>
> (*Guardian*, 24 May 1994)

Hunt saw helping members in terms of 'expert advice on their employment rights and other aspects of their working lives such as training and pensions' (*Guardian*, 24 May 1994). He argued that employers would be happy to recognize unions if they contributed to increased flexibility and efficiency, but concluded that:

> Over the last 15 years trade unions have missed the opportunity to work with the forces of modernisation, rather than against them. Their ideological opposition to the Government's popular and successful reforms of industrial relations and trade union law, such as the prohibition of the closed shop, has left them on the sidelines.
>
> (*Guardian*, 24 May 1994)

Further restriction of the union role has come in the form of **single-union agreements** – limiting negotiating rights to one union rather than several – and **no-strike deals**. We will see later in this section that single-union arrangements are normal in Germany and that German unions regard them as beneficial. In the UK, however, such developments have led to deep philosophical disagreements and some acrimony amongst trade unions. Unions such as the mainly electrical EEPTU were accused of 'selling out' to employers and 'poaching' members by actively negotiating for single-union agreements; and, despite the rhetoric, it is clear that realism has driven most major unions into similar deals (Goss 1994: 142).

Intriguingly, Brown (1994) finds that during the 1980s average pay rises were higher in non-unionized than unionized businesses. Moreover, this was not due to single-union agreements. He finds no evidence that non-unionism in this period was associated with 'progressive' management developments such as HRM. Non-unionism is linked to the absence of a bargaining structure, but Brown argues that removing trade unions leads to worse people management. This is reflected in inferior training, health and safety, and dismissal practices. By their very existence, unions force managers to manage.

For whatever reason, strikes and other cases of reported industrial action are considerably more common in larger organizations. This is not necessarily due to the atmosphere being better in small companies; an obvious corollary is that far fewer people in small firms are members of unions. This is because:

- employers in small companies actively discourage union organization;
- unions are not particularly interested in small groups of staff who

would need far more attention and provide relatively little extra benefit in either monetary or political terms.

During 1996 the UK experienced a new wave of industrial unrest within the Post Office, London Underground and rail companies. The total number of days lost due to industrial action exceeded 500,000 between January and July. This was seen as a reaction to many years of Conservative rule and a re-awakening of union power as a change of government became a strong possibility. Insecurity, stress and overstretched 'lean' organizations led to worker dissatisfaction, and an increase in feelings of anger towards management have also contributed. The IPD have argued that despite the dramatic improvements in British employee relations there is a need for a mechanism to deal with a growing sense of grievance in the workplace. In a similar vein Keith Sisson considers that:

> The British system of 'voluntarism' (leaving employers and unions to sort out their own problems) has failed either to protect workers or to deliver an efficient economy [. . .] This isn't a moral issue: most British managers would perform much better if they had to justify their actions to the workplace.
> (Keith Sisson; quoted in the *Observer*, 28 July 1996)

Such remarks also indicate an increased awareness that British employee relations and industrial organization are out of step with the rest of the European Union. In the next section we consider employee relations in countries which have a tradition of employees and managers as social partners rather than adversaries.

Employee relations in mainland Europe

In common with all western capitalist countries, in different ways and at varying speeds, since the Second World War democratic European states have developed institutional systems to govern employee relations (Van Ruysseveldt *et al.* 1995: 2). Since the signing of the Treaty of Rome in 1958 there have been several attempts to develop community-wide initiatives on employee participation and corporate industrial relations. Progress in harmonizing this area has been slow but there has been a considerable convergence of employment conditions. The resistance of British Conservative governments to any control of social policy at a European level is well known. However, the delay can be attributed to deeper philosophical differences within the EU as a whole. There are two perspectives (Cressey 1993):

- Free-market enthusiasts – particularly in the UK – seek the deregulation and decentralization of employee relations. They emphasize voluntary, non-statutory arrangements.
- Regulatory-minded people in the Commission, European Parliament and Council of Ministers see a need for a harmonized system of employee relations.

The EU already recognizes employees and their representatives as a 'social partner' in its own institutions. It allows representation, consultation and participation within a number of the EU's tripartite bodies. The argument revolves around an extension of this representation to situations beyond the EU's own institutions.

Brewster (1994) describes Europe as a 'heavily unionized continent'. Membership of trade unions varies from over 70 per cent in Denmark to a mere 12 per cent in France (see Table 12.3). In Europe membership is concentrated in organizations employing over 200 staff. In part, this variation reflects the differing traditions of member states, from the free market capitalist model in the UK to the social-market concepts prevalent in Germany. Brewster concludes that, unlike in the UK, unions in Europe 'tend to be more involved and to have more positive and less antagonistic relations with employers' (1994: 63). A 1991 survey questioning senior human resource practitioners about trade union influence in their organizations during the previous three years found that (reported in Brewster 1994):

- 52 per cent of UK and 46 per cent of French respondents said their influence had decreased;
- Swiss, German, Danish, Spanish, Norwegian and Dutch managers, in contrast, said that their importance had increased.

During the mid-1990s, government attempts to meet the requirements of the single currency agreement led to extensive industrial action in several European countries, France being a notable instance. Reductions in public spending and cuts in government borrowing hit state-sector – or state-subsidized – industries hard, producing wage cuts and job losses. In these cases, efforts to forge pacts with trade unions were generally unsuccessful because governments had nothing to offer in return. Throughout Europe, unions have lost political influence. Ironically, in Belgium and Spain their allies in government have been instrumental in the imposition of some of the toughest economic measures.

As mentioned earlier, the Maastricht Treaty has extended employee con-

Table 12.3 Trade union membership in the European Community

Country	Percentage of working population
Denmark	73.2
Belgium	53.0
Ireland	52.4
Luxembourg	49.7
UK	41.5
Italy	39.6
Germany	33.8
Portugal	30.0
Netherlands	25.0
Greece	25.0
Spain	16.0
France	12.0

Source: OECD (1991).

sultation throughout Europe (with the exception of the UK at the time of writing). Works councils are required in all companies employing a minimum of 1,000 workers in two or more countries in the EU, provided there are at least 150 workers at two sites or more. The councils are to be informed of the state of business and consulted on changes to production or working methods, restructuring and planned closures. Under Article 13 of the directive, all such companies had to have works councils in place by 22 September 1996.

After some initial hostility, some prominent British employers have been quick to set up works councils in other countries which also cover their employees in the UK. This is partly due to the loose wording of the agreement, which does not specify the form of such councils, nor their manner of working (*The Financial Times*, 10 November 1995). Whereas French and German companies have modelled their Europe-wide councils on pre-existing national formats, other organizations are obtaining agreements on widely different bases.

German employee relations

At this point it is appropriate to elaborate on the legislative tradition of employee relations in Germany. By comparison with many other countries, the management of people in Germany is tightly controlled by legal processes. Indeed many aspects of people management which can be dealt with in an ad-hoc way elsewhere are strictly regulated in the Federal Republic. As a result of the various codetermination laws in the period since the end of the Second World War, Germany has evolved a system which focuses on industrial democracy and harmony. Abandoning the prewar tradition of small craft-based unions, fifteen single-industry unions were organized largely for blue-collar workers. Together with the Police Trade Union, these unions formed the Deutscher Gewerkschaftsbund (DGB) – the Confederation of German Trade Unions – in 1949.

At the time of German unification in 1990 the unions affiliated to the DGB had almost 8 million members, including IG Metall (Metal-Workers' Union) which, with 3.6 million members in West and East Germany, was the largest trade union in the world (Randlesome 1994: 109). There are also separate associations representing white-collar workers, civil servants and Christian trade unionists.

Unlike **craft** and **general** unions, or **professional** associations, German unions are **industrial**: anyone employed in the industry represented by a particular union may be a member. This includes blue-collar and white-collar, skilled and unskilled, manual or supervisory workers. Consequently, demarcation disputes between different grades in a company cannot occur since all are represented by the same union. Ninety per cent of German employers belong to federations which require them to recognize trade unions (Brewster 1994: 64).

In practical terms, the main instruments of codetermination are the Supervisory Boards and works councils which characterize large companies.

Supervisory boards

Companies employing more than 2,000 workers are obliged to have a supervisory board. This is in addition to the management board, which continues to have final authority. The supervisory board consists of 50 per cent shareholder representatives, with the other 50 per cent being worker representatives elected by the workforce – including both basic and executive staff. Elections take place every four years. The supervisory board oversees management action and monitors and evaluates performance and change. German employers were reluctant to go along with this procedure but most now believe that it functions well, despite the occasional problem. In fact, the number of occasions when the supervisory and management boards fail to agree is limited – largely by means of informal discussions to make sure that they achieve consensus in the official forum. If they completely fail to agree, the chairperson of the supervisory board (a shareholder representative) has the casting vote. The major drawback of the system is that it slows down the process of decision-making.

Works councils

We noted earlier that works councils have been extended to all large companies operating in more than one European country. In Germany, three sets of rights have been given to works councils (Lawrence 1993: 34):

1 **Codetermination right** (*Mitbestimmungsrecht*), the ability to give consent on a number of issues:

- the appointment of an employee to a new position;
- transfers within the organization;
- transfers from one wage group to another;
- determination of starting and finishing times for the working day;
- the introduction of shift working, overtime, etc.

> A German company that has a bursting order book cannot just institute overtime by its own authority. It needs the agreement of the works council to do this and even then it cannot engage in unlimited overtime working. [. . .] quite small issues between management and workforce can only be said to be 'settled' when they have been formally agreed with the works council and written down.
>
> (Lawrence 1993: 36)

2 **Consultation right** (*Mitwirkungsrecht*) over planning issues, including plant closure, new factories, investment decisions and business policy matters.

3 **Information right** (*Informationsrecht*), the right to receive information about company performance and prospects.

Pay negotiations take place between an appropriate employers' federation and the matching union for that industry. Negotiations take place at the *Land* (state) level, with some variation in settlement levels between rich and less affluent states. Bargaining takes place to a predetermined schedule and in a specific order of states (Lawrence 1993: 30). So, for example, in the spring of 1995 Bavarian engineering employers agreed to increases of 11 per cent over the next two years, leading to similar increases in other *Länder* – accompanied by loud protests from a number of companies. Some smaller companies are not members of employers' federations but tend to follow agreements although they are not obliged to do so. A few large organizations, such as Siemens, conduct negotiations directly with their unions.

Until recently, codetermination brought stability into the German employee relations scene:

> From the point of view of organization policy, the trade unions have proved to be extremely stable. Their status as a party to collective bargaining has up to now remained unchallenged because of the high degree of juridification and centralization and their monopoly-like legal privileges in collective bargaining and in calling strikes. Whereas the 'institutionalization of class struggle' could be seen as a fetter on the unions' development of power in the years of sustained high employment, institutional protection now constitutes a bulwark against labour-exclusion strategies.
>
> (Jacobi and Muller-Jentsch 1990: 134)

However, in 1996 some cracks began to appear in these apparently sacrosanct arrangements (*The Financial Times*, 21 October 1996). Viessmann, a mid-sized producer of heating systems, was sued by the IG Metall engineering union on the grounds that it had negotiated new working hours with its employees without involving the union. Faced with the loss of work to a new (and cheaper) factory in the Czech Republic, Viessmann's workers agreed to work thirty-eight rather than thirty-five hours a week without increased pay. This improved efficiency by 8.6 per cent, matching the savings which would have been gained by the company had it transferred its work to the Czech Republic. IG Metall objected because the German system accords negotiating rights for pay and working hours to the trade unions. In this case the union action failed because only some 10 per cent of Viessmann's employees were members of IG Metall.

Other companies have negotiated informal agreements and opt-out clauses which have allowed them to reduce employee costs. There have also been murmurings about the structure of supervisory boards. In fact, the cosy consensus between management and employees is under strain. As we have noted already, the economic pressures, first, of additional taxation to support the unification of East and West Germany and, latterly, of government spending cuts to meet single-currency convergence requirements have caused considerable tensions. Unemployment has climbed rapidly since unification and the combination of a highly valued Deutschmark, high rates of pay and generous social security has led to the export of jobs on a significant scale. Government measures to cut statutory sick pay from 100 per cent to 80 per cent of normal wages caused a particularly angry response from the unions.

Japanese employee relations

A further major influence on the conduct of employee relations comes from Japan. This represents a total contrast with the German approach and emphasizes management dominance. Japanese employee relations methods have relevance in two contexts: Japan itself and transplant factories in the Pacific area, North America and Europe. Nissan, for example, has been particularly active in overseas expansion and – in common with many other Japanese corporations – has a specific attitude towards trade unions (Garrahan and Stewart 1992: 9). It established a factory in Tennessee, USA, where state laws on the 'right to work' effectively neutralized the power of established unions by allowing the freedom not to belong to unions. Nissan campaigned against the Auto Union, with the result that it failed to establish itself. In the UK Nissan took a site in Washington in the north-east of England. The company contracted a single union deal with the Amalgamated Union of Engineering Workers. This gave the union negligible negotiating powers. In fact, the company staff council had more power.

In Japan itself, Nissan destroyed union power in 1953 after a four-month lock-out of employees, coupled with the use of strong-arm tactics. After the capitulation of the independent national auto union, employees were taken back by the company on condition that they joined a company union, the All Nissan Motor Workers' Union. After this episode, employee relations were described by the company as follows: 'Nissan prides itself on 30 years of smooth labour-management relations' (Garrahan and Stewart 1992: 9).

Critics said that Nissan controlled the union, pointing to the history of employee relations since the 1950s. Employee pay was reduced for six years after 1953. It took until 1964 for that level to be achieved again. Thereafter wage claims were always 100 per cent agreed, but this was not too surprising, given that the claims were always modest and restrained. The company gained a massive increase in productivity as a result.

During 1980 union elections, 99 per cent of employees voted, with the elected officials receiving 98 per cent of the total votes cast. The voting process was closely monitored by company officials. Strangest of all to western eyes is the part played by union membership in career progression. A period as a union officer – on secondment from the personnel department – is an expected part of the career route. Pressure is put on staff to belong to the company union and they can be dismissed for belonging to other unions or unacceptable political groups.

Nissan and other major Japanese organizations have a particular strategic approach to employee relations. Organizations elsewhere in the world also tend to adopt strategies which fit their particular business cultures. In the next section we examine the organizational context of employee relations in more detail.

Organizations and employee relations

Earlier in this chapter we observed that traditional industrial relations assumed a formal structure in which management and staff negotiated pay levels and working conditions such as hours of work, grade demarcation, holiday entitlement and sick pay arrangements. In some organizations the same structure was used for grievance and disciplinary matters, agreeing levels of performance, attendance requirements – such as shift hours – and work procedures. Within this mechanism, staff were represented by one or more trade unions or staff associations.

In recent years large organizations in free-market countries have attempted to move away from traditional mechanisms. The focus has switched to individual rather than collective bargaining. This may take place through:

- the introduction of personal contracts, allowing employers to offer pay increases to staff willing to accept such contracts but not to workers wishing to remain as union members;
- organizational change methods such as team briefings, where managers cascade information throughout the organization by means of a series of meetings (usually on a monthly basis) and also collect ideas and criticisms at the same meetings to be funnelled upwards;
- quality circles, which have served to circumvent the traditional union role by emphasising direct dialogue between staff and line management on the subject of improving procedures.

It is not surprising that unions have often resisted the introduction of change methods of this nature because they depend on staff and management talking directly to each other, thereby removing a main source of union power – as the filter or gatekeeper of information and innovation. In such situations, collective bargaining has often been reduced to the primary subjects of pay, holidays and discipline, removing the unions from the discussion of procedures.

Individualized systems stress commitment from employees, yet the fashion for downsizing and restructuring imposes a 'fear of commitment' amongst managers and employees alike (Rousseau 1995: xii). HR policies which emphasize the individual contribute to this fear since they do away with any collective employee defence against the employer. This effectively constitutes a policy of 'divide and rule'. Hendry acknowledges a 'more sophisticated pluralist technique which sees the unitary organization as "bad" because the denial of individual and group interests actually makes for a less effective organization' (1995: 57). In other words, there is a valid criticism that the integrating activities of HRM can erase the healthy diversity which is essential for future development: 'Such paradoxes, discrepancies, and ambiguities highlight the fact that organizational life is beset by paradoxes, and that (mercifully) managers and organizations cannot get a handle completely on human behaviour' (Hendry 1995: 57).

Peters (1987) distinguishes two contradictory philosophies operating in modern business organizations:

- **Minimize human resources.** Workers are pure costs. New methods and equipment are now available globally. Businesses in the developed world can cut employee costs to match those of poorer countries or switch to industries which are not labour intensive. This involves actual and threatened redundancies, transferring operations to lower-wage countries and automation.
- **Increase the value of the people element.** Employees are assets. This approach emphasizes flexibility and creativity and aims to eliminate unnecessary routine by the intelligent use of technology and retraining

workers for more complex or varied tasks. According to Peters, it should be tied to profit-linked bonuses to ensure commitment.

The first approach leads to industrial conflict. Managers must make cuts and be aggressive towards staff. Workers defend their position and oppose change. It is the view which has predominated in New Right thinking and has predominated in the UK under Conservative rule. The second approach is collaborative. It seeks partnership between workers and employers for mutual benefit. It fits the 'social market' philosophy held by many governments in the European Union. Peters argues that both approaches deliver short-term profits but only the second can maintain competitiveness in the long term.

Other management writers advocate a new form of employee relationship based on cooperation. For example, Kanter argues that 'the adversarial mode with its paranoid world view' is unsuitable for the modern world (1989: 127). 'Teaming up' is the route to growth and survival. Corporations need to seek strategic alliances – cooperative arrangements to achieve business goals. Such alliances should be made with unions as well as other businesses. Kanter defines these as **stakeholder alliances** or 'complementary' coalitions. In 1996 the British Labour Party adopted a similar concept as its 'big idea' for the UK's future.

In Case 12.1 we see an example of a 'business partnership' forged by Pacific Telesis and Nevada Bell with the Communications Workers' of America to introduce new technology and cut operating costs. Since these changes affected workforce levels and employee skills, managers felt that the cooperation of the union would determine whether or not they could achieve their strategic goals. Kanter describes this as an example of management-driven labour relations: whereas the union might get a benefit from the process, the partnership was formed through a management initiative in order to achieve management goals (1989: 132).

CASE 12.1 ***Business*** ***partnership in*** ***employee*** ***relations***	The partnership involved a shift in power. It began as an antagonistic, adversarial relationship, with suspicion and conflict being highlighted. As employers and union grew closer, however, the nature of the relationship changed: • Influence shifted from full-time union officials to locally elected officers. • Local decision-making became more important than national union issues. • The treatment of union members on a 'mass' basis was replaced with local bargaining and differentiation between individuals. • 'Common interest forums' provided arenas to define union strategy at a local level. The partnership provided local union officials with regular, direct and informal contact with senior managers within the telecommunications companies. Previously, contact had been through official meetings on a once-a-year basis, or through lower-level managers. Local union officials now sat on a number of common interest committees and acquired a more global understanding of the business than many of the managers. However, direct contact with senior managers led also to the union officers taking local problems directly to the top, cutting out the normal management chain of command. According to Kanter:

vice-presidents say *they* are getting problems brought to them that middle managers used to tackle. And at times, Pacific Bell middle managers find themselves in the position of learning more about emerging company issues from union representatives than from their own superiors.

(Kanter 1989: 146)

This produced a conflict with middle and lower managers, who saw themselves losing their role in the communication chain. Improved communication with union officials produced a delicate 'political' situation which had to be redressed. Having been the **gatekeepers** – policing the relationship between the organization and its boundary with the union and deciding what was communicated and what was not – the managers were sensitive to their loss of power: 'Partnerships . . . simultaneously make the activities involved in 'external' relationships more important and reduce the former gatekeeper's monopoly over them' (Kanter 1989: 149). This was a 'squeeze' which required a redefinition of the middle managers' roles. It was more than a question of hurt feelings: these managers were in a position to wreck the process if they were not brought on board.

(*Source*: based on Kanter, R. M. (1989), *When Giants Learn to Dance*, Simon and Schuster.)

Discussion question
Summarize the benefits and disadvantages of the business partnership for the different stakeholders:

- employers;
- employees;
- national union officials;
- local union officials;
- middle managers.

Participation is also a matter of delegation, involving everyone downwards within the organization as well as the stakeholder partners. It requires a change in behaviour from managers who have previously exercised power in a clear-cut, overtly decisive fashion. A consensus style requires:

- patience;
- a willingness to discuss ideas at an early stage;
- the ability to listen.

Not all managers can make the transition. Partnerships require managers with team leadership skills. They reflect also on union beliefs and attitudes towards employers. Traditionally, according to Galbraith:

It has long been a minor tenet of trade union doctrine that all employers are essentially alike. All seek their own best gain. All, accordingly, are inimical to the interest of the worker. Thus any worker who identifies his interest with that of his boss is making a mistake.

(Galbraith 1967: 266)

Management strategies towards employee relations have been classified in a number of ways (see Table 12.4). These classifications demonstrate the variety of ways in which managers regard employee relations, ranging from authoritarian and anti-unionist to more sophisticated and inclusive

Table 12.4 Strategic management styles towards employee relations

Basic	*Purcell and Sissons (1983)*	*Gunnigle (1992)*
1 Authoritarian. Typical small company style. Boss rules absolutely – staff have simple 'take it or leave it' choice. Works if employees accept the situation, e.g. where there is little or no opportunity to change jobs. Seen in some large organizations.	**1 Traditional.** Firefighting – managers pay little attention to employee relations until trouble arises. Low pay levels. Hostile to unions. Prevails in authoritarian small businesses but seen in larger companies when workers have little choice in their employment.	**1 Anti-union.** Little or no consideration of employee relations. No collective arrangements such as union representation. Low concern for employee needs. Aggressive opposition to collective bargaining and union recognition.
2 Individual. Negotiation between management and individuals. Possible for staff teams to discuss common interests jointly. Non-authoritarian. Emphasis on commitment to company goals. Managers reasonable and approachable. No collective body representing staff.	**2 Paternalist.** More benevolent, humanistic style; close parallels with HRM approach. Employers consider unions unnecessary because conditions are so generous. Employee relations concentrate on getting employees to identify with the objectives of the business.	**2 Paternalist.** Concern for employee needs but rejection of union recognition and collective bargaining. Little sophistication in human resource policies.
3 Collective. Dominant method in western world from 1945 until approximately 1980. Since then, social- and free-market economies have taken different paths. Social-market economies, e.g Germany, have industry- or company-wide trade unions (or staff associations) negotiating with management on behalf of the staff. Free-market economies continue to make extensive use of this approach but management literature and HRM emphasize individual bargaining. Many companies utilize both strategies.	**3 Consultative.** Ideal form of employee relations in some eyes. Emphasis is on informal rather than formal systems of bargaining with continuous dialogue. Unions are fully recognized.	**3 Sophisticated paternalist.** Emphasizes welfare and well-being of individual staff. Sophisticated HR policies for resourcing, development, reward and communication. Rejects unions and collective bargaining. Equates to 'traditional HRM' – values employees because this is seen to benefit organization.
	4 Constitutional. Similar to consultative approach but with an emphasis on formal regulatory agreements to control the relationship between powerful parties on either side. Found in social-market economies and strongly encouraged by European Union social policy.	**4 Sophisticated unionized.** Recognizes trade unions but carefully prescribed union role (e.g. single-union agreement). Mixed collective and individual arrangements, incorporating HR policies. Neo-pluralist model with HRM-type policies designed to foster consensualism and employee commitment.
	5 Opportunistic. Responsibility for employee relations left to individual divisions/subsidiaries, leaving no common approach and an emphasis on unit profitability.	**5 Traditional unionized.** Pluralist approach typified by adversarial industrial relations. Collective bargaining but multiple unions complicate matters.

strategies. In the same way, employees may take various approaches, as we shall see in the next section of this chapter.

Employee strategies

Trade unions in different countries have varying interpretations of their roles and aim for different goals. McIlwee and Roberts, for example, have outlined the major objectives of British trade unions in the twentieth century (1991: 390):

- **Preventing legal interference in the collective bargaining process.** Trade unions in the UK have favoured voluntary collective bargaining and have resisted government attempts to restrict this process – albeit unsuccessfully in the Thatcher era. Unions have been favourably inclined towards (essentially pre-1979) legislation which aimed to protect employees, but have opposed income policies and limitations on industrial action.
- **Improving monetary rewards for members.** Trade unions have pressed for higher wages, especially in periods of high inflation. This is the principal concern of most union members; unions which are successful in this respect are likely to benefit from additional recruitment and retention of existing members.
- **Improving other terms and conditions.** As the nature of work and its rewards change, non-monetary benefits become increasingly important. These include reduction of working hours, earlier retirement, longer holidays, improved pension and sick pay schemes. British unions have been relatively unsuccessful in these respects compared to their continental European counterparts because of greater structural changes in the British economy and a higher uptake of flexibility by UK organizations.
- **Involvement in determining national economic and industrial objectives.** According to McIlwee and Roberts:

  > It is natural that trade unions should wish to be involved in the determination of national and economic objectives and in decision making on industrial strategy because, in the long term, it is going to have an effect on their members.
  >
  > (McIlwee and Roberts 1991: 391)

However, this belief has not been shared by a number of Conservative ministers who have attempted to reduce the influence of trade unionists on economic and other policies with macro-HRM consequences. Accustomed to 'beer and sandwiches' at 10 Downing Street in pre-Thatcher days, these stakeholders have found themselves virtually ignored by New Right governments. However, their (reduced) influence continues through ACAS and Industrial Tribunals:

- **Health and safety at work.** Unions continue to have a significant role in this area despite government attempts to reduce health and safety provisions on the grounds of removing bureaucratic restrictions on enterprise.

- **Protection of job opportunities.** Traditionally, UK unions have fought job cuts in any circumstances, leading to accusations of massive over-staffing in many organizations until the 1980s. Of late, union opposition has been more selective and the 'new realism' has produced a longer-term perspective. Unions have focused increasingly on jobs with a future and have been prepared to negotiate flexible terms with employers in order to preserve work in Britain or to attract jobs from other parts of the EU and elsewhere.
- **Improving public and social services.** The essential purpose of trade unions is to represent members at work. But workers also have other roles: as parents, consumers, tenants, pensioners, the sick, the unemployed. Awareness of this wider context has led to union pressure for changes in society as a whole. This has led unions in the UK into further conflict with Conservative governments, who have described their interest in the public services as being self-serving and backward-looking. Union criticism of the services offered by the newly managerialized NHS has been dismissed with little serious consideration and a barrage of statistics.
- **A voice in government.** British unions have had a direct relationship with the Labour Party since 1900 – initially the party was organized to reflect their views. Many unions contributed funds to the Labour Party and, as the largest source of income, strongly influenced its policies and organization. Conservative legislation in the 1980s allowed members to opt out of their union's political fund, reducing this flow by around 20 per cent.

  The Labour Party itself concluded that identifying too closely with the trade union movement was counterproductive at the end of the twentieth century. The proportion of British voters identifying themselves as 'working class' has fallen dramatically due to government initiatives such as council house sales to tenants and a general improvement in prosperity. The new middle class ('Thatcher's children') are portrayed as being scared of overtly socialist policies which might reduce their economic wellbeing, and are seen to have lost interest in the underprivileged. Although a Labour government might be more receptive to union voices, unions are unlikely to regain the influence they had in the postwar years.
- **Industrial democracy.** The Conservative government opted out of those sections of the Social Chapter which required works councils to be formed in all large companies. However, as we have seen, multinational organizations operating elsewhere in Europe will be compelled to introduce them, thereby giving British unions a role in their operation.

Industrial democracy has also been a feature of recent employee relations legislation in South Africa. The largest union in any company which employs more than 100 people can request the establishment of a workplace forum. Workplace forums can ask employers for information on the state of the company and take part in joint decision-making on a number of topics (*The Financial Times*, 21 November 1995).

The pattern in different countries varies because of the prevailing cultural, historical and legislative factors. These issues are reflected in the nature of employee relations as an activity undertaken by managers, employees and unions.

Employee relations as an activity

In many developed countries the industrial relations of the 1950s to the 1970s depended on the existence of company rules and regulations which served the purpose of clarifying what was expected of both employees and employers. Since then, the move towards flexibility and the empowerment of staff has resulted in 'fuzzier' boundaries between expected and inappropriate behaviour. Employees – particularly managers – have been given greater discretion in decision-making in free-market economies. This has been encouraged by right-wing governments, but within the EU there has been a counterbalance towards formal rules because of the predominance of social-market economies at the heart of the community. Typically, most large organizations continue to have formal rules on the following (ACAS 1987: 10):

- **Timekeeping**:
    - normally expected times of attendance, often with monitoring ('clocking in');
    - sanctions for lateness.

- **Absence**:
    - an approval mechanism for absence;
    - authorization for taking annual leave;
    - a reporting procedure when people are absent from the workplace;
    - the need for medical self-certification or a doctor's certificate.

- **Health and safety**:
    - requirements for appearance or cleanliness, e.g. protective clothing, the wearing of jewellery;
    - special hazards such as chemicals, dangerous machinery;
    - prohibition of smoking, alcohol.

- **Gross misconduct**, offences regarded as being serious enough to lead to dismissal without notice. ACAS (1987: 61) conclude that the following are normally regarded as gross misconduct:
    - theft, fraud, deliberate falsification of records;
    - fighting, assault on another person;
    - deliberate damage to company property;
    - serious inacapability through alcohol or being under the influence of illegal drugs;
    - serious negligence which causes unacceptable loss, damage or injury;

- serious acts of insubordination;
- unauthorized entry to computer records.

- **Use of company facilities**:

  - use of telephone for private calls;
  - admission to company premises outside working hours;
  - use of company equipment, e.g. computers, photocopiers, for personal reasons.

- **Discrimination**:

  - overt discrimination but also sexual harrassment and racial abuse.

How are these rules enforced? Clearly, this is a sensitive issue, requiring some type of formal or informal disciplinary system.

Discipline

> Grievance and discipline handling are one of the personnel roles that few other people want to take over. Ambitious line managers may want to select their own staff without personnel intervention or by using the services of consultants. They may try to brush their personnel colleagues aside and deal directly with trade union officials or organize their own management development, but grievance and discipline is too hot a potato.
>
> (Torrington and Hall 1995: 528)

Torrington and Hall distinguish between three types of discipline:

- **Managerial discipline.** Rules, instructions and behaviour are determined by the manager. Individual performance is controlled as if by the conductor of an orchestra.
- **Team discipline.** Performance depends on mutual dependence: each individual is expected to behave in such a way as to maintain the success of the group. Essentially, this consists in conformity to group norms.
- **Self-discipline.**

Discipline is not only negative, in the sense of being punitive or preventative, it also makes a positive contribution to organizational performance. An effective organization cannot survive if its members behave in an anarchic way. It depends on a mixture of each of these forms of discipline. Within the context of HRM, however, the emphasis has moved away from managerial discipline towards self- and, especially, team discipline. Nevertheless, most organizations continue to have an institutionalized managerial system:

> Managers are not dealing with discipline only when they are rebuking latecomers or threatening to dismiss saboteurs. As well as dealing with the unruly and reluctant, they are developing the co-ordinated discipline of the working team, engendering that *esprit de corps* which makes the whole greater than the sum of the parts.
>
> (Torrington and Hall 1995: 530)

In the UK, the Advisory, Conciliation and Arbitration Service (ACAS) has provided the following model for disciplinary procedures in any size of organization (ACAS 1987: 59):

● **Principles**

- No disciplinary action is to be taken against an employee until the case has been fully investigated.
- Employees should be advised of the nature of the complaint against them and given the opportunity to state their case before any decision is made.
- Every employee may be accompanied by an employee representative or work colleague during a disciplinary interview.
- Employees should not be dismissed for a first breach of discipline except in cases of gross misconduct.
- Employees should have the right to appeal against any disciplinary penalty imposed.

● **Procedure**
In minor cases, the problem should be resolved informally. In more serious or persistent cases, the following (simplified) sequence should occur:

1 When conduct or work performance is not acceptable, employees should first be given a formal oral warning.
2 In the case of a serious offence, or if unsatisfactory conduct continues, the employee should be given a written warning. This should give details of the complaint, the improvement required and the timescale.
3 When there is no improvement, or there has been some action which is serious enough to justify a single written warning but not dismissal, a final written warning is given to the employee. This should detail the complaint, warn of dismissal if there is no acceptable change of behaviour and advise of the right of appeal.
4 If the employee does not heed the warning, the result is normally dismissal. This should be actioned by the appropriate senior manager. The employee should receive a document providing written reasons for dismissal, the date of termination of employment and a statement of the right of appeal.

The ACAS procedure advocates a cautious, carefully recorded and staged approach, giving an employee every opportunity to improve and making the right of appeal clear throughout. The intention is to be fair and also to ensure that there are no grounds to claim unfair dismissal.

Dismissal is the most unpleasant aspect of management. It may arise because of disciplinary issues such as persistent absenteeism, failure of an employee to perform adequately despite support and training, or as a strategic requirement arising from a change in direction by the organization. Most managers regard the 'exiting' process with distaste – often it is more stressful for the sacking manager than the victims.

Conflict

Only a portion of employee relations issues have a disciplinary element. Many cases arise from some form of conflict between management and employees, or between specific individuals. Conflict has both positive and negative aspects, as we can see in Table 12.5. Where does conflict come from? A number of basic psychological causes are apparent, regardless of the overt justification for a dispute (McKenna 1994: 418; Torrington and Hall 1995: 641):

- **Frustration and aggression.** Disagreement often reflects frustration – feelings of being ignored, of being pressurized or of blocked promotion. Any point of difference, no matter how irrelevant, may spark a reaction to frustration. This may appear in the form of verbal aggression seemingly out of proportion to the importance of the supposed dispute. Clearly, the dispute masks problems which are attributable to poor communication, lack of empowerment and mistrust.

- **Different objectives.** Managers have one set of goals, typically including efficiency and cost-effectiveness, whereas employees may be focused on higher pay and longer holidays. Unless there is some mechanism, such as team briefings or quality circles, by which mutual understanding of these goals can be improved, differences are likely to come to a head at some stage.

- **Different values.** These could be political – a difference in belief about the purpose of the business for example – or a disagreement about the manager's right to manage. Many managers believe that they have the authority to issue instructions without being challenged by their staff. On the other hand, some employees consider that managers have this right only if they explain their actions and the consequences, and are prepared to accept questions and criticisms.

- **Jealousy.** Individual employees can be sensitive to other members of staff being paid more than them or getting extra perks. The conflict arises from jealousy or loss of status.

- **Culture.** The tradition of 'us and them' (employees versus management) continues to exist in many organizations, particularly those using an authoritarian style of people management. New staff and management are quickly encouraged to accept the 'normality' of this perspective. In other cases, a change in the management approach disturbs the prevailing employee relations culture. For example, the dispute between London Underground and unions in 1996 seemed to have been exacerbated because of the contrasting styles (and politics) of Ann Burfutt, the Director of Human Resources, and of the union leaders (*The Independent*, 25 July 1996). An abrasive and tough negotiating stance from a woman baffled the traditionally 'male' union negotiators.

Conflict is an inevitable feature of negotiating and bargaining. Trained negotiators are taught to deal with conflict, expecting both negative and positive aspects to appear during the process. This becomes easier to

Table 12.5 Consequences of conflict

Positive	Negative
Clearing the air. Allowing people to air their grievances can sometimes lead to an improved atmosphere after the disagreement has finished. This serves to bring hidden agendas out into the open.	**Wasting time and energy.** A simple decision can be quick to implement, but negotiation can take an inordinate amount of time. Often participants forget the original purpose of the negotiation and get caught up with fighting a war.
Understanding each other's position. When both sides of an agenda are brought out into the open, people must think through their own case in order to express it clearly, and grasp the other point of view in order to challenge it.	**Stress.** Conflicts can become quite personal, abusive and threatening. The postures taken by the two sides can lead to a worsening of the situation, leading to further stress. Mental exhaustion may come from prolonged debate.
Modification of goals. One side may realize how unpopular or impractical the consequences of their argument may be.	**Worsening the situation.** Conflict may highlight problems, dislikes and grievances better left unstated. Tension may escalate the nature of debate into action: strikes, lock-outs, work-to-rule, threatened or implied redundancies. The consequences may be unpleasantness, with worse morale and industrial relations after negotiations than before.

Source: based on Torrington and Hall (1995).

understand when we consider a specific model of negotiation in the final section of this chapter.

Issues of conflict and discipline may be not be resolved at a local level. Many countries have mechanisms by which disputes may be taken to an outside body, usually in the form of industrial tribunals or arbitration bodies.

Tribunals and arbitration systems

> From nowhere, the industrial tribunal has become important [. . .] it offers judgements in some of the thorniest and most controversial issues in everyday life; it points the direction of social evolution and it brings justice, or disappointment to people who become popular heroes and popular villains. In short all human life is there. How much can a boss swear at his employees? How far can the office lizard ogle his women colleagues? What are the boundaries of racial tolerance, as expressed through words and actions in the workplace? A code of permissible conduct at work is taking shape.
>
> (*The Independent on Sunday*, 14 August 1994)

To what extent can differences between employers and workers be resolved by arbitration or legal tribunal? It is the view in many countries that an impartial, legally based view has a significant role to play in a number of circumstances. Industrial tribunals take many forms: in Germany the labour courts make legally binding judgements; in the UK tribunal decisions do not set a precedent in law and cannot establish criminal behaviour. Even in the latter case, however, they have a long-term effect since they establish a set of values which influence the behaviour of others. If there is judgement on a case of significant racial discrimination, for example, the resulting publicity will lead to a moderation of racist behaviour as people fear the possibility of similar action against themselves. In Australia, under the Labour government's thirteen-year accord with the trade unions, the emphasis was on conciliation and cooperation. The Industrial Relations Commission (AIRC) could make binding rulings (as exemplified in Case 12.2).

CASE 12.2
Individual contracts at Weipa

The dispute originated between the mining group CRA and its workers at the Weipa bauxite mine in Queensland. CRA attempted to replace wage rates based on union-negotiated pay awards with individual staff contracts. Over seventy employees had refused to accept the new arrangements and were now complaing about discrimination. They claimed that workers on the new contracts were receiving as much as A$20,000 a year more for the same work. CRA's aluminium subsidiary Comalco admitted that 'differences averaging A$7000 have emerged'.

The dispute escalated into a national disagreement over collective bargaining rights as 3,000 miners in CRA coal mines started a strike, joined by 17,000 others around the country. Port workers began industrial action and public support came from the Metal Trade Federation and the Australian Education Union. The Australian Council of Trade Unions (ACTU) initiated meetings to organize direct action against CRA.

The issue took on a political edge, with ACTU officials arguing that this would be the prevailing industrial relations climate if the opposition came into power. In response, the opposition pointed out that CRA's action had taken place under the Labour government and that they 'would not sanction discrimination against workers doing the same work'.

The dispute ended in November 1995 when a full bench of the Australian Industrial Relations Commission, the country's highest arbitration body, imposed a settlement. They awarded an immediate 8 per cent pay rise to the seventy Weipa workers, backdated to March 1994. They required the ending of industrial action and lifting of all work bans as part of the settlement.

(*Source*: *The Financial Times*, 16 and 22 November 1995)

Discussion questions

1 To what extent does an effective industrial tribunal system rely on an accord or consensus between the different stakeholders?
2 Should all industrial disputes be settled by arbitration?

When the new Liberal-National Party coalition took over, industrial unrest increased markedly. In the first three months alone, four times as many working days were lost through strikes. Twenty thousand trade unionists joined Aboriginal groups outside the Australian Parliament to protest at drastic budget cuts and planned reductions in trade union rights. The accord between government and unions was dismantled and the emphasis changed to banning closed shops, restricting secondary picketing and increased flexibility in the workplace.

In the UK, ACAS plays a similar role to the Australian Industrial Relations Commission in relation to collective disputes. It does not have the same legal sanctions and its role has been weakened during the period of Conservative government. Nevertheless, it has had a highly influential and widely respected role. Funded by the Department of Trade and Industry it has a staff of 600 located in nine offices around the country. Many other countries have similar systems. For example, as we observed in Chapter 2, Case 2.2, South Africa has introduced a Commission for Mediation, Conciliation and Arbitration.

In the UK, ACAS provides the following services:

- **Binding arbitration.** ACAS can appoint an arbitrator provided that the two parties agree to accept the arbitrator's decision. Just 136 requests were received in 1995.
- **Voluntary conciliation.** Around 1,200 collective employment disputes a year are handled through voluntary conciliation. ACAS provides a calm environment and help in defining the important issues. ACAS conciliation staff act as facilitators and do not make judgements or attempt to impose solutions.
- **Mediation.** This is intermediate between arbitration and conciliation. ACAS mediators make advisory recommendations which are aimed at preventing disputes from degenerating into industrial action. These recommendations are not binding on the parties involved.

ACAS also plays a major role in promoting agreed settlements in disputes taken to industrial tribunals. The increasing importance of industrial tribunals in the UK is reflected in the rise in applications from 29,304 in 1988/9 to 88,061 in 1994/5. Of these, only about one-third go to a full hearing by the tribunal – most are settled with ACAS's assistance or withdrawn – and less than half of these are judged in favour of the complainant. Nevertheless this amounted to 24,883 cases in 1994/5. Of the sixty forms of claim under their jurisdiction, the most common is that of unfair dismissal – 39,397 in 1994/5. Trade unions point to the increasing confidence shown by employers in sacking people, particularly in the growing small firms sector. But, of the relatively few judgements on unfair dismissal (4,828), only half of the successful actions are offered compensation and a miniscule proportion (0.2 per cent) have their jobs restored. Compensation is minimal, with a median of £2,773 and a mximum of £22,480 for an employee dismissed after twenty-six years' sevice.

Tribunals are composed of a qualified lawyer as chair and two lay members – one employer and one trade unionist. The tribunals are informal by legal standards but continue to be intimidating for applicants. Generally the panel consists of white, middle-aged men – ethnic minority and female claimants may feel particularly intimidated. As further evidence that industrial tribunals may only be seeing 'the tip of an iceberg', Citizens' Advice Bureaux reported 882,257 requests on employment matters in 1994 (*Guardian*, 16 August 1995).

The negotiating process

Negotiation is an ancient art. It is important in fields as diverse as diplomacy, buying and selling, and arranging relationships (marriages, business partnerships), as well as employee relations. Negotiation is a form of decision-making where two or more parties approach a problem or situation wanting to achieve their own objectives – which may or may not turn out to be the same. In the employee relations arena, negotiation usually takes place within the collective bargaining environment.

Participants enter the process with widely different views: some – typically on the employee side – will view it as being fundamental to industrial democracy, fairness and good business conduct; others see it as a barrier to efficiency – a view more prevalent on the management side. The latter view sees negotiation as compromise and second best to winning – possibly worse than giving in! As can be seen from Table 12.6, the process also has its own jargon.

Negotiation is not simply a matter of 'splitting the difference' so that neither side achieves what it wants. It can produce an outcome which meets both sets of goals. In negotiating, both sides must have some goals in common and some that conflict. For example, employers and employees will all want the business to survive and expand. However, employers might resist high pay rises to keep costs down, whereas the staff side will want increases to boost employee morale. Usually, bargaining takes place because neither side has the power or the authority to force a decision on the other and preserve a harmonious working atmosphere at the same time. Therefore, both sides will open negotiations knowing that they will have to move from the opening position and that there will have to be sacrifices on one item to achieve advantages on another. Even in those ideal circumstances, such as the German model, where deliberate confrontation is not acceptable, there will be an element of conflict between the two sides.

There is also an implicit assumption that the two parties have the same amount of power in the bargaining situation. This is almost certainly not the case and the degree of power will change during the process of negotiation; the location of greatest power may well switch backwards and forwards between the two sides as they achieve positions of advantage. Whatever the actual degree of power, advantages will come from both sides preserving the appearance or illusion of power. There is value, therefore, in playing a game of bluff.

Table 12.6 Communication in collective bargaining

Statement	Actual meaning
We explored all options.	Everybody talked a lot.
A great deal of additional work will be necessary.	Nobody understood it.
The results were inconclusive.	Nothing happened.
While no agreement was reached, definite progress was made.	Nobody budged an inch.
It is hoped that this report will stimulate interest in the problem.	Let somebody else do it next time.

Source: adapted from *Toctanic* (undated, c.1989), unofficial staff publication, British Telecom International.

Many texts imply that the methods of bargaining can only be learned through experience and may well suggest that negotiation, like most inter-personal skills, is instinctive rather than learned. The basic requirement is probably a combination of a competitive, assertive style with a devious and resilient personality. In fact, a study of the bargaining process indicates regular patterns and processes which people tend to go through. Studies of industrial negotiations have indicated that many disputes worsen because of the following:

- there is a lack of clarity about aims or goals by one or both sides;
- there is poor understanding of the detailed situation;
- the apparent dispute is not the real problem.

These points are well illustrated in the case of Timex (see Case 12.3 below), where poor communication, cultural differences and a complete incompat-ibility of goals led to the closure of a factory.

CASE 12.3
Timex

In 1992 Timex was a multinational company with world headquarters in Connecticut, USA. It was controlled by Fred Olsen, a Norwegian entrepreneur and owner of the Olsen shipping line. An electronics components factory in Dundee on the north-east coast of Scotland formed part of the group. The company was faced with falling orders and short-time working, and so negotiations began at the end of that year between local management and unions.

On Christmas Eve 1992 management informed its 343 largely female hourly paid workers that their numbers would have to be halved, at least until the latter part of 1993. Notwith-standing the holiday period, negotiations began immediately between officials of the Amal-gamated Engineering and Electrical Union (AEEW) and managers from the plant. The management side was led by Timex UK President Peter Hall, described in one report as 'the Englishman from Surrey with the executive haircut and the tartan tie'. He had worked for the company for two years, having been headhunted for the Dundee post after his own electronics business had gone into receivership in the south-east of England.

The unions suggested that lay-offs should be organized on a rotating basis, with the company supplementing state benefits. Timex managers did not support the concept of all staff working alternate weeks. They felt that the company should decide who should be laid off. A ballot of members indicated 92 per cent support for a strike, which began on 29 January 1993.

In mid-February, two corporate bosses travelled to the plant with a compromise formula. Among the new 'fringe benefits' proposed were reductions in contributions to employee pension plans and an in-house savings scheme. The AEEU claimed there was a hidden agenda of more significant measures under consideration, including a pay freeze, cuts in holidays and overtime payments, and an increase in working hours from thirty-seven to forty each week.

On 14 February, union members voted to return to work 'under protest', accepting the revised plan for negotiating lay-offs but resisting any erosion of pay and conditions. On 15 February they found the factory gates locked. Two days later they received redundancy notices delivered by taxi. The first members of an alternative workforce were bussed in the following day. The following months saw numerous violent clashes and arrests in the vicinity of the factory. The company unsuccessfully sought legal redress to limit the activities of pickets, who were supported by a number of high-profile politicians and unionists.

As positions polarized, cultural differences between the protagonists became increasingly evident. Timex was an elusive multinational foe with a reputation as a 'slash and burn' employer ready to redeploy in the interests of profit. Olsen was said to keep up-to-date with the smallest detail of his extensive business empire while remaining unimpressed by consensus or prevailing business fashion. Timex had been based in Dundee for forty-six years, entering the globally competitive electronics subcontracting field after watch production ceased in 1983. Dundee was a city in which the demise of traditional industries based on jute and jam-making had contributed to rising unemployment.

The majority of the Timex employees had worked for the company for a long time – ranging from ten to forty years. There was a strong sense of community solidarity extending back over many generations and a tradition of labour activism among women. Non-unionized replacement workers were considered to be 'without dignity or conscience'. Workers were also critical of the AEEW president, Bill Jordan. 'Not for the first time, the focused fervour of a self-sufficient group of workers contrasts sharply with the inevitably distanced pragmatism of their union's top brass.' Within this emotional arena, Timex UK President Peter Hall's tone was described as 'studied, strategic blandness: as far as he is concerned, there is no industrial dispute; he is simply running a business'.

Any hope that Peter Hall was the main obstacle to a negotiated settlement received a major setback in June 1993 when he suddenly resigned. By the next meeting between the two sides Timex management had grown weary of trying to deal with a workforce it did not understand. Senior managers from the United States and union officials could find no common ground. The possible exception was the problem at the heart of the original dispute: a loss of £10 million between 1987 and 1992, coupled with a £2 million shortfall in the first six months of 1993. Timex threatened to close the Dundee factory by Christmas unless the workforce agreed to wage cuts and retraining to introduce conditions similar to those in Japanese companies operating in Britain.

The proposed deal was unanimously rejected and Timex announced 'an orderly withdrawal' from Dundee. Mohammed Saleh, Corporate Director of Human Resources, was reported as telling a press conference: 'I defy anybody to say we are not reasonable . . . It became clear that union members definitely did not want to work under conditions where they would have less wages, or less benefits, than what they had before the strike.' Gavin Laird, General Secretary of AEEW, blamed the situation on the company's exploitation of 'brutal anti-union legislation'. The Scottish Trades Union Congress said responsibility lay with Timex 'management madness'.

The end could not have been more acrimonious. On Sunday evening, 29 August 1993, the Dundee factory was abruptly closed leaving John Monks, then General Secretary-elect of the Trades Union Congress to comment: 'It is typical of Timex that they, in this very sorry and squalid affair, should have pulled out and in a sense done a moonlight flit.' In October 1993 a narrow majority voted to accept a pay-off from Timex as recommended by the AEEW union. This provided one week's pay for every year worked, in return for a promise not to use union funds to pursue claims for unfair dismissal and an end to the boycott of Timex products. Jimmy Airlie, the AEEW union leader, 'fled Dundee amid accusations of blackmail and betrayal'. He commented that, while he understood the bitterness of workers, 'the factory has closed, that was the reality'.

In *Scotland on Sunday* Kamal Ahmed reflected: 'at its simplest the most bitter dispute to hit Britain since the 1980s was over 150 jobs and £30 a week. But at deeper, harsher levels, it became a battle for hearts and minds, a fight to the death between a management's right to manage and a worker's right to earn a decent wage . . . and to strike' (*Scotland on Sunday,* 20 June 1993).

(*Sources: Guardian,* 15 June 1993; *Scotland on Sunday,* 20 June 1993; *The Scotsman,* 15 October 1993.)

Discussion questions

1 What is the main problem underlying this case?
2 List the main parties/ individuals involved and evaluate their:

- objectives;
- degree of flexibility;
- effectiveness as negotiators.

3 What options were open to the negotiators?
4 Who made the final decision?
5 Was there a better way of dealing with the situation?

Models of bargaining

There are several models of the bargaining process, the clearest of which identifies four main stages (Lyons 1988: 110):

1 **Initial positioning.** Both parties set out their positions and requirements in an emphatic, firm way aimed at giving the impression that there is no possibility of budging from those positions. The situation can appear hopeless at this stage.
2 **Testing.** The next stage is a less formal probing of the other side's demands, testing out which are really unmovable and which might bend in the right circumstances.
3 **Concession.** Some tentative proposals and concessions are exchanged on which detailed negotiations can take place.
4 **Settlement.** Finally, agreement is reached and the package of new terms is settled and actioned.

Obviously, the model does not apply in every case – the Timex negotiations went awry from the beginning and came to an end somewhere in the middle of the sequence. Lyons argues that successful negotiation requires specific skills. These skills were visibly missing at Timex, particularly on the management side:

- **Analysis.** The ability to analyse a situation not only in terms of one's own position and goals but also in terms of those of the other side. There should be a long-term perspective – it is clear that one should begin to consider the consequences of the whole process at this basic stage. The analysis must include a decision on which elements can be agreed on an I win/you win basis, as opposed to those which are I win/you lose. It is not worthwhile winning one of the latter if the advantage is trivial in comparison with the longer-term bad feelings that may arise as a consequence. This phase is frequently glossed over but in fact is possibly the most important. It is the stage at which you should work out what the highest and lowest gains you and your opponent are likely to accept. Additionally, there must be a clear understanding of what those on the other side really want as opposed to what you think they might want. Clearly, in the Timex case above we see little understanding of the opposing perspective and no evidence from the management side of a willingness to accept an I win/you win position.

- **Effective argument.** This has to be carefully balanced between being forceful and being reasonable. The whole point of negotiation is to convince the other side of the merits of your argument as against their own. It is a change process. It is important to avoid cheap point-scoring and abuse in order to preserve mutual respect and avoid distraction from irrelevant side issues. Again, the managers at Timex were unable to convince the employees of the merits of their argument and seemingly incapable of understanding the employees' point of view.

- **Signals of cooperation.** These involve the skill of sensing and giving signals of cooperation and possible compromise. Again, these were virtually absent in the Timex case. Kanter found that the participants in successful 'business partnerships' were 'very adept at "reading" signals that indicated whether partner representatives can be trusted' (1989: 156). Union representatives in the Pacific Bell–CWA alliance (discussed in Case 12.1 earlier in this chapter) clearly distinguished between senior managers who were 'serious' and those who were 'just reading the script': 'They looked not for rhetoric but for concrete evidence of management's sincerity, such as one officer who kept people in their jobs despite negative financial implications that could lower his incentive pay' (Kanter 1989: 56). On the 'tit-for-tat' principle, maximum opportunity comes from rewarding cooperation or compromise with a compromise of your own. On the other hand, one does not reward the opposition for sticking to an unmovable position: every offer one makes has to be conditional on cooperation in return. It may be necessary to keep communication going in order for this process to happen. In the case of a complete deadlock, it may even be necessary to have 'talks about talks'. All offers and threats must have credibility – remember that it is not real power that matters but the appearance of it.

- **Attention to detail.** Finally, the conclusion of negotiations requires the ability to attend to detail, making sure that all aspects are taken care of and there is no way for the other side to avoid its agreed obligations.

Summary

'Employee relations' is a relatively new term which broadens the study of industrial relations to include wider aspects of the employment relationship, including non-unionized workplaces, personal contracts and socio-emotional, rather than contractual, arrangements. This is an area with diverse ideological underpinnings and political ramifications. Governments have taken an active part in determining its conduct. In Europe, harmonization is leading to the establishment of works councils across the

EU, giving a new role for collective representation. At an activity level, employee relations covers the resolution of conflict, arbitration and issues of discipline.

Further reading

Van Ruysseveldt, Huiskamp and van Hoof's (1995) *Comparative Industrial & Employment Relations*, translated from the Dutch, provides an excellent view of modern employee relations across (mostly) northern Europe. Blyton and Turnbull's (1994) *The Dynamics of Employee Relations* is unusual in setting out to give an interesting account of British employee relations and actually achieving the goal. Hayes (1991) *Interpersonal Skills: Goal-directed Behaviour at Work* provides a summary of the qualities required by the good negotiator.

Review questions

1 What are the key differences between unitarist and pluralist views of employee relations?
2 What is meant by the employment relationship? To what extent is it reasonable to say that employee relations should encompass all employment relationships?
3 Discuss the view that employee relations is an outmoded concept which has no place in organizations managed according to the principles of HRM.
4 To what degree are the institutions and methods of British employee relations distinct from the European norm?
5 Are works councils a handicap or a benefit to business efficiency?
6 What purposes can be served by industrial tribunals?
7 What qualities are required by skilled negotiators?
8 Is conflict healthy in a working organization?

Problems for discussion and analysis

1 Middletown Council covers a large urban area bordered by open country. Most of its 300 staff are located in the main office complex, Delta House, located in the old town centre. A new shopping mall has opened immediately between the council offices and the old market, transforming a derelict area into a fashionable district. The staff are delighted since they now work in a pleasant and prestigious locality with a massive choice of shops and eating places nearby.

   The council has been re-elected after promising a considerable improvement in services. However, all available funds have been devoted to maintaining things as they are. After much debate the councillors have decided that costs could be cut dramatically by renting out Delta House to a commercial firm and transferring the staff to much cheaper accommodation at the edge of town. The savings could be used to pay for the new services promised in the election.

The staff are unionized and have a reputation for resisting changes, no matter how small. How would you advise the council to proceed?

2   Euro Vehicles manufactures vans and other light commercial vehicles. Due to severe competition and a declining market, the workforce has been reduced from 11,300 to 2,800 in the last three years and the remaining employees are fearful of further redundancy. There are three unions in the two remaining plants, representing clerical, engineering and supervisory staff. Partly as a result of the recent cuts they are all suspicious of management intentions. Management is authoritarian, based on a rigid departmental structure, and values technical competence and seniority over anything else. Most of the managers have been promoted from the engineering and production side of the company and are in their forties and fifties.

The company's production is largely devoted to basic van models built to a 15-year-old design and sold to large utility companies at a very keen price. Marketing is almost non-existent and the Research and Development department was closed as a cost-cutting measure three years ago. The company is currently owned by a large conglomerate which left the management alone until recently but with strict, detailed financial controls. Consequently, the company has been consistently profitable, but with a shrinking level of production and increasingly outdated manufacturing equipment. The conglomerate has decided that this 'hands-off' approach is no longer satisfactory. It is prepared to make a major investment but only if it can be convinced that this will be effectively managed.

You have been brought in as a consultant to look at the current organization and to recommend changes which would improve the situation. How would you go about this? What are the implications for employee relations?

13

Conclusion

This section provides a final overview of the status and significance of HRM. We examine evidence for its adoption and influence in modern business.

We began this volume with an analysis of the concept of HRM. We found that interpretations of human resource management range from formal models to comparatively loose portrayals of the territory with which HRM should be concerned. There is general agreement on its underlying philosophy, linking people management to business objectives in a strategic, integrated and coherent way. Beyond that, however, commentators and practitioners interpret HRM in different ways, depending on personal agendas and vested interests. As a result HRM ranges from soft, humanistic attempts to win over staff and achieve heartfelt commitment, to hard-nosed extraction of maximum effort at minimum cost.

Given that HRM is manifested in diverse and sometimes contradictory ways, how prevalent is it? We can ask the following questions:

- Has HRM been **meaningfully** implemented and, if so, to what extent?
- What form does this take?
- Who are the principal driving forces?
- Is HRM here to stay and, if not, what next?

Regardless of the rationale or the nature of its practice, HRM has become a common label for various forms and functions of people management (Blyton and Turnbull 1992; Storey 1995). In English-speaking countries, the term has replaced 'personnel management' in many contexts. For example, academic courses, journals and textbooks which were formerly 'personnel management' are now described as 'human resource management'. However, and particularly at practitioner level, relabelling does not necessarily mean that either the approach or the content has changed (Sisson 1995: 87). The diverse interpretations of HRM are apparent when we compare practice in different countries and organizations. We noted earlier that 'personnel' and 'human resources' can co-exist, and many organizations throughout the developed world follow North American practice, using the terms interchangeably.

Although the label is common, there is little evidence that the original models of HRM have had much influence. Blyton and Turnbull argue that 'the rhetoric has outstripped the reality' (1992: vii). Studies in the UK, for example, show that its introduction has been a slow process (Guest and Hoque 1993). Often it is nothing more than a cosmetic exercise, changing the nameplate on the Personnel office door to Human Resources:

> in the UK, there is widespread agreement that, in one way or another, the adoption of HRM has so far been limited: limited to a small number of (largely foreign-owned) 'exemplar' companies; limited in the sense of organizations adopting HRM in a very partial and piecemeal way; and limited in many cases to a mere re-labelling of existing activity and positions.
>
> (Blyton and Turnbull 1992: 1)

The implementation of HRM

Since the nature of human resource management remains a matter of debate, it is scarcely surprising that practitioners interpret it in a variety of ways. Some organizations have taken pragmatic, local initiatives based on specific problems and solutions developed by their own managers. Others have sought guidance and advice from consultants, academics and professional associations. In either case, it is relevant to ask if it is a prescriptive, ideal model of people management or simply a description of 'leading-edge' reality in competitive organizations? (Beardwell and Holden 1994: 17).

Part of the confusion comes from the indistinct boundaries between HRM and a plethora of other fashionable management programmes. Often HRM is used as a label for a collection of different people management techniques, described by Legge as 'symbiotic buzz-words' (1995a: 34). A specific people management initiative may be regarded as HRM or, alternatively, bundled up with total quality management, customer care, business process re-engineering, and so on.

Recent years have seen an increasing momentum in the implementation of radical management developments. Managers may use a number of simultaneous initiatives without any real awareness or understanding that they are part of 'HRM'. Indeed, a small study of major organizations produced evidence of 'strategic HRM' being applied, but none of them used the term! (M. Armstrong 1994).

> One cannot help but be impressed by the widespread awareness among practitioners of such experimentation; meetings with managers at all levels even in conventional mainstream organizations soon reveal the fact that current 'flavours' have permeated the managerial consciousness and imagination in a way that was never the case with, for example, OD [organizational development], job enrichment, QWL [quality of working life] and other much-vaunted 'movements' of previous decades which some critics cite as equivalents.
>
> (Storey 1989: 1)

Many of these concepts are presented as 'quick fixes' which are found to be attractive by senior managers, with little time before objectives have to be achieved or contracts run out.

The driving forces of HRM

Whether as a label or a variable combination of specific initiatives, we can justifiably ask if the uptake of HRM has been driven by practitioners – people involved in practical people management – and then attracted wider attention, or if it is the creation of academics and consultants, with some (and only some) practitioners following on. What is apparent is that the practitioners involved in the introduction of HRM are often line or general managers rather than personnel managers. Clearly, there are many 'stakeholders' in HRM. These include managerialists, senior managers, academics and the personnel profession.

Managerialists

Management power increased significantly in the 1980s, especially in English-speaking countries with New Right governments. Keenoy calls HRM 'a deliberate and brilliant ambiguity' (1990: 371), suspecting a hidden political agenda arising from right-wing government policies. This perspective sees HRM as a reflection of Thatcherite and Reaganite policies which were translated into a wave of managerialism, first in industry and then in the public sector.

Certainly, it is evident that politicians take a particular interest in people management when its development affects their view of society. At a 'macro' level, as we observed in Chapter 2, this is illustrated by such examples as the UK Conservative government's hostility to European 'social protection' laws and Singapore's strict employment legislation. The UK is following some of the same trends as other European countries (see Table 13.1). But managerialism's new legitimacy is most clearly seen in

Table 13.1 Human resource trends in Europe

Trends in common	Higher profile for the human resource management function
	Greater sharing of HRM responsibilities with line managers
	Focus on training and development
	Increasing variability in pay
	Slow but clear decentralization of pay determination (and other aspects of HRM)
	Lesser focus on trade unions
	More and wider communication with employees through a range of channels
	Greater flexibility in employment practices
Continued variation	Trade union recognition
	Employee participation
	Equal opportunities
	State regulation

Source: adapted from Hegewisch and Brewster (1993).

the public sector, where government has imposed 'market conditions' and new management structures. Ironically, business concepts such as HRM have been adopted most widely in organizations which are not true 'businesses' at all.

Senior managers

The strategic nature of HRM, conventionally owned and driven from the top, has been of great interest to senior managers. It is compatible with the power needs of top managers who want the reins in their own hands. In effect, HRM is part of the fashionable 'ideas industry' which fuels modern management. In our discussion of the management of change we saw that HRM has been associated with programmes such as TQM, culture change, downsizing and business process re-engineering. Ideas for increasing the effectiveness of business management come and go in a constant stream. Management education and the writings of management gurus both provide ideas and legitimize their adoption. The concepts they spawn flow in tidal waves across the face of industry. Managerial behaviour follows current fads, conforming to each change in fashion as if they were skirt lengths or hairstyles.

Senior executives do not have a consistent view of HRM – any more than they have a shared understanding of management. Many do not perceive any distinction between general management and managing people. Even less do they wish to be involved with fine academic distinctions between different models of HRM: 'As chief executive I have to have the organization I want, and if it doesn't marry up with any particular model that the world of HRM has thrown up, well, too bad' (quoted in M. Armstrong 1994). The actual 'doing' of HRM is passed to middle managers, who are responsible for its implementation and can be held (conveniently) accountable for any failures. People policies and practices must be integrated and coherent for HRM to be effective, but this division of labour leads to a significant weakness: it offers scope for a dislocation between strategic intentions and the conduct of people management at ground level.

Academics

Market forces have given academics an added interest in HRM (Townley 1994: 22; Legge 1995a: 48). With the reduction in the perceived importance of industrial relations due to government action in a number of countries, academics have had to look elsewhere for research funding and new courses to teach. HRM offers an opportunity for people interested in work psychology and industrial sociology to continue with the subjects that interest them – but under a more marketable label. Townley, for example, regards academics as 'participant constructors' rather than neutral observers. In her view HRM has been 'constructed' as a discipline in order to attract (often private) finance to investigate a new phenomenon – HRM itself – which appears to meet the requirements of flexibility and the free market. HRM has become an academic cottage industry, churning out degree courses, collected papers, journals, texts and professorial chairs. Paradoxically, some of the most successful products of this industry have been attempts to 'deconstruct' the contradictions and rhetoric of HRM itself (Legge 1995a: 49)!

The personnel profession

Personnel practitioners have long held ambiguous views on the subject of HRM. Opinion in the profession has swung between various extremes:

- **Ignore it.** It will go away. It's just another fad, which will be replaced by another soon enough.
- **Embrace it.** It will give us prestige. We can repackage personnel management as a marketing exercise. Lots more money.
- **Believe in it.** Always a minority position. People are **really** the most valuable resources? So how come I 'm not paid as much as the finance manager?
- **Live with it.** OK, so it's an American import, a fad and something economists will never understand. But it gives me a bit more clout right now.

Generally, the human resources label has been presented as a move from a personnel (low-status) to a central (high-status) function. In France, for example, the personnel function was viewed as an inferior management role to be avoided by aspiring *grandes écoles* graduates. Recently, however, status has grown, together with changes in title from *'chef du personnel'* to *'responsable des relations sociales'* and now *'directeur des ressources humaines'* (Barsoux and Lawrence 1990: 70).

How typical are these jobs? Millward *et al.* (1992) found that a mere 1 per cent of UK specialists used 'human resource' in their titles. However, casual examination of quality newspapers as far afield as Britain, New Zealand and South Africa indicates fairly common use of the term 'human resource management' in job advertisements, suggesting that this study may be misleading. In general, the term is more commonly used in larger organizations – particularly multinationals – and by senior rather than junior staff. In terms of status, Marginson *et al.* (1993a) found that only 30 per cent of respondent organizations in their UK survey had a full-time human resource (or personnel) director on the main board. Organizations with overseas headquarters were more likely (54 per cent) to do so. Marginson *et al.* saw no relationship between board-status and organizational size or structure. It appears to be down to company history and the personal beliefs of the chief executive and non-executive directors.

Moreover, change initiatives – particularly business process re-engineering – frequently lead to a questioning of the need for any personnel or human resource specialists. Storey (1995: 384) finds this to be a common theme at consultant-organized conferences. Of course, this is consistent with HRM models which place the responsibility for people management in the hands of line managers. Together with marketing and research, it is difficult to measure the effect that HR specialists have on the wellbeing of a company. Paperwork-obsessed personnel administrators ignorant of wider business issues do not help. They make ripe targets for short-termists working to 'zero-based budgeting' and city analysts with no industrial experience.

The impact of HRM

Is there any evidence that the implementation of HRM has a significant effect on national or organizational economic performance? After all, this is the justification implicit in HRM models for valuing the human resource above all others. At the moment, we must conclude that we simply do not know. There are several reasons for this state of affairs:

- **Insufficient research.** This is due not so much to lack of effort as to the absence of clear, agreed frameworks within which to conduct comparative research. The root cause of this is HRM's own ambiguity. How can we look for evidence of HRM and its effects if we have no agreement on what it is?
- **Intangibility.** If people are an 'intangible resource' we have an insurmountable problem – by definition intangibles are unmeasurable!
- **Confusion with other management initiatives.** We have observed already that it is difficult to untangle the effects of true 'HRM' from those of other strategic initiatives. HRM is accompanied almost invariably by other packaged programmes such as TQM.
- **Situational effects.** HRM has not been implemented uniformly. It is found mainly in specific areas. In private industry, it has been adopted by large, sophisticated and often non-unionized organizations. These businesses have particular characteristics which are appropriate for HRM. The classic examples of success come from greenfield sites, which provide a 'clean slate' with no previous practices or cultural history to prevent management action. HRM may not be appropriate in firms which have strong unions or depend on a low-skilled workforce (Hollinshead and Leat 1995: 319).

Unfortunately, what is clear is that the central tenet of 'soft' HRM – the belief that employees are valuable assets and not just costs – is rarely translated into action. The practices associated with HRM are often introduced for reasons of expediency rather than any serious belief in its principles. Indeed, it is arguable that the practice of HRM is rife with hypocrisy and rhetoric. Many organizations in free-market countries feel that competitive forces make it impossible to commit themselves to their employees. People management in these firms is firmly focused on cost-cutting. A conflict arises from the inherent contradiction between typical HRM themes such as encouraging long-term employee commitment and short-term cost-effectiveness. Employees are the people who are left:

> to make sense of the paradoxes and mixed messages with which they are faced, who try to understand the underlying message of customer delight when no attempt is made to provide them with the skills necessary to deliver

it, who are rewarded and promoted for delivering short-term financial targets and who see the people who try hardest to understand customers' needs penalised for the time they take to do so.

(Gratton, *Financial Times: Mastering Management*, 1995)

This leads to the question of whether HRM is no more than a matter of fine words. Employees quickly learn to mistrust official rhetoric and instead practise the art of 'sense-making': looking for cues which indicate the route to success, or at least survival. Informal messages are transmitted by means of the choice of people who are rewarded and those whose skills are developed. For example, large-scale redundancies determined at short notice by senior managers have followed soothing statements about the importance of human resources to an organization's future.

A Harris survey of 1,000 employees in the UK, reported at the 1995 conference of the Institute of Personnel and Development (IPD), found that this fundamental breach of the 'psychological contract' has led to considerable worker dissatisfaction. According to Ewart Wooldridge, IPD vice-president on employee relations: 'All too often the guru-speak about empowerment has been used as an excuse to heap more work on people, rather than offering any genuine influence in how a business is run' (*Guardian*, 27 October 1995). The traditional psychological contract between employers and employees offered relative job security and a career structure in return for loyalty and commitment. The employers' part of the bargaining was no longer on offer in many of the organizations surveyed. As a consequence, the survey found that two-thirds of employees felt they were expected to work harder, but 42 per cent felt negative or indifferent about going to work; 44 per cent described relationships between management and workers as poor or, at best, fair.

What next?

Are people managers on a constant treadmill? Can we expect a never-ending succession of fashionable ideas? There are enough up-and-coming authors and consultants to drive the process. Some of them have been generated by the ideas industry itself: a generation of middle managers evicted by downsizing and delayering. At the same time there are a few hopeful signs of disillusion with simplistic approaches – a call for pragmatism which recognizes the complexities involved in managing people. But 'pragmatic management' implies experience, expertise and common sense. It sounds boring. It is not likely to satisfy the ambitious. Sooner or later, HRM will find itself replaced by a new flavour of the month.

In the past, new management concepts have generally come from North America. However, this is not a sanctified rule. The worldwide economy is changing, with ever-stronger regional groupings challenging individual nation-states in importance. East Asia and the European Union appear destined to be major influences at the beginning of the twenty-first century and neither is dominated by US-style free-market ideas. Whereas American concepts reign in business schools, people are being managed increasingly through methods forged within different cultural ideologies.

If the collectivist traditions of the east and the Social Chapter of the EU can foster philosophies of people management which value employees more than the 'hard HRM' of the free market, so much the better. Only time will tell.

Further reading

For advanced students, *Human Resource Management: A Critical Text*, edited by Storey (1995), provides an excellent survey of the field. The contributors are acknowledged experts and each chapter reviews a specific topic critically. Legge's (1995b) *Human Resource Management: Rhetorics and Realities* takes a personal and critical view on the subject and is also well worth reading.

References

ACAS (1987) *Discipline at Work: The ACAS Advisory Handbook*, Advisory Conciliation and Arbitration Service.

ACAS (1990) *Appraisal Related Pay*, ACAS Advisory Booklet no. 14, Advisory, Conciliation and Arbitration Service.

Adams, A. (1992) *Bullying at Work*, Virago Press.

Adams, K. (1991) 'Externalisation vs specialisation: what is happening to personnel?', *Human Resource Management Journal* 1(4): 40–54.

Akinnusi, D. (1991) 'Personnel management in Africa', in C. Brewster and S. Tyson (eds) *International Comparisons in Human Resource Management*, Pitman.

Allen, N. J. and Meyer, M. P. (1990) 'The measurement of antecedents of affective, continuance and normative commitment to the organisation', *Journal of Occupational Psychology* 63: 1–8.

Amoroso, B. (1990) 'Development and crisis of the Scandinavian model of labour relations in Denmark', in G. Baglioni and C. Crouch (eds) *European Industrial Relations: The Challenge of Flexibility*, Sage.

Andrisani, P. and Nestel, G. (1976) 'Internal–external control as contributor to and outcome of work experience', *Journal of Applied Psychology* 61: 156–65.

Ansoff, H. I. (1968) *Corporate Strategy*, Penguin.

Argyle, M. (1989) *The Social Psychology of Work*, 2nd edition, Penguin.

Argyle, M. (1991) *Cooperation: The Basis of Sociability*, Routledge.

Argyris, C. (1957) *Personality and Organization*, Harper & Row.

Argyris, C. and Taylor, G. (1951) 'The member-centered conference as a research method, II', *Human Organization* 10(1) (spring): 22–7.

Armstrong, M. (1987) 'Human resource management: a case of the emperor's new clothes?', *Personnel Management* (August): 31–4.

Armstrong, M. (1992) *Human Resource Management: Strategy and Action*, Kogan Page.

Armstrong, M. (1994) 'The reality of strategic HRM', paper presented at the Strategic Direction of Human Resource Management Conference, Nottingham Trent University, 14–15 December.

Armstrong, P. (1995) 'Accountancy and HRM', in J. Storey (ed.) *Human Resource Management: A Critical Text*, Routledge.

Arnold, J., Robertson, I. T., and Cooper, C. L. (1991) *Work Psychology*, Pitman.

Ashton, D. and Felstead, A. (1995) 'Training and development', in J. Storey (ed.) *Human Resource Management: A Critical Text*, Routledge.

Atkinson, J. (1984) 'Manpower strategies for flexible organisations', *Personnel Management* (August): 28–31.

Barsoux, J.-L. and Lawrence, P. (1990) *Management in France*, Cassell.

Bartram, D. (1991) 'Addressing the abuse of psychological tests', *Personnel Management* (April): 34–9.

Beardwell, I. and Holden, L. (eds) (1994) *Human Resource Management: A Contemporary Perspective*, Pitman.

Beattie, D. F. and Tampoe, T. F. (1990) 'Human resource planning for ICL', *Long Range Planning* 23(1).

Beaumont, P. B. (1992) 'The US human resource management literature: a review', in G. Salaman (ed.) *Human Resource Strategies*, Sage.

Becker, G. S. (1965) 'A theory of the allocation of time', *Economic Journal* 75(299): 493–517.

Beer M., Spector B., Lawrence, P. R., Quinn-Mills, D. and Walton, R. G. (1984) *Managing Human Assets*, Free Press.

Belbin, M. (1993) *Team Roles at Work*, Butterworth-Heinemann.

Ben-Tovim, G., Gabriel, J., Law, I. and Stredder, K. (1992) 'A political analysis of local struggles for racial equality', in P. Braham, A. Rattansi and R. Skellington (eds) *Racism and Antiracism*, Sage.

Bertsch, B. and Williams, R. (1994) 'How multinational CEOs make change programmes stick', *Long Range Planning* 27(5) (October): 12–24.

Bevan, S. and Thompson, M. (1992) *Merit Pay, Performance Appraisals and Attitudes to Women's Work*, IMS Publications.

Blanksby, M. and Iles, P. (1990) 'Recent developments in assessment centre theory, practice and operation', *Personnel Review* 19(6): 33–42.

Blau, P. M. and Schoenherr, R. A. (1971) *The Structure of Organizations*, Basic Books.

Bleicher, K. (1994) 'Integrative management in a time of transformation', *Long Range Planning* 27(5) (October): 136–44.

Bloom, A. (1987) *The Closing of the American Mind*, Penguin.

Blyton, P. and Turnbull, P. (1992) *Reassessing Human Resource Management*, Sage.

Blyton, P. and Turnbull, P. (1994) *The Dynamics of Employee Relations*, Macmillan.

Bourantas, D. and Papalexandris, N. (1990) 'Sex differences in leadership: leadership styles and subordinate satisfaction', *Journal of Managerial Psychology* 5: 7–10.

Bowen, W. A. and Finegan, T. A. (1969) *The Economics of Labor Force Participation*, Princeton University Press.

Bower, M. (1966) *The Will to Manage*, McGraw-Hill.

Boyatzis, R. E. (1982) *The Competent Manager*, John Wiley & Sons.

Brading, E. and Wright, V. (1990) 'Performance-related pay', *Personnel Management* Factsheet, June.

Braham, R., Rattansi, A. and Skellington, R. (eds) (1992) *Racism and Antiracism*, Sage.

Braverman, H. (1974) *Labor and Monopoly Capital: The Degradation of Work in the Twentieth Century*, Monthly Review Press.

Breakwell, G. M. (1990) *Interviewing*, BPS/Routledge.

Brewster, C. (1994) 'European HRM: reflection of, or challenge to, the American concept?', in P. S. Kirkbride (ed.) *Human Resource Management in Europe: Perspectives for the 1990s*, Routledge.

Brewster, C. (1995) 'HRM: the European dimension', in J. Storey (ed.) *Human Resource Management: A Critical Text*, Routledge.

Brewster, C. and Bournois, F. (1991) 'A European Perspective on Human Resource Management', *Personnel Review* 20(6).

Brewster, C. and Larsen, H. H. (1993) 'Human resource management in Europe: evidence from ten countries', in A. Hegewisch and C. Brewster (eds) *European Developments in Human Resource Management*, Kogan Page.

Brewster, C. and Tyson, S. (eds) (1991) *International Comparisons in Human Resource Management*, Pitman.

Briggs, P. (1991) 'Organisational commitment: the key to Japanese success', in C. Brewster and S. Tyson (eds) *International Comparisons in Human Resource Management*, Pitman.

Brown, W. (1994) *Bargaining for Full Employment*, Employment Policy Institute.

Brunsson, N. (1989) *The Organization of Hypocrisy: Talk, Decisions and Action in Organizations*, Wiley.

Bryman, A. (1992) *Charisma and Leadership in Organizations*, Sage.

Buchanan, D. and Boddy, D. (1992) *The Expertise of the Change Agent*, Prentice-Hall.

Bunge, M. and Ardila, R. (1987) *Philosophy of Psychology*, Springer-Verlag.

Burke, G. and Peppard, J. (eds) (1995) *Examining Business Process Re-engineering: Current Perspectives and Research Directions*, Kogan Page.

Burns, P. and Dewhurst, I. (eds) (1989) *Small Business and Entrepreneurship*, Macmillan.

Burns, T. and Stalker, G. M. (1961) *The Management of Innovation*, Tavistock Publications.

Butler, R. (1991) *Designing Organizations: A Decision-Making Perspective*, Routledge.

Byham, W. (1984) 'Assessing employees without resorting to a "centre"', *Personnel Management* 55 (October).

Campbell, J. P., Dunnette, M., Lawler, E. and Weick, K. (1970) *Managerial Behavior, Performance and Effectiveness*, McGraw-Hill.

Carnall, C. (1991) *Managing Change*, Routledge.

Chandler, A. (1962) *Strategy and Structure*, MIT Press.

Checkland, P. B. (1981) *Systems Thinking, Systems Practice*, John Wiley.

Chung, T. Z. (1991) 'Culture: a key to management communication between the Asian-Pacific area and Europe', *European Management Journal* 9(4) (December): 419–24.

Claydon, T. (1994) 'Human resource management and the labour market', in I. Beardwell and L. Holden (eds) *Human Resource Management: A Contemporary Perspective*, Pitman.

Cole, W., Shears, P. and Tiley, J. (1990) *Law in a Business Context*, Chapman & Hall.

Commission of the EC, (1992) 'Community charter of the fundamental social rights of workers', *Social Europe* 1/92 (Brussels): 7–11.

Cooke, S. and Slack, N. (1991) *Making Management Decisions,* 2nd edition, Prentice-Hall.

Cox, J. and Tapsell, J. (1991) 'The writing on the wall graphology and its validity in personality assessments', paper presented at the British Psychological Society Conference, Cardiff.

Cressey, P. (1993) 'Employee participation', in M. Gold (ed.) (1993) *The Social Dimension: Employment Policy in the European Community*, Macmillan.

Crittan, P. (1993) *Investing in People: Towards Corporate Capability*, Butterworth-Heinemann.

Crofts, A. (1991) 'Learning to lead', *Management Today* 68 (June).

Curran, J. and Stanworth, J. (1988) 'The small firm – a neglected area of management', in A. G. Cowling, M. J. K. Stanworth, R. D. Bennett, J. Curran and P. Lyons *Behavioural Sciences for Managers*, 2nd edition, Edward Arnold.

Daft, R. L. (1989) *Organization Theory and Design*, 2nd edition, West Publishing Co.

Davidson, M. J. and Earnshaw, J. (1991) 'Policies, practices and attitudes towards sexual harassment in UK organisations', *Women in Management Review & Abstracts* 6(6): 15–21.

Dawson, P. (1994) *Organizational Change: A Processual Approach*, Paul Chapman Publishing.

Deal, T. and Kennedy, A. (1982) *Corporate Cultures: The Rites and Rituals of Corporate Life*, Addison-Wesley.

Dominelli, L. (1992) 'An uncaring profession: an examination of racism in social work', in P. Braham, A. Rattansi and R. Skellington (eds) *Racism and Antiracism: Inequalities, Opportunities and Policies*, Sage in association with the Open University Press.

Drenth, P. (1978) 'Personnel selection', in P. B. Warr (ed.) *Psychology at Work*, 2nd edition, Penguin.

Drucker, P. F. (1954) *The Practice of Management*, Harper & Row.

Due, J., Madsen, J. S. and Jense, C. S. (1991) 'The social dimension: convergence or diversification of industrial relations in the Single European Market?', *Industrial Relations Journal* 22(2) (summer): 85–102.

Dulewicz, V. (1991) 'Improving assessment centres', *Personnel Management* (June): 50–5.

Eccles, A. (1989) 'Brief case: if we're so smart, why are they winning?', *Long Range Planning* (October): 144–6.

Eiser, J. R. (1994) *Attitudes, Chaos and the Connectionist Mind*, Blackwell.

English, G. (1991) 'Tuning up for performance management', *Training & Development Journal* (April).

Fayol, H. (1949) *General Industrial Management*, Pitman.

Filella, J. (1991) 'Is there a Latin model in the management of human resources', *Personnel Review* 20(6): 15–24.

Flanders, A. (1970) *Management and Unions*, Faber & Faber.

Flanders, M. L. (1994) *Breakthrough: The Career Woman's Guide to Shattering the Glass Ceiling*, Paul Chapman Publishing.

Fleishman, E. A. and Quaintance, M. K.(1984) *Taxonomies of Human Performance*, Academic Press.

Fletcher, C. and Williams, R. (1992) 'The route to performance management', *Personnel Management* (October): 42–7.

Foley, P. (1989) 'Small business success – a market survey', in P. Foley and H. Green (eds) *Small Business Success*, Paul Chapman Publishing.

Foley, P. and Green, H. (eds) (1989) *Small Business Success*, Paul Chapman Publishing.

Fossum, J. and Fitch, M. (1985) 'The effects of individual and contextual attributes on the sizes of recommended salary increases', *Personnel Psychology* 38 (autumn): 587–602.

Fowler, A. (1987) 'When chief executives discover HRM', *Personnel Management* (January): 3.

Fowler, A. (1991) 'How to identify training needs', *Personnel Management Plus* (November): 22.

Fowler, A. (1993) 'How to manage cultural change', *Personnel Management Plus* (November): 25–6.

French, W. L. and Bell, C. H. (1990) *Organization Development: Behavioral Science Interventions for Organization Improvement*, 4th edition, Prentice-Hall.

Furnham, A. (1990) *The Protestant Work Ethic: The Psychology of Work-related Beliefs and Behaviours*, Routledge.

Furnham, A. (1992) *Personality at Work*, Routledge.

Galbraith, J. K. (1967) *The New Industrial State*, Hamish Hamilton.

Garfield, S. (1994) *The End of Innocence: Britain in the Time of AIDS*, Faber & Faber.

Garrahan, P. and Stewart, P. (1992) *The Nissan Enigma: Flexibility at Work in the Local Economy*, Mansell.

Garvin, D. (1993) 'Building a learning organization', *Harvard Business Review* (July–August): 78–91.

Gaugler, E. (1988) 'HR management: an international comparison', *Personnel* (August): 24–30.

Giddens, A. (1989) *Sociology*, Polity Press.

Giles, E. and Williams, R. (1991) 'Can the personnel department survive quality management?', *Personnel Management* (April).

Glover, J. (1988) *I: The Philosophy and Psychology of Personal Identity*, Penguin.

Gold, M. (1993) 'Overview of the social dimension', in M. Gold (ed.) *The Social Dimension: Employment Policy in the European Community*, Macmillan.

Goss, D. (1994) *Principles of Human Resource Management*, Routledge.

Gouldner, A. W. (1954) *Patterns of Industrial Bureaucracy*, Free Press.

Graham, H. T and Bennett, R. (1992) *Human Resources Management*, 7th edition, M&E Handbook Series, Pitman.

Griffin, R. W. and Bateman, T. S. (1986) 'Job satisfaction and organizational commitment', in C. L. Cooper and I. T. Robertson (eds) *International Review of Industrial and Organizational Psychology, 1986*, John Wiley.

Grint, K. (1995) 'Utopian re-engineering', in G. Burke and J. Peppard (eds) *Examining Business Process Re-engineering: Current Perspectives and Research Directions*, Kogan Page.

Guest, D. (1987) 'Human resource management and industrial relations', *Journal of Management Studies* 24(5): 503–21.

Guest, D. (1989) 'Personnel and HRM: can you tell the difference?', *Personnel Management* (January): 48–51.

Guest, D. (1992) 'Right enough to be dangerously wrong: an analysis of the *In Search of Excellence* phenomenon', in G. Salaman (ed.) *Human Resource Strategies*, Sage.

Guest, D. (1993) 'Current perspectives on human resource management in the United Kingdom', in C. Brewster (ed.) *Current Trends in Human Resource Management in Europe*, Kogan Page.

Guest, D. (1995) 'Human resource management, trade unions and industrial relations', in J. Storey (ed.) *Human Resource Management: A Critical Text*, Routledge.

Guest, D. and Hoque, K. (1993) 'The mystery of the missing human resource manager', *Personnel Management* (June): 40–1.

Guha, K. (1995) 'Management training', *Career Choice* (Financial Times Guide): 22.

Gunz, H. (1990) 'The dual meaning of managerial careers: organizational and individual levels of analysis', *Journal of Management Studies* 26 (May): 3.

Haire, M. (1959) 'Psychological problems relevant to business and industry', *Psychological Bulletin* 56: 169–94.

Haire, M., Ghiselli, E. E. and Porter, L. W. (1966) *Managerial Thinking: An International Study*, John Wiley.

Hamblin, A. C. (1974) *Evaluation and Control of Training*, McGraw-Hill.

Hammer, M. (1990) 'Re-engineering work: don't automate, obliterate', Harvard Business Review (November–December): 119–31.

Hammer, M. and Champy, J. (1993) *Reengineering the Corporation: A Manifesto for Business Revolution*, Harper Business.

Hammond, V. (1993) 'Women and development', *Training and Development* (December): 10–11.

Handy, C. (1989) *The Age of Unreason*, Business Books.

Handy, C. (1993) *Understanding Organizations*, 4th edition, Penguin.

Hart, T. J. (1993) 'Human resource management: time to exorcise the militant tendency', *Employee Relations* 15(3): 29–36.

Hayes, J. (1991) *Interpersonal Skills: Goal-directed Behaviour at Work*, HarperCollins.

Hayes, J. and Nutman, P. (1981) *Understanding the Unemployed: The Psychological Effects of Unemployment*, Tavistock Publications.

Heasman, K. (1993) 'The case against ageism', *NATFHE Journal* (autumn): 28.

Hegewisch, A. and Brewster, C. (1993) *European Developments in Human Resource Management*, Kogan Page.

Heilbroner, R. L. (1953) *The Worldly Philosopher*, Simon & Schuster.

Helman, C. G. (1990) *Culture, Health and Illness*, 2nd edition, Butterworth-Heinemann.

Hendry, C. (1994a) 'The Single European Market and the HRM response', in P. S. Kirkbride (ed.) *Human Resource Management in Europe: Perspectives for the 1990s*, Routledge.

Hendry, C. (1994b) 'Developing a human resources strategy: a case study in organizational process', paper presented at the Strategy Direction of Human Resource Management Conference, Nottingham Trent University, 14–15 December.

Hendry, C. (1995) *Human Resource Management: A Strategic Approach to Employment*, Butterworth-Heinemann.

Herbert, T. and Jones, G. E. (eds) (1995) *Post-war Wales*, University of Wales Press.

Herriot, P. and Fletcher, C. (1990) 'Candidate-friendly selection for the 1990s', *Personnel Management* (February): 32–5.

Hewitson, J. (1996) *Clinging to the Edge*, Mainstream Publishing.

Hinton, P. R. (1993) *The Psychology of Interpersonal Perception*, Routledge.

Hoerr, J. (1991) 'What should unions do?', *Harvard Business Review* (May–June): 30–45.

Hofstede, G. (1980) *Culture's Consequences: International Differences in Work-related Values*, Sage.

Hofstede, G. (1994) *Cultures and Organizations*, HarperCollins (amended paperback edition of the 1991 McGraw-Hill publication).

Hofstede, G. and Bond, M. H. (1988) 'The Confucius connection: from cultural roots to economic growth', *Organizational Dynamics* 16(4): 4–21.

Hollinsead, G. and Leat, M. (1995) *Human Resource Management: An International and Comparative Perspective*, Pitman.

Hood, C. (1986) *Administrative Analysis: An Introduction to Rules, Enforcement and Organisations*, Wheatsheaf.

Hornaday, R. W. (1990) 'Dropping the E-word from small business research', *Journal of Small Business Research* (October): 22–33.

Howitt, D. and Owusu-Bempah, J. (1990) 'Racism in a British journal', *Psychologist* (September): 396–9.

Hoxie, R. F. (1923) *Trade Unionism in the United States*, 2nd edition, Appleton-Century Crofts; reproduced in W. E. J. McCarthy (ed.) (1972) *Trade Unions*, Penguin.

Huczynski, A. and Buchanan, D. (1991) *Organizational Behaviour*, Prentice-Hall.

Hui, C. H. (1988) 'Measurement of individualism–collectivism', *Journal of Research in Personality* 22: 17–36.

Hui, C. H. (1990) 'Work attitudes, leadership styles, and managerial behaviours in different cultures', in R. W. Brislin (ed.) *Applied Cross-cultural Psychology*, Sage.

Humm, M. (1989) *The Dictionary of Feminist Theory*, Harvester Wheatsheaf.

Husband, C. (1991) 'Race, conflictual politics and anti-racist social work: lessons from the past for action in the 90's', in Northern Curriculum Development Project *Setting the Context for Change*, Central Council for Education and Training in Social Work, Leeds.

Husbands, R. (1992) 'Sexual harassment law in employment: an international perspective', *International Labour Review* 131(6): 535–59.

Hyman, R. (1988) 'Flexible specialization: miracle or myth?', in R. Hyman and W. Streek (eds) *New Technology and Industrial Relations*, Blackwell.

Iles, P. and Salaman, G. (1995) 'Recruitment, selection and assessment', in J. Storey (ed.) *Human Resource Management: A Critical Text*, Routledge.

ILO (1995) *World Labour Report 1995*, International Labour Organization.

Jacobi, O. and Muller-Jentsch (1990) 'West Germany: continuity and structural change', in G. Baglioni and C. Crouch (eds) *European Industrial Relations: The Challenge of Flexibility*, Sage.

Jahoda, M. (1982) *Employment and Unemployment: A Social-psychological Analysis*, Cambridge University Press.

Janis, I. L. (1982) *Victims of Groupthink*, Houghton Mifflin.

Jennings, D. and Wattam, S. (1994) *Decision Making: An Integrated Approach*, Pitman.

Jones, M. R. (1995) 'The contradictions of business process re-engineering', in G. Burke and J. Peppard (eds) *Examining Business Process Re-engineering: Current Perspectives and Research Directions*, Kogan Page.

Kahn, H. (1979) *World Economic Development: 1979 and Beyond*, Westview.

Kahneman, D., Knetch, J. L., and Thaler, R. H. (1986) 'Fairness as a constraint of profit-seeking: Entitlements in the market', *American Economic Review* 76: 728–41.

Kanter, R. M. (1984) *The Change Masters*, Simon & Schuster.

Kanter, R. M. (1989) *When Giants Learn to Dance*, Simon & Schuster.

Kaplan, R. E. (1984) 'Trade routes: the manager's network of relationships', *Organizational Dynamics* (spring).

Keenoy, T. (1990) 'HRM: a case of the wolf in sheep's clothing?', *Personnel Review* 19(2): 3–9.

Keenoy, T. and Anthony, P. (1992) 'Metaphor, meaning and morality', in P. Blyton and P. Turnbull (eds) *Reassessing Human Resource Management*, Sage.

Kessler, I. (1995) 'Reward systems', in J. Storey (ed.) *Human Resource Management: A Critical Text*, Routledge.

Kilburn, D. (1993) 'The sun sets Japan's lifers', *Management Today* (September): 45.

Kline, P. (1993) *The Handbook of Psychological Testing*, Routledge.

Kobayashi, N. (1992) 'Japan's global and regional roles', *Business & the Contemporary World* 4(4) (autumn): 18–24.

Kochan, T. and Dyer, L. (1995) 'HRM: an American view', in J. Storey (ed.) *Human Resource Management: A Critical Text*, Routledge.

Kotter, J. P. (1982) 'What effective managers really do', *Harvard Business Review* (November–December).

Kotter, J. P. (1990) 'What leaders really do', *Harvard Business Review* (May–June): 103–11.

Kotter, J. P. and Schlesinger, L. A. (1979) 'Choosing strategies for change', *Harvard Business Review* 57(2): 106–14.

Kram, K. E. (1983) 'Phases of the mentor relationship', *Academy of Management Journal* 26(4).

Kuhn, T. S. (1962) *The Structure of Scientific Revolutions*, Chicago University Press.

Kunda, G. (1991) 'Ritual and the management of corporate culture. A critical perspective', paper presented at the 8th International Standing Conference on Organizational Symbolism, Copenhagen, June.

Labour Market Trends, December 1995, HMSO.

Lawrence, P. (1993) 'Human resource management in Germany', in S. Tyson, P. Lawrence, P. Poirson, L. Manzolini and C. F. Vincente (eds) *Human Resource Management in Europe: Strategic Issues and Cases*, Kogan Page.

Lawton, A. and Rose, A. (1991) *Organisation and Management in the Public Sector*, Pitman.

Leeds, C., Kirkbride, P. S. and Durcan, J. (1994) 'The cultural context of Europe: a tentative mapping', in P. S. Kirkbride (ed.) *Human Resource Management in Europe: Perspectives for the 1990s*, Routledge.

Legge, K. (1989) 'Human resource management: a critical analysis', in J. Storey (ed.) *New Perspectives on Human Resource Management*, Routledge.

Legge, K. (1995a) 'HRM: rhetoric, reality and hidden agendas', in J. Storey (ed.) *Human Resource Management: A Critical Text*, Routledge.

Legge, K. (1995b) *Human Resource Management: Rhetorics and Realities*, Macmillan Business.

Lengnick-Hall, C. A. and Lengnick-Hall, M. L. (1988) 'Strategic HRM – a review of the literature and a proposed typology', *Academy of Management Review* 13(3): 454–70.

Lewis, C. (1985) *Employee Selection*, Hutchinson.

Lewis, P. (1991) 'Eight steps to the successful appointment of a training consultant', *Journal of European Industrial Training* 15(6): 25–9.

Lindbeck, A. and Snower, D. (1988) *The Insider–Outsider Theory of Unemployment and Employment*, MIT Press.

London, M. and Stumpf, S. A. (1984) *Managing Careers*, Addison-Wesley.

Long, P. (1986) *Performance Appraisal Revisited*, Institute of Personnel Management.

Lopes, P. F. (1993) 'Fine-tuning re-engineering with workflow automation, blueprint and tool', *Industrial Engineering* (August): 51–3.

Lustgarten, L. and Edwards, J. (1992) 'Racial inequality and the limits of law', in P. Braham, A. Rattansi and R. Skellington (eds) *Racism and Antiracism*, Sage.

Lyons, P. (1988) 'Social interaction', in A. G. Cowling, M. J. K. Stanworth, R. D. Bennett, J. Curran and P. Lyons *Behavioural Sciences for Managers*, 2nd edition, Edward Arnold.

Mabey, C. and Iles, P. (eds) (1994) *Managing Learning*, Routledge in association with the Open University.

Mabey, W. (1989) 'The majority of large companies use occupational tests', *Guidance and Assessment Review* 5 (3).

McCormick, E. J. and Ilgen, D. (1987) *Industrial and Organizational Psychology*, 8th edition, Unwin Hyman.

McGregor, D. (1960) *The Human Side of Enterprise*, McGraw-Hill.

McIlwee, T. and Roberts, I. (1991) *Human Resources Management*, Elm Publications.

Mackay, J. (1992) 'Tying the knot: the human side of acquisitions', *Human Resources* (autumn): 10–14.

McKenna, E. (1994) *Business Psychology and Organisational Behaviour*, Lawrence Erlbaum Associates.

Margerison, C. (1991) *Making Management Development Work*, McGraw-Hill.

Marginson, P., Edwards, P. K., Armstrong, P. and Purcell, J. (1993a) *Executive Summary of Findings. Second Company Level, Industrial Relations Survey*, Industrial Relations Research Unit (mimeo).

Marginson, P., Edwards, P. K., Armstrong, P., Purcell, J. and Hubbard, N. (1993b) *Report of the Initial Findings from the Second Company-Level Industrial Relations Survey*, Warwick Papers in Industrial Relations, no. 45, University of Warwick.

Marginson, P., Edwards, P., Martin, R., Purcell, J. and Sisson, K. (1988) *Beyond the Workplace: Managing Industrial Relations in the Multi-establishment Enterprise*, Blackwell.

Maslow, A. H. (1954) *Motivation and Personality*, Harper & Row.

Meek, V. L. (1988) 'Organizational culture: origins and weaknesses', *Organization Studies* 9(4): 453–73.

Metcalf, H., Modood, T. and Virdee, S. (1996) *Asian Self-Employment*, Policy Studies Institute.

Miles, R. and Snow, C. (1978) *Organizational Strategy, Structure and Process*, McGraw-Hill.

Miller, A. F., Jr, and Hanson, M. (1991) The smile on the face of a leadership tiger', *Personnel Management* (October): 54–7.

Miller, P. (1989) 'Managing corporate identity in the diversified business', *Personnel Management* (March): 36–9.

Mills, A. J. and Murgatroyd, S. J. (1991) *Organizational Rules: A Framework for Understanding Organizational Action*, Open University.

Millward, N., Stevens, M., Smart, D. and Hawes, W. R. (1992) *Workplace Industrial Relations in Transition*, Dartmouth.

Mintzberg, H. (1973) *The Nature of Managerial Work*, Harper & Row.

Mintzberg, H. (1994) *The Rise and Fall of Strategic Planning*, Prentice-Hall.

Mintzberg, H. and Waters, J. A. (1985) 'Of strategies deliberate and emergent', *Strategic Management Journal* 6: 257–72.

Molander, C. and Winterton, J. (1994) *Managing Human Resources*, Routledge.

Morgan, G. (1986) *Images of Organization*, Sage.

Morris, L. (1987) 'The household in the labour market', in C. C. Harris (ed.) *Redundancy and Recession*, Blackwell.

Mosel, J. N. and Goheen, H. W. (1958) 'The validity of the employment recommendation questionnaire in personnel selection', *Personnel Psychology* 2: 487–90.

Moss, G. (1992) 'Different European perspectives on selection techniques: the case of graphology in business', in Vickerstaff, S. (ed.) *Human Resource Management in Europe: Text and Cases*, Chapman & Hall.

Mowday, R., Steers, R. and Porter, L. (1979) 'The measurement of organizational commitment', *Journal of Vocational Behaviour* 14: 224–47.

Moynahan, B. (1993) 'Creating harassment-free work zones', *Training & Development* (May): 67–70.

Mullins, L. J. (1996) *Management and Organisational Behaviour*, 4th edition, Pitman.

Murliss, H. (1987) 'Performance-related pay in the public sector', *Public Money* (March): 29–33.

Murphy, K. R. (1994) 'Meta-analysis and validity generalization', in N. Anderson and P. Herriot (eds) *Assessment and Selection in Organizations: Methods and Practice for Recruitment and Appraisal*, First Update and Supplement 1994, Wiley.

Murphy, K. R. and Cleveland, J. N. (1995) *Understanding Performance Appraisal: Social, Organizational and Goal-based Perspectives*, Sage.

Neale, A. and Haslam, C. (1994) *Economics in a Business Context*, 2nd edition, Chapman & Hall.

Needle, D. (1994) *Business in Context: An Introduction to Business and its Environment*, 2nd edition, Chapman & Hall.

Nelkin, D. and Tancredi, L. (1989) *Dangerous Diagnostics*, Basic Books.

Noon, M. (1992) 'HRM: a map, model or theory?', in P. Blyton and P. Turnbull (eds) *Reassessing Human Resource Management*, Sage.

Noonan, C. (1985) *Practical Export Management: Developing International Business*, George Allen & Unwin.

Nowack, K. M. (1991) 'A true training needs analysis', *Training & Development Journal* (April): 69–73.

OECD (1991) *Employment Outlook*, OECD.

Offe, C. (1985) *Disorganized Capitalism*, Polity and Blackwell.

Olie, R. (1990) 'Culture and integration problems in international mergers and acquisitions', *European Management Journal* 8(2).

Papalexandris, N. (1991) 'A comparative study of human resource management in selected Greek and foreign-owned subsidiaries in Greece', in C. Brewster and S. Tyson *International Comparisons in Human Resource Management*, Pitman.

Pascale, R.T. (1990) *Managing on the Edge: How Successful Companies Use Conflict to Stay Ahead*, Penguin.

Pascale, R. T. and Athos, A. G. (1981) *The Art of Japanese Management*, Simon & Schuster.

Pedler, M., Boydell, T. H. and Burgoyne, J. G. (1989) 'Towards a learning company', *Management Education and Development* 2(3): 19–41.

Perkins, D. and Snapes, A. (1992) 'Developing the best managers: an assessment centre for general managers in the NHS', in S. Vickerstaff (ed.) *Human Resource Management in Europe: Text and Cases*, Chapman & Hall.

Peters, T. J. (1987) *Thriving on Chaos*, Alfred A. Knopf.

Peters, T. J. and Waterman, R. H. (1982) *In Search of Excellence*, Harper & Row.

Philp, T. (1990) *Appraising Performance for Results*, McGraw-Hill.

Pieper, R. (ed.) (1990) *Human Resource Management: An International Comparison*, de Gruyter.

Pinchot, G. (1985) *Intrapreneuring: Why You Don't Have to Leave the Corporation to Become an Entrepreneur*, Harper & Row.

Poirson, P. (1993) 'The characteristics and dynamics of human resource management in France', in S. Tyson *et al.* (1993) *Human Resource Management in Europe*, Kogan Page.

Poole, M. (1990) 'Editorial: human resource management in an international perspective', *International Journal of Human Resource Management* 1(1) (June): 1–16.

Porter, M. J. (1990) *The Competitive Advantage of Nations*, Free Press.

Pratt, K. J. and Bennett, S. G. (1989) *Elements of Personnel Management*, 1st edition, Chapman & Hall.

Pratt, K. J. and Bennett, S. G. (1990) *Elements of Personnel Management*, 2nd edition, Chapman & Hall.

Prochaska, J. and DiClemente, C. (1986) 'Towards a comprehensive model of change', in W. R. Miller and N. Heather (eds) *Treating Addictive Behaviours: Processes of Change*, Plenum Press.

Purcell, J. (1989) 'The impact of corporate strategy on human resource management', in J. Storey (ed.) *New Perspectives on Human Resource Management*, Routledge.

Purcell, J. (1995) 'Corporate strategy and its link with human resource strategy', in J. Storey (ed.) *Human Resource Management: A Critical Text*, Routledge.

Purcell, J. and Sisson, K. (1983) 'Strategies and practice in the management of industrial relations', in G. S. Bain (ed.) *Industrial Relations in Britain*, Blackwell.

Raelin, J. A. (1985) *The Clash of Cultures: Managers Managing Professionals*, 1st edition, Harvard Business School Press.

Raelin, J. A. (1991) *The Clash of Cultures: Managers Managing Professionals*, 2nd edition, Harvard Business School Press.

Rainbird, H. and Maguire, M. (1993) 'When corporate need supersedes employee development', *Personnel Management* (February): 34–7.

Randlesome, C. (1994) *The Business Culture in Germany*, Butterworth-Heinemann.

Ransom, D. (1994) 'Maquila sunrise', *New Internationalist* 251 (January): 7.

Reichheld, F. F. (1996) *The Loyalty Effect*, Harvard Business School/Bain & Co., Inc.

Revans, R. W. (1972) 'Action learning – a management development programme', *Personnel Review* (autumn).

Rice, A. K., Hull, J. M. and Trist, E. L. (1950) 'The representation of labour turnover as a social process', *Journal of Human Relations* 3.

Robertson, I. T. and Makin, P. J. (1986) 'Management selection in Britain: a survey and critique', *Journal of Occupational Psychology* 59(1).

Rodger, A. (1953) *The Seven Point Plan*, National Institute of Industrial Psychology.

Ronen, S. and Shenkar, O. (1985) 'Clustering countries on attitudinal dimensions: a review and synthesis', *Academy of Management Review* 10(7): 445–54.

Ross, R. and Schneider, R. (1992) *From Equality to Diversity: A Business Case for Equal Opportunities*, Pitman.

Rost, J. and Smith, A. (1992) 'Leadership: a postindustrial approach', *European Management Journal* 10(2): 193–200.

Rothwell, S. (1992) 'The development of the international manager', *Personnel Management* (January): 33–5.

Rousseau, D. M. (1995) *Psychological Contracts in Organizations: Understanding Written and Unwritten Agreements*, Sage.

Russell, C., Mattson, J., Devlin, S. and Atwater, D. (1990) 'Predictive validity of biodata items generated from retrospective life experience essays', *Journal of Applied Psychology* 75: 569–80.

Sadler, P. and Milner, K. (1993) *The Talent-Intensive Organisation: Optimising Your Company's Human Resource Strategies*, Economist Intelligence Unit.

Salaman, G. (ed.) (1992) *Human Resource Strategies*, Sage.

Salaman, G. and Butler, J. (1994) 'Why managers won't learn', in C. Mabey and P. Iles (eds) (1994) *Managing Learning*, Routledge/Open University.

Salancik, G. R. (1977) 'Commitment and control of organizational behavior and beliefs', in B. M. Staw and G. R. Salancik (eds) *New Directions in Organizational Behavior*, St Clair Press.

Sampson, A. (1995) *Company Man: The Rise and Fall of Corporate Life*, HarperCollins.

Sapsford, D. and Tzannatos, Z. (1993) *The Economics of the Labour Market*, Macmillan.

Sayal, A. (1990) 'Black women and mental health', *Psychologist* (January): 24–7.

Scase, R. and Goffee, R. (1990) 'Women in management: towards a research agenda', *International Journal of Human Resource Management* 1(1): 107–25.

Schein, E. H. (1985) *Organizational Culture and Leadership: A Dynamic View*, Jossey-Bass.

Schein, E. H. (1988) *Organizational Psychology*, 3rd edition, Prentice-Hall.

Shackleton, V. and Newell, S. (1991) 'Management selection: a comparative survey of methods used in top British and French companies', *Journal of Occupational Psychology* 64 (March): 23–36.

Simon, H. A. (1955) 'Recent advances in organization theory', *Research Frontiers in Politics and Government*, Brookings Institution, Washington, DC.

Sisson, K. (1990) 'Introducing the *Human Resource Management Journal*', *Human Resource Management Journal* 1(1): 7–24.

Sisson, K. (1995) 'Human resource management and the personnel function', in J. Storey (ed.) *Human Resource Management: A Critical Text*, Routledge.

Sisson, K., Waddington, J. and Whitson, C. (1992) *The Structure of Capital in the European Community: The Size of Companies and the Implications for Industrial Relations*, Warwick Papers in Industrial Relations, No. 38, Warwick University.

Sivanandan, A. (1991) 'Black struggles against racism', in Northern Curriculum Development Project *Setting the Context for Change: Anti-Racist Social Work Education*, Central Council for Education and Training in Social Work, Leeds.

Sloman, M. (1993) 'Training to play a lead role', *Personnel Management* (July): 40–4.

Sloman, M. (1994) 'Coming in from the cold: a new role for trainers', *Personnel Management* (January).

Smith, M. (1948) *An Introduction to Industrial Psychology*, 4th edition, Cassell.

Smith, M. (1991) 'Selection in organizations', in M. Smith (ed.) *Analysing Organizational Behaviour*, Macmillan.

Smith, M. and Robertson, I. T. (1993) *The Theory and Practice of Systematic Personnel Selection*, 2nd edition, Macmillan.

Smith, M., Gregg, M. and Andrews, R. (1989) *Selection & Assessment: A New Appraisal*, Pitman.

Snow, C. C., Miles, R. E. and Coleman, H. J. (1992) 'Managing 21st century organizations', *Organizational Dynamics* (winter).

Snyder, M. (1974) 'The self-monitoring of expressive behaviour', *Journal of Personality and Social Psychology* 30: 526–37.

Sonnenfeld, J. and Kotter, J. P (1982) 'The maturation of career theory', *Human Relations* 35: 19–46.

Sonnenfeld, J. A., Peiperl, M. A. and Kotter, J. P. (1988) 'Strategic determinants of managerial labor markets: a career systems view', *Human Resource Management* 27(4) (winter): 369–88; reprinted in G. Salaman (ed.) *Human Resource Strategies*, Sage).

Sparrow, P. (1994) 'Organizational competencies: creating a strategic behavioural framework for selection and assessment', in N. Anderson and P. Herriot (eds) *Assessment and Selection in Organizations: Methods and Practice for Recruitment and Appraisal*, First Update and Supplement 1994, Wiley.

Sparrow, P. and Hiltrop, J.-M. (1994) *European Human Resource Management in Transition*, Prentice-Hall.

Stacey, R. D. (1993) *Strategic Management and Organisational Dynamics*, Pitman.

Steedman, H. and Wagner, K. (1987) 'A second look at productivity, machinery and skills in Britain and Germany', *National Institute Economic Review* (November): 57–71.

Sternberg, R. J. (1994) 'Thinking styles: theory and assesment at the interface between intelligence and personality', in R. J. Sternberg and P. Ruzgis (eds) *Personality and Intelligence*, Cambridge University Press.

Stevens, J. and Walsh, T. (1991) 'Training and competitiveness', in J. Stevens and R. Mackay (eds) *Training and Competitiveness*, NEDO/ Kogan Page.

Stewart, R. (1983) *The Reality of Management*, 2nd edition, Heinemann.

Storey, J. (ed.) (1989) *New Perspectives on Human Resource Management*, Routledge.

Storey, J. (1992) *Developments In The Management Of Human Resources*, Blackwell.

Storey, J. (1994a) 'How new-style management is taking hold', *Personnel Management* (January): 32–5.

Storey, J. (1994b) *New Wave Manufacturing Strategies: Organizational and Human Resource Management Dimensions*, Paul Chapman Publishing.

Storey, J. (ed.) (1995) *Human Resource Management: A Critical Text*, Routledge.

Straw, J. M. (1989) *Equal Opportunities: The Way Ahead*, Institute for Personnel Management.

Thompson, J. L. (1993) *Strategic Management: Awareness and Change*, 2nd edition, Chapman & Hall.

Thompson, P. and McHugh, D. (1990) *Work Organisations: A Critical Introduction*, Macmillan.

Thomson, R. and Mabey, C. (1994) *Developing Human Resources*, Butterworth-Heinemann.

Thurley, K. and Wirdenius, H. (1990) *Towards European Management*, Pitman.

Tichy, N. M., Fombrun, C. J. and Devanna, M. A. (1982) 'Strategic human resource management', *Sloan Management Review* 23(2): 47–61.

Tinaikar, R., Hartman, A. and Nath, R. (1995) 'Rethinking business process re-engineering: a social constructivist perspective', in G. Burke and J. Peppard (eds) *Examining Business Process Re-engineering: Current Perspectives and Research Directions*, Kogan Page.

Torrington, D. (1994) *International Human Resource Management*, Prentice-Hall.

Torrington, D. and Hall, L. (1991) *Personnel Management: A New Approach*, 2nd edition, Prentice-Hall.

Torrington, D. and Hall, L. (1995) *Personnel Management: HRM in Action*, 3rd edition, Prentice-Hall.

Townley, B. (1989) 'Selection and appraisal: reconstituting "social relations"?', in J. Storey (ed.) *New Perspectives on Human Resource Management*, Routledge.

Townley, B. (1994) *Reframing Human Resource Management*, Sage.

Townsend, R. (1970) *Up The Organization*, Michael Joseph.

Triandis, H. C. (1990) 'Theoretical concepts that are applicable to the analysis of ethnocentrism', in R. W. Brislin (ed.) *Applied Cross-cultural Psychology*, Sage.

Triandis, H. C. (1995) 'A theoretical framework for the study of diversity', in M. M. Chemers, S. Oskamp and M. A. Costanzo (eds) *Diversity in Organizations: New Perspectives for a Changing Workplace*, Sage.

Trice, H. M. and Beyer, J. M. (1984) 'Studying organizational cultures through rites and rituals', *Academy of Management Review* 9. 653–69.

Tuckman, B. W. (1965) 'Development sequences in small groups', *Psychological Bulletin* 63.

Tylor, E. B. (1871) *Primitive Culture*, Henry Holt.

Tyson, S. (1995) *Human Resource Strategy*, Pitman.

Tyson, S., Lawrence, P., Poirson, P., Manzolini, L. and Vincente, C. F. (1993) *Human Resource Management in Europe: Strategic Issues and Cases*, Kogan Page.

UNIDO (1993) *United Nations Industrial Development Organization, Annual Report 1993*, UNIDO.

Uvalic, M. (1991) *The PEPPER Report*, Commission of the European Communities/European University Institute, Brussels and Florence; reprinted in S. Vickerstaff (ed.) (1992) *Human Resource Management in Europe*, Chapman & Hall.

van de Vliet, Anita (1993) 'Assess for success', *Management Today* (July): 60–5.

Van Ours, J. and Ridder, G. (1992) 'Vacancies and the recruitment of new employees', *Journal of Labor Economics* 10(2) (April): 138–55.

Van Ruysseveldt, J., Huiskamp, R. and van Hoof, J. (1995) *Comparative Industrial and Employment Relations*, Sage.

Vicente, C. S. (1993) 'Human resource management in Spain: strategic issues, the economic and social framework', in S. Tyson, P. Lawrence, P. Poirson, L. Manzolini and C. F. Vicente *Human Resource Management in Europe: Strategic Issues and Cases*, Kogan Page.

Vicere, A. and Freeman, V. (1990) 'Executive education in major corporations', *Journal of Management Development* 9(1).

Vickerstaff, S. (1992) *Human Resource Management in Europe: Text and Cases*, Chapman & Hall.

Vroom, V. and Yetton, P. W. (1973) *Leadership and Decision Making*, University of Pittsburg Press.

Walker, P. (1991) *Staying Power: An Autobiography*, Bloomsbury.

Warr, P. (1987) *Psychology at Work*, 2nd edition, Penguin Books.

Watson, T. J. (1994) *In Search of Management: Culture, Chaos and Control in Managerial Work*, Routledge.

Webster, E. C. (1964) *Decision Making in the Employment Interview*, Industrial Relations Centre, McGill University, Montreal.

Webster, W. (1990) *Not a Man to Match Her: The Marketing of a Prime Minister*, Women's Press.

Weisner, W.H. and Cronshaw, S.F. (1988) 'A meta-analytic investigation of the impact of interview format and degree of structure on the validity of the employment interview', *Journal of Occupational Psychology* 61: 275–90.

Whipp, R. (1992) 'HRM, competition and strategy', in P. Blyton and P. Turnbull (eds) *Reassessing Human Resource Management*, Sage.

White, R. and Lippitt, R. (1953) 'Leader behaviour and member reaction in three "social climates"', in D. Cartwright and A. Zander (eds) *Group Dynamics*, Row, Peterson.

Whitehill, A. M. (1990) *Japanese Management: Tradition and Transition*, Routledge.

Wickens, P. (1987) *The Road to Nissan*, Macmillan.

Willmott, H. (1993) 'Strength is ignorance; slavery is freedom: managing culture in modern organizations', *Journal of Management Studies* 30(4).

Willmott, H. (1995) 'Will the turkeys vote for Christmas? The re-engineering of human resources', in G. Burke and J. Peppard (eds) *Examining Business Process Re-engineering: Current Perspectives and Research Directions*, Kogan Page.

Wilson, F. M. (1995) *Organizational Behaviour and Gender*, McGraw-Hill.

Wood, D. (1983) 'Uses and abuses of personnel consultants', *Personnel Management* (October): 407.

Wood, R. and Baron, H. (1992) 'Psychological testing free from prejudice', *Personnel Management* (December): 34–7.

Wood, S. (ed.) (1989) *The Transformation of Work?*, Routledge.

Woodward, J. (1980) *Industrial Organization: Theory and Practice*, 2nd edition, Oxford University Press.

Wright, M. and Storey, J. (1994) 'Recruitment', in I. Beardwell and L. Holden (eds) *Human Resource Management*, Pitman.

Wright, P. C. and Bean, S. A. (1993) 'Sexual harassment: an issue of employee effectiveness', *Journal of Managerial Psychology* 8(2): 306.